THE MAMMOTH BOOK OF PRIVATE LIVES

The Emotional & Domestic Worlds
of the Famous through
their Letters

Edited by
Jon E. Lewis

Robinson
.LONDON

For Penny, Tristram and Freda Lewis-Stempel.
As always. SWALK

Robinson Publishing Ltd
7 Kensington Church Court
London W8 4SP

First published in the UK by Robinson Publishing 1999

Collection copyright © J. Lewis-Stempel 1999

Front cover painting: "Girl Reading a Letter at an Open Window"
by Jan Vermeer.

All rights reserved. This book is sold subject to the condition that it shall
not, by way of trade or otherwise, be lent, re-sold, hired out or otherwise
circulated in any form of binding or cover other than that in which it is
published and without a similar condition including this condition being
imposed on the subsequent purchaser.

A copy of the British Library Cataloguing in Publication Data
is available from the British Library.

ISBN 1–84119–071–3
Typeset by FSH London.
Printed and bound in the EC.

THE MAMMOTH BOOK OF PRIVATE LIVES

Also available

The Mammoth Book of Ancient Wisdom
The Mammoth Book of Armchair Detectives & Screen Crimes
The Mammoth Book of Arthurian Legends
The Mammoth Book of Battles
The Mammoth Book of Best New Horror 99
The Mammoth Book of Best New Science Fiction 12
The Mammoth Book of British Kings & Queens
The Mammoth Book of Cats
The Mammoth Book of Chess
The Mammoth Book of Comic Fantasy
The Mammoth Book of Dogs
The Mammoth Book of Erotica
The Mammoth Book of Gay Erotica
The Mammoth Book of Heroic and Outrageous Women
The Mammoth Book of Historical Detectives
The Mammoth Book of Historical Erotica
The Mammoth Book of Historical Whodunnits
The Mammoth Book of How It Happened
The Mammoth Book of International Erotica
The Mammoth Book of Jack the Ripper
The Mammoth Book of Lesbian Short Stories
The Mammoth Book of Men O'War
The Mammoth Book of Mindbending Puzzles
The Mammoth Book of New Erotica
The Mammoth Book of New Sherlock Holmes Adventures
The Mammoth Book of Nostradamus and Other Prophets
The Mammoth Book of Seriously Comic Fantasy
The Mammoth Book of Sports & Games
The Mammoth Book of Tasteless Lists
The Mammoth Book of the Third Reich at War
The Mammoth Book of True Crime (new edition)
The Mammoth Book of True War Stories
The Mammoth Book of Unsolved Crimes
The Mammoth Book of War Diaries and Letters
The Mammoth Book of the Western
The Mammoth Book of the World's Greatest Chess Games

CONTENTS

INTRODUCTION   vii

THE LETTERS   1

Marcus Tullius Cicero   1   Horace Walpole   114
Mark Antony   2   Samuel Richardson   118
Agrippina the Younger   3   Samuel Johnson   121
Pliny the Younger   5   David Hume   125
St Jerome   8   James Boswell   126
Abelard and Heloïse   10   The Duke of Queensberry   137
Petrarch   29   George Washington   139
Pope Pius II   32   Wolfgang Amadeus Mozart   141
Leonardo da Vinci   34   William Cobbett   144
Queen Catherine of Aragon   36   Charles Lamb   146
Albrecht Dürer   37   Napoleon Bonaparte   154
Babar the Conqueror   41   William Wordsworth   157
King Henry VIII and Anne Boleyn   43   Samuel Taylor Coleridge   167
Pietro Aretino   49   William Blake   172
Viscount Lisle   51   Jane Austen   175
Sir Thomas More   53   Lord Nelson   177
Queen Elizabeth I   55   Fanny Burney   181
Sir Philip Sidney   58   William Godwin   192
Sir Walter Raleigh   59   Lord Byron   194
King James I and George Villiers   62   John Keats   206
John Donne   66   William Hazlitt   212
James Howell   68   Mary Shelley   215
Queen Henrietta Maria   70   Thomas Carlyle and Jane Baillie Welsh   224
Oliver Cromwell   72   Joey Grimaldi   234
John Dryden   75   Charlotte Brontë   235
Madame de Sévigné   76   Abraham Lincoln   238
Cotton Mather   79   Queen Victoria   244
Nell Gwyn   81   Henry David Thoreau   246
John Evelyn and Samuel Pepys   82   Sydney Smith   251
Lady Mary Wortley Montagu   84   Karl Marx and Friedrich Engels   252
Jonathan Swift   97   Napoleon Dana   258
Anthony Henley   104   Elizabeth Barrett and Robert Browning   260
Thomas Sheridan   104   Gustave Flaubert   264
Lord Chesterfield   107   George Sand   269
Benjamin Franklin   112   Charles Dickens   271

CONTENTS

Frederick Douglass	276	Jack London	373
John Clare	284	Robert Graves	374
Fyodor Dostoyevsky	287	Wilfred Owen	378
Harriet Beecher Stowe	292	Ivor Gurney	381
Camille Corot	303	Rosa Luxemburg	387
Friedrich Nietzsche	304	E.M. Forster	392
Louisa May Alcott	305	T.E. Lawrence	396
Lewis Carroll	312	F. Scott Fitzgerald	403
Cardinal Newman	318	Ernest Hemingway	411
Mark Twain	319	Vita Sackville-West	414
Gerard Manley Hopkins	322	John Steinbeck	422
Claude Monet	324	Jawaharlal Nehru	426
Eliza Savage and Samuel Butler	325	Dylan Thomas	429
General Charles Gordon	327	James Agee	434
Winston Churchill	328	Lion Feuchtwanger	436
Joseph Conrad	330	James Thurber	438
Oscar Wilde	333	Albert Einstein	443
Emile Zola	337	Sir Jock Delves Broughton	445
Erik Satie	340	Evelyn Waugh	449
Edith Wharton	340	Martin Bormann	454
Alban Berg	343	Edith Sitwell	459
D.H. Lawrence	346	Malcolm Lowry	464
Robert Falcon Scott	353	Humphrey Bogart	474
Virginia Woolf	355	Groucho Marx	475
Rupert Brooke	360	Harry S. Truman	479
Paul Claudel	363	E.B. White	480
André Gide	364	Malcolm X	481
George Bernard Shaw	365	Elvis Presley	484
Katherine Mansfield	370	Monica Lewinsky	486

SOURCES	489
ACKNOWLEDGMENTS	497

INTRODUCTION

The pleasure in reading other people's mail is primarily a guilty one. It is the privileged chance to eavesdrop, unobserved, on the lives of others. The enjoyment is illicit but difficult to resist. Privacy is fine for oneself, but it takes a saint-like soul not to be interested in what happens in the shuttered rooms of someone else's existence. And not to wish to break into those sancta. Letter reading appeals to the snoop in all of us.

This snooping is most readily aroused when the letter writer is famous. Which is perhaps just as well, for of all the letters ever written, those of the famous have tended to be those preserved. A letter from an aunt or friend might end up as a taper for the fire, but few would consign an epistle from Napoleon, George Washington, Jane Austen or Oliver Cromwell to such a fate.

At its most virtuous the display of the private lives of the famous through their letters serves to illuminate both them and their part in history. Henry VIII's pained love letter to his mistress Anne Boleyn (for whom he would divorce his wife and thus unleash the English Reformation), Samuel Taylor Coleridge's agonized missive on his opium addiction, Hemingway's correspondence with Scott Fitzgerald outlining his personal vision of heaven, Cicero's note of relief that dinner with dictator Julius Caesar passed off smoothly, homosexual James I's doting letters to his court favourite George "Steenie" Villiers (subsequently elevated to the mighty Duke of Buckingham), all add to our measure of the men and their times. At a pinch, the private letters of the famous can also stand as social history, providing insights into the manners, mores, beliefs and lifestyles of an age. Mozart's letters to his wife contain sexual ribaldry some might think a twentieth-century invention (but which has existed since time immemorial), while Cotton Mather's are brimful of the Protestant fundamentalism that caused witch-hunt hysteria in the New England of the 1690s.

At its basest, the publishing of private correspondence of the famous tarnishes the reputations of the great without – in the case of the dead – the possibility of a fair response. Then again, perhaps it is only those with something to hide who have something to fear. Certainly, the letters of the famous can sometimes make disturbing reading for anyone inclined to idolatry. T. E. Lawrence's pathetic homoerotic love letter to a young American soldier sits ill with the manufactured legend of "Lawrence of Arabia", Harry Truman's threat to inflict bodily harm ("you'll need a supporter below") on the critic who had the temerity to criticize his daughter's singing is hardly statesmanlike, while any picture of Karl Marx as a super-intellectual – a body-less brain almost – will be shattered by his complaints to his collaborator Engels about his carbuncles.

As it happens, the main purpose of Marx's voluminous correspondence with the rich Engels was Marx's continuous requests for a loan; in this he was desperately ordinary, for begging letters, historically, are the commonest form of letter; the second commonest being refusals of which Abraham Lincoln's famous high-minded epistolary "No" to his stepbrother is almost a model.

Almost inevitably, the greatest – and most fecund – letter writers amongst the famous are those who are professional writers – Coleridge, Byron, Swift, Dickens, Steinbeck, Scott Fitzgerald. Such people form the bulk of the letterists selected for this anthology. And almost half of them are women. For, as Jane Austen wrote in *Northanger Abbey*, "Everybody allows... that the habit of writing... letters is peculiarly female." For centuries, indeed, letter writing was the only literary activity allowed women, and not a few women – Madame de Sévigné, habituée of the court of Louis XIV, and Lady Mary Wortley Montagu among them – became famous primarily for their published *belles-lettres*.

Not all the letters collected here are strictly private affairs. Some correspondents have clearly written with one eye on future publication (Marcus Cicero comes to mind), while letters of complaint to august bodies are obviously intended to be read by many though few can be so amusingly written as Groucho Marx's to the board of directors of a company in which he had invested shares. Letters to newspapers are *de facto* public, hence the importance of the newspaper to the 'open letter' writer such as Emile Zola with his famous "J'accuse", castigating the French government in the anti-Semitic Dreyfus case, and Frederick Douglass's open letter to his former slave master. Both helped changed the destiny of nations. If such letters only tangentially reveal the emotional and domestic lives of their authors, I have included them because they illustrate a transcendent truth. There is nothing so dangerous as a letter – a point underlined by Albert Einstein's top secret letter to President Roosevelt requesting permission to make the A-bomb, and in another way by Dylan Thomas's desperate missive to his wife, Caitlin, after she had discovered a letter by him to another woman.

It is said that the telephone has all but killed letter writing as an art form or even as a private form of communication beyond "Wish you were here" postcards and thank-you notes. And yet it is perhaps a promising portent for those of us who like to leaf through the epistles of the famous that the penultimate letter in this book is an e-mail (that from Monica Lewinsky to Linda Tripp, one which almost brought down a president), a form of communication which burgeons in the dawn of the new millennium. And electronic mail is still mail for all its instant, sparkling hi-technology. The form has changed, but the words remain written.

If the letters collected in this anthology span a great arc in time, from 45BC to AD1998, the topics covered are almost limitless. There are letters of love, war, family intrigue, employment requests (including that from Leonardo da Vinci to the Duke of Milan), rural life, poverty, artistic endeavour, spiritual awakening, health, gossip, last letters from the condemned and the spurned, letters written in madness (the poet John Clare in the asylum, "I have quite forgotten who you are"), sadness and badness. There are also plain oddities, such as Nazi leader Martin Bormann's boasting of his gaining of a mistress – to his beloved wife (who wrote back in approval, suggesting the setting up of a *ménage à trois*), and Elvis Presley's missive to President Nixon asking to be made an FBI Special Agent in the war against drugs.

To paraphrase Scott Fitzgerald, the famous are different from you and me. They do everything in life in bold and italics and uppercase. Their letters only prove this.

THE LETTERS

MARCUS TULLIUS CICERO

CICERO (106–43BC) WAS PRE-EMINENT AMONG Roman orators and letter-writers. He opposed Julius Caesar in the internecine struggle for mastery of Rome, throwing himself on Caesar's mercy when the dictator emerged victorious from the battle of Pharsalia, 48BC. In 43BC after Caesar's death, Cicero delivered his speeches against Mark Antony, *the Philippics*, for which he was executed, his severed head and hands being put on public display.

To Atticus (45BC)

Oh, what a formidable guest to have had! and yet *je ne m'en plains pas*, because he was in a very agreeable mood. But after his arrival at Philippus's house on the evening of the second day of the Saturnalia the whole establishment was so crowded with soldiers that even the room where Caesar himself was to dine could hardly be kept clear from them; it is a fact that there were 2,000 men! Of course I was nervous about what might be the case with me next day, and so Cassius Barba came to my assistance; he set some men on guard. The camp was pitched out of doors; my villa was made secure. On the third day of the Saturnalia he stayed at Philippus's till near one and admitted nobody (accounts with Balbus, I suppose), then took a walk on the beach. After two to the bath: then he heard about Mamurra; he made no objection. After the toilet he sat down to dinner. He was under the "emetic cure", and consequently he ate and drank *sans peur*; and with much satisfaction. And certainly everything was very good, and well served; nay more, I may say that

> Though the cook was good,
> 'Twas Attic salt that flavoured best the food.

There were three dining-rooms besides, where there was a very hospitable reception for the gentlemen of his *suite*; while the inferior class of freedmen and slaves had abundance at any rate; for as to the better class, they had a more refined table. In short, I think I acquitted myself like a man. The guest however was not the sort of person to whom you would say "I shall be most delighted if you will come here again on your way back", once is enough. Nothing was said *au grand sérieux*; much on "literary" chat. In short, he was greatly pleased, and seemed to enjoy himself. He told me that he should be one day at Puteoli, and the next near Baiae. Here you have the story of his visit – or, I may call it, his *billeting* – which, as I told you, was a thing one would shrink from, but did not give much trouble. I am for Tusculum next after a short stay here.

When he was passing Dolabella's house, but nowhere else, the whole guard was paraded in arms on either side of him as he rode, I have it from Nicias.

MARK ANTONY

ANTONY (*c.* 80–30BC) WAS ONE OF THE "TRIUMVIRS" who ruled the Roman Empire after the assassination of Julius Caesar. He became infatuated with the Egyptian queen Cleopatra, divorcing his wife – Octavia, sister of co-triumvir Octavianus Augustus – for her. Antony and Cleopatra later committed suicide, after losing in battle to Augustus.

To Octavianus Augustus (33BC)

What's upset you? Because I go to bed with Cleopatra? But she's my wife, and I've been doing so for nine years, not just recently. And, anyway, is Livia *your* only pleasure? I expect that you will have managed, by the time you read this, to have hopped into bed with Tertulla, Terentilla, Rufilla, Salvia Titisenia, or the whole lot of them. Does it really matter where, or with what women, you get your excitement?

AGRIPPINA THE YOUNGER

THE THIRD WIFE OF THE ROMAN EMPEROR CLAUDIUS, Agrippina (?–AD59) intrigued successfully to win the throne for her son Nero, poisoning his rivals and enemies. Her influence, however, proved intolerable and the new emperor, with the bidding of his mistress Poppaea Sabina, ordered her execution for treason. Agrippina's letter pleading for clemency from her son fell on deaf ears and she was strangled.

To her son, Emperor Nero (AD59)

I do wonder that barren Silana has no sense of maternal affection. One who has never borne a son naturally would not know how to bear the loss of one. Nature renders either hateful or indifferent those objects that we do not ourselves experience. . . . I am amazed that even the most skilful sorcery of words could make you pay the least attention to such barbarous inhumanity...

Don't you know, my son, the affection all mothers naturally bear their children? Our love is unbounded, incessantly fed by that tenderness unknown to all but ourselves. Nothing should be more dear to us than what we have bought with the risk of our lives; nothing mare precious than what we have endured such grief and pain to procure. These are so acute and unbearable that if it were not for the vision of a successful birth, which makes us forget our agonies, generation would soon cease.

Do you forget that nine full months I carried you in my womb and nourished you with my blood? How likely is it, then, that I would destroy the dear child who cost me so much anguish to bring into the world? It may be that the just gods were angry at my excessive love of you, and used this way to punish me.

Unhappy Agrippina! You are suspected of a crime of which nobody could really think you guilty... What does the title of empress mean to me, if I am accused of a crime that even the basest of women would abhor? Unhappy are those who breathe the air of the court. The wisest of people are not secure from storms in that harbour. There even a calm is dangerous. But why blame the court? Can that be the cause of my being suspected of parricide?...

Tell me, why should I plot against your life? To plunge myself into a worse fate? That's not likely. What hopes could induce me to build upon your downfall? I know that the lust for empire often corrupts the laws of nature; that justice has no sword to punish those who offend in this way; and that ambition disregards wrong so long as it succeeds in its aim... Nay, to what deity could I turn for absolution after I had committed so black a deed?...

What difficulties have I not surmounted to crown your brow with laurels? But I insult your gratitude by reminding you of my services. My innocence ought not to defend itself but to rely wholly on your justice.

Farewell

PLINY THE YOUNGER

GAIUS PLINIUS CAECILIUS SECUNDUS PLINY (c. AD61–113), Roman lawyer and statesman, nephew of the polymath Elder Pliny. Nine books of Pliny's letters were published in his lifetime; a tenth, dealing with his correspondence with Emperor Trajan while acting as imperial representative in Bithynia and Pontus, was published posthumously.

❦

To Cornelius Tacitus (c. AD104)

Gaius Cornelius Tacitus (c. 55–120), Roman historian. The letter refers to Pliny's adventures during the eruption of Vesuvius in AD 79, and to the death of his uncle, Pliny the Elder, then in charge of the Roman fleet at Misenum, who had gone to investigate the eruption, landing at Stabiae where he perished from volcanic gases.

So the letter which you asked me to write on my uncle's death has made you eager to hear about the terrors and hazards I had to face when left at Misenum, for I broke off at the beginning of this part of my story. 'Though my mind shrinks from remembering ... I will begin.'

After my uncle's departure I spent the rest of the day with my books, as this was my reason for staying behind. Then I took a bath, dined, and then dozed fitfully for a while. For several days past there had been earth tremors which were not particularly alarming because they are frequent in Campania: but that night the shocks were so violent that everything felt as if it were not only shaken but overturned. My mother hurried into my room and found me already getting up to wake her if she were still asleep. We sat down in the forecourt of the house, between the buildings and the sea close by. I don't know whether I should call this courage or folly on my part (I was only seventeen at the time) but I called for a volume of Livy and went on reading as if I had nothing else to do. I even went on with the extracts I had been making. Up came a friend of my uncle's who had just come from Spain to join him. When he saw us sitting there and me actually reading, he scolded us both – me for my foolhardiness and my mother for allowing it. Nevertheless, I remained absorbed in my book.

By now it was dawn, but the light was still dim and faint. The buildings round us were already tottering, and the open space we were in was too small for us not to be in real and imminent danger if the house collapsed. This finally decided us to leave the town. We were followed by a panic-stricken mob of people wanting to act on someone else's decision in preference to their own (a point in which fear looks like prudence), who hurried us on our way by pressing hard behind in a dense crowd. Once beyond the buildings we stopped, and there we had some extraordinary experiences which thoroughly alarmed us. The carriages we had ordered to be brought out began to run in different directions though the ground was quite level, and would not remain stationary even when wedged with stones. We also saw the sea sucked away and apparently forced back by the earthquake: at any rate it receded from the shore so that quantities of sea creatures were left stranded on dry sand. On the landward side a fearful black cloud was rent by forked and quivering bursts of flame, and parted to reveal great tongues of fire, like flashes of lightning magnified in size.

At this point my uncle's friend from Spain spoke up still more urgently: "If your brother, if your uncle is still alive, he will want you both to be saved; if he is dead, he would want you to survive him – why put off your escape?" We replied that we would not think of considering our own safety as long as we were uncertain of his. Without waiting any longer, our friend rushed off and hurried out of danger as fast as he could.

Soon afterwards the cloud sank down to earth and covered the sea; it had already blotted out Capri and hidden the promontory of Misenum from sight. Then my mother implored, entreated and commanded me to escape as best I could – a young man might escape, whereas she was old and slow and could die in peace as long as she had not been the cause of my death too. I refused to save myself without her, and grasping her hand forced her to quicken her pace. She gave in reluctantly, blaming herself for delaying me. Ashes were already falling, not as yet very thickly. I looked round: a dense black cloud was coming up behind us, spreading over the earth like a flood. "Let us leave the road while we can still see," I said, "or we shall be knocked down and trampled underfoot in the dark by the crowd behind." We had scarcely sat down to rest when darkness fell, not the dark of a moonless or cloudy night, but as if the lamp had been put out in a closed room. You could hear the shrieks of women, the wailing of infants, and the shouting of men; some were calling their parents, others their children or their wives, trying to recognize them by their voices. People bewailed their own fate or that of their relatives, and there were some who prayed for death in their terror of dying. Many besought the aid of the gods, but still more imagined there were no gods left, and that the universe was plunged into eternal darkness for evermore. There were people, too, who added to the real perils by inventing fictitious dangers: some reported that part of Misenum had collapsed or another part was on fire, and though their tales were false they found others to believe them. A gleam of light returned, but we took this to be a warning of the approaching flames rather than daylight. However, the flames remained some distance off; then darkness came on once more and ashes began to fall again, this time in heavy showers. We rose from time to time and shook them off, otherwise we should have been buried and crushed beneath their weight. I could boast that not a groan or cry of fear escaped me in these perils, had I not derived some poor consolation in my mortal lot from the belief that the whole world was dying with me and I with it.

At last the darkness thinned and dispersed into smoke or cloud; then there was genuine daylight, and the sun actually shone out, but yellowish as it is during an eclipse. We were terrified to see everything changed, buried deep in ashes like snowdrifts. We returned to Misenum where we attended to our physical needs as best we could, and then spent an anxious night alternating between hope and fear. Fear predominated, for the earthquakes went on, and several hysterical individuals made their own and other people's calamities seem ludicrous in comparison with their frightful predictions. But even then, in spite of the dangers we had been through and were still expecting, my mother and I had still no intention of leaving until we had news of my uncle.

Of course these details are not important enough for history, and you will read them without any idea of recording them; if they seem scarcely worth putting in a letter, you have only yourself to blame for asking for them.

❧

To his wife, Calpurnia (n.d.)

You cannot believe how much I miss you. I love you so much and we are not used to separations. So I stay awake most of the night thinking of you, and by day I find my feet carrying me (a true word, carrying) to your room at the times I usually visited you; then finding it empty I depart, as sick and sorrowful as a lover locked out. The only time I am free from this misery is when I am in court and wearing myself out with my friends' lawsuits. You can judge then what a life I am leading, when I find my rest in work and distraction in troubles and anxiety.

ST JEROME

PROPERLY EUSEBIUS SOPHRONIUS HIERONYMOUS (c. 342–420) and secretary to Pope Damascus, St Jerome led a pilgrimage to the Holy Land in 385, where he settled in Bethlehem. There he pursued many literary labours, notably the first translation of the Bible from Hebrew into Latin.

To Asella (August 385)

Jerome departed for the Holy Land under a cloud caused by a scandalous rumour concerning his relationship with a nun Paula; in this letter, to another holy woman, he defended himself.

Before I became acquainted with the family of the saintly Paula, all Rome resounded with my praises. Almost everyone concurred in judging me worthy of the episcopate. Damasus, of blessed memory, spoke no words but mine. Men called me holy, humble, eloquent.

Did I ever cross the threshold of a light woman? Was I ever fascinated by silk dresses, or glowing gems, or rouged faces, or display of gold? Of all the ladies in Rome but one had power to subdue me, and that one was Paula. She mourned and fasted, she was squalid with dirt, her eyes were dim from weeping. For whole nights she would pray to the Lord for mercy, and often the rising sun found her still at her prayers. The psalms were her only songs, the Gospel her whole speech, continence her one indulgence, fasting the staple of her life. The only woman who took my fancy was one whom I had not so much as seen at table. But when I began to revere, respect, and venerate her as her conspicuous chastity deserved, all my former virtues forsook me on the spot.

Oh! envy, that dost begin by tearing thyself! Oh! cunning malignity of Satan, that dost always persecute things holy! Of all the ladies in Rome, the only ones that caused scandal were Paula and Mdanium, who, despising their wealth and deserting their children, uplifted the cross of the Lord as a standard of religion. Had they frequented the baths, or chosen to use perfumes, or taken advantage of their wealth and position as widows to enjoy life and to be independent, they would have been saluted as ladies of high rank and saintliness. As it is, of course, it is in order to appear beautiful that they put on sackcloth and ashes, and they endure fasting and filth merely to go down into the Gehenna of fire! As if they could not perish with the crowd whom the mob applauds! If it were Gentiles or Jews who thus assailed their mode of life, they would at least have the consolation of failing to please only those whom

Christ Himself has failed to please. But, shameful to say, it is Christians who thus neglect the care of their own households, and disregarding the beams in their own eyes, look for motes in those of their neighbors. They pull to pieces every profession of religion, and think that they have found a remedy for their own doom, if they can disprove the holiness of others, if they can detract from every one, if they can show that those who perish are many, and sinners, a great multitude...I write this in haste, dear Lady Asella, as I go on board, overwhelmed with grief and tears; yet I thank my God that I am counted worthy of the world's hatred...Men call me a mischief-maker, and I take the title as a recognition of my faith. For I am but a servant, and the Jews still call my master a magician. The Apostle [St Paul] likewise, is spoken of as a deceiver. There hath no temptation taken me but such as is common to man. How few distresses have I endured, I who am yet a soldier of the cross! Men have laid to my charge a crime of which I am not guilty; but I know that I must enter the kingdom of heaven through evil report as well as through good.

Salute Paula and Eustochium, who, whatever the world may think, are always mine in Christ. Salute Albina, your mother, and Marcella, your sister; Marcellina also, and the holy Felicitas; and say to them all: "We must all stand before the judgment seat of Christ, and there shall be revealed the principle by which each has lived."

And now, illustrious model of chastity and virginity, remember me, I beseech you, in your prayers, and by your intercessions calm the waves of the sea.

ABELARD AND HELOÏSE

IN 1115 THE PHILOSOPHER PETER ABELARD (1079–1142) was appointed lecturer in the cathedral school of Notre Dame, Paris, where he fell in love with the beautiful seventeen-year-old niece of Canon Fulbert, Heloïse. On the discovery of their affair, they fled to Brittany, where Heloïse gave birth to a son, but later they returned to Paris to be married. This was not to the approval of Heloïse's relatives, who castrated Abelard – he then fled in shame to the abbey of St Denis to become a monk. Heloïse (1098–1164) herself took the veil and became a nun at Argenteuil. They compiled a famous collection of their correspondence and were reunited after death when they were buried in the same tomb at Abelard's monastic retreat, the Paraclete. In 1800 their remains were taken to Paris, to be interred in one sepulchre in Père Lachaise Cemetery.

Heloïse to Abelard (c. 1122)

> To her Lord, her Father, her Husband, her Brother, his Servant, his Child, his Wife, his Sister, and to express all that is humble, respectful and loving to her Abelard, Heloïse writes this.

A consolatory letter of yours to a friend happened some days since to fall into my hands; my knowledge of the writing and my love of the hand gave me the curiosity to open it. In justification of the liberty I took, I flattered myself I might claim a sovereign privilege over everything which came from you. Nor was I scrupulous to break through the rules of good breeding when I was to hear news of Abelard. But how dear did my curiosity cost me! What disturbance did it occasion, and how surprised I was to find the whole letter filled with a particular and melancholy account of our misfortunes! I met with my name a hundred times; I never saw it without fear – some heavy calamity always followed it. I saw yours too, equally unhappy.

These mournful but dear remembrances put my heart into such violent motion that I thought it was too much to offer comfort to a friend for a few slight disgraces, but such extraordinary means as the representation of our sufferings and revolutions. What reflections did I not make! I began to consider the whole afresh, and perceived myself pressed with the same weight of grief as when we first began to be miserable. Though length of time ought to have closed up my wounds, yet the seeing them described by your hand was sufficient to make them all open and bleed afresh...

My tears, which I could not restrain, have blotted half your letter; I wish they had effaced the whole, and that I had returned it to you in that condition; I should then have been satisfied with the little time I kept it; but it was demanded of me too soon.

I must confess I was much easier in my mind before I read your letter. Surely all the misfortunes of lovers are conveyed to them through the eyes: upon reading your letter I feel all mine renewed. I reproached myself for having been so long without venting my sorrows, when the rage of our unrelenting enemies still burns with the same fury. Since length of time, which disarms the strongest hatred, seems but to aggravate theirs; since it is decreed that your virtue shall be persecuted till it takes refuge in the grave – and even then, perhaps, your ashes will not be allowed to rest in peace – let me always meditate on your calamities, let me publish them through all the world, if possible, to shame an age that has not known how to value you...

Let me have a faithful account of all that concerns you; I would know everything, be it ever so unfortunate. Perhaps by mingling my sighs with yours I may make your sufferings less, for it is said that all sorrows divided are made lighter.

Tell me not by way of excuse you will spare me tears; the tears of women shut up in a melancholy place and devoted to penitence are not to be spared. And if you wait for an opportunity to write pleasant and agreeable things to us, you will delay writing too long. Prosperity seldom chooses the side of the virtuous, and fortune is so blind that in a crowd in which there is perhaps but one wise and brave man it is not to be expected that she should single him out. Write to me then immediately and wait not for miracles; they are too scarce, and we too much accustomed to misfortunes to expect a happy turn. I shall always have this, if you please, and this will always be agreeable to me, that when I receive any letter from you I shall know you still remember me...

I have your picture in my room; I never pass it without stopping to look at it; and yet when you are present with me I scarce ever cast my eyes on it. If a picture, which is but a mute representation of an object, can give such pleasure, what cannot letters inspire? They have souls; they can speak; they have in them all that force which expresses the transports of the heart; they have all the fire of our passions, they can raise them as much as if the persons themselves were present; they have all the tenderness and the delicacy of speech, and sometimes even a boldness of expression beyond it.

We may write to each other; so innocent a pleasure is not denied us. Let us not lose through negligence the only happiness which is left us, and the only one perhaps which the malice of our enemies can never ravish from us. I shall read that you are my husband and you shall see me sign myself your wife. In spite of all our misfortunes you may be what you please in your letter. Letters were first invented for consoling such solitary wretches as myself. Having lost the substantial pleasures of seeing and possessing you, I shall in some measure compensate this loss by the satisfaction I shall find in your writing. There I shall read your most sacred thoughts; I shall carry them always about with me, I shall kiss them every moment; if you can be capable of any jealousy let it be for the fond caresses I shall bestow upon your letters, and envy only the happiness of those rivals.

That writing may be no trouble to you, write always to me carelessly and without study; I had rather read the dictates of the heart than of the brain. I cannot live if you will not tell me that you still love me; but that language ought to be so natural to you, that I believe you cannot speak otherwise to me without violence to yourself. And since by this melancholy relation to your friend you have awakened all my sorrows, 'tis but reasonable you should allay them by some tokens of your unchanging love...

You cannot but remember (for lovers cannot forget) with what pleasure I have passed whole days in hearing your discourse. How when you were absent I shut myself from everyone to write to you;

how uneasy I was till my letter had come to your hands; what artful management it required to engage messengers. This detail perhaps surprises you, and you are in pain for what may follow. But I am no longer ashamed that my passion had no bounds for you, for I have done more than all this. I have hated myself that I might love you. I came hither to ruin myself in a perpetual imprisonment that I might make you live quietly and at ease.

Nothing but virtue, joined to a love perfectly disengaged from the senses, could have produced such effects. Vice never inspires anything like this: it is too much enslaved to the body. When we love pleasures we love the living and not the dead. We leave off burning with desire for those who can no longer burn for us. This was my cruel uncle's notion; he measured my virtue by the frailty of my sex, and thought it was the man and not the person I loved. But he has been guilty to no purpose. I love you more than ever; and so revenge myself on him. I will still love you with all the tenderness of my soul till the last moment of my life. If, formerly, my affection for you was not so pure, if in those days both mind and body loved you, I often told you even then that I was more pleased with possessing your heart than with any other happiness, and the man was the thing I least valued in you.

You cannot but be entirely persuaded of this by the extreme unwillingness I showed to marry you, though I knew that the name of wife was honourable in the world and holy in religion; yet the name of your mistress had greater charms because it was freer. The bonds of matrimony, however honourable, still bear with them a necessary engagement, and I was very unwilling to be necessitated to love always a man who would perhaps not always love me. I despised the name of wife that I might live happy with that of mistress; and I find by your letter to your friend you have not forgotten that delicacy of passion which loved you always with the utmost tenderness – and yet wished to love you more!

You have very justly observed in your letter that I esteemed those public engagements insipid which form alliances only to be dissolved by death, and which put life and love under the same unhappy necessity. But you have not added how often I have protested that it was infinitely preferable to me to live with Abelard as his mistress than with any other as Empress of the World. I was happier obeying you than I should have been as lawful spouse of the King of the Earth. Riches and pomp are not the charm of love. True tenderness makes us separate the lover from all that is external to him, and setting aside his position, fortune, or employments, consider him merely as himself...

It is not love, but the desire of riches and position which makes a woman run into the embraces of an indolent husband. Ambition, and not affection, forms such marriages. I believe, indeed, they may be followed with some honours and advantages, but I can never think that this is the way to experience the pleasures of affectionate union, nor to feel those subtle and charming joys when hearts long parted are at last united. These martyrs of marriage pine always for larger fortunes which they think they have missed. The wife sees husbands richer than her own, and the husband wives better portioned than his. Their mercenary vows occasion regret, and regret produces hatred. Soon they part – or else desire to. This restless and tormenting passion for gold punishes them for aiming at other advantages by love than love itself.

If there is anything that may properly be called happiness here below, I am persuaded it is the union of two persons who love each other with perfect liberty, who are united by a secret inclination, and satisfied with each other's merits. Their hearts are full and leave no vacancy for any other passion; they enjoy perpetual tranquillity because they enjoy content...

What rivalries did your gallantries of this kind occasion me! How many ladies lay claim to them? 'Twas a tribute their self-love paid to their beauty. How many have I seen with sighs declare their passion for you when, after some common visit you had made them, they chanced to be complimented for the Sylvia of your poems. Others in despair and envy have reproached me that I had no charms but what your wit bestowed on me, nor in anything the advantage over them but in being beloved by you. Can you believe me if I tell you, that notwithstanding my sex, I thought myself peculiarly happy in having a lover to whom I was obliged for my charms and took a secret pleasure in being admired by a man who, when he pleased, could raise his mistress to the character of a goddess. Pleased with your glory only, I read with delight all those praises you offered me, and without reflecting how little I deserved, I believed myself such as you described, that I might be more certain that I pleased you.

But oh! where is that happy time? I now lament my lover, and of all my joys have nothing but the painful memory that they are past. Now learn, all you my rivals who once viewed my happiness with jealous eyes, that he you once envied me can never more be mine. I loved him; my love was his crime and the cause of his punishment. My beauty once charmed him; pleased with each other, we passed our brightest days in tranquillity and happiness. If that were a crime, 'tis a crime I am yet fond of, and I have no other regret save that against my will I must now be innocent.

But what do I say? My misfortune was to have cruel relatives whose malice destroyed the calm we enjoyed; had they been reasonable I had now been happy in the enjoyment of my dear husband. Oh! how cruel were they when their blind fury urged a villain to surprise you in your sleep! Where was I – where was your Heloïse then? What joy should I have had in defending my lover; I would have guarded you from violence at the expense of my life. Oh! whither does this excess of passion hurry me? Here love is shocked and modesty deprives me of words.

But tell me whence proceeds your neglect of me since my being professed? You know nothing moved me to it but your disgrace, nor did I give my consent, but yours. Let me hear what is the occasion of your coldness, or give me leave to tell you now my opinion. Was it not the sole thought of pleasure which engaged you to me? And has not my tenderness, by leaving you nothing to wish for, extinguished your desires?...

Is it so hard for one who loves to write?... all I desire is such letters as the heart dictates, and which the hand cannot transcribe fast enough. How did I deceive myself with hopes that you would be wholly mine when I took the veil...

Why should I conceal from you the secret of my call? You know it was neither zeal nor devotion that brought me here. Your conscience

16

is too faithful a witness to permit you to disown it. Yet here I am, and here I will remain; to this place an unfortunate love and a cruel relation have condemned me. But if you do not continue your concern for me, if I lose your affection, what have I gained by my imprisonment? What recompense can I hope for? The unhappy consequences of our love and your disgrace have made me put on the habit of chastity, but I am not penitent of the past. Thus I strive and labour in vain. Among those who are wedded to God I am wedded to a man; among the heroic supporters of the Cross I am the slave of a human desire; at the head of a religious community I am devoted to Abelard alone.

What a monster am I! Enlighten me, O Lord, for I know not if my despair of Thy grace draws these words from me! I am, I confess, a sinner, but one who, far from weeping for her sins, weeps only for her lover; far from abhorring her crimes, longs only to add to them; and who, with a weakness unbecoming my state, please myself continually with the remembrance of past delights when it is impossible to renew them.

Good God! What is all this? I reproach myself for my own faults,' I accuse you for yours, and to what purpose? Veiled as I am, behold in what a disorder you have plunged me! How difficult it is to fight for duty against inclination. I know what obligations this veil lays upon me but I feel more strongly what power an old passion has over my heart...

Oh, for pity's sake help a wretch to renounce her desires – her self – and if possible even to renounce you! If you are a lover – a father, help a mistress, comfort a child! These tender names must surely move you; yield either to pity or to love; If you gratify my request I shall continue a religious, and without longer profaning my calling.

I am ready to humble myself with you to the wonderful goodness of God, who does all things for our sanctification, who by His grace purifies all that is vicious and corrupt, and by the great riches of His mercy draws us against our wishes, and by degrees opens our eyes to behold His bounty which at first we could not perceive...

A heart which has loved as mine cannot soon be indifferent. We fluctuate long between love and hatred before we can arrive at tranquillity, and we always flatter ourselves with some forlorn hope that we shall not be utterly forgotten.

Yes, Abelard, I conjure you by the chains I bear here to ease the weight of them, and make them as agreeable as I would they were to me. Teach me the maxims of Divine Love; since you have forsaken me I would glory in being wedded to Heaven. My heart adores that title and disdains any other; tell me how this Divine Love is nourished, how it works, how it purifies.

When we were tossed on the ocean of the world we could hear of nothing but your verses, which published everywhere our joys and pleasures. Now we are in the haven of grace is it not fit you should discourse to me of this new happiness, and teach me everything that might heighten or improve it? Show me the same complaisance in my present condition as you did when we were in the world. Without changing the ardour of our affections let us change their objects; let us have our songs and sing hymns; let us lift up our hearts to God and have no transports but for His glory!

I expect this from you as a thing you cannot refuse me. God has a peculiar right over the hearts of great men He has created. When He pleases to touch them He ravishes them, and lets them not speak nor breathe but for His glory. Till that moment of grace arrives, O think of me – do not forget me – remember my love and fidelity and constancy: love me as your mistress, cherish me as your child, your sister, your wife! Remember I still love you, and yet strive to avoid loving you. What a terrible saying is this! I shake with horror, and my heart revolts against what I say. I shall blot all my paper with tears. I end my long letter wishing you, if you desire it (would to Heaven I could!), for ever adieu!

Abelard to Heloïse (c. 1122)

Could I have imagined that a letter not written to yourself would fall into your hands, I had been more cautious not to have inserted anything in it which might awaken the memory of our past misfortunes. I described with boldness the series of my disgraces to a friend, in order to make him less sensible to a loss he had sustained.

If by this well-meaning device I have disturbed you, I purpose now to dry up those tears which the sad description occasioned you to shed; I intend to mix my grief with yours, and pour out my heart before you: in short, to lay open before your eyes all my trouble, and the secret of my soul, which my vanity has hitherto made me conceal from the rest of the world, and which you now force from me, in spite of my resolutions to the contrary.

It is true, that in a sense of the afflictions which have befallen us, and observing that no change of our condition could be expected; that those prosperous days which had seduced us were now past, and there remained nothing but to erase from our minds, by painful endeavours, all marks and remembrances of them. I had wished to find in philosophy and religion a remedy for my disgrace; I searched out an asylum to secure me from love. I was come to the sad experiment of making vows to harden my heart.

But what have I gained by this? If my passion has been put under a restraint my thoughts yet run free. I promise myself that I will forget you, and yet cannot think of it without loving you. My love is not at all lessened by those reflections I make in order to free myself. The silence I am surrounded by makes me more sensible to its impressions, and while I am unemployed with any other things, this makes itself the business of my whole vocation. Till after a multitude of useless endeavours I begin to persuade myself that it is a superfluous trouble to strive to free myself; and that it is sufficient wisdom to conceal from all but you how confused and weak I am.

I remove to a distance from your person with an intention of avoiding you as an enemy; and yet I incessantly seek for you in my mind; I recall your image in my memory, and in different disquietudes I betray and contradict myself. I hate you! I love you! Shame presses me on all sides.

I am at this moment afraid I should seem more indifferent than you fare, and yet I am ashamed to discover my trouble. How weak are we in ourselves if we do not support ourselves on the Cross of

Christ. Shall we have so little courage, and shall that uncertainty of serving two masters which afflicts your heart affect mine too? You see the confusion I am in, how I blame myself and how I suffer.

Religion commands me to pursue virtue, since I have nothing to hope for from love. But love still preserves its dominion over my fancies and entertains itself with past pleasures. Memory supplies the place of a mistress. Piety and duty are not always the fruits of retirement; even in deserts, when the dew of heaven falls not on us, we love what we ought no longer to love.

The passions, stirred up by solitude, fill these regions of death and silence; it is very seldom that what ought to be is truly followed here and that God only is loved and served. Had I known this before I had instructed you better. You call me your master; it is true you were entrusted to my care. I saw you, I was earnest to teach you vain sciences; it cost you your innocence and me my liberty.

Your uncle, who was fond of you, became my enemy and revenged himself on me. If now, having lost the power of satisfying my passion, I had also lost that of loving you, I should have some consolation. My enemies would have given me that tranquillity which Origen purchased with a crime. How miserable am I! I find myself much more guilty in my thoughts of you, even amidst my tears, than in possessing you when I was in full liberty. I continually think of you; I continually call to mind your tenderness.

In this condition, O Lord! if I run to prostrate myself before your altar, if I beseech you to pity me, why does not the pure flame of the Spirit consume the sacrifice that is offered? Cannot this habit of penitence which I wear interest Heaven to treat me more favourably? But Heaven is still inexorable, because my passion still lives in me; the fire is only covered over with deceitful ashes, and cannot be extinguished but by extraordinary grace. We deceive men, but nothing is hidden from God.

You tell me that it is for me you live under that veil which covers you; why do you profane your vocation with such words? Why provoke a jealous God with a blasphemy? I hoped after our separation you would have changed your sentiments; I hoped too that God would have delivered me from the tumult of my senses. We commonly die to the affections of those we see no more, and they to ours; absence is the tomb of love. But to me absence is an unquiet remembrance of what I once loved which continually torments me. I flattered myself that when I should see you no more you would rest in my memory without troubling my mind; that Brittany and the sea would suggest other thoughts; that my fasts and studies would by degrees delete you from my heart. But in spite of severe fasts and redoubled studies, in spite of the distance of 300 miles which separates us, your image, as you describe yourself in your veil, appears to me and confounds all my resolutions.

What means have I not used! I have armed my hands against myself; I have exhausted my strength in constant exercises; I comment upon Saint Paul; I contend with Aristotle: in short, I do all I used to do before I loved you, but all in vain; nothing can be successful that opposes you. Oh! do not add to my miseries by your constancy... Why use your eloquence to reproach me for my flight and for my silence? Spare the recital of our assignations and your constant exactness to them; without calling up such disturbing thoughts I have enough to suffer. What great advantages would philosophy give us over other men, if by studying it we could learn to govern our passions? What efforts, what relapses, what agitations do we undergo! And how long are we lost in this confusion, unable to exert our reason, to possess our souls, or to rule our affections?...

How can I separate from the person I love the passion I should detest? Will the tears I shed be sufficient to render it odious to me? I know not how it happens, there is always a pleasure in weeping for a beloved object. It is difficult in our sorrow to distinguish penitence from love. The memory of the crime and the memory of the object which has charmed us are too nearly related to be immediately separated. And the love of God in its beginning does not wholly annihilate the love of the creature.

But what excuses could I not find in you if the crime were excusable? Unprofitable honour, troublesome riches, could never tempt me: but those charms, that beauty, that air, which I yet behold at this instant, have occasioned my fall. Your looks were the beginning of my guilt; your eyes, your discourse, pierced my heart; and in spite of that ambition and glory which tried to make a defence, love was soon the master.

God, in order to punish me, forsook me. You are no longer of the world; you have renounced it: I am a religious devoted to solitude; shall we not take advantage of our condition? Would you destroy my piety in its infant state? Would you have me forsake the abbey into which I am but newly entered? Must I renounce my vows? I have made them in the presence of God; whether shall I fly from His wrath should I violate them? Suffer me to seek ease in my duty...

Regard me no more, I entreat you, as a founder or any great personage; your praises ill agree with my many weaknesses. I am a miserable sinner, prostrate before my Judge, and with my face pressed to the earth I mix my tears with the earth. Can you see me in this posture and solicit me to love you? Come, if you think fit, and in your holy habit thrust yourself between my God and me, and be a wall of separation. Come and force from me those sighs and thoughts and vows I owe to Him alone. Assist the evil spirits and be the instrument of their malice. What cannot you induce a heart to do whose weakness you so perfectly know?

Nay, withdraw yourself and contribute to my salvation. Suffer me to avoid destruction, I entreat you by our former tender affection and by our now common misfortune. It will always be the highest love to show none; I here release you from all your oaths and engagements. Be God's wholly, to whom you are appropriated; I will never oppose so pious a design. How happy shall I be if I thus lose you! Then shall I indeed be a religious and you a perfect example of an abbess.

Make yourself amends by so glorious a choice; make your virtue a spectacle worthy of men and angels. Be humble among your children, assiduous in your choir, exact in your discipline, diligent in your reading; make even your recreations useful.

Have you purchased your vocation at so light a rate that you should not turn it to the best advantage? Since you have permitted yourself to be abused by false doctrine and criminal instruction, resist not those good counsels which grace and religion inspire me with.

I will confess to you I have thought myself hitherto an abler master to instil vice than to teach virtue. My false eloquence has only set off false good. My heart, drunk with voluptuousness, could only suggest terms proper and moving to recommend that. The cup of sinners overflows with so enchanting a sweetness, and we are naturally so much inclined to taste it, that it needs only to be offered to us.

On the other hand the chalice of saints is filled with a bitter draught and nature starts from it. And yet you reproach me with cowardice for giving it to you first. I willingly submit to these accusations. I cannot enough admire the readiness you showed to accept the religious habit; bear therefore with courage the Cross you so resolutely took up. Drink of the chalice of saints, even to the bottom, without turning your eyes with uncertainty upon me; let me remove far from you and obey the Apostle who hath said "Fly!"

You entreat me to return under a pretence of devotion. Your earnestness in this point creates a suspicion in me and makes me doubtful how to answer you. Should I commit an error here my words would blush, if I may say so, after the history of our misfortunes. The Church is jealous of its honour, and commands that her children should be induced to the practice of virtue by virtuous means. When we approach God in a blameless manner, then we may with boldness invite others to Him.

But to forget Heloïse, to see her no more, is what Heaven demands of Abelard; and to expect nothing from Abelard, to forget him even as an idea, is what Heaven enjoins on Heloïse. To forget, in the case of love, is the most necessary penance, and the most difficult. It is easy to recount our faults; how many, through indiscretion, have made themselves a second pleasure of this instead of confessing them with humility. The only way to return to God is by neglecting the creature we have adored, and adoring the God whom we have neglected. This may appear harsh, but it must be done if we would be saved.

To make it more easy consider why I pressed you to your vow before I took mine; and pardon my sincerity and the design I have of meriting your neglect and hatred if I conceal nothing from you. When I saw myself oppressed by my misfortune I was furiously jealous, and regarded all men as my rivals. Love has more of distrust than assurance. I was apprehensive of many things because of my many defects, and being tormented with fear because of my own example I imagined your heart so accustomed to love that it could not be long without entering on a new engagement. Jealousy can easily believe the most terrible things.

I was desirous to make it impossible for me to doubt you. I was very urgent to persuade you that propriety demanded your withdrawal from the eyes of the world; that modesty and our friendship required it; and that your own safety obliged it. After such a revenge taken on me you could expect to be secure nowhere but in a convent.

I will do you justice: you were very easily persuaded. My jealousy secretly rejoiced in your innocent compliance; and yet, triumphant as I was, I yielded you up to God with an unwilling heart. I still kept my gift as much as was possible, and only parted with it in order to keep it out of the power of other men. I did not persuade you to religion out of any regard to your happiness, but condemned you to it like an enemy who destroys what he cannot carry off. And yet you heard my discourses with kindness, you sometimes interrupted me with tears, and pressed me to acquaint you with those convents I held in the highest esteem. What a comfort I felt in seeing you shut up. I was now at ease and took a satisfaction in considering that you continued no longer in the world after my disgrace, and that you would return to it no more.

But still I was doubtful. I imagined women were incapable of steadfast resolutions unless they were forced by the necessity of vows. I wanted those vows, and Heaven itself for your security, that I might no longer distrust you. Ye holy mansions and impenetrable retreats! from what innumerable apprehensions have ye freed me? Religion and piety keep a strict guard around your grates and walls. What a haven of rest this is to a jealous mind! And with what impatience did I endeavour after it!

I went every day trembling to exhort you to this sacrifice; I admired, without daring to mention it then, a brightness in your beauty which I had never observed before. Whether it was the bloom of a rising virtue, or an anticipation of the great loss I was to suffer, I was not curious in examining the cause, but only hastened your being professed. I engaged your prioress in my guilt by a criminal bribe with which I purchased the right of burying you. The professed of the house were alike bribed and concealed from you, at my directions, all their scruples and disgusts. I omitted nothing, either little or great; and if you had escaped my snares I myself would not have retired; I was resolved to follow you everywhere. The shadow of myself would always have pursued your steps and continually have occasioned either your confusion or your fear, which would have been a sensible gratification to me.

But, thanks to Heaven, you resolved to take the vows. I accompanied you to the foot of the altar, and while you stretched out your hand to touch the sacred cloth I heard you distinctly pronounce those fatal words that for ever separated you from man. Till then I thought your youth and beauty would foil my design and force your return to the world. Might not a small temptation have changed you? Is it possible to renounce oneself entirely at the age of two-and-twenty? At an age which claims the utmost liberty, could you think the world no longer worth your regard? How much did I wrong you, and what weakness did I impute to you? You were in my imagination both light and inconstant. Would not a woman at the noise of the flames and the fall of Sodom involuntarily look back in pity on some person? I watched your eyes, your every movement, your air; I trembled at everything. You may call such self-interested conduct treachery, perfidy, murder. A love so like to hatred should provoke the utmost contempt and anger.

It is fit you should know that the very moment when I was convinced of your being entirely devoted to me, when I saw you were infinitely worthy of all my love, I imagined I could love you no more. I thought it time to leave off giving you marks of my affection, and I considered that by your Holy Espousals you were now the peculiar care of Heaven, and no longer a charge on me as my wife. My jealousy seemed to be extinguished. When God only is our rival we have nothing to fear; and being in greater tranquility than ever before, I even dared to pray to Him to take you away from my eyes.

But it was not a time to make rash prayers, and my faith did not warrant them being heard. Necessity and despair were at the root of my proceedings, and thus I offered an insult to Heaven rather than a sacrifice. God rejected my offering and my prayer, and continued my punishment by suffering me to continue my love. Thus I bear alike the guilt of your vows and of the passion that preceded them, and must be tormented all the days of my life.

If God spoke to your heart as to that of a religious whose innocence had first asked Him for favours, I should have matter of comfort; but to see both of us the victims of a guilty love, to see this love insult us in our very habits and spoil our devotions, fills me with horror and trembling. Is this a state of reprobation? Or are these the consequences of a long drunkenness in profane love?

We cannot say love is a poison and a drunkenness till we are illuminated by grace; in the meantime it is an evil we dote on. When we are under such a mistake, the knowledge of our misery is the first step towards amendment. Who does not know that 'tis for the glory of God to find no other reason in man for His mercy than man's very weakness? When He has shown us this weakness and we have bewailed it, He is ready to put forth His omnipotence and assist us. Let us say for our comfort that what we suffer is one of those terrible temptations which have sometimes disturbed the vocations of the most holy.

God can grant His presence to men in order to soften their calamities whenever He shall think fit. It was His pleasure when you took the veil to draw you to Him by His grace. I saw your eyes, when you spoke your last farewell, fixed upon the Cross. It was more than six months before you wrote me a letter, nor during all that time did I receive a message from you. I admired this silence, which I durst not blame, but could not imitate. I wrote to you, and you returned me no answer: your heart was then shut, but this garden of the spouse is now opened; He is withdrawn from it and has left you alone.

By removing from you He has made trial of you; call Him back and strive to regain Him. We must have the assistance of God, that we may break our chains; we are too deeply in love to free ourselves.

Our follies have penetrated into the sacred places; our amours have been a scandal to the whole kingdom. They are read and admired; love which produced them has caused them to be described. We shall be a consolation to the failings of youth for ever; those who offend after us will think themselves less guilty. We are criminals whose repentance is late; oh, let it be sincere! Let us repair as far as is possible the evils we have done, and let France, which has been the witness of our crimes, be amazed at our repentance. Let us confound all who would imitate our guilt; let us take the side of God against ourselves, and by so doing prevent His judgement.

Our former lapses require tears, shame, and sorrow to expiate them. Let us offer up these sacrifices from our hearts, let us blush and let us weep. If in these feeble beginnings, O Lord, our hearts are not entirely Thine, let them at least feel that they ought to be so.

Deliver yourself, Heloïse, from the shameful remains of a passion which has taken too deep root. Remember that the least thought for any other than God is an adultery. If you could see me here with my meagre face and melancholy air, surrounded with numbers of persecuting monks, who are alarmed at my reputation for learning and offended at my lean visage, as if I threatened them with a reformation, what would you say of my base sighs and of those unprofitable tears which deceive these credulous men? Alas! I am humbled under love, and not under the Cross. Pity me and free yourself. If your vocation be, as you say, my work, deprive me not of the merit of it by your continual inquietudes.

Tell me you will be true to the habit which covers you by all inward retirement. Fear God, that you may be delivered from your frailties; love Him that you may advance in virtue. Be not restless in the cloister, for it is the peace of saints. Embrace your bands, they are the chains of Christ Jesus; He will lighten them and bear them with you, if you will but accept them with humility.

Without growing severe to a passion that still possesses you, learn from your misery to succour your weak sisters; pity them upon consideration of your own faults. And if any thoughts too natural should importune you, fly to the foot of the Cross and there beg for mercy – there are wounds open for healing; lament them before the dying Deity.

At the head of a religious society be not a slave, and having rule over queens, begin to govern yourself. Blush at the least revolt of your senses. Remember that even at the foot of the altar we often sacrifice to lying spirits, and that no incense can be more agreeable to them than the earthly passion that still burns in the heart of a religious.

If during your abode in the world your soul has acquired a habit of loving, feel it now no more save for Jesus Christ. Repent of all the moments of your life which you have wasted in the world and on pleasure; demand them of me, 'tis a robbery of which I am guilty; take courage and boldly reproach me with it.

I have been indeed your master, but it was only to teach sin. You call me your father; before I had any claim to the title, I deserved that of parricide. I am your brother, but it is the affinity of sin that brings me that distinction. I am called your husband, but it is after a public scandal.

If you have abused the sanctity of so many holy terms in the superscription of your letter to do me honour and flatter your own passion, blot them out and replace them with those of murderer, villain, and enemy, who has conspired against your honour, troubled your quiet, and betrayed your innocence. You would have perished through my means but for an extraordinary act of grace, which, that you might be saved, has thrown me down in the middle of my course.

This is the thought you ought to have of a fugitive who desires to deprive you of the hope of ever seeing him again. But when love has once been sincere, how difficult it is to determine to love no more! 'Tis a thousand times more easy to renounce the world than love. I hate this deceitful, faithless world; I think no more of it; but my wandering heart still eternally seeks you, and is filled with anguish at having lost you, in spite of all the powers of my reason. In the meantime, though I should be so cowardly as to retract what you have read, do not suffer me to offer myself to your thoughts save in this last fashion.

Remember my last worldly endeavours were to seduce your heart; you perished by my means and I with you: the same waves swallowed us up. We waited for death with indifference, and the same death had carried us headlong to the same punishments. But Providence warded off the blow, and our shipwreck has thrown us into a haven.

There are some whom God saves by suffering. Let my salvation be the fruit of your prayers; let me owe it to your tears and your exemplary holiness. Though my heart, Lord, be filled with the love of Thy creature, Thy hand can, when it pleases, empty me of all love save for Thee.

To love Heloïse truly is to leave her to that quiet which retirement and virtue afford. I have resolved it: this letter shall be my last fault. Adieu.

If I die here I will give orders that my body be carried to the house of the Paraclete. You shall see me in that condition, not to demand tears from you, for it will be too late; weep rather for me now and extinguish the fire which burns me.

You shall see me in order that your piety may be strengthened by horror of this carcase, and my death be eloquent to tell you what you brave when you love a man. I hope you will be willing, when you have finished this mortal life, to be buried near me. Your cold ashes need then fear nothing, and my tomb shall be the more rich and renowned.

PETRARCH

FRANCESCO PETRARCA (1304–74), ITALIAN RENAISsance scholar and poet. Most famous for his perfection of the sonnet, his works include *Canzoniere*, the epic poem *Africa*, and the prose history *De Viris Illustribus*.

To "Socrates" (May/June 1349)

The "pestilence" was the Black Death, a form of bubonic plague which killed around a third of Europe's 25 million population.

Oh, brother, brother, brother! (That may seem a new way to begin a letter, but in fact it's very ancient; it was used by Cicero nearly 1,400 years ago.) Alas, my loving brother, what shall I say? How can I begin? Where shall I turn? Everywhere is woe, terror everywhere. You may see in me what you have read in Virgil of the great city, with "everywhere tearing pain, everywhere fear and the manifold images of death". Oh, brother, would that I had never been born or that I had already met my death! And if that is my present wish, what, think you, shall I say if I shall reach extreme old age? How I hope I do not! But if it comes, I fear not a longer life, but a long death...

I think that my complaints will be excused, if one reflects that I am not mourning some slight distress but that dreadful year 1348, which not merely robbed us of our friends, but robbed the whole world of its peoples. And if that were not enough, now this following year reaps the remainder, and cuts down with its deadly scythe whatever survived that storm. Will posterity credit that there was a time when, with no deluge from heaven, no worldwide conflagration, no wars or other visible devastation, not merely this or that territory but almost the whole earth was depopulated? When was such a disaster ever seen, ever heard of? In what records can we read that houses were emptied, cities abandoned, countrysides untilled, fields heaped with corpses and a vast, dreadful solitude over all the world? Consult the historians, they are silent. Interrogate the physicists; they are dumfounded. Ask the philosophers; they shrug their shoulders, they wrinkle their brows; finger to lip, they command silence. Posterity, will you believe what we who lived through it can hardly accept? We should think we were dreaming, had we not the testimony of our opened eyes, encountering on our city walks only funerals, and on our return finding our home empty of our dear ones. Thus we learn that our troubles are real and true. Oh how happy will be future times, unacquainted with such miseries, perhaps counting our testimony as fabulous!

I don't deny that we deserve these evils and even worse. But our ancestors deserved them too; may our descendants not deserve them likewise! Why then, most just of judges, should the punishment of thy avenging sword fall particularly on our times? Why, in times when guilt abounded, was punishment withheld? While all sinned alike, now we alone bear the lash...

Can it be that God has no care for the mortal lot?

Surely thou dost care for us and for our affairs, O God: but there is some hidden, unknown reason why, through all the centuries, we have seemed to be the creatures most severely to be punished. Not that justice is the less just because it is concealed; for the depth of thy judgements is inscrutable and inaccessible to human senses. So either we are the worst of all beings, which I should like to deny but dare not; or God is exercising and purging us with present evils for our future good; or there is something at the root which we are totally unable to conceive. Anyway, however hidden the reasons, the results are very evident.

There remained for me here a survivor of the wrecks of last year, a man distinguished above all, and, on my word, great of soul and wise in judgement. This was Paganino da Milano. After several trials of his worth, I found him most congenial. I judged that as my friend he was worthy to be friend to us all, thus I began to regard him as another Socrates. He had your sincerity, your good fellowship; and – the happiest quality in a friend – we shared good fortune and bad, laid bare our inmost feelings, honestly avowed our secrets...

Now he too was suddenly snatched away by the pestilence that ravages the world. He dined in the evening with friends, and afterward he spent some time with me in talk and in friendly discussion of our affairs. That night he was attacked. He bore his sufferings with a stout spirit; and in the morning death came swiftly. And that no evil should be spared him, within three days his children and his whole family followed him to the grave. Oh mortals, strain strive, and sweat, range the earth and sea for riches you will not attain, for glory that will not last! The life we lead is a sleep, and all its businesses resemble those in dreams. Only death shatters the sleep, the dream. Oh, may such an awakening be granted us! But live, meanwhile; and farewell.

But to turn from public griefs to our private ones, hardly a year and a half has gone by since, departing for Italy, I left you in tears by the tearful fountain of the Sorgue. Look no farther back; count these few

31

days, and think what we were and what we are. Where now are those sweet friends, where are the loved faces, where the caressing words, the gay and gentle conversation? What lightning bolt destroyed them, what earthquake overthrew them, what tempest submerged them, what abyss swallowed them? We were a close-knit band; and now we are almost alone. We must make new friendships. Where shall we find them? And to what end, if the human race is almost extinguished, if, as I surmise, the end of the world is at hand?...

POPE PIUS II

ENEA SILVIO DE PICCOLOMINI (1405–64), SCHOLAR AND diplomat, was elected Pope in 1458, at which he rejected his earlier decadence in favour of a stringent Christianity.

❧

To Cardinal Rodrigo Borgia (11 June 1460)

Despite Pius II's reprimand, Borgia continued his dissolute ways. He later bribed his way onto the papal throne as Alexander VI.

Dear Son:

We have learned that your Worthiness, forgetful of the high office with which you are invested, was present from the seventeenth to the twenty-second hour, four days ago, in the gardens of John de Bichis, where there were several women of Siena, women wholly given over to worldly vanities. Your companion was one of your colleagues whom his years, if not the dignity of his office, ought to have reminded of his duty. We have heard that the dance was indulged in in all wantonness; none of the allurements of love were lacking, and you conducted yourself in a wholly worldly manner. Shame forbids mention of all that took place, for not only the things themselves but their very names are unworthy of your rank. In order that your lust might be all the more unrestrained, the husbands, fathers, brothers, and kinsmen of the young women and girls were not invited to be present. You and a few servants were the leaders and inspirers of this orgy.

It is said that nothing is now talked of in Siena but your vanity, which is the subject of universal ridicule. Certain it is that here at the baths, where Churchmen and the laity are very numerous, your name is on everyone's tongue. Our displeasure is beyond words, for your conduct has brought the holy state and office into disgrace; the people will say that they make us rich and great, not that we may live a blameless life, but that we may have means to gratify our passions. This is the reason the princes and the powers despise us and the laity mock us; this is why our own mode of living is thrown in our face when we reprove others. Contempt is the lot of Christ's vicar because he seems to tolerate these actions.

You, dear son, have charge of the bishopric of Valencia, the most important in Spain; you are a chancellor of the Church, and what renders your conduct all the more reprehensible is the fact that you have a seat among the cardinals, with the Pope, as advisors of the Holy See. We leave it to you whether it is becoming to your dignity to court young women, and to send those whom you love fruits and wine, and during the whole day to give no thought to anything but sensual pleasures. People blame us on your account, and the memory of your blessed uncle, Calixtus, likewise suffers, and many say he did wrong in heaping honours upon you. If you try to excuse yourself on the ground of your youth, I say to you: you are no longer so young as not to see what duties your offices impose upon you.

A cardinal should be above reproach and an example of right living before the eyes of all men, and then we should have just grounds for anger when temporal princes bestow uncomplimentary epithets upon us; when they dispute with us the possession of our property and force us to submit ourselves to their will. Of a truth we inflict these wounds upon ourselves, and we ourselves are the cause of these troubles, since we by our conduct are daily diminishing the authority of the Church. Our punishment for it in this world is dishonour, and in the world to come well-deserved torment.

May, therefore, your good sense place a restraint on these frivolities, and may you never lose sight of your dignity; then people will not call you a vain gallant among men. If this occurs again we shall be compelled to show that it was contrary to our exhortation, and that it caused us great pain; and our censure will not pass over you without causing you to blush. We have always loved you and thought you worthy of our protection as a man of an earnest and modest character. Therefore, conduct yourself henceforth so that we may retain this our opinion of you, and may behold in you only the example of a well-ordered life. Your years, which are not such as to preclude improvement, permit us to admonish you paternally.

LEONARDO DA VINCI

THE RENAISSANCE GENIUS LEONARDO DA VINCI (1452–1519) was born near Florence, Italy, the illegitimate son of a Florentine nobleman. At the age of thirty he left Florence, decadent under the Medici, for Milan, where he was obliged to write to Lodovico Sforza seeking employment.

❧

To Lodovico Sforza, Duke of Milan (1482)

Having, most illustrious lord, seen and considered the experiments of all those who pose as masters in the art of inventing instrument is of war, and finding that their inventions differ in no way from those in common use, I am emboldened, without prejudice to anyone, to solicit an appointment of acquainting your Excellency with certain of my secrets.

1. I can construct bridges which are very light and strong and very portable, with which to pursue and defeat the enemy; and others more solid, which resist fire or assault, yet are easily removed and

placed in position; and I can also burn and destroy those of the enemy.

2. In case of a siege I can cut off water from the trenches and make pontoons and scaling ladders and other similar contrivances.

3. If by reason of the elevation or the strength of its position a place cannot be bombarded, I can demolish every fortress if its foundations have not been set on stone.

4. I can also make a kind of cannon which is light and easy of transport, with which to hurl small stones like hail, and of which the smoke causes great terror to the enemy, so that they suffer heavy loss and confusion.

5. I can noiselessly construct to any prescribed point subterranean passages either straight or winding, passing if necessary underneath trenches or a river.

6. I can make armoured wagons carrying artillery, which shall break through the most serried ranks of the enemy, and so open a safe passage for his infantry.

7. If occasion should arise, I can construct cannon and mortars and light ordnance in shape both ornamental and useful and different from those in common use.

8. When it is impossible to use cannon I can supply in their stead catapults, mangonels, trabocchi and other instruments of admirable efficiency not in general use – in short, as the occasion requires I can supply infinite means of attack and defence.

9. And if the fight should take place upon the sea I can construct many engines most suitable either for attack or defence and ships which can resist the fire of the heaviest cannon, and powders or weapons.

10. In time of peace, I believe that I can give you as complete satisfaction as anyone else in the construction of buildings both public and private, and in conducting water from one place to another.

I can further execute sculpture in marble, bronze or clay, also in painting I can do as much as anyone else, whoever he may be.

Moreover, I would undertake the commission of the bronze horse, which shall endue with immortal glory and eternal honour the auspicious memory of your father and of the illustrious house of Sforza.–

And if any of the aforesaid things should seem to anyone impossible or impracticable, I offer myself as ready to make trial of them in your park or in whatever place shall please your Excellency, to whom I commend myself with all possible humility.

QUEEN CATHERINE OF ARAGON

THE YOUNGEST DAUGHTER OF KING FERDINAND AND Queen Isabella of Aragon, Catherine of Aragon (1485–1536) married the Prince of Wales, heir of Henry VII in 1501; on the Prince's premature death she was betrothed to her brother-in-law, the future Henry VIII.

⁂

To her father, King Ferdinand II of Aragon (c. 1506)

Ferdinand II of Aragon (1452–1516), first monarch of all Spain. Henry VII (1457–1509), first Tudor king of England, kept his daughter-in-law in penury.

My Lord,
...I have written many times to Your Highness, supplicating you to order a remedy for my extreme necessity, of which [letters] I have never had an answer. Now I supplicate Your Highness, for the love of Our Lord, that you consider how I am your daughter, and that after Him (our Saviour) I have no other good nor remedy, except in Your Highness; and how I am in debt in London, and this not for extravagant things, nor yet by relieving my own people, who greatly

need it, but only [for] food; and how the King of England, my lord, will not cause them to be satisfied, although I myself spoke to him and all those of his Council, and that with tears: but he said, that he is not bound to give me anything, and that even the food he gives me is of his good will; because Your Highness has not kept promise with him in the money of my marriage-portion. I told him that I believed that in time to come Your Highness would discharge it. He told me that was yet to see, and that he did not know it. So that, my lord, I am in the greatest trouble and anguish in the world. On the one part, seeing all my people that they are ready to ask alms; on the other, the debts that I have in London.

About my own person I have nothing for chemises; wherefore, by Your Highness' life, I have now sold some bracelets to get a dress of black velvet, for I was all but naked; for since I departed thence I have had nothing but two new dresses, for till now, those I brought from thence have lasted me. Although now I have got nothing but dresses of brocade... Calderon, who brings this letter, has served me very well. He is now going to be married. I have not wherewith to recompense him. I supplicate Your Highness to do me so great a favour as to command him to be paid there, and have him recommended; for I have such care for him, that any favour that Your Highness may do him I should receive as most signal. Our Lord guard the life and royal estate of Your Highness, and increase it as I desire.

> From Richmond, the 22nd of April.
> The humble servant of Your Highness,
> who kisses your hands,
> *The Princess of Wales*

ALBRECHT DÜRER

ALBRECHT DÜRER (1471–1528), PAINTER AND ENGRAVER, born in Nuremburg, Germany where he was apprenticed under Michael Wolgemut, the illustrator of the Nuremburg Chronicle. One of Dürer's first major commissions on founding his own workshop was *The Assumption of the Virgin* for Jacob Heller.

❧

To Jacob Heller (24 August 1508)

Dear Herr Jacob,

I have safely received your letter, that is to say, the last but one, and I gather from it that you wish me to execute your panel well, which is just what I myself have in mind to do. In addition, you shall know how far it has got on; the wings have been painted in stone colours on the outside, but they are not yet varnished; inside they are wholly underpainted, so that [the assistants] can begin to carry them out.

The middle panel I have outlined with the greatest care and at cost of much time; it is also coated with two very good colours upon which I can begin to underpaint it. For I intend, so soon as I hear you approve, to underpaint it some four, five, or six times over, for clearness and durability's sake, also to use the very best ultramarine for the painting that I can get. And no one shall paint a stroke on it except myself, wherefore I shall spend much time on it. I therefore assume that you will not mind, and have decided to write you my proposed plan of work [but I must add] that I cannot without loss carry out said work [in such elaborate fashion] for the fee of 130 Rhenish florins; for I must spend such money and lose time over it. However, what I have promised you I will honourably perform: if you don't want the picture to cost more than the price agreed, I will paint it in such a way that it will still be worth much more than you paid for it. If, however, you will give me 200 florins I will follow out my plan of work. Though if hereafter somebody was to offer me 400 florins I would not paint another, for I shall not gain a penny over it, as a long time is spent on it. So let me know your intention, and when I have heard it I will go to the Imhofs [the great Nuremburg banking house] for 50 florins, for I have as yet received no money on the work.

Now I commend myself to you. I want you also to know that in all my days I have never begun any work that pleased me better than this picture of yours which I am painting. Till I finish it I will not do any other work; I am only sorry that the winter will so soon come upon us. The days grow so short that one cannot do much.

I have still one thing to ask you; it is about the Madonna that you saw in my house; if you know of any one near you who wants a picture pray offer it to him. If a proper frame were put to it, it would be a beautiful picture, and you know that it is neatly done. If I had to paint it for someone, I would not take less than 50 florins. I will let you have it cheap. But as it is already done it might be damaged in the house. So I would give you full power to sell it for me cheap for 30 florins, indeed rather than that it should not be sold I would even let it go for 25 florins. I have certainly lost much food over it.

Many good nights. Given at Nürnberg on Bartholomew's day 1508.

❧

To Jacob Heller (26 August 1509)

First my willing service to you, dear Herr Jacob Heller. In accordance with your last letter, I am sending the picture well packed and seen to in all needful points. I have handed it over to Hans Imhof and he has paid me another 100 florins. Yet believe me, on my honour, I am still losing my own money over it besides losing the time which I have bestowed upon it. Here in Nürnberg they were ready to pay 300 florins for it, which extra 100 florins would have done nicely for me had I not sent [the picture] in order to please and serve you. For I value keeping your friendship at more than 100 florins, I would also rather have this painting at Frankfurt, than anywhere else in all Germany.

If you think that I have behaved unfairly in not leaving the payment to your own free will, you must bear in mind that this would not have happened if you had not written by Hans Imhof that I might keep the picture as long as I liked. I should otherwise gladly have left it to you even if thereby I had suffered a greater loss still. But I have confidence in you that, supposing I had promised to make you something for about 10 florins and it cost me 20, you yourself would not wish me to lose by it. So pray be content with the fact that I took 100 florins less from you than I might have got for the picture – for I tell you that they wanted to take it from me, so to speak, by force.

I have painted it with great care, as you will see, using none but the best colours I could get. It is painted with good ultramarine under, and over, and over that again, some five or six times; and then after it was finished I painted it again twice over so that it may last a long time. Since you will keep it clean I know it will remain bright and fresh 500 years, for it is not done as men are wont to paint. So have it kept clean and don't let it be touched or sprinkled with holy water. I feel sure it will not be criticized, or only for the purpose of annoying me; and I believe it will please you well.

No one shall ever compel me to paint a picture again with so much labour. Herr Georg Tausy besought me of his own accord to paint him a Madonna in a landscape with the same care and of the same size as this picture, and he would give me 400 florins for it. That I flatly refused to do, for it would have made a beggar of me. Of ordinary pictures I will in a year paint a pile which no one would believe it possible for one man to do in the time. But painstaking drudgery does not get along so speedily. So henceforth I shall stick to my engraving, and had I done so before I should today have been a richer man by 1,000 florins.

I may tell you also that, at my own expense, I have had for the middle panel a new frame made which has cost me more than 6 florins. The old one I have broken off, for the joiner had made it crudely; but I have not had it gilded, for you would not have it. It would be a very good thing to have the bands unscrewed so that the picture may not crack.

If the picture is set up, let it be made to hang forward two or three finger breadths, for then it will be well visible, on account of the glare. And when I come over to you, say in one, or two, or three years' time, the picture must be taken down [to see] whether it has dried out, and then I would varnish it over anew with a special varnish, which no one else can make; it will then last another 100 years longer than it would before. But don't let anybody else varnish it, for all other varnishes are yellow, and the picture would be ruined for you. And if a thing, on which I have spent more than a year's work, were ruined it would be grief to me. And when you unpack it, be present yourself lest it be damaged. Deal carefully with it, for you will hear from your own and from foreign painters how it is done.

Give my greeting to your painter Martin Hess. My wife asks you for a *Trinkgeld*, but that is as you please, I screw you no higher. And now I hold myself commended to you. Read by the sense, for I write in haste. Given at Nürnberg on Sunday after Bartholomew's 1509.

BABAR THE CONQUEROR

ZAHIR AL-DIN MUHAMMAD (1483–1530), BABAR the Conqueror, invaded India to establish the Mughal empire. Defeated in the process were the Afghans of Ibrahim Lodi and the Hindu Rajput confederacy; both continued resistance, including an assassination attempt on Babar in December 1526.

To a friend (1527)

The details of the momentous events of Friday the 16th of the first Rabi in the date 933 [21 December 1526] are as follows: The ill-omened old woman Ibrahim's mother heard that I ate things from the hands of Hindustanis – the thing being that three or four months earlier, as I had not seen Hindustani dishes, I had ordered Ibrahim's cooks to be brought and out of fifty or sixty had kept four. Of this she heard, sent to Atawa for Ahmad the taster, and, having got him, gave a *tula* of poison, wrapped in a square of paper, into the hand of a slave woman who was to give it to him. That poison Ahmad gave to the Hindustani cooks in our kitchen, promising them four *parganas* if they would get it somehow into the food.

Following the first slave woman, that ill-omened old woman sent a second to see if the first did or did not give the poison she had received to Ahmad. Well was it that Ahmad put the poison not into the cooking pot but on a dish! He did not put it into the pot because I had strictly ordered the tasters to compel any Hindustanis who were present while food was cooking in the pots, to taste that food. Our graceless tasters were neglectful when the food was being dished up. Thin slices of bread were put on a porcelain dish; on these less than half of the paper packet of poison was sprinkled, and over this buttered fritters were laid. It would have been bad if the poison had been strewn on the fritters or thrown into the pot. In his confusion, the man threw the larger half into the fireplace.

On Friday, late after the afternoon prayer, when the cooked meats were set out, I ate a good deal of a dish of hare and also much fried carrot, took a few mouthfuls of the poisoned Hindustani food without noticing any unpleasant flavour, took also a mouthful or two of dried meat. Then I felt sick. As some dried meat eaten on the previous day had had an unpleasant taste, I thought my nausea due to the dried meat. Again and again my heart rose; after retching two or three times I was near vomiting on the tablecloth. At last I saw it would not do, got up, went retching every moment of the way to the water-closet, and, on reaching it, vomited much. Never had I vomited after food, used not to do so indeed while drinking.

I became suspicious; I had the cooks put in ward and ordered some of the vomit to be given to a dog and the dog to be watched. It was somewhat out-of-sorts near the first watch of the next day; its belly was swollen and however much people threw stones at it and turned it over, it did not get up. In that state it remained till mid-day; it then got up; it did not die. One or two of the braves who also had eaten of that dish vomited a good deal next day; one was in a very bad state. In the end all escaped. "An evil arrived but happily passed on! God gave me new birth! I am coming from that other world; I am born today of my mother; I was sick; I live; through God, I know today the worth of life!"

I ordered Paymaster Sl. Muhammad to watch the cook; when he was taken for torture, he related the above particulars one after another.

Monday being court day, I ordered the grandees and notables, amirs and wazirs, to be present and that those two men and two women should be brought and questioned. They related the particulars of the affair. The taster I had cut in pieces, the cook skinned alive; one of the women I had thrown under an elephant, the other shot with a matchlock. The old woman I had kept under guard; she will meet her doom, the captive of her own act.

On Saturday I drank a bowl of milk, on Sunday 'araq in which stamped clay was dissolved. On Monday I drank milk in which were dissolved stamped clay and the best theriac, a strong purge. As on the first day, Saturday, something very dark like parched bile was voided.

Thanks be to God! no harm has been done. Till now I had not known so well how sweet a thing life can seem! As the line has it, "He who has been near to death knows the worth of life." Spite of myself, I am all upset whenever the dreadful occurrence comes back to my mind. It must have been God's favour gave me life anew; with what words can I thank him?

Although the terror of the occurrence was too great for words, I have written all that happened, with detail and circumstance, because I said to myself, "Don't let their hearts be kept in anxiety!" Thanks be to God! there may be other days yet to see! All has passed off well and for good; have no fear or anxiety in your minds.

KING HENRY VIII

HENRY VIII (1491–1547), KING OF ENGLAND from 1509. He first married Catherine of Aragon,

but when she failed to bear him a male child he determined to nullify the marriage. Furthermore, he had also
set his affections on Lady Anne Boleyn, the niece of
the Duke of Norfolk. She refused to consummate the
relationship until Henry began negotiations for divorce
from Catherine.

To Anne Boleyn (c. 1522)

To My Mistress

As the time seems very long since I heard from you, or concerning
your health, the great love I have for you constrains me to send this
bearer, to be better informed both of your health and pleasure,
particularly because, since my last parting with you, I have been told
that you have entirely changed the mind in which I left you, and that
you neither mean to come to court with your mother, nor any other
way; which report, if true, I cannot enough marvel at, being persuaded
in my own mind that I have never committed any offence against you.

And it seems hard, in return for the great love I bear you, to be kept
at a distance from the person and presence of the woman in the world
that I value the most; and if you loved with as much affection as I hope
you do, I am sure that the distance of our two persons would be equally
irksome to you – though this does not belong so much to the mistress
as to the servant.

Consider well, my mistress, how greatly your absence afflicts me. I
hope it is not your will that it should be so. But if I heard for certain
that you yourself desire it, I could but mourn my ill fortune, and
strive by degrees to abate of my folly. And so, for lack of time, I make
an end of this rude letter, beseeching you to give the bearer credence
in all he will tell you from me.

Written by the hand of your entire servant,

H.R.

To Anne Boleyn (n.d.)

By revolving in my mind the contents of your last letters, I have put myself into great agony, not knowing how to interpret them – whether to my advantage (as I understand some of them) or not. I beseech you earnestly to let me know your real mind as to the love between us two. It is needful for me to obtain this answer, having been for a whole year wounded with the dart of love, and not yet assured whether I shall succeed in finding a place in your heart and affection.

This uncertainty has hindered me of late from declaring you my mistress, lest it should prove that you only entertain for me an ordinary regard. But if you please to do the duty of a true and loyal mistress, and give up yourself heart and body to me, who will be, as I have been, your most loyal servant (if your rigour does not forbid me), I promise you that not only the name shall be given you, but also that I will take you for my mistress, casting off all others that are in competition with you out of my thoughts and affections, and serving you only.

I beg you to give an entire answer to this my rude letter, that I may know on what and how far I may depend; but if it does not please you to answer me in writing, let me know some place where I may have it by word of mouth, and I will go thither with all my heart.

No more, for fear of tiring you.

Written by the hand of him who would willing remain

Yours,
H. REX

To Anne Boleyn (1528)

My Mistress and My Friend,

My heart and I surrender ourselves into your hands, and we supplicate to be commended to your good graces, and that by absence your affections may not be diminished to us. For that would be to augment our pain, which would be a great pity, since absence gives enough and more than I ever thought could be felt. This brings to my mind a fact in astronomy, which is, that the further the poles are from the sun, notwithstanding, the more scorching is his heat. Thus it is with our love; absence has placed distance between us, nevertheless fervour increases – at least on my part. I hope the same from you, assuring you that in my case the anguish of absence is so great, that it would be intolerable were it not for the firm hope I have of your indissoluble affection towards me.

In order to remind you of it, and because I cannot in person be in your presence, I sent you the thing which comes nearest that is possible; that is to say, my picture, and the whole device, which you already know of, set in bracelets, wishing myself in their place when it pleaseth you. This is from the hand of your servant and friend.

H.R.

To Anne Boleyn (1528)

The reasonable request in your last letter, with the pleasure also that I take to know them true, causes me to send you these news. The legate whom we most desire arrived at Paris on Sunday or Monday last, so that I trust by the next Monday to hear of his arrival at Calais. And then I trust within a while after to enjoy that which I have so longed for, to God's pleasure, and both our comforts.

No more to you at this present, mine own darling, for lack of time. But I would that you were in my arms, or I in yours – for I think it long since I kissed you.

Written after the killing of a hart, at eleven of the clock; purposing with God's grace, to-morrow, mighty timely, to kill another, by the hand which, I trust, shortly shall be yours.

HENRY R.

Anne Boleyn to Henry VIII (6 May 1536, from the Tower of London)

Despite Henry VIII's declarations of love for Anne Boleyn she fell out of his favour, particularly after her failure to produce a male heir. She was falsely arrested and tried for incest with her brother, along with adulterous relations with four commoners. Her appeal for justice was to no avail, and she was beheaded on 19 May 1536. Eleven days later Henry VIII married Jane Seymour. Boleyn's daughter later ruled as Elizabeth I.

Sir,

Your Grace's displeasure, and my Imprisonment are Things so strange to me, as what to Write, or what to Excuse, I am altogether ignorant; whereas you sent unto me (willing me to confess a Truth, and so obtain your Favour) by such a one, whom you know to be my ancient and professed Enemy; I no sooner received the Message by him, than I rightly conceived your Meaning; and if, as you say, confessing Truth indeed may procure my safety, I shall with all Willingness and Duty perform your Command.

But let not your Grace ever imagine that your poor Wife will ever be brought to acknowledge a Fault, where not so much as Thought thereof proceeded. And to speak a truth, never Prince had Wife more Loyal in all Duty, and in all true Affection, than you have found in *Anne Boleyn*, with which Name and Place could willingly have contended my self, as if God, and your Grace's Pleasure had been so pleased. Neither did I at any time so far forge my self in my Exaltation, or received Queenship, but that I always looked for such an Alteration as now I find; for the ground of my preferment being on no surer Foundation than your Grace's Fancy, the least Alteration, I knew, was fit and sufficient to draw that Fancy to some other subject.

You have chosen me, from a low Estate, to be your Queen and Companion, far beyond my Desert or Desire. If then you found me worthy of such Honour, Good your Grace, let not any light Fancy, or bad Counsel of mine Enemies, withdraw your Princely Favour from me; neither let that Stain, that unworthy Stain of a Disloyal Heart towards your good Grace, ever cast so foul a Blot on your most Dutiful Wife, and the Infant Princess your Daughter:

Try me, good King, but let me have a Lawful Trial, and let not my sworn Enemies sit as my Accusers and Judges, yes, let me receive an open Trial, for my Truth shall fear no open shame; then shall you see, either mine Innocency cleared, your Suspicion and Conscience satisfied, the Ignominy and Slander of the World stopped, or my Guilt openly declared. So that whatsoever God or you may determine of me, your Grace may be freed from an open Censure; and mine Offence being so lawfully proved, your Grace is at liberty, both before God and Man, not only to execute worthy Punishment on me as an unlawful Wife, but to follow your Affection already settled on that party, for whose sake I am now as I am, whose Name I could some good while since have pointed unto: Your Grace being not ignorant of my Suspicion therein.

But if you have already determined of me, and that not only my Death, but an Infamous Slander must bring you the enjoying of your desired Happiness; then I desire of God, that he will pardon your great Sin therein, and likewise mine Enemies, the Instruments thereof; that he will not call you to a strict Account for your unprincely and cruel usage of me, at his General Judgment-Seat, where both you and my self must shortly appear, and in whose Judgment, I doubt not, (whatsover the World may think of me) mine Innocence shall be openly known, and sufficiently cleared.

My last and only Request shall be, That my self may only bear the Burthen of your Grace's Displeasure, and that it may not touch the Innocent Souls of those poor Gentlemen, who (as I understand) are likewise in strait Imprisonment for my sake. If ever I have found favour in your Sight; if ever the Name of Anne Boleyn hath been pleasing to your Ears, then let me obtain this Request; and I will so leave to trouble your Grace any further, with mine earnest Prayers to the Trinity to have your Grace in his good keeping, and to direct you in all your actions.

Your most Loyal and ever Faithful Wife, *Anne Boleyn*
From my doleful Prison the Tower, this 6th of May.

PIETRO ARETINO

THE POET AND WIT PIETRO ARETINO (1492–1557) WAS born in Arezzo, Italy. His works include the bawdy *Sonetti Lussuriosi*, which incurred the disfavour of Pope Leo X. It is said that Aretino died from injuries received after falling off a stool laughing at his sister's misadventures.

To his landlord (c. 1530)

I should think it a sin of ingratitude, gentle sir, if I did not repay with praise a part of my debt to the divine site on which your house is built and where I dwell with the utmost pleasure in life, for it is set in a place which neither hither nor thither nor higher nor lower could better. Certainly, whoever built it gave it the most proper and pre-eminent place on the whole Grand Canal, and, as this is the patriarch of all avenues and Venice the Pope of all cities, I may truthfully say that I enjoy the most beautiful street and the most delightful view in the world.

I never go to the window but I see thousands of people and as many gondolas going to market. The *piazze* to my right are the Beccarie and the Pescaria; on the left, the Bridge and the Fondaco dei Tedeschi; while, facing them both, rises the Rialto, crowded with traders. Here I see boats full of grapes, game and birds in the shops, and kitchen gardens on the pavements. Rivers and irrigated fields I no longer care to see, now that I can watch the water at dawn covered with every manner of thing that is in season. It is a joy to study the bearers of this grand plenty of fruits and greens and to watch them dispensing them to the porters who carry them to their stalls.

But all this is nothing to the sight of twenty or twenty-five sailboats, heaped up with melons like a little island, and the multitude thronging about them to reckon and weigh and smell their beauty. Of the beautiful housewives shining in silks and gold and jewels, and seated proudly under the poop, I will say nothing, lest I slight their pomp. But I will say that I hold my sides when I listen to the boatmen shouting, jeering, and roaring at those who are rowed by lackeys without scarlet hose.

And what man could hold his water if he saw, as Giulio Camillo and I saw, a boatload of Germans upset in the dead of winter, just as they came out of a tavern? Giulio is a wag and he says that the side door of this house, being dark, narrow, and brutal to climb, is like the terrible name I have made for myself by venting the truth; but he adds: anyone who knows me finds in my pure, frank, and natural friendship the same calm contentment that he feels when he comes out on the portico of my palace and leans on my balcony. Moreover, to add to the delight of my eye, here are the orange groves that gild the base of the Palazzo dei Camerlinghi on one side, and on the other the *rio* and bridge of San Giovanni Grisostomo; and the winter sun cannot rise without saluting my bed, my study, my kitchen, my chambers, and my hall...

In sum, if I could satisfy touch and the other senses as I satisfy sight, the house would be a heaven, for I enjoy every recreation here that can please the eye. Nor must I forget the great gentlemen, both foreign and native, who pass my door, nor my heavenly rapture when the Bucentaur goes by, nor the regattas, nor the festivals which convert the Canal into a continual triumph for my eye, which is lord of all it surveys. And what shall I say of the lights which appear in the evening like scattered stars? Or of the night music which tickles my ear with sweet harmonies? It would be easier to describe your profound judgment in letters and public affairs than to exhaust the delights that I enjoy merely in gazing.

Therefore, if there be any faint breath of talent in the trifles I have written, I owe it to the innuence, neither of shadow nor of light nor yet of verdure nor of violets, but to the joy I feel in the airy felicity of your mansion, in which may God grant me to number, in vigour and health, the years a respectable man may hope to live.

VISCOUNT LISLE

Arthur Plantagenet, Viscount Lisle (148?–1542), illegitimate son of Edward IV, was the Governor of Calais between 1533 and 1540. Some 3,000 letters to and from Lisle's Calais household survive.

Sir John Russell to Lord Lisle (6 August 1533)

The king was Henry VIII.

Right honourable and my singular good Lord, in my heartiest manner I commend me unto your good Lordship. And very glad I am to hear of the good report of you, how well you are beloved and how well you use yourself there, which is great comfort and pleasure to your friends here. Howbeit, I would fain know how you like the town and the country there, and the air thereabout. My Lord, news here is none, but that thanked be God the King's Highness is merry and in good health, and I never saw him merrier of a great while than he is now; and the best pastime in hunting, the red deer that I have seen And for cheer, what at my Lord Marquess of Exeter's, Mr Treasurer's, and at Mr Weston's, I never saw more delicate nor better cheer in my life. The King was minded to go to Farnham, and from thence to East Hampstead and so to Windsor And now he cometh not there because of the Sweat, and he was fain to remove from Guildford to Sutton, Mr Weston's house, because of the Sweat in likewise And now within this viij days his Grace cometh again to Windsor. And soon after the Queen removeth from thence to Greenwich, where her Grace taketh her chamber.

My Lord, your Lordship was so good unto me at your departing that you promised to provide me of iij tun of wine, whereof I heartily desire your Lordship to be so good unto me as to send me one tun of French wine to Bridewell, to one Gayes, skinner; for I can get none in London that is aught for no money...

If there be any pleasure or service I may do you, you may command me, as he that is your own assuredly, to the best of my little power; as knoweth our Lord, who preserve your lordship and send you good honourable and long life.

From Sutton, the vj[th] day of August. I pray you that I may be commended unto my good lady your wife.

Your owen to comande
J. Russell

❧

Lord Edmund Howard to Lady Lisle (c. 1535)

Howard was the father of Catherine Howard, the fifth wife of Henry VIII.

Madame so it is I have this night after midnight taken sour medicine, for the which I heartily thank you, for it hath done me much good, and hath caused the stone to break, so that now I void much gravel. But for all that, your said medicine hath done me little honesty, for it made me piss my bed this night, for the which my wife hath sore beaten me, and saying it is children's parts to bepiss their bed. Ye have made me such a pisser that I dare not this day go abroad, wherefore I beseech you to make mine excuse to my Lord and Master Treasurer, for that I shall not be with you this day at dinner. Madame, it is showed me that a wing or a leg of a stork, if I eat thereof, will make me that I shall never piss more in bed, and though my body be simple yet my tongue shall be ever good, and especially when it speaketh of women; and sithence such a medicine will do such a great cure God send me a piece thereof.

all youres,
Edmund Howard

John Husee to Lord Lisle (21 August 1537)

Husee was Lisle's agent in London. Lisle had sent to Sir William Fitzwilliam, the Lord Admiral and Lord Privy Seal, what he hoped was an appropriate gift-cum-bribe: a seal – the aquatic sort.

...touching my Lord Admiral, he hath him commended most heartily unto your lordship, and thanketh you for the seal. And his lordship saith that he will send your lordship venison shortly. Your lordship shall understand that I kept the seal here at Wapping v weeks and more, for none of my Lord Admiral's men would receive her. She spent me some day in fish vj^d, and yet she had not dined. I could never speak with my Lord Admiral till the King came to Grafton, and there I delivered him your letter. And when his lordship had read the same he said it required no answer, and how that he wist not where to keep the seal, but desired me at my coming to London to kill it and deliver it to Osburne his man and cause him to bake it and send the same to my Lady his wife, and so it is done. I perceive he will keep nothing that shall put him to cost.

SIR THOMAS MORE

SIR THOMAS MORE (1478–1535), LORD CHANCELLOR of England, author of *Utopia*. On the breach with Rome he refused to recognize Henry VIII as head of the English church and was beheaded on 6 July 1535. His last letter, written "with a coal" was to his daughter Margaret, wife of the biographer William Roper.

To Margaret Roper (5 July 1535)

Dorothy Coly and Joan Alleyne were Margaret Roper's maids.

Our Lord bless you good daughter and your good husband and your little boy and all yours and all my children and all my godchildren and all our friends. Recommend me when you may to my good daughter Cecily, whom I beseech our Lord to comfort, and I send her my blessing and to all her children and pray her to pray for me. I send her an handkercher and God comfort my good son her husband. My good daughter Daunce hath the picture in parchment that you delivered me from my Lady Conyers, her name is on the back side. Show her that I heartily pray her that you may send it in my name to her again for a token from me to pray for me.

I like special well Dorothy Coly, I pray you be good unto her. I would wit whether this be she that you wrote me of. If not I pray you be good to the tother, as you may in her affliction and to my good daughter Joan Alleyne to give her I pray you some kind answer, for she sued hither to me this day to pray you be good to her.

I cumber you good Margaret much, but I would be sorry, if it should be any longer than tomorrow, for it is St Thomas's Eve, and the utas of St Peter and therefore tomorrow long I to go to God, it were a day very meet and convenient for me. I never liked your manner toward me better than when you kissed me last for I love when daughterly love and dear charity hath no leisure to look to worldly courtesy.

Farewell my dear child, and pray for me, and I shall for you and all your friends that we may merrily meet in heaven. I thank you for your great cost.

I send now unto my good daughter Clement her algorism stone and I send her and my good son and all hers God's blessing and mine.

I pray you at time convenient recommend me to my good son John More. I liked well his natural fashion. Our Lord bless him and his good wife my loving daughter, to whom I pray him to be good, as he hath great cause, and that if the land of mine come to his hand, he break not my will concerning his sister Daunce. And our Lord bless Thomas and Austen and all that they shall have.

QUEEN ELIZABETH I

ELIZABETH I (1533–1603), DAUGHTER OF HENRY VIII and Anne Boleyn, acceded to the throne of England in 1558. She allowed marriage negotiations with several foreign suitors, although with no intention of completion, and was content instead to see the succession fall on James VI of Scotland, her nephew and fellow Protestant.

❧

To King Erik of Sweden (25 February 1561)

King Erik had offered his hand in marriage in August 1560, an offer diplomatically rejected in this reply.

Most Serene Prince Our Very Dear Cousin,

A letter truly yours both in the writing and sentiment was given us on 30 December by your very dear brother, the Duke of Finland. And while we perceive therefrom that the zeal and love of your mind towards us is not diminished, yet in part we are grieved that we cannot gratify your Serene Highness with the same kind of affection. And that indeed does not happen because we doubt in any way of your love and honour, but, as often we have testified both in words and writing, that we have never yet conceived a feeling of that kind of affection towards anyone. We therefore beg your Serene Highness again and again that you be pleased to set a limit to your love, that it advance not beyond the laws of friendship for the present nor disregard them in the future. And we in our turn shall take care that whatever can be required for the holy preservation of friendship between Princes we will always perform towards your Serene Highness. It seems strange for your Serene Highness to write that you understand from your brother and your ambassadors that we have entirely determined not to marry an absent husband; and that we will give you no certain reply until we shall have seen your person.

We certainly think that if God ever direct our heart to consideration of marriage we shall never accept or choose any absent husband how powerful and wealthy a Prince soever. But that we are not to give you an answer until we have seen your person is so far from the thing itself that we never even considered such a thing. But I have always given both to your brother, who is certainly a most excellent prince and deservedly very dear to us, and also to your ambassador likewise the same answer with scarcely any variation of the words, that we do not conceive in our heart to take a husband, but highly commend this single life, and hope that your Serene Highness will no longer spend time in waiting for us.

God keep your Serene Highness for many years in good health and safety. From our Palace at Westminster, 25 February

Your Serene Highness' sister and cousin,
Elizabeth

To John Harrington (1575)

Harrington, a teenager, was Elizabeth's godson. The letter accompanied a copy of her speech to Parliament.

Boy Jack

I have made a clerk write fair my poor words for thine use. As it cannot be such striplings have entrance into Parliament Assembly yet.

Ponder them in thy hours of leisure, and play with them till they enter thine understanding; so shalt thou hereafter, perchance, find some good fruits hereof when thy godmother is out of remembrance; and I do this because thy father was ready to serve and love us in trouble and thrall.

To James VI of Scotland (c. 1 February 1586)

James VI had suggested that his mother, Mary Queen of Scots, imprisoned by Elizabeth for traitorous activities, should be placed in the custody of a neutral power.

Be not carried away, my dear brother, with the lewd persuasions of such as instead of informing you of my too needful and helpless cause of defending the breath that God hath given me, to be better spent than spilt by the bloody invention of traitors' hands, may perhaps make you believe that either the offence was not so great, or if that cannot serve them, for the over-manifest trial which in public and by the greatest and most in this land hath been manifestly proved, yet they will make that her life may be saved and mine safe, which would God were true, for when you make view of my long danger endured these four – well-nigh five – months' time to make a taste of, the greatest wits amongst my own, and then of French, and last of you, will grant with me, that if need were not more than my malice she should not have her merit.

And now for a good conclusion of my long-tarried-for answer. Your commissioners tells me that I may trust her in the hand of some indifferent prince, and have all her cousins and allies promise she will no more seek my ruin. Dear brother and cousin, weigh in true and equal balance whether they lack not much good ground when such stuff serves for their building. Suppose you I am so mad to trust my life in another's hand and send it out of my own? If the young master of Gray, for currying favour with you, might fortune to say it, yet old master Melvin hath years enough to teach him more wisdom than to tell a prince of any judgment such a contrarious frivolous maimed reason. Let your councillors, for your honour, discharge their duty so much to you as to declare the absurdity of such an offer; and, for my part, I do assure myself too much of your wisdom, as, though like a most natural son you charged them to seek all means they could devise with wit or judgment to save her life, yet I can not, nor do not, allege any fault to you of these persuasions, for I take it you will remember that advice or desires ought ever agree with the surety of the party sent to and honour of the sender, which when both you weigh, I doubt not but your wisdom will excuse my need, and wait my necessity, and not accuse me either of malice or of hate.

And now to conclude. Make account, I pray you, of my firm friendship, love and care, of which you may make sure account, as one that never minds to fail from my word, nor swerve from our league, but will increase, by all good means, any action that may make true show of my stable amity; from which, my dear brother, let no sinister whispers, no busy troublers of princes' states persuade to leave your surest, and stick to unstable stays. Suppose them to be but the echoes of those whose stipendiaries they be, and will do more for their gain than for your good. And so, God hold you ever in his blessed keeping, and make you see your true friends. Excuse my not writing sooner, for pain in one of my eyes was only the cause.

Your most assured loving sister and cousin,
Elizabeth R.

To my dear brother and cousin, the king of Scots.

SIR PHILIP SIDNEY

SIR PHILIP SIDNEY (1554–86), POET AND SOLDIER, SON of Sir Henry Sidney, the Lord Deputy of Ireland.

To Edmund Molyneux (31 May 1578)

Molyneux was secretary to Sir Henry Sidney.

Mr Mollineax

Few woordes are beste. My lettres to my Father have come to the eys of some. Neither can I condemne any but yow for it. If it be so you have plaide the very knave with me; and so I will make yow know if I have good proofe of it. But that for so muche as is past. For that is to come, I assure yow before God, that if ever I know yowdo so muche as reede any lettre I wryte to my Father, without his commandement, or my consente, I will thruste my Dagger into you. And truste to it, for I speake it in earnest. In the meane time farwell. From Courte this laste of May 1578.

By me
Philippe Sidney.

SIR WALTER RALEIGH

SIR WALTER RALEIGH (1552–1618), POET, SOLDIER, AND navigator. A favourite of Queen Elizabeth I, he fell from grace on the accession of James I, and was sentenced to death on 11 December 1603. He wrote the following valedictory letter to his wife from the Tower of London, but was then reprieved. The sentence, however, was carried out in 1618 after Raleigh led an abortive expedition to find gold along the Orinoco.

To his wife, Elizabeth (December 1603)

Elizabeth ('Bessy') Raleigh was a former maid-in-honour to Elizabeth I.

You shall receave, deare wief, my last words in these my last lynes. My love I send you, that you may keepe it when I am dead; and my councell, that you may remember it when I am noe more. I would not, with my last Will, present you with sorrowes, deare Besse. Lett them goe to the grave with me, and be buried in the dust. And, seeing it is not the will of God that ever I shall see you in this lief, beare my destruccion gentlie and with a hart like yourself.

First, I send you all the thanks my hart cann conceive, or my penn expresse, for your many troubles and cares taken for me, which – though they have not taken effect as you wished – yet my debt is to you never the lesse; but pay it I never shall in this world.

Secondlie, I beseich you. for the love you bare me living that you doe not hide yourself many dayes, but by your travell seeke to helpe your miserable fortunes, and the right of your poore childe. Your mourning cannot avayle me that am but dust.

You shall understand that my lands were conveyed to my child, *bonâ fide*. The wrightings were drawn at Midsummer was twelvemonethes, as divers can wittnesse. My honest cosen Brett can testifie so much, and Dalberie, too, cann remember somewhat therein. And I trust my bloud will quench their mallice that desire my slaughter; and that they will not alsoe seeke to kill you and yours with extreame poverty. To what frind to direct thee I knowe not. for all mine have left mee in the true tyme of triall: and I plainly perceive that my death was determyned from the first day. Most sorry I am (as God knoweth) that, being thus surprised with death, I can leave you noe better estate. I meant you all myne office of wynes, or that I could purchase by selling it; half my stuffe. the jewells, but some few, for my boy. But God hath prevented all my determinations; the great God that worketh all in all. If you can live free from want, care for no more; for the rest is but vanity. Love God. and beginne betymes to repose yourself on Him; therein shall you find true and lastinge ritches, and endles comfort. For the rest, when you have travelled and wearied your thoughts on all sorts of worldly cogitations, you shall sit downe by Sorrow in the end. Teach your sonne alsoe to serve and feare God, while he is young: that the feare of God may grow upp in him. Then will God be a husband unto you, and a father unto him; a husband and a father which can never be taken from you.

Bayly oweth me two hundred pounds, and Adrion six hundred pounds. In Gersey, alsoe, I have much owinge me. The arrearages of the wynes will pay my debts. And, howsoever, for my soul's healthe, I beseech you pay all poore men. When I am gonne, no doubt you shal be sought unto by many, for the world thinks that I was very ritch; but take heed of the pretences of men and of their affections; for they laste but in honest and worthy men. And no greater misery cann befall you in this life then to become a pray, and after to be despised. I speak it (God knowes) not to disswad you from marriage – for that willbe best for you – both in respect of God and the world. As for me, l am no more your's, nor you myne. Death hath cutt us asunder; and God hath devided me from the world, and you from me.

Remember your poore childe for his father's sake, that comforted you and loved you in his happiest tymes.

Gett those letters (if it bee possible) which I writt to the Lords, wherein I sued for my lief, but God knoweth that itt was for you and yours that I desired it, but itt is true that I disdaine myself for begging itt. And know itt (deare wief) that your sonne is the childe of a true man, and who, in his own respect, despiseth Death, and all his misshapen and ouglie formes.

I cannot wright much. God knowes howe hardlie I stole this tyme. when all sleep; and it is tyme to separate my thoughts from the world. Begg my dead body, which living was denyed you; and either lay itt att Sherborne if the land continue, or in Exiter church, by my father and mother. I can wright noe more. Tyme and Death call me awaye.

The everlasting, infinite powerfull, and inscrutable God, that Almightie God that is goodnes itself, mercy itself, the true lief and light, keep and yours, and have mercy on me, and teach me to forgeve my persecutors and false accusers; and send us to meete in His glorious kingdome. My true wief, farewell. Blesse my poore boye; pray for me. My true God hold you both in His armes.

Written with the dyeing hand of sometyme thy husband, but now (alasse!) overthrowne.

Your's that was; but nowe not my owne,
W. Ralegh.

KING JAMES I

JAMES I (1566–1625), KING OF SCOTLAND FROM 1567, king of England from 1603, son of Mary, Queen of Scots.

※

To George Villiers, Marquis of Buckingham (1622)

George Villiers (1592–1628), English courtier and statesman, a favourite of the homosexual James I, who heaped upon him wealth and titles, eventually that of Duke of Buckingham.

My only sweet and dear child,

I am now so miserable a coward, as I do nothing but weep and mourn; for I protest to God, I rode this afternoon a great way in the park without speaking to anybody, and the tears trickling down my cheeks, as now they do, that I can scarcely see to write. But, alas! what shall I do at our parting? The only small comfort that I can have will be to pry into thy defects with the eye of an enemy, and of every mote to make a mountain; and so harden my heart against thy absence. But this little malice is like jealousy, proceeding from a sweet root; but in one point it overcometh it, for, as it proceeds from love, so it cannot but end in love.

Sweet heart! be earnest with Kate to come and meet thee at New Hall within eight or ten days after this. Cast thee to be here tomorrow, as near as about two in the afternoon as thou canst, and come galloping hither. Remember thy picture, and suffer none of the Council to come here – for God's sake! Write not a word again, and let no creature see this letter. The Lord of heaven and earth bless thee, and my sweet daughter, and my sweet little grandchild, and all thy blessed family, and send thee a happier return – both now and thou knowest when – to thy dear dad and Christian gossip.

James R.

To Prince Charles and George Villiers
(17 March 1623)

Prince Charles, accompanied by George Villiers, had been despatched to Madrid to secure the hand of the Infanta.

My Sweet Boys,

I write now, my seventh letter, unto you, upon the 17th of March, sent in my ship called the *Adventure*, to my two boys adventurers, who God ever bless. And now to begin with him, *a Jove principium*, I have sent you my Baby, two of your chaplains fittest for this purpose, Mawe and Wrenn, together, with all stuff and ornaments fit for the service of God. I have fully instructed them, so as all their behaviour and service shall, I hope, prove decent, and agreeable to the purity of the primitive Church, and yet as near the Roman form as can lawfully be done, for it hath ever been my way to go with the Church of Rome *usque ad aras*. All the particularities hereof I remit to the relation of your before named chaplains. I send you also your robes of the order, which ye must not forget to wear upon St. George's Day, and dine together in them, if they can come in time, which I pray God they may, for it will be a goodly sight for the Spaniards to see my two boys dine in them: I send you also the jewels as I promised, some of mine and such of yours, I mean both of you, as are worthy the sending. For my Baby's presenting his mistress, I send him an old double cross of Lorrain, not so rich as ancient, and yet not contemptible for the value; a good looking-glass, with my picture in it, to be hung at her girdle, which ye must tell her ye have caused it so to be enchanted by art magic, as whensoever she shall be pleased to look in it, she shall see the fairest lady that either her brother or your father's dominions can afford; ye shall present her with two fair long diamonds, set like an anchor, and a fair pendant diamond hanging at them; ye shall give her a goodly rope of pearls; ye shall give her a carquant or collar, thirteen great balls rubies, and thirteen knots or conques of pearls, and ye shall give her a head-dressing of two and twenty great pear pearls; and ye shall give her three goodly pear pendants diamonds, whereof the biggest to be worn at a needle on the midst of her forehead, and one in every ear; and for my Baby's own wearing, ye have two good jewels of your own, your round broach of diamonds, and your triangle diamond with the great round pearl; and I send you for your wearing, the three brethren, that ye know full well, but newly set, and the mirrour of France, the fellow of the Portugal diamond, which I would wish you to wear alone in your hat, with a little black feather; ye have also good diamond buttons of your own, to be set to a doublet, or jerkin. As for your I [?], it may serve for a present to a don. As for thee, my sweet Gossip, I send thee a fair table diamond, which I would once have given thee before, if thou would have taken it, for wearing in thy hat, or where thou pleases; and if my Baby will spare thee the two long diamonds in form of an anchor, with the pendant diamond, it were fit for an admiral to wear, and he hath enough better jewels for his mistress, though he's of thine own thy good old jewel, thy three pinders diamonds, the picture-case I gave Kate, and the great diamond chain I gave her, who would have sent thee the least pin she had, if I had not staid her. If my Baby will not spare the anchor from his mistress, he may well lend thee his round broach to wear, and yet he shall have jewels to wear in his hat, for three great days. And now for the form of my Baby's presenting of his jewels to his mistress, I leave that to himself, with Steenie's advice, and my Lord of Bristol's; only I would not have them presented all at once, but at the more sundry times the better, and I would have the rarest and richest kept hindmost. I have also sent four other crosses, of meaner value, with a great pointed diamond in a ring, which will save charges in presents to dons, according to their quality; but I will send with the fleet, divers other jewels for presents, for saving of charges, whereof we have too much need; for till my Baby's coming away, there will be no need of giving of presents to any but to her. Thus ye see, bow, as long as I want the sweet comfort of my boys' conversation, I am forced, yea, and delight to converse with them by long letters. God bless you both, my sweet boys, and send you, after a successful journey, joyful and happy return in the arms of your dear dad.

James R.

George Villiers to James I (25 April 1623)

Dere dad, gossope, and steward,

Though your babie him selfe hath sent word what neede he hath of more jewells, yeet will I by this berer, who can make more speede then Carlile, againe acquaint your majestie therewith and give my poure and sausie opinion what will be fittest more to send. Hetherto you have bine so spareing that, whereas you thought to have sent him suffitientlie for his one wareing, to present his mistris, who I ame sure shall shortlie now louse that title, and to lend me, that I to the contrarie have bine forsed to lend him. You neede not aske who made me able to doe it. Sir, he hath neyther chaine nor hattband, and I beseech you consider first how rich they are in jewells here, then in what a poure equipage he came in, how he hath no other meanes to appere like a kings sonne, how they are usefullests at such a time as this, when they may doe your selfe, your sone and the nation honor, and lastlie how it will neyther caust nor hasard you anie thinge. These resons I hope, since you have ventured allredie your cheefest jewell, your sonne, will serve to perswade you to lett louse theese more after him, first your best hattband, the Portingall dimond, the rest of the pendant dimonds to make up a necles to give his mistris, and the best rope of perle, with a rich chaine or tow for him selfe to waire, or els your doge must want a coller, which is the redie way to put him into it. There are manie other jewells which are of so meane qualitie as they deserve not that name, but will save much in your purs and serve verie well for presents. They had never so good and greate an occation to take the aire out of there boxses as at this time. God knowes when they shall have such another, and they had neede some times to gett nerer the sonne to continue them in their perfection. Here give me leave humbly on my knees to give your majestie thankes for that rich jewell you sent me in a box by my lord Vahan; and give him leave to kiss your hands from me, who tooke the paines to draw it. My reward to him is this: he spent his time well, which is the thinge wee should all most desier and is the glorie I covett most here in your service, which sweet Jesus grant me and your blessing.

> Your majestie's most humble slave
> and doge,
> *Steenie*.

James I to George Villiers (1625)

My own sweet and dear child,

Notwithstanding of your desiring me to write yesterday, yet had I written in the evening, if at my coming in out of the park such a drowsiness had not come upon me, as I was forced to sit and sleep in my chair half an hour. And yet I cannot content myself without sending you this billet, praying God that I may have a joyful and comfortable meeting with you, and that we may make at this Christenmass a new marriage, ever to be kept hereafter; for, God so love me, as I desire only to live in this world for your sake, and that I had rather live banished in any part of the earth with you, than live a sorrowful widow-life without you.

And so God bless you, my sweet child and wife, and grant that ye may ever be a comfort to your dear dad and husband.

> *James R.*

JOHN DONNE

JOHN DONNE (1572–1631), ENGLISH POET. HE WAS appointed Dean of St Paul's in 1621.

To Sir Henry Goodyer (4 October 1622)

Goodyer was one of Donne's patrons.

almost at midnight

Sir,

All our moralities are but our outworks, our Christianity is our Citadel; a man who considers duty but the dignity of his being a man, is not easily beat from his outworks, but from his Christianity never; and therefore I dare trust you, who contemplates them both. Every distemper of the body now, is complicated with the spleen, and when we were young men we scarce ever heard of the spleen. In our declinations now, every accident is accompanied with heavy clouds of melancholy; and in our youth we never admitted any. It is the spleen of the minde, and we are affected with vapors from thence; yet truly, even this sadnesse that overtakes us, and this yeelding to the sadnesse, is not so vehement a poison (though it be no Physick neither) as those false waies, in which we sought our comforts in our looser daies. You are able to make rules to your self, and our B. Saviour continue to you an ability to keep within those rules. And this particular occasion of your present sadnesse must be helped by the rule, for, examples you will scarce finde any, scarce any that is not encombred and distressed in his fortunes. I had locked my self, sealed and secured my self against all possibilities of falling into new debts, and in good faith, this year hath thrown me £400 lower than when I entred this house. I am a Father as well as you, and of children (I humbly thank God) of as good dispositions; and in saying so, I make account that I have taken my comparison as high as I could goe; for in good faith, I beleeve yours to be so: but as those my daughters (who are capable of such considerations) cannot but see my desire to accommodate them in this world, so I think they will not murmure if heaven must be their Nunnery, and they associated to the B. virgins there: I know they would be content to passe their lives in a Prison, rather than I should macerate my self for them, much more to suffer the mediocrity of my house, and my means, though that cannot preferre them: yours are such too, and it need not that patience, for your fortune doth not so farre exercise their patience. But to leave all in Gods hands, from whose hands nothing can be wrung by whining but by praying, nor by praying without the *Fiat voluntas tua*. Sir, you are used to my hand, and, I think have leisure to spend some time in picking out sense, in ragges; else I had written lesse, and in longer time. Here is room for an *Amen*; the prayer – so I am going to my bedside to make for all you and all yours, with

Your true friend and servant in Christ Jesus
J. Donne.

JAMES HOWELL

HOWELL (1593–1666), SCHOLAR, POLITICIAN AND royalist spy. Imprisoned by Parliament during the Civil War, he was created Historiographer Royal to Charles II at the Restoration. He wrote forty-one books, among them *Instructions for Forreine Travel* (1642) and *Epsistolae Ho-Elianae; or Familiar Letters* (1645–55).

To Lady Scroop (25 August 1628)

Lady Scroop was the aunt of George Villiers, the Duke of Buckingham; the latter was assassinated by a disaffected lieutenant, John Felton, on 23 August.

Madam,

I lay yesternight at the Post-house at *Stilton*, and this morning betimes the Post-master came to my Bed's-head and told me the D. of *Buckingham* was slain: My Faith was not then strong enough to believe it, till an hour ago I met in the way with my Lord of *Rutland* (your Brother) riding Post towards *London*; it pleas'd him to alight, and shew me a Letter, wherein there was an exact relation of all the circumstances of this sad Tragedy.

Upon *Saturday* last, which was but next before yesterday, being *Bartholomew Eve*, the Duke did rise up in a well-dispos'd humour out of his bed, and cut a Caper or two, and being ready, and having been under the Barber's hand (where the murderer had thought to have done the deed, for he was leaning upon the window all the while), he went to breakfast, attended by a great company of Commanders, where *Mons. Soubize* came to him, and whisper'd him in the ear that *Rochel* was reliev'd: The Duke seem'd to slight the news, which made some think that *Soubize* went away discontented. After breakfast, the Duke going out, Col. *Fryer* stept before him, and stopping him upon some business, and Lieut. *Felton* being behind, made a thrust with a common tenpenny knife over *Fryer's* arm at the Duke, which lighted so fatally, that he slit his heart in two, leaving the knife sticking in the body. The Duke took out the knife, and threw it away; and laying his hand on his Sword, and drawn it half out, said, The Villain hath kill'd me (meaning, as some think, Col. *Fryer*), for there had been some difference 'twixt them; so, reeling against a chimney, he fell down dead. The Dutchess being with Child, hearing the noise below, came in her night-geers from her Bed-chamber, which was in an upper room, to a kind of rail, and thence beheld him weltering in his own blood. *Felton* had lost his hat in the croud, wherein there was a Paper sow'd, wherein he declar'd, that the reason which mov'd him to this Act was no grudge of his own, tho' he had been far behind for his pay, and had been put by his Captain's place twice, but in regard he thought the Duke an Enemy to the *State*, because he was branded in Parliament; therefore what he did was for the publick good of his Country. Yet he got clearly down, and so might have gone to his horse, which was ty'd to a hedge hard by; but he was so amaz'd that he miss'd his way, and so struck into the pastry, where, altho' the cry went that some *Frenchman* had done't, he thinking the word was *Felton*, boldly confess'd, 'twas he that had done the deed, and so he was in their hands. *Jack Stamford* would have run at him, but he was kept off by Mr *Nicholas*; so being carry'd up to a Tower, Capt. *Mince* tore off his Spurs, and asking how he durst attempt such an Act, making him believe the Duke was not dead, he answer'd boldly, that he knew he was dispatch'd, for 'twas not he, but the hand of Heaven that gave the stroke; and tho' his whole body had been cover'd over with Armour of Proof, he could not have avoided it. Capt. *Cha. Price* went post presently to the King four miles off, who being at prayers on his knees when it was told him, yet never stirr'd, nor was he disturb'd a whit till all divine service was done. This was the relation, as far as my memory could bear, in my Lord of *Rutland's* Letter, who will'd me to remember him to your Ladyship, and tell you that he was going to comfort your niece (the Dutchess) as fast as he could. And so I have sent the truth of this sad story to your Ladyship, as fast as I could by this Post, because I cannot make that speed myself, in regard of some business I have to dispatch for my Lord in the way: So I humbly take my leave, and rest—

Your Ladyship's most dutiful Servant.
J. H.

QUEEN HENRIETTA MARIA

HENRIETTA MARIA (1609–69) QUEEN CONSORT OF KING Charles I (1600–49). During the English Civil War she fled England for Holland, where she raised money for the Royalist cause, partly by selling her own and the Crown's jewels.

❧

To her son, Prince Charles, the future Charles II (1641)

Charles

    I am sorry I must begin my first letter with chiding you, because I hear that you will not take *physic*. I hope it was only for this day, and that to-morrow you will do it; for if you will not, I must come to you and make you take it, for it is for your health.

I have given order to my Lord of Newcastle, to send me word to-night whether you will or not; therefore I hope you will not give me the pain to come.

And so I rest

Your affectionate Mother,
Henrietta Marie [sic]

To my dear son, the Prince.

To Charles I (1642)

My Dear Heart,

After much trouble, we have at last procured some money, but only a little as yet, for the fears of the merchants are not entirely passed away. It was written from London, that I had carried off my jewels secretly, and against your wish, and that if money was lent me upon them, that would be no safety for them; so that all this time, when we were ready to conclude anything, our merchants drew back. At last, it was necessary to show your power, signed under your own hand, about which I have written to you before, and immediately we concluded our business...

I have given up your pearl buttons, and my little chain has done you good. You cannot imagine how handsome the buttons were, when they were out of the gold, and strung into a chain, and many as large as my great chain. I assure you, that I gave them up with no small regret. Nobody would take them in pledge, but only buy them. You may judge, now, when they know that we want money, how they keep their foot on our throat. I could not get for them more than half of what they are worth. I have six weeks time in which to redeem them, at the same price.

My great chain, and that cross which I had bought from the Queen my mother, is only pledged. With all these, I could not get any more money than what I send you.

I will send to-morrow to Antwerp, to pawn your ruby collar, for as to that, in Holland, they will not have it. For the largest collar, I am waiting a reply from Denmark. Every day, hopes are given me that those of Amsterdam will lend me money…

OLIVER CROMWELL

CROMWELL (1599–1658) WAS PARLIAMENT'S MOST effective cavalry leader during the English Civil War. He was Lord Protector of England, 1653–8.

❧

To Colonel Valentine Walton (2 July 1644)

Walton was Cromwell's brother-in-law. The letter was written immediately after the battle of Marston Moor.

To my loving Brother, Colonel Valentine Walton…

It's our duty to sympathize in all mercies; and to praise the Lord together in chastisements or trials, that so we may sorrow together.

Truly England and the Church of God hath had a great favour from the Lord, in this great victory given unto us, such as the like never was since this war began. It had all the evidences of an absolute victory obtained by the Lord's blessing upon the Godly Party principally. We never charged but we routed the enemy. The Left Wing, which I commanded, being our own horse, saving a few Scots in our rear, beat all the Prince's horse. God made them as stubble to our swords. We charged their regiments of foot with our horse, and routed all we charged. The particulars I cannot relate now; but I believe, of twenty thousand the Prince hath not four thousand left. Give glory, all the glory, to God.

Sir, God hath taken away your eldest son by a cannon-shot. It brake his leg. We were necessitated to have it cut off, whereof he died.

Sir, you know my own trials this way [Cromwell's son had been killed shortly before]: but the Lord supported me with this, That the Lord took him into the happiness we all pant for and live for. There is your precious child full of glory, never to know sin or sorrow any more. He was a gallant young man, exceedingly gracious. God give you His comfort. Before his death he was so full of comfort that to Frank Russel and myself he could not express it, "It was so great above his pain." This he said to us. Indeed it was admirable. A little after, he said, One thing lay upon his spirit. I asked him, What that was? He told me it was, That God had not suffered him to be any more the executioner of His enemies. At his fall, his horse being killed with the bullet, and as I am informed three horses more, I am told he bid them, Open to the right and left, that he might see the rogues run. Truly he was exceedingly beloved in the Army, of all that knew him. But few knew him; for he was a precious young man, fit for God. You have cause to bless the Lord. He is a glorious Saint in Heaven; wherein you ought exceedingly to rejoice. Let this drink up your sorrow; seeing these are not feigned words to comfort you, but the thing is so real and undoubted a truth. You may do all things by the strength of Christ. Seek that, and you shall easily bear your trial. Let this public mercy to the Church of God make you to forget your private sorrow. The Lord be your strength: so prays

Your truly faithful and loving brother,
Oliver Cromwell

To his wife (12 April 1651)

Written from Edinburgh, during Cromwell's campaign against Prince Charles.

My Dearest,

I praise the the Lord I am increased in strength in my outward man but that will not satisfy me except I get a heart to love and serve my Heavenly Father better; and get more of the light of His countenance, which is better than life, and more power over my corruptions: in these hopes I wait, and am not without expectation of a gracious return; Pray for me; truly do I daily for thee, and the dear family; and God Almighty bless you with all His spiritual blessings.

Mind poor Betty of the Lord's great mercy. Oh, I desire her not only to seek the Lord in her necessity, but indeed and in truth to turn to the Lord; and to keep close to Him; and to take heed of a departing heart, and of being cozened with worldly vanities and worldly company, which I doubt she is too subject to. I earnestly and frequently pray for her and for him. Truly they are dear to me, very dear; and I am in fear lest Satan should deceive them, knowing how weak our hearts are, and how subtle the adversary is, and what way the deceitfulness of our hearts and the vain world make for his temptations. The Lord give them truth of heart to Him. Let them seek Him in truth, and they shall find Him.

My love to the dear little ones; I pray for grace for them. I thank them for their letters; let me have them often.

Beware of my Lord Herbert's resort to your house. If he do so, it may occasion scandal, as if I were bargaining with him. Indeed, be wise, you know my meaning. Mind Sir Henry Vane of the business of my estate. Mr Floyd knows my whole mind in that matter.

If Dick Cromwell and his wife be with you, my dear love to them. I pray for them; they shall, God willing, hear from me. I love them very dearly. Truly I am not able to write much. I am weary; and rest. Thine.

John Dryden

J OHN DRYDEN (1631–1700), ENGLISH POET LAUREATE.
Honor Dryden was his cousin.

To Honor Dryden (May 1653)

Madame,

If you have received the lines I sent by the reverend Levite, I doubt not but they have exceedingly wrought upon you; for beeing so longe in a Clergymans pocket, assuredly they have acquired more Sanctity then theire Author meant them. Alasse Madame, for ought I know they may become a Sermon ere they could arrive at you; and believe it having you for the text it could scarcely proove bad, if it light upon one that could handle it indifferently. But I am so miserable a preacher that though I have so sweet and copious a subject, I still fall short in my expressions And instead of an use of thanksgiveing I am allways makeing one of comfort, that I may one day againe have the happinesse to kisse your faire hand, but that is a message I would not so willingly do by letter as by word of mouth. This is a point I must confesse I could willingly dwell longer on, and in this case what ever I say you may confidently take for gospell. But I must hasten. And indeed Madame (Beloved I had almost sayd) hee had need hasten who treats of you; for to speake fully to evry part of your excellencyes requires a longer houre then most persons have allotted them. But in a word your selfe hath been the best Expositor upon the text of your own worth, in that admirable Comment you wrote upon it, I meane your incomparable letter. By all thats good (and you Madame are a great part of my Oath) it hath put me so farre besides my selfe that I have scarce patience to write prose: my pen is stealing into verse every time I kisse your letter. I am sure the poore paper smarts for my Idolatry, which by wearing it continually neere my brest will at last bee burnt and martyrd in those flames of adoration it hath kindled in mee. But I forgett Madame what rarityes your letter came fraught with besides words; You are such a Deity that commands worship by provideing the Sacrifice: you are pleasd Madame to force mee to write by sending me Materialls, and compell mee to my greatest happinesse. Yet though I highly vallue your Magnificent presents, pardon mee if I must tell the world they are but imperfect Emblemes of your beauty; For the white and red of waxe and paper are but shaddowes of that vermillion and snowe in your lips and forehead. And the silver of the Inkhorne if it presume to vye whiteness with your purer Skinne, must confesse it selfe blacker than the liquor it containes. What then do I more than retrieve your own guifts? and present you that paper adulterated with blotts which you gave spotlesse?

> For since t'was mine the white hath lost its hiew
> To show t'was n'ere it selfe but whilst in you;
> The Virgin Waxe hath blusht it selfe to red
> Since it with mee hath lost its Maydenhead.
> You (fairest Nymph) are waxe; oh may you bee
> As well in softnesse so as purity;
> Till Fate and your own happy choise reveale
> Whom you so farre shall blesse to make you scale.

Fairest Valentine the unfeigned wishe of your humble votary,

Jo: Dryden.

Cambridge
May the
To the faire hands
of Madame Honor Dryden
these crave admittance

MADAME DE SÉVIGNÉ

MADAME DE SÉVIGNÉ (1626–96) FRENCH LETTER-writer, gossip, and attendant at the court of Louis XIV, "the Sun King". Nearly 1,000 letters from her, mostly to her children and family, survive.

To her cousin, the Marquis de Coulanges
(15 December 1670)

In December 1670 the French court was stunned to discover that "La Grande Mademoiselle", the ungainly niece of Louis XIII, had secured an engagement to the soldier-adventurer Duc de Lauzun.

What I am about to communicate to you is the most astonishing thing, the most surprising, the most marvellous, the most miraculous, most triumphant, most baffling, most unheard of, most singular, most extraordinary, most unbelievable, most unforeseen, biggest, tiniest, rarest, commonest, the most talked about, the most secret up to this day, the most brilliant, the most enviable, in fact a thing of which only one example can be found in past ages, and, moreover, that example is a false one; a thing nobody can believe in Paris (how could anyone believe it in Lyons?), a thing that makes everybody cry "mercy on us" a thing that fills Mme de Rohan and Mme de Hauterive with joy, in short a thing that will be done on Sunday and those who see it will think they are seeing visions – a thing that will be done on Sunday and perhaps not done by Monday. I can't make up my mind to say it. Guess, I give you three tries. You give up? Very well, I shall have to tell you. M. de Lauzun is marrying on Sunday, in the Louvre – guess who? I give you four guesses, ten, a hundred. Mme de Coulanges will be saying: That's not so very hard to guess, it's Mlle de La Vallière. Not at all, Madame, Mlle de Retz, then? Not at all, you're very provincial: Of course, how silly we are, you say: It's Mlle Colbert. You're still further away. Then it must be Mlle de Créquy? You're nowhere near. I shall have to tell you in the end: he is marrying, on Sunday, in the Louvre, with the King's permission, Mademoiselle, Mademoiselle de... Mademoiselle... guess the name. He's marrying Mademoiselle, of course! Honestly, on my honour, on my sworn oath! Mademoiselle, the great Mademoiselle, Mademoiselle, daughter of the late Monsieur, Mademoiselle, granddaughter of Henri IV, Mademoiselle d'Eu, first cousin of the King, destined for the throne, the only bride in France worthy of Monsieur [Louis XIV's brother]. If you shout aloud, if you say we have lied, that it is false, a fine old story, too feeble to imagine, you are perfectly right.

We did as much ourselves. Goodbye, letters coming by this post will show you whether we are telling the truth or not.

To her cousin, the Marquis de Coulanges
(19 December 1670)

What you might call a bolt from the blue occurred yesterday evening at the Tuileries, but I must start the story further back. You have heard as far as the joy, transports, ecstasies of the Princess and her fortunate lover. Well, the matter was announced on Monday, as you were told. Tuesday was spent in talk, astonishment, compliments. On Wednesday Mademoiselle made a settlement on M. de Lauzun, with the object of bestowing on him the titles, names and honours needed for mention in the marriage contract, and that was enacted on the same day. So, to go on with, she bestowed on him four duchies: first the earldom of Eu, which is the highest peerage in France and gives him first precedence, the duchy of Montpensier, which name he bore all day yesterday, the duchy of SaintFargeau and that of Châtellerault, the whole estimated to be worth twenty-two millions. Then the contract was drawn up, in which he took the name of Montpensier. On Thursday morning, that is yesterday, Mademoiselle hoped that the King would sign the contract as he had promised, but by seven in the evening His Majesty, being persuaded by the Queen, Monsieur and divers greybeards that this business was harmful to his reputation, decided to break it off, and after summoning Mademoiselle and M. de Lauzun, declared to them, in the presence of Monsieur le Prince, that he forbade their thinking any more about this marriage. M. de Lauzun received this order with all the respect, all the submissiveness, all the stoicism and all the despair that such a great fall required. As for Mademoiselle, according to her mood she burst into tears, cries, violent outbursts of grief, exaggerated lamentations, and she remained in bed all day, taking nothing but broth. So much for a beautiful dream, a fine subject for a novel or a tragedy, but above all for arguing and talking for ever and ever. And that is what we are doing day and night, evening and morning.

"Mademoiselle" and de Lauzun's eventual marriage was not a success.

COTTON MATHER

THE PURITAN CLERGYMAN COTTON MATHER (1663–1728) was born in Boston, Massachussetts, the son of Increase Mather. He published 382 books, with his *Memorable Providences Relating to Witchcraft and Possessions* (1685) doing much to fan the religious intolerances of New Englanders. He was an instigator of the Salem witch hunt.

To John Higginson (1682)

To Ye Aged and beloved, Mr John Higginson

There be now at sea a ship called Welcome, which has on board 100 or more of the heretics and malignants called Quakers, with W. Penn, who is the chief scamp, at the head of them. The General Court has accordingly given sacred orders to Master Malachi Huscott, of the brig Porpoise, to waylay the said Welcome slyly as near the Cape of Cod as may be, and make captive the said Penn and his ungodly crew, so that the Lord may be glorified and not mocked on the soil of this new country with the heathen worship of these people. Much spoil can be made of selling the whole lot to Barbados, where slaves fetch good prices in rum and sugar, and we shall not only do the Lord great good by punishing the wicked, but we shall make great good for His Minister and people.

Yours in the bowels of Christ,
Cotton Mather

To John Cotton Mather (5 August 1692)

Reverend Sir,

Our good God is working of miracles. Five witches were lately executed, impudently demanding of God a miraculous vindication of their innocency. Immediately upon this, our God miraculously sent in five Andover witches, who made a most ample, surprising, amazing confession of all their villainies, and declared the five newly executed to have been of their company, discovering many more, but all agreeing in Burroughs being their ringleader, who, I suppose, this day receives his trial at Salem, whither a vast concourse of people is gone, my father this morning among the rest. Since those, there have come in other confessors; yea, they come in daily. About this prodigious matter my soul has been refreshed with some little short of miraculous answers of prayer, which are not to be written; but they comfort me with a prospect of a hopeful issue.

The whole town yesterday turned the lecture into a fast, kept in our meeting-house; God give a good return. But in the morning we were entertained with the horrible tidings of the late earthquake at Jamaica, on the 7th of June last. When, on a fair day, the sea suddenly swelled, and the earth shook and broke in many places; and in a minute's time, the rich town of Port-Royal, the Tyrus of the whole English America, but a very Sodom for wickedness, was immediately swallowed up, and the sea came rolling over the town. No less than seventeen-hundred souls of that one town are missing, besides other incredible devastations all over the island, where houses are demolished, mountains overturned, rocks rent, and all manner of destruction inflicted. The Non-conformist minister there escaped wonderfully with his life. Some of our poor New England people are lost in the ruins, and others have their bones broke. Forty vessels were sunk – namely all whose cables did not break; but no New England ones. Behold, an accident speaking to all our English America. I live in pains, and want your prayers.

Bestow them, dear Sir, on Your,
Cotton Mather

NELL GWYN

ELEANOR GWYN (1650–87), ORANGE-SELLER AND ACT-ress, born in Hereford, England. She was mistress to Charles II, by whom she had two illegitimate children, the Lords Beauclerk and Burford.

To Laurence Hyde (May/June 1682)

Hyde was a politician; the letter was probably written to him when he was on a diplomatic mission to The Hague.

pray Deare Mr Hide forgive me for not writeing to you before now for the reasone is I have bin sick three months & sinse I recovered I have had nothing to intertaine you withall nor have nothing now worth writing but that I can holde no longer to let you know I never have ben in any companie without drinking your health, for I love you with all my soule. the pel mel is now to me a dismale plase sinse I have uterly lost Sir Car Scrope never to be recovred agane for he tould me he could not live allwayes at this rate & so begune to be a littel uncivil, which I could not sufer from an uglye *baux garscon*. Ms Knights Lady mothers dead & she has put up a scrutchin no beiger then my Lady grins scunchis. My lord Rochester is gon in the cuntrei. Mr Savil has got a misfortune, but is upon recovery & is to mary an hairres, who I thinke wont wont have an ill time ont if he holds up his thumb. My lord of Dorscit apiers wonse in three munths, for he drinkes aile with Shadwell & Mr Haris at the Dukes house all day long. my Lord Burford remimbers his sarvis to you. my Lord Bauclaire isis goeing into france. we are a goeing to supe with the king at whithall & my lady Harvie. the King remembers his sarvis to you. now lets talke of state affairs, for we never caried things so cunningly as now for we dont know whether we shall have pesce or war, but I am for war and for no other reason but that you may come home. I have a thousand merry conseets, but I cant make her write um & therfore you must take the will for the deed. god bye. your most loveing obedunt faithfull & humbel

sarvant
E. G.

JOHN EVELYN

JOHN EVELYN (1620–1706), ENGLISH DIARIST, AUTHOR, civil servant.

To Samuel Pepys (22 July 1700)

Samuel Pepys (1633–1703), Admiralty official, diarist; the letter was written when both diarists were in the very twilights of their lives.

I could no longer suffer this old servant of mine to pass and repass so near Clapham without a particular account of your health and all your happy family. You will now inquire what I do here? Why, as the patriarchs of old, I pass the days in the fields, among horses and oxen, sheep, cows, bulls, and sows, *et cetera pecora campi*. We have, thank God I finished our hay harvest prosperously. I am looking after my hinds, providing carriage and tackle against reaping time and sowing. What shall I say more? *Venio ad voluptates agricolarum*, which Cicero, you know, reckons amongst the most becoming diversions of old age; and so I render it. This without: now within doors, never was any matron more busy than my wife, disposing of our plain country furniture for a naked old extravagant house, suitable to our employments. She has a dairy, and distaffs, for *lac, linum, et lanam*, and is become a very Sabine. But can you thus hold out? Will my friend say; is philosophy, Gresham College, and the example of Mr Pepys, and agreeable conversation of York Buildings, quite forgotten and abandoned? No, no! *Naturam expellas furca tamen usque recurret.* Know I have been ranging of no fewer than thirty large cases of books, destined for a competent standing library, during four of five days wholly destitute of my young coadjutor, who, upon some pretence of being much engaged in the mathematics, and desiring he may continue his course at Oxford till the beginning of August, I have wholly left it to him. You will now suspect something by this disordered hand; truly I was too happy in these little domestic affairs, when, on the sudden, as I was about my books in the library, I found myself sorely attacked with a shivering, followed by a feverish indisposition, and a strangury, so as to have kept, not my chamber only, but my bed, till very lately, and with just so much strength as to scribble these lines to you. For the rest, I give God thanks for this gracious warning, my great age calling upon me *sarcinam componere* every day expecting it, who have still enjoyed a wonderful course of bodily health for forty years...

Samuel Pepys to John Evelyn (7 August 1700)

I have no herds to mind, nor will my doctor allow me any book here. What then, will you say, too, are you doing? Why, truly nothing that will bear naming, and yet I am not, I think, idle; for who can, that has so much of past and to come to think on, as I have? And thinking, I take it, is working, though many forms beneath what my lady and you are doing. But pray remember what o'clock it is with you and me; and be not now, by overstirring, too bold with your present complaint, any more than I dare be with mine which, too, has been no less kind in giving me my warning, than the other to you, and to neither of us, I hope, and, through God's mercy, dare say, either unlooked for or unwelcome. I wish, nevertheless, that I were able to administer anything towards the lengthening that precious rest of life which God has thus long blessed you, and, in you, mankind, with; but I have always been too little regardful of my own health, to be a prescriber to others. I cannot give myself the scope I otherwise should in talking now to you at this distance, on account of the care extraordinary I am now under from Mrs Skinner's being suddenly fallen very ill; but ere long I may possibly venture at entertaining you with something from my young man in exchange – don't say in payment, for the pleasure you gratify me with from yours, whom I pray God to bless with continuing but what he is! and I'll ask no more for him.

LADY MARY WORTLEY MONTAGU

LADY MARY WORTLEY MONTAGU (1689–1762), ENGLISH writer and society hostess. She accompanied her husband, Edward Wortley Montagu, on his embassy to Constantinople, from where she wrote the "Turkish Letters" through which she would become famous. She was instrumental in introducing the smallpox vaccination – a practice she witnessed in Turkey – to Britain. She spent the last two decades of her life living alone in Italy and France.

To Edward Wortley Montagu (28 March 1710)

At the time of this letter, Lady Mary was the unmarried youngest daughter of the Earl (later Duke) of Kingston. She married Wortley Montagu – against her father's wishes – in 1712.

Perhaps you'l be surprizd at this Letter. I have had manny debates with my selfe before I could resolve on it. I know it is not Acting in

Form, but I do not look upon you as I do upon the rest of the world. and by what I do for you, you are not to judge my manner of acting with others. You are Brother to a Women I tenderly lov'd. My protestations of freindship are not like other people's. I never speak but what I mean, and when I say I love, it is for ever. I had that real concern for Mrs Wortley I look with some regard on every one that is related to her. This and my long Acquaintance with you may in some measure excuse what I am now doing.

I am surprizd at one of the Tatlers you sent me. Is it possible to have any sort of Esteem for a person one beleives capable of having such triffling Inclinations? Mr Bickerstaff has very wrong notions of our sex* can say there are some of us that despises charms of show, and all the pageantry of Greatnesse, perhaps with more ease than any of the Philosophers. In contemning the world they seem to take pains to contemn it. We dispise it, without takeing the pains to read lessons of Morrality to make us do it. At least I know I have allwaies look'd upon it with contempt without being at the Expence of one serious refflection to oblige me to it. I carry the matter yet farther. Was I to chuse of £2,000 a year or twenty thousand, the first would be my choice. There is something of an unavoidable embarras in makeing what is calld a great figure in the world, that takes off from the happynesse of Life. I hate the noise and hurry inseparable from great Estates and Titles, and look upon both as blessings that ought only to be given to Fools, for tis only to them that they are blessings.

The pritty Fellows you speak of, I own entertain me sometimes, but is it impossible to be diverted with what one dispises? I can laugh at a puppet shew, at the same time I know there is nothing in it worth my attention or regard. General Notions are generally wrong. Ignorance and Folly are thought the best foundations for Virtue, as if not knowing what a Good Wife is was necessary to make one so I confesse that can never be my way of reasoning. As I allwaies forgive an Injury when I think it not done out of malice, I can never think my selfe oblig'd by what is done without design. Give me leave to say

---

*Bickerstaff (aka Steele), the editor of the *Tatler*, had declared that it had been named in honour of 'the fair sex'.

it (I know it sounds Vain): I know how to make a Man of sense happy. but then that man must resolve to contribute something towards it himselfe. I have so much Esteem for you I should be very sorry to hear you was unhappy, but for the world I would not be the Instrument of makeing you so, which (of the humour you are) is hardly to be avoided if I am your Wife. You distrust me. I can neither be easy nor lov'd where I am distrusted, nor do I believe your passion for me is what you pretend it; at least I'm sure, was I in love I could not talk as you do.

Few Women would have spoke so plainly as I have done, but to dissemble is among the things I never do. I take more pains to approve my conduct to my selfe than to the world, and would not have to accuse my selfe of a minute's deceit. I wish I lov'd you enough to devote my selfe to be for Ever miserable for the pleasure of a day or two's happynesse. I cannot resolve upon it – You must think otherwise of me or not at all.

I don't injoin you to burn this Letter. I know you will. Tis the first I ever writ to one of your sex and shall be the last. You must never expect another. I resolve against all correspondence of this kind. My resolutions are seldom made and never broken.

❧

To her sister, the Countess of Mar (18 April 1717), from Adrianople, Turkey

I wrote to you, dear sister, and to all my other English correspondents, by the last ship, and only Heaven can tell when I shall have another opportunity of sending to you; but I cannot forbear to write again, though perhaps my letter may lie upon my hands these two months. To confess the truth, my head is so full of my entertainment yesterday, that 'tis absolutely necessary for my own repose to give it some vent. Without farther preface, I will then begin my story.

I was invited to dine with the Grand-Vizier's lady, and it was with a great deal of pleasure I prepared myself for an entertainment which was never before given to any Christian. I thought I should very little satisfy her curiosity (which I did not doubt was a considerable motive to the invitation) by going in a dress she was used to see and therefore dressed myself in the court habit of Vienna, which is much more magnificent than ours. However, I chose to go *incognito* to avoid any disputes about ceremony, and went in a Turkish coach, only attended by my woman that held up my train, and the Greek lady who was my interpretess. I was met at the court door by her black eunuch, who helped me out of the coach with great respect, and conducted me through several rooms, where her she-slaves, finely dressed, were ranged on each side. In the innermost I found the lady sitting on her sofa, in a sable vest. She advanced to meet me, and presented me half a dozen of her friends with great civility. She seemed a very good looking woman, near fifty years old. I was surprised to observe so little magnificence in her house, the furniture being all very moderate; and, except in her habits and number of her slaves, nothing about her appeared expensive. She guessed at my thoughts and told me she was no longer of an age to spend either her time or money in superfluities; that her whole expense was charity, and her whole employment praying to God. There was no affectation in this speech; both she and her husband are entirely given up to devotion. He never looks upon any other woman; and, what is much more extraordinary, touches no bribes, notwithstanding the example of all his predecessors. He is so scrupulous on this point, he would not accept Mr Wortley's present, till he had been assured over and over that it was a settled perquisite of his place at the entrance of every ambassador.

She entertained me with all kind of civility till dinner came in. which was served, one dish at a time, to a vast number, all finely dressed after their manner, which I don't think so bad as you have perhaps heard it represented. I am a very good judge of their eating, having lived three weeks in the house of an *effendi* at Belgrade, who gave us very magnificent dinners, dressed by his own cooks. The first week they pleased me extremely; but I own I then began to grow weary of their table, and desired our own cook might add a dish or two after our manner. But I attribute this to custom, and am very much inclined to believe that an Indian, who had never tasted of either, would prefer their cookery to ours. Their sauces are very high, all the roast very much done. They use a great deal of very rich spice. The soup is served for the last dish; and they have at least as great a variety of ragouts as we have. I was very sorry I could not eat of as many as the good lady would have had me, who was very earnest in serving me of every thing. The treat concluded with coffee and perfumes, which is a high mark of respect; two slaves kneeling *censed* my hair, clothes, and handkerchief. After this ceremony, she commanded her slaves to play and dance, which they did with their guitars in their hands, and she excused to me their want of skill, saying she took no care to accomplish them in the art.

I returned her thanks, and soon after took my leave. I was conducted back in the same manner I entered, and would have gone straight to my own house; but the Greek lady with me earnestly solicited me to visit the *kiyaya's* lady, saying, he was the second officer in the empire, and ought indeed to be looked upon as the first, the Grand-Vizier having only the name, while he exercised the authority. I had found so little diversion in the Vizier's *harem*, that I had no mind to go into another. But her importunity prevailed with me, and I am extremely glad I was so complaisant.

All things here were with quite another air than at the Grand-Vizier's, and the very house confessed the difference between an old devotee and a young beauty. It was nicely clean and magnificent. I was met at the door by two black eunuchs, who led me through a long gallery between two ranks of beautiful young girls, with their hair finely plaited, almost hanging to their feet all dressed in fine light damasks, brocaded with silver. I was sorry that decency did not permit me to stop to consider them nearer. But that thought was lost upon my entrance into a large room, or rather pavilion, built round with gilded sashes, which were most of them thrown up, and the trees planted near them gave an agreeable shade, which hindered the sun from being troublesome. The jessamines and honeysuckles that twisted round their trunks, shed a soft perfume, increased by a white marble fountain playing sweet water in the lower part of the room, which fell into three or four basins with a pleasing sound. The roof was painted with all sorts of flowers, falling out of gilded baskets, that seemed tumbling down. On a sofa, raised three steps, and covered with fine Persian carpets, sat the *kiyaya's* lady, leaning on cushions of white satin, embroidered; and at her feet sat two young girls about twelve years old, lovely as angels, dressed perfectly rich, and almost covered with jewels. But they were hardly seen near the fair *Fatima* (for that is her name), so much her beauty effaced every thing I have seen, nay, all that has been called lovely either in England or Germany. I must own that I never saw anything so gloriously beautiful, nor can I recollect a face that would have been taken notice of near hers. She stood up to receive me, saluting me after their fashion, putting her hand to her heart with a sweetness full of majesty that no court breeding could ever give. She ordered cushions to be given me, and took care to place me in the corner, which is the place of honour. I confess, though the Greek lady had before given me a great opinion of her beauty, I was so struck with admiration, that I could not for some time speak to her, being wholly taken up in gazing. That surprising harmony of features! that lovely bloom of complexion unsullied by art! the unutterable enchantment of her smile! – But her eyes! – large and black, with all the soft languishment of the blue! every turn of her face discovering some new grace.

After my first surprise was over, I endeavoured, by nicely examining her face, to find out some imperfection, without any fruit of my search, but my being clearly convinced of the error of that vulgar notion, that a face exactly proportioned, and perfectly beautiful, would not be agreeable; nature having done for her, with more success, what Apelles is said to have essayed, by a collection of the most exact features, to form a perfect face. Add to all this a behaviour so full of grace and sweetness, such easy motions, with an air so majestic, yet free from stillness or affectation, that I am persuaded, could she be suddenly transported upon the most polite throne of Europe, nobody would think her other than born and bred to be a queen, though educated in a country we call barbarous. To say all in a word, our most celebrated English beauties would vanish near her.

She was dressed in a *caftan* of gold brocade, flowered with silver, very well fitted to her shape, and showing to admiration the beauty of her bosom, only shaded by the thin gauze of her shift. Her drawers were pale pink, her waistcoat green and silver, her slippers white satin, finely embroidered: her lovely arms adorned with bracelets of diamonds, and her broad girdle set round with diamonds; upon her head a rich Turkish handkerchief of pink and silver, her own fine black hair hanging a great length in various tresses, and on one side of her head some bodkins of jewels. I am afraid you will accuse me of extravagance in this description. I think I have read somewhere that women always speak in rapture when they speak of beauty, and I cannot imagine why they should not be allowed to do so. I rather think it a virtue to be able to admire without any mixture of desire or envy. The gravest writers have spoken with great warmth of some celebrated pictures and statues. The workmanship of Heaven certainly excels all our weak imitations, and, I think, has a much better claim to our praise. For my part, I am not ashamed to own I took more pleasure in looking on the beauteous Fatima, than the finest piece of sculpture could have given me.

She told me the two girls at her feet were her daughters, though she appeared too young to be their mother. Her fair maids were ranged below the sofa, to the number of twenty, and put me in mind of the pictures of the ancient nymphs. I did not think all nature could have furnished such a scene of beauty. She made them a sign to play and dance. Four of them immediately began to play some soft airs on instruments, between a lute and a guitar which they accompanied with their voices, while the others danced by turns. This dance was very different from what I had seen before. Nothing could be more artful, or more proper to raise *certain ideas*. The tunes so soft! – the motions so languishing! – accompanied with pauses and dying eyes! half-falling back, and then recovering themselves in so artful a manner, that I am very positive the coldest and most rigid prude upon earth could not have looked upon them without thinking of *something not to be spoken of*. I suppose you may have read that the Turks have no music but what is shocking to the ears; but this account is from those who never heard any but what is played in the streets, and is just as reasonable as if a foreigner should take his ideas of English music from the *bladder and string*, or the *marrow-bones and cleavers*. I can assure you that the music is extremely pathetic; 'tis true I am inclined to prefer the Italian, but perhaps I am partial. I am acquainted with a Greek lady who sings better than Mrs Robinson, and is very well skilled in both, who gives the preference to the Turkish. 'Tis certain they have very fine natural voices; these were very agreeable. When the dance was over, four fair slaves came into the room with silver censers in their hands, and perfumed the air with amber, aloes-wood, and other scents. After this they served me coffee upon their knees in the finest japan china, with *soucoups* of silver gilt. The lovely Fatima entertained me all this while in the most polite agreeable manner, calling me often *Guzél sultanum*, or the beautiful sultana, and desiring my friendship with the best grace in the world, lamenting that she could not entertain me in my own language.

When I took my leave, two maids brought in a fine silver basket of embroidered handkerchiefs; she begged I would wear the richest for her sake, and gave the others to my woman and interpretess. I retired through the same ceremonies as before, and could not help thinking I had been some time in Mahomet's paradise, so much was I charmed with what I had seen. I know not how the relation of it appears to you. I wish it may give you part of my pleasure; for I would have my dear sister share in all the diversions of,

Yours, etc

To the Countess of Mar (c. September 1727)

Lady Mary's son, Edward, had recently run away from school at Westminster and reached as far as Gibraltar.

This is a vile world, dear sister, and I can easily comprehend that whether one is at Paris or London, one is stifled with a certain mixture of fool and knave, that most people are composed of. I would have patience with a parcel of polite rogues, or your downright honest fools; but father Adam shines through his whole progeny. So much for our inside – then our outward is so liable to ugliness and distempers, that we are perpetually plagued with feeling our own decays and seeing those of other people. Yet, sixpenny worth of common sense, divided among a whole nation, would make our lives roll away glibly enough; but then we make laws, and we follow customs. By the first we cut off our own pleasures, and by the second we are answerable for the faults and extravagances of others. All these things, and five hundred more, convince me (as I have the most profound veneration for the Author of Nature) that we are here in an actual state of punishment; I am satisfied I have been one of *the* condemned ever since I was born; and, in submission to the divine justice, I don't at all doubt but I deserved it in some pre-existent state. I will still hope that I am only in purgatory; and that after whining and grunting a certain number of years, I shall be translated to some more happy sphere, where virtue will be natural, and custom reasonable; that is, in short, where common sense will reign. I grow very devout as you see, and place all my hopes in the next life, being totally persuaded of the nothingness of this. Don't you remember how miserable we were in the little parlour at Thoresby? we then thought marrying would put us at once into possession of all we wanted. Then came being with child, &c., and you see what comes of being with child. Though, after all, I am still of opinion that it is extremely silly to submit to ill-fortune. One should pluck up a spirit, and live upon cordials when one can have no other nourishment. These are my present endeavours, and I run about, though I have five thousand pins and needles running into my heart. I try to console myself with a small damsel, who is at present everything I like – but, alas! she is yet in a white frock. At fourteen, she may run away with the butler: – there's one of the blessed consequences of great disappointments; you are not only hurt by the thing present, but it cuts off all future hopes, and makes your very expectations melancholy.

Quelle vie!!!

To her daughter, the Countess of Bute
(28 January 1753), sent from Louvere, Italy

Dear Child –

You have given me a great deal of satisfaction by your account of your eldest daughter. I am particularly pleased to hear she is a good arithmetician; it is the best proof of understanding; the knowledge of numbers is one of the chief distinctions between us and brutes. If there is any thing in blood, you may reasonably expect your children should be endowed with an uncommon share of good sense. Mr Wortley's family and mine have both produced some of the greatest men that have been born in England: I mean Admiral Sandwich, and my grandfather, who was distinguished by the name of Wise William. I have heard Lord Bute's father mentioned as an extraordinary genius, though he had not many opportunities of showing it; and his uncle the present Duke of Argyll has one of the best heads I ever knew. I will therefore speak to you as supposing Lady Mary not only capable, but desirous of learning; in that case by all means let her be indulged in it. You will tell me I did not make it a part of your education; your prospect was very different from hers. As you had much in your circumstances to attract the highest offers, it seemed your business to learn how to live in the world, as it is hers, to know how to be easy out of it. It is the common error of builders and parents to follow some plan they think beautiful (and perhaps is so), without considering that nothing is beautiful which is displaced. Hence we see so many edifices raised that the raisers can never inhabit; being too large for their fortunes. Vistas are laid open over barren heaths, and apartments contrived for a coolness very agreeable in Italy, but killing in the north of Britain; thus every woman endeavours to breed her daughter a fine lady, qualifying her for a station in which she will never appear, and at the same time incapacitating her for that retirement, to which she is destined. Learning, if she has a real taste for it, will not only make her contented, but happy in it. No entertainment is so cheap as reading, nor any pleasure so lasting. She will not want new fashions, nor regret the loss of expensive diversions, or variety of company, if she can be amused with an author, in her closet. To render this amusement complete, she should be permitted to learn the languages. I have heard it lamented that boys lose so many years in mere learning of words: this is no objection to a girl, whose time is not so precious: she cannot advance herself in any profession, and has therefore more hours to spare; and as you say her memory is good, she will be very agreeably employed this way. There are two cautions to be given on this subject: first, not to think herself learned, when she can read Latin, or even Greek. Languages are more properly to be called vehicles of learning than learning itself, as may be observed in many schoolmasters, who, though perhaps critics in grammar, are the most ignorant fellows upon earth. True knowledge consists in knowing things, not words. I would no farther wish her a linguist than to enable her to read books in their originals, that are often corrupted, and are always injured by translations. Two hours' application every morning will bring this about much sooner than you can imagine, and she will have leisure enough beside, to run over the English poetry, which is a more important part of a woman's education than it is generally supposed. Many a young damsel has been ruined by a fine copy of verses, which she would have laughed at if she had known it had been stolen from Mr Waller. I remember, when I was a girl, I saved one of my companions from destruction, who communicated to me an epistle, she was quite charmed with. As she had naturally a good taste, she observed the lines were not so smooth as Prior's or Pope's but had more thought and spirit than any of theirs. She was wonderfully delighted with such a demonstration of her lover's sense and passion, and not a little pleased with her own charms, that had force enough to inspire such elegancies. In the midst of this triumph I showed her, that they were taken from Randolph's poems, and the unfortunate transcriber was dismissed with the scorn he deserved. To say truth, the poor plagiary was very unlucky to fall into my hands; that author being no longer in fashion, would have escaped any one of less universal reading than myself. You should encourage your daughter to talk over with you what she reads; and as you are very capable of distinguishing, take care she does not mistake pert folly for wit and humour, or rhyme for poetry, which are the common errors of young people, and have a train of ill consequences.

The second caution to be given her (and which is most absolutely necessary) is to conceal whatever learning she attains, with a much solicitude as she would hide crookedness or lameness: the parade of it can only serve to draw on her the envy, and consequently the most inveterate hatred, of all he and she fools, which will certainly be at least three parts in four her acquaintance. The use of knowledge in our sex, beside the amusement of solitude, is to moderate the passions, and learn to be contented with a small expense, which are the certain effects of a studious life; and it may be preferable even to that fame which men have engrossed to themselves, and will not suffer us to share. You will tell me I have not observed this rule myself; but you are mistaken: it is only inevitable accident that has given me any reputation that way. I have always carefully avoided it, and even thought it a misfortune. The explanation of this paragraph would occasion a long digression, which I will not trouble you with, it being my present design only to say what I think useful for the instruction of my granddaughter, which I have much at heart. If she has the same inclination (I should say passion) for learning that I was born with, history, geography, and philosophy will furnish her with materials to pass away cheerfully a longer life than is allotted to mortals. I believe there are few heads capable of making Sir Isaac Newton's calculations, but the result of them is not difficult to be understood by a moderate capacity. Do not fear this should make her affect the character of Lady — , or Lady —, or Mrs —: those women are ridiculous, not because they have learning, but because they have it not. One thinks herself a complete historian, after reading Echard's Roman History; another a profound philosopher, having got by heart some of Pope's *unintelligible* essays; and a third an able divine on the strength of Whitfield's sermons: thus you hear them screaming politics and controversy.

It is a saying of Thucydides, that ignorance is bold, and knowledge reserved. Indeed it is impossible to be far advanced in it, without being more humbled by a conviction of human ignorance, than elated by learning. At the same time I recommend books, I neither exclude work nor drawing. I think it as scandalous for a woman not to know how to use a needle, as for a man not to know how to use a sword.

I was once extremely fond of my pencil, and it was a great mortification to me when my father turned off my master, having made a considerable progress for the short time I learnt. My over eagerness in the pursuit of it had brought a weakness in my eyes, that made it necessary to leave off; and all the advantage I got was the improvement of my hand. I see, by hers, that practice will make her a ready writer; she may attain it by serving you for a secretary, when your health or affairs make it troublesome to you to write yourself; and custom will make it an agreeable amusement to her. She cannot have too many for that station of life which will probably be her fate. The ultimate end of your education was to make you a good wife (and I have the comfort to hear that you are one): hers ought to be, to make her happy in a virgin state. I will not say it is happier; but it is undoubtedly safer than any marriage. In a lottery, where there is (at the lowest computation) ten thousand blanks to a prize, it is the most prudent choice, not to venture. I have always been so thoroughly persuaded of this truth, that, notwithstanding the flattering views I had for you (as I never intended you a sacrifice to my vanity), I thought I owed you the justice to lay before you all the hazards attending matrimony; you may recollect I did so in the strongest manner. Perhaps you may have more success in the instructing your daughter: she has so much company at home, she will not need seeking it abroad, and will more readily take the notions, you think fit to give her. As you were alone in my family, it would have been thought a great cruelty to suffer you no companions of your own age, especially having so many near relations, and I do not wonder their opinions influenced yours. I was not sorry to see you not determined on a single life, knowing it was not your father's intention, and contented myself with endeavouring to make your home so easy that you might not be in haste to leave it.

I am afraid you will think this is a very long insignificant letter. I hope the kindness of the design will excuse it, being willing to give you every proof in my power that I am,

Your most affectionate mother,

M. *Wortley*

JONATHAN SWIFT

JONATHAN SWIFT (1667–1745) WAS AUTHOR OF THE satirical novel *Gulliver's Travels*. In 1708 he met Esther Vanhomrigh (l690–1723) who became infatuated with him, with unhappy result for herself. Swift immortalized her as Vanessa in the poem *Cadenus and Vanessa*, in which he makes clear his distancing from her.

Esther Vanhomrigh to Jonathan Swift
(1 September 1712)

Had I a correspondent in China, I might have had an answer by this time. I never could think till now that London was so far off in your thoughts and that twenty miles were by your computation equal to some thousands. I thought it a piece of charity to undeceive you in this point and to let you know, if you'll give yourself the trouble to write, I may probably receive your letter in a day. 'Twas that made me venture to take pen in hand the third time. Sure you'll not let it be to no purpose. You must needs be extremely happy where you are, to forget your absent friends; and I believe you have formed a new system and think there is no more of this world, passing your sensible horizon. If this be your notion I must excuse you; if not, you can plead no other excuse; and if it be so, I must reckon myself of another world; but I shall have much ado to be persuaded till you send me some convincing arguments of it. Don't dally in a thing of this consequence, but demonstrate that 'tis possible to keep up a correspondence between friends, though in different worlds, and assure one another, as I do you, that

I am

Your most obedient & humble servant
E. Van Homrigh

Esther Vanhomrigh to Jonathan Swift (June 1713)

'Tis unexpressible the concern I am in ever since I heard from Mr Lewis that your head is so much out of order. Who is your physician? For God sake don't be persuaded to take many slops. Satisfy me so much as to tell me what medicines you have taken and do take. How did you find yourself whilst a shipboard? I fear 'tis your voyage has discomposed you, and then so much business following so immediately, before you had time to recruit' – twas too much. I beg, make all haste imaginable to the country for I firmly believe that air and rest will do you more good than anything in the world besides. If I talk impertinently, I know you have goodness enough to forgive me when you consider how great an ease 'tis for me to ask these questions, though I know it will be a great while before I can be answered – I am sure I shall think it so. Oh! what would I give to know how you do at this instant. My fortune is too hard: your absence was enough, without this cruel addition.

Sure the powers above are envious of your thinking so well, which makes them at some times strive to interrupt you. But I must confine my thoughts, or at least stop from telling them to you, or you'll chide, which will still add to my uneasiness. I have done all that was possible to hinder myself from writing to you till I heard you were better, for fear of breaking my promise, but 'twas all in vain; for had [I] vowed neither to touch pen, ink or paper, I certainly should have some other invention. Therefore I beg you won't be angry with me for doing what is not in my power to avoid.

Pray make Parvisol write me word what I desire to know, for I would not for the world have you hold down your head. I am impatient to the last degree to hear how you are. I hope I shall soon have you here.

To Esther Vanhomrigh (8 July 1713)

I stayed but a fortnight in Dublin, very sick, and returned not one visit of a hundred that were made me – but all to the Dean, and none to the Doctor. I am riding here for life, and think I am something better, and hate the thoughts of Dublin, and prefer a field-bed and earthen floor before the great house there, which they say is mine. I had your last spleenatic letter. I told you when I left England, I would endeavour to forget everything there, and would write as seldom as I could. I did indeed design one general round of letters to my friends, but my health has not yet suffered me. I design to pass the greatest part of the time I stay in Ireland here in the cabin where I am now writing, neither will I leave the kingdom till I am sent for; and if they have no further service for me discontent, and was horribly melancholy while they were installing me; but it begins to wear off, and change to dulness. My river walk is extremely pretty, and my canal in great beauty, and I see trouts playing in it.

I know not any one thing in Dublin; but Mr Ford is very kind, and writes to me constantly what passes among you. I find you are likewise a good politician; and I will say so much to you, that I verily think, if the thing you know of had been published just upon the Peace, the Ministry might have avoided what hath since happened. But I am now fitter to look after willows, and to cut hedges, than meddle with affairs of state. I must order one of the workmen to drive those cows out of my Island, and make up the ditch again; a work much more proper for a country vicar than driving out factions and fencing against them. And I must go and take my bitter draught to cure my head, which is spoilt by the bitter draughts the public hath given me.

How does Davila go on? Johnny Clark is chosen portreeve of our town of Trim; and we shall have the assizes there next week, and fine doings; and I must go and borrow a horse to meet the judges, and Joe Beaumont and all the boys that can get horses will go too. Mr Warburton has but a thin school. Mr Percival has built up the other side of his house, but people whisper that it is but scurvily built. Mr Steers is come to live in Mr Melthorp's house, and 'tis thought the widow Melthorp will remove to Dublin.

Nay, if you do not like this sort of news, I have no better. So go to your Dukes and Duchesses, and leave me to Goodman Bumford and Patrick Dolan of Clonduggan.

Adieu

Esther Vanhomrigh to Jonathan Swift (1720)

Believe me 'tis with the utmost regret that I now complain to you, because I know your good nature such, that you cannot see any human creature miserable without being sensibly touched. Yet what can I do? I must either unload my heart and tell you all its griefs, or sink under the unexpressible distress I now suffer by your prodigious neglect of me. 'Tis now ten long, long weeks since I saw you, and in all that time I have never received but one letter from you, and a little note with an excuse. Oh – how have you forgot me! You endeavour by severities to force me from you; nor can I blame you, for with the utmost distress and confusion I behold myself the cause of uneasy reflections to you. Yet I cannot comfort you, but here declare that 'tis not in the power of art, time or accident to lessen the unexpressible passion which I have for—. Put my passion under the utmost restraint, send me as distant from you as the earth will allow, yet you cannot banish those charming ideas, which will ever stick by me whilst I have the use of memory. Nor is the love I bear you only seated in my soul, for there is not a single atom of my frame that is not blended with it. Therefore don't flatter yourself that separation will ever change my sentiments, for I find myself unquiet in the midst of silence, and my heart is at once pierced with sorrow and love. For Heaven's sake tell me what has caused this prodigious change in you, which I have found of late. If you have the least remains of pity for me left, tell me tenderly. No; don't tell it, so that it may cause my present death; and don't suffer me to live a life like a languishing death, which is the only life I can lead if you have lost any of your tenderness for me.

Esther Vanhomrigh to Jonathan Swift (1720)

Tell me sincerely if you have once wished with earnestness to see me since I wrote to you. No, so far from that, you have not once pitied me, though I told you how I was distressed. Solitude is insupportable to a mind which is not easy. I have worn out my days in sighing, and my nights with watching and thinking of -,-,-,-, who thinks not of me. How many letters must I send you before I shall receive an answer? Can you deny me in my misery the only comfort which I can expect at present? Oh! that I could hope to see you here, or that I could go to you. I was born with violent passions, which terminate all in one – that unexpressible passion I have for you. Consider the killing emotions which I feel from your neglect of me, and shew some tenderness for me, or I shall lose my senses. Sure, you cannot possibly be so much taken up but you might command a moment to write to me and force your inclinations to do so great a charity.

I firmly believe, could I know your thoughts, (which no human creature is capable of guessing at, because never anyone living thought like you), I should find that you have often in a rage willed me religious, hoping then I should have paid my devotions to Heaven. But that would not spare you, for was I an enthusiast, still you'd be the deity I should worship. What marks are there of a deity but what you are to be known by? You are present everywhere; your dear image is always before my eyes; sometimes you strike me with that prodigious awe, I tremble with fear; at other times a charming compassion shines through your countenance, which revives my soul. Is it not more reasonable to adore a radiant form one has seen, than one only described?

To Robert Percival (3 January 1730)

Percival was a former neighbour of Swift's.

S–,

Seeing your frank on the outside, and the address in the same hand, it was obvious who was the writer, and before I opened it, a worthy friend being with me, I told him the subject of the difference between us: That your Tythes being generally worth 5 or 6ll a year, and by the terror of your Squireship frighting my Agent, to take what you graciously thought fit to give, you wronged me of half my due every year... That having held from your father an Island worth three pence a year, which I planted, and pay^d two Shillings annually for, and being out of possession of the s^d Island seven or eight years, there could not possibly be above 4^s due to you; for which you have thought fit to stop 3 or 4 years of Tyth at your own rate of 2^{ll}–5^s a year (as I remember) and still continue to stop it, on pretence that the s^d Island was not surrendered to you in form; although you have cutt down more Plantations of Willow and Abeilles than would purchase a dozen such Islands. I told my friend, that this talent of Squires formerly prevayled very much in the County of Meath; that as to your self, from the badness of your Education against all my advice and endeavors, and from the case of your Nature, as well as another circumstance which I shall not mention, I expected nothing from you that became a Gentleman. That I had expostulated this scurvy matter very gently with you, that I conceived this letter was answer: that from the prerogative of a good estate the practice of lording over a few Irish wretches, and from the natural want of better thinking, I was sure your answer would be extremely rude and stupid, full of very bad language in all senses: That a Bear in a wilderness will as soon fix on a Philosopher as on a Cotteger; and a Man wholly voyd of education, judgment, or distinction of person has no regard in his insolence but to the passion of fear; and how heartily I wished, that to make you shew your humility, your quarrell had been rather with a Captain of Dragoons than the Dean of St Patricks.

All this happened before my opening your Letter; which being read, my friend told me I was an ill guesser... That you affirm you despise me onely as a Clergy-man, by your own Confession: And that you had good reason, because Clergymen pretend to learning, wherein you value your self as what you are an utter Stranger to.

I took some pains in providing and advising about your Education, but since you have made so ill use of my rules; I cannot deny according to your own Principles that your usage of me is just... You are wholly out of my danger; the weapons I use will do you no hurt, and to that which would keep a nicer man in aw, you are insensible. A needle against a stone wall can make no impression.

Your faculty lyes in making bargains: stick to that; leave your Children a better estate than your father left you; as he left you much more than your Grandfather left him. Your father and you are much wiser than I, who gave amongst you fifty years purchase for land, for which I am not to see one farthing. This was intended as an Encouragement for a Clergyman to reside among you, whenever any of your posterity shall be able to distinguish a Man from a Beast. One thing I desire you will be set right in; I do not despise All Squires. It is true I despise the bulk of them. But, pray take notice, that a Squire must have some merit before I shall honor him with my contempt. For, I do not despise a Fly, a Maggot, or a Mite.

If you send me an answer to this, I shall not read it, but open it before company, and in their presence burn it; for no other reason but the detestation of bad spelling, no grammar, and that pertness which proceeds from ignorance and an invincible want of tast.

I have ordered a Copy of this Letter to be taken with an intention to print it, as a mark of my esteem for you; which however perhaps I shall not pursue; For I could willingly excuse our two names from standing in the same paper, since I am confident you have as little desire of Fame, as I have to give it you.

I wish many happy new years to you and your family and am with truth Your friend and humble Serv[t]

J: Swift

Let me add something serious; that, as it is held an imprudent thing to provoke valour, so I confess it was imprudent in me to provoke rudeness: which, as it was my own standing rule never to do except in cases where I had power to punish it, so my error proceeded from a better opinion of you than you have thought fit to make good ... for with every fault in your Nature, your education, and your understanding, I never imagined you so utterly devoyd of knowing some little distinction between persons.

ANTHONY HENLEY

HENLEY (?–1745) WAS A MEMBER OF PARLIAMENT FOR Southampton, relinquishing his seat in 1734. Before stepping down he wrote this letter to his constituents after they had complained to him about the Excise Bill.

To his constituents (1734)

Gentlemen,

I received yours and am surprised by your insolence in troubling me about the Excise. You know, what I very well know, that I bought you. And I know, what perhaps you think I don't know, you are now selling yourselves to Somebody Else; and I know, what you do not know, that I am buying another borough. May God's curse light upon you all: may your houses be as open and common to all Excise Officers as your wifes and daughter were to me, when I stood for your scoundrell corporation.

Yours, etc.,
Anthony Henley

THOMAS SHERIDAN

SHERIDAN (1687–1738) WAS AN IRISH SCHOOLTEACHER and a friend of the satirist Swift. Sheridan's grandson was the dramatist Richard Brinsley Sheridan, author of *The Rivals* (1775).

To Dean Jonathan Swift (15 July 1735)

A translation of Sheridan's spoof Latin, by Sir Walter Scott, is below.

De armis ter De An,

Urit tome sum time ago an diam redito anser it thus. A lac a de mi illinc ducis in it, is notabit fit fora de an; it is more fit fora puppi. I lusit toti. Irritato ripam flet an Dicti toral e ver ibit. Dic is abest. Dic is a serpenti se. Dic is a turdi se. Dic is a fartor. Dic is pisti se. Dic is a vix en. Dic is as qui ter in nasti fusti musti cur. Dic is arantur. Dic is ab a boni se. Sed Ito Dicti cantu cum in as a dans in mas ter an dans ab ori ora minuet. Da me I fido sed Dic. Quis mi ars se diu puppi. Ure as turdi rufi an sed I. Ure a tori villa in sed Dic. Ure fit fora gallus sed I; an dume dia dans in. Ure aras calli cur sed Dic. Dicti sed I ure regis a farto me.

Tanti vi sed I tanti vi
Hi fora Dic in apri vi.

Ime Dic as te mas amo use foralis angor. I recollecta piper, sed I, an dat rumpetur, an da sume cur, an ad rumor, an das qui re, an ab lac a more in ure cum pani, an da de al more me ac in a gesto uti. It is ali ad a me sed Dic, as suras istinc. Sensu caseso I caeno more.

I cum here formo ni. Itis apparent I canta ve mi maerent, mi tenentis tardi. I cursum e veri de nota peni cani res. I ambit. Mi stomachis a cor morante ver re ad ito digesta me ale in a minute. I eat nolam, noram, no dux, I generali eat a quale carbone dedat super an da qualis as fine abit as arabit. I es ter de I eat atro ut at abit. De vilis in mi a petite. A crustis mi de lite. (I neu Eumenides ago eat tuenti times more.) As unde I eat offa buccas fatas mi arsis. On nam unde I eat sum pes. A tu es de I eat apud in migra num edit. A venis de I eat sum pasti. Post de notabit. Afri de abit ab re ad. A Satur de sum tripes.

Luis is mus ter in an armi an de sines carri in it as far as I tali, sum se germani. It do es alarum mus; De vel partum. I fani nues is fito ritu me directo me at cava ni Virgilu a. Miser vice tomi da ter an, Capta in Pari, Doctor de lanij, Major Folli ut; an mi complemento mi de armis tresses, especiali fiRLL.

I amat ure re verens his cervice forever an de ver.

Dear Mister Dean,

You writ to me some time ago, and I am ready to answer it thus. Alacka-day, my ill ink, deuce is in it, is not a bit fit for a Dean; it is more fit for a puppy. I'll use it to Tighe. I writ a Tory pamphlet, and Dick Tighe tore all, every bit. Dick is a beast. Dick is a serpent, I say, Dick is a turd, I say. Dick is a farter. Dick is pist, I say. Dick is a vixen. Dick is a squittering, nasty, fusty, musty cur. Dick is a ranter. Dick is a baboon, I say. Said I to Dick Tighe, can't you come in as a dancing-master, and dance a bory or a minuet? Damme if I do, said Dick. K— my a—, said I, you puppy. You're a sturdy ruffian, said I. You're a Tory villain, said Dick. You're fit for a gallows, said I, and you may die a-dancing. You're a rascally cur, said Dick. Dick Tighe, said I, your rage is a fart to me.

> Tantivy! said I, untivy,
> Hy! for a Dick in a privy.

I made Dick as tame as a mouse for all his anger. I recollect a piper, said I, and a trumpeter, and a shoemaker, and a drummer, and a squire, and a blackamore in your company, and a deal more making a jest o' you, Tighe. It is all a lie, a damme, said Dick, as sure as I stink. Since you say so, I say no more.

I come here for money. It is apparent I can't have my May-rent, my tenant is tardy. I curse him every day, not a penny can I raise. I am bit. My stomach is a cormorant, ever ready to digest a meal every minute. I eat no lamb, no ram, no ducks. I generally eat a quail carbonaded at supper, and a quail is as fine a bit as a rabbit. Yesterday I eat a trout at a bit. Devil is in my appetite. A crust is my delight. I knew you, many days ago, eat twenty times more. A' Sunday I eat of a buck as fat as my — is; on a Monday I eat some peas; a Tuesday I eat a pudding, my gran made it; a' Wednesday I eat some pasty; Post-day not a bit; a' Friday a bit of bread; a' Saturday, some tripes.

Lewis is mustering an army, and designs carrying it as far as Italy, some say Germany. It does alarm us; devil part 'em. If any news is fit to write, you may direct to me at Cavan in Virginia. My service to my daughter Anne, Captain Parry, Doctor Delany, Major Folliott;

and my compliment to my dear mistresses, especially Worrall.

I am at your Reverence his service for ever and ever.

LORD CHESTERFIELD

PHILIP DORMER STANHOPE, 4TH EARL OF CHESTERFIELD (1694–1773), was an English statesman, who served as an Irish Lord-lieutenant and Secretary of State in the ministry of Henry Pelham. Chesterfield wrote many letters of advice to his son, Philip, encouraging him in manners and morals. When Philip predeceased him, dying in 1768 at the age of thirty-six, Chesterfield sought to similarly guide his godson and heir presumptive.

To his son (c. 1740 when the recipient was eight)

Dear boy,

You behaved yourself so well at Mr Boden's last Sunday, that you justly deserve commendation: besides, you are encouraging me to give you some rules of politeness and good-breeding, being persuaded that you will observe them.

Know then, that as learning, honour and virtue are absolutely necessary to gain you the esteem and admiration of mankind, politeness and good-breeding are equally necessary to make you welcome and agreeable in conversation and common life. Great talents, such as honour, virtue, learning, and parts, are above the generality of the world, who neither possess them themselves, nor judge of them rightly in others: but all people are and consider themselves to be judges of all the lesser talents, such as civility, affability, and an obliging, agreeable address and manner; because they feel the good effects of them, as making society easy and pleasing.

Good-sense must, in many cases, determine good-breeding; because the same thing that would be civil at one time, and to one person, may be quite otherwise at another time, and to another person: but there are some general rules of good-breeding that hold always true, and in all cases. As, for example, it is always extremely rude to answer only Yes, or No, to anybody, without adding, Sir, my Lord, or Madam, according to the quality of the person you speak to...

It is likewise extremely rude, not to give the proper attention and a civil answer when people speak to you; or to go away, or be doing something else, while they are speaking to you; for that convinces them that you despise them, and do not think it worth your while to hear or answer what they say. I dare say I need not tell you how rude it is, to take the best place in a room, or to seize immediately upon what you like at table, without offering first to help others, as if you considered nobody but yourself. On the contrary, you should always endeavour to procure all the conveniences you can to the people you are with. Besides being civil, which is absolutely necessary, the perfection of good-breeding is, to be civil with ease, and in a gentlemanlike manner. For this, you should observe the French people, who excel in it, and whose politeness seems as easy and natural as any other part of their conversation; whereas the English are often awkward in their civilities, and, when they mean to be civil, are too much ashamed to get it out.

But, pray, do you remember never to be ashamed of doing what is right: you would have a great deal of reason to be ashamed, if you were not civil; but what reason can you have to be ashamed of being civil? And why not say a civil and obliging thing as easily and naturally as you would ask what o'clock it is? This kind of bashfulness, which is justly called by the French *mauvaise honte*, is the distinguishing character of an English booby, who is frightened out of his wits when people of fashion speak to him; and, when he is to answer them, blushes, stammers, can hardly get out what he would say, and becomes really ridiculous from a groundless fear of being laughed at: whereas, a real well-bred man would speak to all the Kings in the world with as little concern and as much ease as he would speak to you.

Remember, then, to be civil, and to be civil with ease (which is properly called good-breeding), is the only way to be beloved and well received in company; that to be ill-bred and rude is intolerable, and the way to be kicked out of company; and that to be bashful is ridiculous. As I am sure you will mind and practise all this, I expect that, when you are *novennis*, you will not only be the best scholar, but the best-bred boy in England of your age.

Adieu!

To his son (6 August 1741)

I warned you in my last, against those disagreeable tricks and awkwardnesses which many people contract when they are young, by the negligence of their parents, and cannot get quit of them when they are old; such as odd motions, strange postures, and ungenteel carriage. But there is likewise an awkwardness of the mind, that ought to be, and with care may be, avoided: as, for instance, to mistake or forget names; to speak of Mr What-d'ye-call-him, or Mrs Thingum, or How-d'ye-call-her, is excessively awkward and ordinary... To begin a story or narration, when you are not perfect in it, and cannot go through with it, but are forced, possibly, to say, in the middle of it, "I have forgot the rest," is very unpleasant and bungling. One must be extremely exact, clear, and perspicuous in everything one says; otherwise, instead of entertaining or informing others, one only tires and puzzles them.

The voice and manner of speaking, too, are not to be neglected: some people almost shut their mouth when they speak, and mutter so, that they are not to be understood, others speak so fast, and sputter, that they are not to be understood either; some always speak as loud as if they were talking to deaf people; and others so low that one cannot hear them. All these habits are awkward and disagreeable; and are to be avoided by attention: they are the distinguishing marks of the ordinary people, who have had no care taken of their education. You cannot imagine how necessary it is to mind all these little things; for I have seen many people with great talents, ill received, for want of having these talents too; and others well received, only from their little talents, and who had no great ones.

To his son (5 September 1746)

As women are a considerable part, or at least a pretty numerous part, of company; and as their suffrages go a great way towards establishing a man's character in the fashionable part of the world (which is of great importance to the fortune and figure he proposes to make in it), it is necessary to please them. I will therefore, upon this subject, let you into a certain *arcana*, that will be very useful for you to know, but which you must, with the utmost care, conceal, and never seem to know. Women, then, are only children of a larger growth; they have an entertaining tattle and sometimes wit, but for solid, reasoning good-sense, I never in my life knew one that had it, or who reasoned or acted consequentially for four-and-twenty hours together.

Some little passion or humour always breaks in upon their best resolutions. Their beauty neglected or controverted, their age increased, or their supposed understandings depreciated, instantly kindles their little passions, and overturns any system of consequential conduct, that in their most reasonable moments they might have been capable of forming. A man of sense only trifles with them, plays with them, humours and flatters them, as he does with a sprightly, forward child; but he neither consults them about, nor trusts them with, serious matters; though he often makes them believe that he does both; which is the thing in the world that they are proud of; for they love mightily to be dabbling in business (which by the way, they always spoil), and being justly distrustful, that men in general look upon them in a trifling light, they almost adore that man, who talks more seriously to them, and who seems to consult and trust them; I say, who seems, for weak men really do, but wise ones only seem to do it.

No flattery is either too high or too low for them. They will greedily swallow the highest, and gratefully accept of the lowest; and you may safely flatter any woman, from her understanding down to the exquisite taste of her fan. Women who are either indisputably beautiful, or indisputably ugly, are best flattered upon the score of their understandings; but those who are in a state of mediocrity, are best flattered upon their beauty, or at least their graces; for every woman who is not absolutely ugly, thinks herself handsome; but, not hearing often that she is so, is the more grateful and the more obliged to the few who tell her so; whereas a decided and conscious beauty looks upon every tribute paid to her beauty, only as her due; but wants to shine, and to be considered on the side of her understanding; and a woman who is ugly enough to know that she is so, knows that she has nothing left for it but her understanding, which is consequently (and probably in more senses than one) her weak side.

But these are secrets which you must keep inviolably, if you would not, like Orpheus, be torn to pieces by the whole sex; on the contrary, a man who thinks of living in the great world, must be gallant, polite, and attentive to please the women. They have, from the weakness of men, more or less influence in all Courts; they absolutely stamp every man's character in the *beau monde*, and make it either current, or cry it down, and stop it in payments. It is, therefore, absolutely necessary to manage, please, and flatter them; and never to discover the least marks of contempt, which is what they never forgive; but in this they are not singular, for it is the same with men; who will much sooner forgive an injustice than an insult.

Every man is not ambitious, or covetous, or passionate; but every man has pride enough in his composition to feel and resent the least slight and contempts. Remember, therefore, most carefully to conceal your contempt, however just, wherever you would not make an implacable enemy. Men are much more unwilling to have their weaknesses and imperfections known, than their crimes; and, if you hint to a man that you think him silly, ignorant, or even ill-bred or awkward, he will hate you more, and longer, than if you tell him plainly that you think him a rogue. Never yield to that temptation, which to most young men is very strong, of exposing other people's weaknesses and infirmities, for the sake of either diverting the company, or of showing your own superiority. You may get the laugh on your side by it, for the present; but you will make enemies by it for ever; and even those who laugh with you then will, upon reflection, fear, and consequently hate you; besides that, it is ill-natured, and a good heart desires rather to conceal than expose other people's weaknesses or misfortunes. If you have wit, use it to please, and not to hurt: you may shine like the sun in the temperate zones, without scorching. Here it is wished for: under the line it is dreaded.

These are some of the hints which my long experience in the great world enables me to give you; and which, if you attend to them, may prove useful to you in your journey through it. I wish it may be a prosperous one; at least, I am sure that it must be your own fault if it is not.

BENJAMIN FRANKLIN

BENJAMIN FRANKLIN (1706–90), AMERICAN SCIENTIST and statesman, one of the architects of the Declaration of Independence, 1776.

To unknown (25 June 1745)

My dear friend:–

I know of no Medicine fit to diminish the violent natural inclination you mention; and if I did, I think I should not communicate it to you. Marriage is the proper Remedy. It is the most natural State of Man, and therefore the State in which you will find solid Happiness. Your Reason against entering into it at present appears to be not well founded. The Circumstantial Advantages you have in View by Postponing it, are not only uncertain, but they are small in comparison with the Thing itself, *the being married and settled.* It is the Man and Woman united that makes the complete human Being. Separate she wants his force of Body and Strength of Reason; he her Softness, Sensibility and acute Discernment. Together they are most likely to succeed in the World. A single Man has not nearly the value he would have in that State of Union. He is an incomplete Animal. He resembles the odd Half of a Pair of Scissors.

If you get a prudent, healthy wife, your Industry in your Profession, with her good Economy, will be a Fortune sufficient.

But if you will not take this Counsel, and persist in thinking a Commerce with the Sex is inevitable, then I repeat my former Advice that in your Amours you should *prefer old Women to young ones.* This you call a Paradox, and demand my reasons. They are these:

1. Because they have more Knowledge of the world, and their Minds are better stored with observations; their Conversation is more improving, and more lastingly agreeable.

2. Because when Women cease to be handsome, they study to be good. To maintain their Influence over Man, they supply the Diminution of Beauty by an Augmentation of Utility. They learn to do a thousand Services, small and great, and are the most tender and useful of all Friends when you are sick. Thus they continue amiable. And hence there is hardly such a thing to be found as an old Woman who is not a good Woman.

3. Because there is no hazard of children, which irregularly produced may be attended with much inconvenience.

4. Because through more Experience they are more prudent and discreet in conducting an Intrigue to prevent Suspicion. The Commerce with them is therefore safer with regard to your reputation; and regard to theirs, if the Affair should happen to be known, considerate People might be inclined to excuse an old Woman, who would kindly take care of a young Man, form his manners by her good Councils, and prevent his ruining his Health

and Fortune among mercenary Prostitutes.

5. Because in every Animal that walks upright, the Deficiency of the Fluids that fill the Muscles appears first in the highest Part. The Face first grows lank and wrinkled; then the Neck; then the Breast and Arms; the lower parts continuing to the last as plump as ever; so that covering all above with a Basket, and regarding only what is below the Girdle, it is impossible of two Women to know an old from a young one. And as in the Dark all Cats are grey, the Pleasure of Corporal Enjoyment with an old Woman is at least equal and frequently superior, every Knack being by Practice capable by improvement.

6. Because the sin is less. The Debauching of a Virgin may be her Ruin, and make her for Life unhappy.

7. Because the compunction is less. The having made a young Girl *miserable* may give you frequent bitter Reflections; none of which can attend making an old Woman *happy*.

8th & lastly. They are so grateful!!!

Thus much for my Paradox. But still I advise you to marry immediately; being sincerely

Your Affectionate Friend,
Benj. Franklin

HORACE WALPOLE

HORACE WALPOLE (1717–97) WAS THE SON OF SIR Robert, the first British prime minister. After Cambridge, where he was friends with the poet Thomas Gray, Walpole entered politics, but his *métier* was writing, and his novel *Castle of Otranto* (1764) set the fashion for Gothic romance. Walpole's letters, intended for publication, run to forty-eight volumes; with one correspondent alone, Madame de Deffand, he exchanged more than 1,600 letters.

~⚜~

To Thomas Gray (19 November 1765), from Paris

Thomas Gray (1716–71), poet, author of the *Elegy Written in a Country Churchyard*.

You are very kind to inquire so particularly after my gout: I wish I may not be too circumstantial in my answer; but you have tapped a dangerous topic; I can talk gout by the hour. It is my great mortification, & has disappointed all the hopes that I had built on temperance & hardiness. 1 have resisted like a hermit, & exposed myself to all weathers & seasons like a smugler; & in vain. I have however still so much of the obstinacy of both professions left, that I think I shall continue, & cannot obey you in keeping myself warm. I have gone thro my second fit under one blanket, & already go about in a silk wastecoat with my bosom unbuttoned. In short, I am as prejudiced to my regimen, tho so ineffectual, as I coud have been to all I expected from it. The truth is, I am almost as willing to have the gout as to be liable to catch cold; & must run up stairs & down, in & out of doors when I will, or I cannot have the least satisfaction. This will convince you how readily I comply with another of your precepts, walking as soon as I am able – 1 have had little indulgence for myself on that head. Wine I drink with my water, because I cannot drink the filthy water here by itself; I began with brandy, but soon grew to nauseate it. The greatest change I have made, is in leaving off Tea – I doubt, only because I took an aversion to it. I own I am much better since. This is the Detail: the general history is, that I was seized with the gout in one foot at the End of June, soon had it in both, with great torment, & then without it's going out of my feet, in head, Stomach, both wrists & both Shoulders. Nine weeks passed before I coud even walk without a Stick; yet the state of convalescence, as it has been in my second fit, was much worse &

more uneasy than the height of the pain from the constant sickness at my Stomach. I came hither, mended miraculously with the Sea & the journey, but caught cold in a fortnight, & have had six weeks more of pain in both feet, and such sickness that I have been very near starved: besides such swelled legs, that they were as much too big for my body, as before they would have been too little for any other person's alive. I have not got the better of every thing but the weakness, & am only thrown or tumble down ten times a day. For receipts, you may trust me for making use of none; I would not see a physician at the worst, but have quacked myself as boldly, as Quacks treat others: I laughed at your idea of quality receipts, it came so apropos: there is not a Man or Woman here that is not a perfect old nurse, & who does not talk gruel & anatomy with equal fluency & ignorance. One instance shall serve; Madame de Bouzols, Marshal Berwick's daughter, assured me there was nothing so good for the gout as to preserve the parings of my nails in a bottle close stopped. When I try any illustrious Nostrum, I shall give the preference to this.

So much for the Gout! I told you what was coming. As to the Ministry, I know & care very little about them. I told you & told them long ago, that if ever a change happened, I would bid adieu to Politics forever. Do me the justice to allow that I have not altered with the Times. I was so impatient to put this resolution in execution, that I hurried out of England, before I was sufficiently recovered. I shall not run the same hazard again in haste; but will stay here till I am perfectly well, & the Season of warm weather coming on or arrived, tho the Charms of Paris have not the least attraction for me, nor would keep me here an hour on their own account. For the City itself, I cannot conceive where my eyes were: It is the ugliest, beastly Town in the Universe. I have not seen a mouthfull of verdure out of it, nor have they any thing green but their treillage & window shutters. Trees cut into fire-shovels & stuck into pedestals of chalk, compose their country. Their boasted knowledge of Society is reduced to talking of their suppers, & every malady they have about them, or know of. The Dauphin is at the point of death; every morning the Physicians frame an account of him, & happy is he or She, who can produce a copy of this lie, called a *bulletin*. The night before last, one of these was produced at supper where I was; it was read, & said, he had had une *evacuation foetide* – I beg your pardon, tho you are not at Supper. The Old Lady of the House, who by the way is quite blind, was the Regent's mistress for a fortnight, & is very agreeable, called out, Oh! they have forgot to mention that he threw down his chamberpot, and was forced to change his bed. There were present several Women of the first rank, as Madame de la Valière, who you remember Duchesse de Vaujour, & who is still miraculously pretty tho fifty three, a very handsome Madame de Forcalquier, & others – nor was this conversation at all particular to that evening. They talk of a *Chienne chaude*, or the *dangerous* time of a Woman's age, as they would talk of a knotting bag.

Their gaiety is not greater than their Delicacy – but I will not expatiate. In short, they are another people from what they were. They may be growing wise, but the intermediate passage is Dullness. Several of the Women are agreeable, & some of the Men; but the Latter are in general vain & ignorant. The Savants, I beg their pardons, the Philosophes, are insupportable. Superficial, over-bearing, & fanatic; they preach incessantly, & their avowed doctrine is Atheism; you would not believe how openly – Dont wonder therefore, if I should return a Jésuit. Voltaire himself does not satisfy them: One of their Lady-Devotes said of Him; il est Bigot; c'est un Deiste.

I am as little pleased with their taste in trifles. Crebillon is entirely out of fashion, & Marivaux a proverb; *Marivauder*, & *Marivaudage* are established terms for being prolix & tiresome. I thought that We were fallen, but they are ten times lower.

Notwithstanding all I have said, I have found two or three Societies that please me; am amused with the novelty of the whole, & should be sorry not to have come. The Dumenil is, if possible, superior to what you remember; I am sorry not to see the Clairon, but several persons whose judgments seem the soundest, prefer the Former. Preville is admirable in low comedy: the Mixture of Italian Comedy and Comic Operas prettily written, & set to Italian music, at the same Theatre, is charming, & gets the better both of their operas & French Comedy, the latter of which is seldom full, with all it's merit. Petit maîtres are obsolete, like our Lords Foppington – Tout le monde est Philosophe – When I grow very sick of this last nonsense, I go and compose myself at the Chartreuse, where I am almost tempted to prefer Le Soeur to every Painter I know – Yet what new old Treasures are come to light, routed out of the Louvre, own into new lumber-rooms at Versailles! – but I have not room to tell you what I have seen! I will keep this and other chapters for Strawberry.* adieu! and thank you.

Yrs ever
HW.

Old Mariette has shown me a print by Diepenbecke of the D. & Dss of Newcastle at dinner with their family: you wd oblige me if you would look into all their Grace's folios, & see if it is not a frontispiece to some one of them. Then He has such a Petitot of Madame d'Olonne! The Pompadour offered him fifty Louis's for it – Alack! so would I!

---

*Strawberry Hill, Walpole's Gothic cottage in Twickenham.

SAMUEL RICHARDSON

RICHARDSON (1689–1761) WAS THE AUTHOR OF *Letters Written to and for Particular Friends* (1741), and the epistolary novels *Pamela* (1749) and *Clarissa* (1748).

From a country gentleman in town to his brother in the country (n.d.)

Dear Brother,

I have this day been satisfying a curiosity, I believe natural to most people, by seeing an execution at Tyburn: The sight has had an extraordinary effect upon me, which is more owing to the unexpected oddness of the scene, than the affecting concern which is unavoidable in a thinking person, at a spectacle so awful, and so interesting, to all who consider themselves of the same species with the unhappy sufferers.

That I might the better view the prisoners, and escape the pressure of the mob, which is prodigious, nay, almost incredible, if we consider the frequency of these executions in London, which is once a month; I mounted my horse, and accompanied the melancholy cavalcade from Newgate to the fatal tree. The criminals were five in number. I was much disappointed at the unconcern and carelessness that appeared in the faces of three of the unhappy wretches: The countenances of the other two were spread with that horror and despair which is not to be wonder'd at in men whose period of life is so near, with the terrible aggravation of its being hastened by their own voluntary indiscretion and misdeeds. The exhortation spoken by the bell-man, from the wall of St Sepulchre's churchyard, is well intended; but the noise of the officers, and the mob, was so great, and the silly curiosity of people climbing into the cart to take leave of the criminals, made such a confused noise, that I could not hear the words of the exhortation when spoken; tho' they are as follow:

"All good people pray heartily to God for these poor sinners, who now are going to their deaths; for whom this great bell doth toll.

"You that are condemned to die, repent with lamentable tears. Ask mercy of the Lord for the salvation of your own souls, thro' the merits, death, and passion, of Jesus Christ, who now sits at the right-hand of God, to make intercession for as many of you as penitently return unto him.

"*Lord have mercy upon you! Christ have mercy upon you!*" – which last words the bell-man repeats three times.

All the way up Holborn the crowd was so great, as, at every twenty or thirty yards, to obstruct the passage; and wine, notwithstanding a the good order against that practice, was brought the malefactors, who drank greedily of it, which I thought did not suit well with their deplorable circumstances: After this, the three thoughtless young men, who at *first* seemed not enough concerned, grew most shamefully daring and wanton; behaving themselves in a manner that would have been ridiculous in men in any circumstance whatever: They swore, laugh'd, and talked obscenely; and wish'd their wicked companions good luck, with as much assurance as if their employment had been the most lawful.

At the place of execution, the scene grew still more shocking; and the clergyman who attended was more the subject of ridicule, than of their serious attention. The psalm was sung amidst the curses and quarrelling of hundreds of the most abandon'd and profligate of mankind: Upon whom (so stupid are they to any sense of decency) all the preparation of the unhappy wretches seems to serve only for the subject of a barbarous kind of mirth, altogether inconsistent with humanity. And as soon as the poor creatures were half-dead, I was much surprised, before such a number of peace-officers, to see the populace fall to haling and pulling the carcases with so much earnestness, as to occasion several warm rencounters, and broken heads. These, I was told, were the friends of the persons executed, or such as, for the sake of tumult, chose to appear so, and some persons sent by private surgeons to obtain bodies for dissection. The contests between these were fierce and bloody, and frightful to look at: so that I made the best of my way out of the croud, and, with some difficulty, rode back among a large number of people, who had been upon the same errand with myself. The face of every one spoke a kind of mirth, as if the spectacle they had beheld had afforded pleasure instead of pain, which I am wholly unable to account for.

In other nations, common criminal executions are said to be little attended by any beside the necessary officers, and the mournful friends, but here, all was hurry and confusion, racket and noise, praying and oaths, swearing and singing psalms; I am unwilling to impute this difference in our own from the practice of other nations, to the cruelty of our natures; to which, foreigners, however, to our dishonour, ascribe it. In most instances, let them say what they will, we are humane beyond what other nations can boast; but in this, the behaviour of my countrymen is past my accounting for; every street and lane I passed through, bearing rather the face of a holiday, than of that sorrow which I expected to see, for the untimely deaths of five members of the community.

One of their bodies was carried to the lodging of his wife, who not being in the way to receive it, they immediately hawked it about to every surgeon they could think of, and when none would buy it, they rubb'd tar all over it, and left it in a field hardly cover'd with earth.

This is the best description I can give you of a scene that was no way entertaining to me, and which I shall not again take so much pains to see. I am, dear brother,

Yours affectionately

SAMUEL JOHNSON

Dr JOHNSON (1709–84), ONE OF THE MOST EMINENT literary figures of his day, was the compiler of the *Dictionary of the English Language*, a work that took him eight years to complete.

To the Earl of Chesterfield (7 February 1755)

My Lord. –

I have been lately informed, by the proprietor of the World, that two papers, in which my Dictionary is recommended to the public, were written by your Lordship. To be so distinguished is an honour, which, being very little accustomed to favours from the great, I know not well how to receive, or in what terms to acknowledge.

When, upon some slight encouragement, I first visited your Lordship, I was overpowered, like the rest of mankind, by the enchantment of your address, and could not forbear to wish that I might boast myself *Le vainqueur du vainqueur de la terre;* – that I might obtain that regard for which I saw the world contending; but I found my attendance so little encouraged that neither pride nor modesty would suffer me to continue it. When I had once addressed your Lordship in public I had exhausted all the art of pleasing which a retired and uncourtly scholar can possess. I had done all that I could; and no man is well pleased to have his all neglected, be it ever so little.

Seven years, my Lord, have now passed since I waited in your outward rooms, or was repulsed from your door; during which time I have been pushing on my work through difficulties, of which it is useless to complain, and have brought it at last to the verge of publication, without one act of assistance, one word of encouragement, or one smile of favour. Such treatment I did not expect, for I never had a Patron before.

The shepherd in Virgil grew at last acquainted with Love, and found him a native of the rocks.

Is not a Patron, my Lord, one who looks with unconcern on a man struggling for life in the Water and, when he has reached ground encumbers him with help? The notice which you have been pleased to take of my labours had it been early, had been kind; but it has been delayed till I am indifferent, and cannot enjoy it; till I am solitary, and cannot impart it; till I am known and do not want it. I hope it is no very cynical asperity not to confess obligations where no benefit has been received, or to be unwilling that the public should consider me as owing that to a Patron, which Providence has enabled me to do for myself.

Having carried on my work thus far with so little obligation to any favourer of learning. I shall not be disappointed though I should conclude it, if less be possible with less; for I have been long awakened from that dream of hope, in which I once boasted myself with so much exultation, my Lord, – Your Lordship's most humble, most obedient servant,

Sam. Johnson.

To Hester Thrale (19 June 1783)

Hester Thrale was the wife of Johnson's friend, the brewer Henry Thrale.

Dear Madam

I am sitting down in no cheerful solitude to write a narrative which would once have affected you with tenderness and sorrow, but which you will perhaps pass over now with the careless glance of frigid indifference. For this diminution of regard however, I know not whether I ought to blame you, who may have reasons which I cannot know, and I do not blame myself, who have for a great part of human life done you what good I could, and have never done you evil.

I had been disordered in the usual way, and had been relieved by the usual methods, by opium and catharticks, but had rather lessened my dose of opium.

On Monday the 16th I sat for my picture, and walked a considerable way with little inconvenience. In the afternoon and evening I felt myself light and easy, and began to plan schemes of life. Thus I went to bed, and in a short time waked and sat up, as has long my custom, when I felt a confusion and indistinctness in my head, which lasted I suppose about half a minute; I was alarmed, and prayed God, that however he might afflict my body, he would spare my understanding. This prayer, that I might try the integrity of my faculties, I made in Latin verse. The lines were not very good, but I knew them not to be very good: I made them easily, and concluded myself to be unimpaired in my faculties.

Soon after I perceived that I had suffered a paralytick stroke, and that my speech was taken from me. I had no pain, and so little dejection in this dreadful state, that I wondered at my own apathy, and considered that perhaps death itself when it should come would excite less horrour than seems now to attend it.

In order to rouse the vocal organs I took two drams. Wine has been celebrated for the production of eloquence. I put myself into violent motion, and I think repeated it; but all was vain. I then went to bed, and, strange as it may seem, I think slept. When I saw light, it was time to contrive what I should do. Though God stopped my speech he left me my hand, I enjoyed a mercy which was not granted to my dear Friend Lawrence, who now perhaps overlooks me as I am writing, and rejoices that I have what he wanted. My first note was necessarily to my servant, who came in talking, and could not immediately comprehend why he should read what I put into his hands.

I then wrote a card to Mr Allen, that I might have a discreet friend at hand to act as occasion should require. In penning this note I had some difficulty, my hand, I knew not how nor why, made wrong letters. I then wrote to Dr Taylor to come to me, and bring Dr Heberden, and I sent to Dr Brocklesby, who is my neighbour. My physicians are very friendly and very disinterested, and give me great hopes, but you may imagine my situation. I have so far recovered my vocal powers, as to repeat the Lord's Prayer with no very imperfect articulation. My memory, I hope, yet remains as it was; but such an attack produces solicitude for the safety of every faculty. . . . I suppose you may wish to know how my disease is treated by the physicians. They put a blister upon my back, and two from my ear to my throat, one on a side. The blister on the back has done little, and those on the throat have not risen. I bullied and bounced (it sticks to our last sand) and compelled the apothecary to make his salve according to the Edinburgh Dispensatory, that it might adhere better. I have two on now of my own prescription. They likewise give me salt of hartshorn, which I take with no great confidence, but am satisfied that what can be done is done for me.

O God! give me comfort and confidence in Thee: forgive my sins; and if it be Thy good pleasure, relieve my diseases for Jesus Christ's sake. Amen.

I am almost ashamed of this querulous letter, but now it is written, let it go.

> I am, Madam Your most humble servant
> *Sam. Johnson*

DAVID HUME

DAVID HUME (1711–76), SCOTTISH PHILOSOPHER, AUTHOR of *A Treatise on Human Nature* and *Essays Moral and Political*.

❧

To Sir Gilbert Elliot (16 October 1769)

...I have been settled here [Edinburgh] two Months, and am here Body & Soul, without casting the least Thought of Regreat to London, or even to Paris. I think it improbable that I shall ever in my Life cross the Tweed, except perhaps a Jaunt to the North of England, for Health or Amusement. I live still, and must for a twelvemonth, in my old House in James's Court, which is very chearful, and even elegant, but too small to display my great Talent for Cookery, the Science to which I intend to addict the remaining Years of my Life; I have just now lying on the Table before me a Receipt for making *Soupe a la Reine*, copy'd with my own hand. For Beef and Cabbage (a charming Dish), and old Mutton and old Claret, no body excels me. I make also Sheep head Broth in a manner that Mr Keith speaks of it for eight days after, and the Duc de Nivernois would bind himself Apprentice to my Lass to learn it. I have already sent a Challenge to David Moncrief. You will see, that in a twelvemonth he will take to the writing of History, the Field I have deserted: For as to the giving of Dinners, he can now have no farther Pretensions. I should have made a very bad use of my Abode in Paris, if I coud not get the better of a mere provincial like him. All my Friends encourage me in this Ambition; as thinking it will redound very much to my Honour.

I am delighted to see the daily and hourly Progress of Madness and Folly and Wickedness in England. The Consummation of these Qualities are the true Ingredients for making a fine Narrative in History; especially if followed by some signal and ruinous

Convulsion, as I hope will soon be the Case with that pernicious People. He must be a very bad Cook indeed, that cannot make a palatable Dish from the whole. You see in my Reflexions and Allusions I still mix my old and new Profession together. I am Dear Sir Gilbert

Your most obedient humble Servant,
David Hume

Edinburgh
16 of Octʳ 1769

P.S. I beg my Respects to Lady Elliot.

JAMES BOSWELL

JAMES BOSWELL (1740–95) WAS THE AUTHOR OF *THE Life of Samuel Johnson*. In 1764 he perpetrated an outrageous piece of gatecrashing, introducing himself to both Rousseau and Voltaire during a European tour.

∗∗∗

To The Reverend William Temple (28 December 1764)

Temple, vicar of Penryn in Cornwall, and Boswell met at Edinburgh University. Their correspondence continued for thirty-seven years.

My Dear Temple;

  Think not that I insult you, when you read the full tale of my supreme Felicity. After thanking you for your two letters of the month of October, I must pour forth the Exultation of a heart swelling with Joy. Call me Bombast. Call me what you please. Thus will I talk. No other stile can give the most distant expression of the feelings of Boswell. If I appear ridiculous, it is because our Language is deficient.

I compleated my Tour thro' the German Courts. At all of them I found state and Politeness. At Baaden Durlach I found Worth, Learning and Philosophy united in the Reigning Marggrave. He is a Prince whose character deserves to be known over Europe. He is the best Sovereign, the best Father, the most amiable Man. He has travelled a great deal. He has been in England and he speaks the language in amazing Perfection.

During the time that I stayed at his Court, I had many, many conversations with him. He shewed me the greatest distinction. The Inspector of his Cabinet, His Library-keeper, and the Officers of his court had orders to do every thing in their power to render my stay agreeable. Madame La Marggrave, who paints in perfection and has a general taste for the fine arts, treated me in the most gracious manner.

The Marggrave told me how happy he was to have me with him. I asked him if I could do any thing that might shew my gratitude.

He replied, "I shall write to you sometimes. I shall be very happy to receive your letters." He was in earnest. I have already been honoured with a letter from His Most Serene Highness. I have promised to return and pass some weeks at his court. He is not far from France.

I have been with Rousseau. He lives in the Village of Môtiers Travers in a beautiful Valley surrounded with immense mountains. I went thither from Neufchatel. I determined to put my real merit to the severest test, by presenting myself without any recommendation before the Wild, illustrious Philosopher.

I wrote him a letter in which I told him all my worth, and claimed his regard as what I had a title to. *"Ouvrez donc votre Porte, Monsieur, à un Homme qui ose vous assurer qu'il merite d'y entrer."* Such was my bold and manly stile. He received me, altho' he was very ill. *"Je suis malade, souffrant, hors d'etat de recevoir des visites. Cependant Je ne puis me refuser à celle de Monsieur Boswell pourvu que par égard pour mon etat il veuille bien la faire courte."*

I found him very easy and unaffected. At first he complained and lamented the state of humanity. But I had address enough to bring him upon Subjects which pleased him, and he grew very animated, quite the amiable St Preux at fifty. He is a genteel man, has a fine countenance and a charming voice.

You may beleive I had a difficult task enough to come up to the Idea which I had given him of myself. I had said all that my honest Pride believed. My letter was a piece of true Oratory. You shall see it when we meet. No other man in Europe could have written such a letter, and appeared equal to all it's praise.

I stayed at this time three days in the Village, and was with M. Rousseau every day. A week after, I returned and stayed two days. He is extremely busy. The Corsicans have actually applied to him to give them a set of Laws. What glory for him. He said, "*C'est au dessus de mes forces; mais pas au dessus de mon Zèle.*"

He is preparing to give a compleat and splendid Edition of all his works. When I was sure of his good opinion on my own merit, I shewd him a Recommendation which My Lord Marischal had given me. I talked to him with undisguised confidence; I gave him a written sketch of my life. He studied it, and he loved me with all my failings. He gave me some Advices which will influence the rest of my existence. He is to corespond with me while he lives. When I took leave of him, he embraced me with an elegant cordiality and said, "*Souvenez vous toujours de moi. Ii y a des points ou nos Ames sont liés.*"

On my arrival at Geneva I received a letter from him, with a letter of Recommendation to an intimate freind of his at the Court of Parma, a man of uncommon value. He has left the letter open for me to read, altho' it contains his most important concerns and the kindest effusions of his heart. Is not this treating me with a regard which my Soul must be proud of? I must give you a sentence of this letter.

"*Je suis bien aise que M. Boswell et vous fassiez connoissance. Je crois que vous m'en saurrez gré tous deux. Dans la première lettre qu'il m'écrivit ii me marqua qu'il etoit un Homme d'un merite singuliere. J'evus la curiosite de voir celui qui parloit ainsi de luimeme, et Je trouvois qu'il m'avoit dit vrai.*"

And whence do I now write to you, My Freind? From the Chateau of M. de Voltaire. I had a letter for him from a Suiss Colonel at the Hague. I came hither Monday and was presented to him. He received me with dignity and that air of a man who has been much in the world, which a Frenchman acquires in perfection. I saw him for about half an hour before dinner. He was not in spirits. Yet he gave me some brilliant Sallies. He did not dine with us, and I was obliged to post away immediately after dinner, because the Gates of Geneva shut before five, and Ferney is a good hour from Town.

I was by no means satisfy'd to have been so little time with the Monarch of French Literature. A happy scheme sprung up in my adventurous mind. Madame Denis, the niece of M. de Voltaire, had been extremely good to me. She is fond of our language. I wrote her a letter in English begging her interest to obtain for me the Privilege of lodging a night under the roof of M. de Voltaire who, in opposition to our Sun, rises in the evening. I was in the finest humour and my letter was full of wit. I told her, "I am a hardy and a vigourous Scot. You may mount me to the highest and coldest Garret. I shall not even refuse to sleep upon two chairs in the Bed-chamber of your maid. I saw her pass thro' the room where we sat before dinner."

I sent my letter on Tuesday by an Express. It was shewn to M. de Voltaire who with his own hand wrote this answer in the Character of Madam Denis. "You will do us much honour and pleasure. We have few beds; But you will (*shall*) not sleep on two chairs. My uncle, tho' very sick, hath guessed at your merit. I know it better; for I have seen you longer."

Temple, I am your most Obedient. How do you find yourself? Have you got such a thing as an old freind in this world? Is he to be valued or is he not?

I returned yesterday to this enchanted castle. The Magician appeared a very little before dinner. But in the evening he came into the drawing room in great spirits. I placed myself by him. I touched the keys in unison with his Imagination. I wish you had heard the Music. He was all Brilliance. He gave me continued flashes of Wit. I got him to speak english which he does in a degree that made me, now and then, start up and cry, "Upon my soul this is astonishing."

When he talked our language He was animated with the Soul of a Briton. He had bold flights. He had humour. He had an extravagance; he had a forcible oddity of stile that the most comical of our dramatis Personae could not have exceeded. He swore bloodily as was the fashion when he was in England. He hum'd a Ballad, He repeated nonsense.

Then he talked of our Constitution with a noble enthusiasm. I was proud to hear this from the mouth of an illustrious Frenchman.

At last we came upon Religion. Then did he rage. The Company went to Supper. M. de Voltaire and I remained in the drawing room with a great Bible before us; and if ever two mortal men disputed with vehemence we did. Yes, upon that occasion He was one Individual and I another. For a certain portion of the time there was a fair opposition between Voltaire and Boswell. The daring bursts of his Ridicule confounded my understanding. He stood like an Orator of ancient Rome. Tully was never more agitated than he was. He went too far. His aged frame trembled beneath him. He cried, "O I am very sick; My head turns round," and he let himself gently fall upon an easy chair. He recovered.

I resumed our Conversation, but changed the tone. I talked to him serious and earnest. I demanded of him an honest confession of his real sentiments. He gave it me with candour and with a mild eloquence which touched my heart. I did not beleive him capable of thinking in the manner that he declared to me was "from the bottom of his heart." He exprest his veneration – his love – of the Supreme Being, and his entire resignation to the will of Him who is Allwise. He exprest his desire to resemble the Authour of Goodness, by being good himself. His sentiments go no farther. He does not inflame his mind with grand hopes of the immortality of the Soul. He says it may be; but he knows nothing of it. And his mind is in perfect tranquillity.

I was moved; I was sorry. I doubted his Sincerity. I called to him with emotion, "Are you sincere? are you really sincere?" He answered, "Before God I am."

Then with the fire of him whose Tragedies have so often shone on the Theatre of Paris, he said, "I suffer much. But I suffer with

Patience and Resignation; not as a Christian – But as a Man."

Temple, was not this an interesting Scene? Would a Journey from Scotland to Ferney have been too much to obtain such a remarkable Interview? I have given you the great lines. The whole Conversation of the evening is fully recorded, and I look upon it as an invaluable Treasure. One day the Public shall have it. It is a Present highly worthy of their Attention. I told M. de Voltaire that I had written eight quarto Pages of what he had said. He smiled and seemed pleased.

Our important Scene must not appear till after his death. But I have a great mind to send over to London a little Sketch of my Reception at Ferney, of the splendid manner in which M. de Voltaire lives and of the brilliant conversation of this celebrated Authour at the age of Seventy-two. The Sketch would be a letter, addressed to you, full of gayety and full of freindship. I would send it to one of the best Public Papers or Magazines. But this is probably a flight of my overheated mind. I shall not send the Sketch unless you approve of my doing so.

Before I left Britain, I was idle, dissipated, ridiculous and regardless of Reputation. Often was I unworthy to be the freind of Mr Temple. Now I am a very different Man. I have got a character which I am proud of. Speak thou who hast known me from my earliest years, couldst thou have imagined eight years ago that thy Companion in the Studies of Antiquity who was debased by an unhappy education in the smoak of Edinburgh, couldst thou have imagined him to turn out the Man that he now is?

We are now, my freind, united in the strictest manner. Let us do nothing of any consequence without the consent of each other.

And must I then marry a Dutchwoman? Is it already marked in the rolls of Heaven? Must the proud Boswell yield to a tender inclination? Must he in the strength and vigour of his youth resign his liberty for life to one Woman? Rather (say you) shall not my freind embrace the happiness which Fortune presents to him? Will not his Pride be gratified by the Attachment of a Lady who has refused many advantageous offers? Must he not marry to continue his ancient family? and where shall he find a more amiable wife? Is he not a man of a most singular character? and would not an ordinary woman be insupportable to him?

Should he not thank the Powers above for having shewn him Zélide, a young Lady free from all the faults of her sex, with Genius, with good humour, with elegant accomplishments? But, My Dear Temple, she is not by half so rich as I thought. She has only £400 a year.

Besides, I am not pleased with her conduct. We had agreed to corespond, and she directed me to send my letters to the care of her Bookseller. I wrote to her from Berlin a long letter. She did not answer it. I was apprehensive that I had talked too severely of her faults, and wrote her from Anhalt-Dessau begging pardon for my too great freedom. Still I remain unanswer'd.

Her father is a very worthy Man. He and I corespond and we write to each other of his Daughter in a strange mysterious manner. I have trusted him upon honour with a letter to her. So I shall be sure that she receives it and shall see how she behaves. After all, when I consider my unhappy constitution, I think I should not marry, at least for some time, and when I do, should chuse a healthy, chearfull woman of rank and fortune. I am now well because I am agitated by a variety of new scenes. But when I shall return to the uniformity of Scotland, I dread much a relapse into the gloomy distemper. I must endeavour by some scheme of ambition, by elegant Study and by rural occupations to preserve my mind. Yet I own that both of us are sadly undetermin'd. However, I hope the best.

My worthy Father has consented that I shall go to Italy. O my freind what a rich Prospect spreads before me. My letter is already so long that I shall restrain my enthusiastic sallies. Imagine my Joy. On Tuesday morning I set out for Turin. I shall pass the rigourous Alps with the resolution of Hannibal. I shall be four months in Italy and then return thro' France. I expect to pass some time at Paris.

Forgive me, Temple, for having delayed to mention your concerns till allmost at the end of my letter. You are sure how much I suffer from your uneasiness. I wish I could be as sure of releiving you. I know well the great, and can have no confidence in them. Lord Eglintoune would forget to do anything. I have written to Lady

Northumberland begging she may get Bob put upon whole Pay. Lord Warkworth was in General Craufurd's Regiment and both my Lord and My Lady had a great esteem of the General. I have told her Ladyship that the General had promised to take care of the young Lieutenant and that if her Ladyship puts him again in Commission "in so doing you will fullfill the intentions of Him who is no more, whose memory you must ever regard. May I add that your Ladyship will give me a pleasure – a comfort – which I can hardly express. Were I at present as rich as I shall probably be, the Brother of my freind should not depend for a Commission on the uncertain favour of any Great Person alive."

She may be angry at this last period. It ought to please, it ought to rouse her. "O Madam! be truly great. Be generous to the unfortunate. If your Ladyship will befreind the Young Man sincerely, I beg to be honoured with a line," etc; I own to you I have but little hopes from her Ladyship. We shall see. I have not been mean enough to flatter her. That I am determined never to practice.

I have also written to Mr Mitchell, late envoy at the Court of Berlin, who is just recalled. He is an old freind of my Father's, and a man of the strictest Probity and the warmest Generosity. I have told him your Story as I did to Lady Northumberland.

O my Temple! how do I glory in displaying the conduct of my freind. If Mr Mitchell can aid Us, he will. I would hope he may serve either your Father or Brother. I have solicited him for Both. Why am I not in power? I may be so perhaps, yet, before I die.

Temple, I am again as loyal as ever. I abhorr a despotic Tyrant. But I revere a limited Monarch. Shall I be a British Courtier? Am I worthy of the Confidence of my King? May George the Third chuse that the most honest and most amiable of his Subjects should stand continually in his Royal Presence? I will if he says, "You shall be independent." Churchill's death is awefull. The lines which Characterise him are excellent. Temple, this is a noble letter. Fare you well, My ever Dear Freind.

James Boswell

To the Reverend William Temple (8 February 1768)

The heiress Catherine Blair married her cousin, Sir William Maxwell in 1776.

My dear friend,

All is over between Miss Blair and me. I have delayed writing till I could give you some final account. About a fortnight after she went to the country, a report went that she was going to be married to Sir Alexander Gilmour, Member of Parliament for the county of Midlothian, a young man about thirty, who has £1,600 a year of estate, was formerly an officer in the guards, and is now one of the Clerks of the Board of Green Cloth, £1,000 a year – in short a noble match, though a man of expence and obliged to lead a London life. After the fair agreement between her and me, which I gave you fully in my last, I had a title to know the truth. I wrote to her seriously and told her that if she did not write me an answer I should believe the report to be true. After three days, I concluded from her silence that she was at last engaged. I endeavoured to laugh off my passion and I got Sir Alexander Gilmour to frank a letter to her, which I wrote in a pleasant strain, and amused myself with the whim. Still, however, I was not absolutely certain, as her conduct has been so prudent all along. At last she comes to town, and who comes too but my old rival the Nabob? I got acquainted with Mr Fullarton, and he and I joked a good deal about our heiress. Last night he proposed that he and I should go together and pay her a visit for the first time after her return from the country. Accordingly we went and I give you my word, Temple, it was a curious scene. However, the Princess behaved exceedingly well, though with a reserve more than ordinary. When we left her, we both exclaimed, "Upon my soul, a fine woman!" I began to like the Nabob much; so I said to him, "I do believe, Mr Fullarton, you and I are in the same situation here. Is it possible to be upon honour, and generous in an affair of this kind?" We agreed it was. Each then declared he was serious in his love for Miss B. and each protested he never before believed the other in earnest. We agreed to deal by one another in a fair and candid manner. I carried him to sup at a lady's, a cousin of mine, where we stayed till half an hour past eleven. We then went to a tavern and the good old claret was set before us. He told me that he had been most assiduous in attending Miss Blair; but she never gave him the least encouragement and declared he was convinced she loved me as much as a woman could love a man. With equal honesty I told all that has past between her and me, and your observation on the *wary mother*. "What," said he, "did Temple say so? If he had lived twenty years in the country with them, he could not have said a better thing." I then told him Dempster's humorous saying that all Miss B's connections were in an absolute confederacy to lay hold of every man who has a £1,000 a year, and how I called their system a *Salmond Fishing*. "You have hit it," said he, "we're all kept in play; but I am positive you are the fish and Sir Alexander is only a mock salmon to force you to jump more expeditiously at the bait." We sat till two this morning. We gave our words as men of honour that we would be honest to each other; so that neither should suffer needlessly and, to satisfy ourselves of our real situation, we gave our words that we should both ask her this morning, and I should go first. Could there be anything better than this? The Nabob talked to me with the warmth of the Indies, and professed the greatest pleasure on being acquainted with me.

Well, Temple, I went this morning and she made tea to me alone. I then asked her seriously if she was to be married to Sir Alexander. She said "it was odd to believe every thing people said, and why did I put such question? &c." I said that she knew very well I was much in love with her, and that if I had any chance I would take a good deal of trouble to make myself agreeable to her. She said I need not take the trouble, and I must not be angry, for she thought it best to tell me honestly. "What then," said I, "have I no chance?" "No," said she. I asked her to say so upon her word and upon honour. She fairly repeated the words. So I think, Temple, I had enough.

She would not tell me whether she was engaged to the knight. She said she would not satisfy an idle curiosity. But I own I had no doubt of it. What amazed me was that she and I were as easy and as good friends as ever. I told her I have great animal spirits and bear it wonderfully well. But this is really hard. I am thrown upon the wide world again. I don't know what will become of me.

Before dinner, the Nabob and I met, and he told me that he went and, in the most serious and submissive manner, begged to know if she was engaged. She would give him no satisfaction and treated him with a degree of coldness that overpowered him quite, poor man.

Such is the history of the lovers of this cruel Princess, who certainly is a lucky woman to have had a sovereign sway over so many admirers. I have endeavoured to make merry on my misfortune.

A Crambo Song on losing my Mistress.

Although I be an honest *Laird*,
In person rather strong and brawny,
For me the Heiress never car'd,
For she would have the Knight, Sir Sawney.

And when with ardent vows, I swore
Loud as Sir Jonathan Trelawney,
The Heiress shewed me to the door,
And said, she'd have the Knight, Sir Sawney.

She told me, with a scornful look,
I was as ugly as a Tawney;
For she a better fish could hook,
The rich and gallant Knight, Sir Sawney.

N.B. I can find no more rhimes to Sawney.

Now that all is over, I see many faults in her, which I did not see before. Do you not think she has not feeling enough, nor that ingenuous spirit which your friend requires? The Nabob and many other people are still of opinion that she has not made sure of Sir Sawney, and that all this may be finesse. But I cannot suspect so young a creature of so much artifice and whatever may be in it, I am honourably off, and you may wonder at it, but I assure you I am very easy and chearful. I am, however, resolved to look out for a good wife, either here or in England. I intend to be in London in March. My address will be at Mr Dilly's, Bookseller. But I expect to hear from you before I set out, which will not be till the 14th of March. I rejoice to hear that Mrs Temple is in a good way. My best wishes ever attend you and her.

I am your most affectionate friend.
James Boswell

11 February. I have allowed my letter to lie by till this day. The heiress is a good Scots lass. But I must have an English woman. My mind is now twice as enlarged as it has been for some months. You cannot say how fine a woman I may marry, perhaps a Howard or some other of the noblest in the kingdom.

THE DUKE OF QUEENSBERRY

CHARLES DOUGLAS, THE THIRD DUKE OF QUEENSBERRY (1698–1778), sometime Lord Justice General of England.

To Soubise (8 November 1772)

Soubise was Douglas's black servant.

Soubise (I wish I could call you good Soubise), I desire you will tell Mr Angelo that I am much obliged to him for his kind offer of a shooting horse, which I will very readily accept of on condition that he will give me leave to pay for him when we meet.

I will now say a few words to you about yourself. You may have observed that I have never of late said much to you on that subject, not that I was blind to your faults nor imposed upon by your cunning false professions, but that I found advice made no impression on you, & therefore for some time I have expected no good from it. The unmerited kindness & indulgence you have met with ought, from gratitude as well as from self-interest, to have induced you to endeavour by good behaviour to deserve the continuance of the goodness of your friends. You may still regain my good opinion (which you have forfeited) if you can get the better of an evil disposition you have given way to. In order to correct one's faults it is necessary in the first place to be sensible of them, I will therefore tell you what yours are. Prosperity seems really to have turned your head. You are full of pride and arrogance, which are despicable qualities even in persons of high rank & fortune, & in you are quite ridiculous. Reflect what your condition would have been if Captain Douglas had not brought you here from Jamaica. You would probably have been at this very time a slave, working half-naked among sugar canes. You are now, by the kindness of your friends, in a situation much above what you had any pretensions to, but that should rather inspire you with modest gratitude than with foolish pride. You are self-conceited, & aim at being on a level with the fashionable fine gentleman of the age, which must lead into all the vices and follies of it, and must soon bring distress and ruin upon you. Accustom yourself to speak truth, and to adhere strictly to it at all times & upon all occasions, even in the confession of a fault, for endeavouring to disguise guilt by lying is an aggravation of it. In short, a liar is a shameful and dishonest character, detested & distrusted by all mankind. I have now laid your faults open before you, & if you have a grain of reason and common sense you must be convinced of the necessity of a total change to prevent the fatal consequences of an inconsiderate dissipated course of life. After the trouble I have now taken for your sake, you cannot doubt of my being

Your well-wisher
Queensberry &c

Our own waggon goes to London with some goods, and will be there on Wednesday next, & will set out from thence either that night or

Thursday morning early. If Mr Angelo will send the horse to our house on Wednesday care will be taken of him to bring him safe here.

GEORGE WASHINGTON

THE FIRST PRESIDENT OF THE UNITED STATES OF America, Washington (1732–99) led the American ("Continental") forces during the War of Independence. Although his soldiers were ill-equipped and ill-trained, under Washington's disciplined command they inflicted early defeats on the British Redcoats and survived the difficult winter at Valley Forge in 1777–8. In 1781 Washington forced the surrender of Cornwallis at Yorktown, which effectively ended the War.

❧

To his wife Martha [nicknamed Patsy] (18 June 1775)

My Dearest:

I am now set down to write to you on a subject which fills me with inexpressible concern, and this concern is greatly aggravated and increased, when I reflect upon the uneasiness I know it will give you. It has been determined in Congress, that the whole army raised for the defence of the American cause shall be put under my care, and that it is necessary for me to proceed immediately to Boston to take upon me the command of it.

You may believe me, my dear Patsy, when I assure you, in the most solemn manner, that so far from seeking this appointment, I have used every endeavour in my power to avoid it not only from my unwillingness to part with you and the family, but from consciousness of its being a trust too great for my capacity, and that I should enjoy more real happiness in one month with you at home, than I have the most distant prospect of finding abroad, if my stay were to be seven times seven years. But as it has been a kind of destiny, that has thrown me upon this service, I shall hope that my undertaking is designed to answer some good purpose. You might, and I suppose did perceive from the tenor of my letters, that I was apprehensive I could not avoid this appointment, as I did not pretend to intimate when I should return. That was the case. It was utterly out of my power to refuse this appointment, without exposing my character to such censures, as would have reflected dishonour upon myself, and given pain to my friends. This, I am sure, could not, and ought not, to be pleasing to you, and must have lessened me considerably in my own esteem. I shall rely ,therefore, confidently on that Providence, which has heretofore preserved and been bountiful to me, not doubting but that I shall return safe to you in the fall. I shall feel no pain from the toil or the danger of the campaign: my unhappiness will flow from the uneasiness I know you will feel from being left alone. I therefore beg, that you will summon your whole fortitude, and pass your time as agreeably as possible. Nothing will give me so much sincere satisfaction as to hear this, and to hear it from your own pen. My earnest and ardent desire is, that you would pursue any plan that is most likely to produce content and a tolerable degree of tranquillity: as it must add greatly to my uneasy feelings to hear, that you are dissatisfied or complaining at what I really could not avoid.

As life is always uncertain and common prudence dictates to every man the necessity of settling his temporal concerns, while it is in his power, and while the mind is calm and undisturbed, I have, since I came to this place for I have not the time to do it before I left home got Colonel Pendleton to draft a will for me, by the directions I gave him, which I will now enclose. The provision made for you in case of my death will, I hope, be agreeable.

I shall add nothing more, as I have several letters to write, but to desire that you will remember me to your friends, and to assure you that I am with the most unfeigned regard, my dear Patsy, your affectionate, &c.

G. *Washington*

WOLFGANG AMADEUS MOZART

IN 1781 THE COMPOSER MOZART (1756–91) SECRETLY became engaged to Konstanze Weber, only telling his father after the event. Leopold Mozart, concerned that marriage would divert his son from his lucrative musical labours, was not pleased.

To his father, Leopold Mozart (15 December 1781)

Dearest Father,

You ask me for an explanation of the words with which I ended my last letter! Oh, how gladly would I have opened my heart to you long since; but I held back lest you should reproach me for *thinking of such a thing unseasonably* – although thinking can never be unseasonable... To marry! – You are alarmed by the idea? But I entreat you, dearest, most beloved Father, to listen to me! I was obliged to disclose my intentions to you, now permit me also to disclose my reasons, which indeed are forcible ones. Nature's voice speaks within me as loudly as in any other man, and perhaps louder than in many a tall, strong lout. I cannot lead the same life as most young men do nowadays. Firstly, I have too much religion, secondly, too much love of my neighbour and sense of honour, to be able to seduce an innocent girl, and thirdly, too much horror and disgust, dread and fear of diseases, and too much regard for my health, to be running after whores. Thus I can swear that until now I have had no dealings of this kind with any woman. If it had happened I would not conceal it from you, for it is always natural enough for a man to err, and to err *once* would be mere weakness – though I would not trust myself to promise that I should be satisfied with a single error if I once indulged myself in this respect – but I can stake my life on this assurance to you. I am well aware that this reason, powerful though it always is, has not sufficient weight. But my temperament is more disposed towards a tranquil, domestic life than towards rowdiness; moreover from youth up I have never been accustomed to attend to my own affairs, such as linen, clothes, etc. – and I can think of nothing more necessary to me than a wife. I assure you that I am often put to needless expense because I do not give heed to anything – I am quite persuaded that with a wife (and the same income I have by myself) I should manage better than I do as it is. And how many needless expenses would be saved! One incurs others in their stead, that is true – but one knows what they are, one can allow for them – in short, one leads a well-ordered life. In my eyes a bachelor is only half alive – my eyes are like that, I cannot help it. I have considered and reflected sufficiently on the matter, and my mind is made up. But who then is the object of my love? Do not be alarmed again, I implore you; but surely she is not a Weber? – Yes, a Weber – but not Josepha – not Sophie. – It is *Konstanze*, the middle one. I never met such different natures in any family as in this one. The eldest daughter is a lazy, coarse, perfidious creature and as sly as a fox. Madame Lange [Aloysia, his former love] is a false, malicious creature and a coquette. The youngest – is still too young to be anything at all – is nothing more than a kindhearted but too frivolous girl! May God preserve her from seduction. The middle one, however, namely my dear, kind Konstanze, is the martyr among them, and perhaps for that very reason the most warm-hearted, the cleverest, and in short the best of them all. She attends to everything in the house, and yet can do nothing right. Oh, dearest Father, I could fill whole pages if I were to describe to you all the scenes the two of us have witnessed in that house… She is not ugly, but she is far from beautiful. Her only beauties are a pair of little black eyes and a lovely figure. She has no wit, but enough good sense to be able to carry out her duties as wife and mother. She is not inclined to extravagance… and most of what a woman needs she can make for herself, and she dresses her own hair every day as well – understands housekeeping, has the kindest heart in the world – I love her, and she loves me with all her heart. Tell me, could I wish myself a better wife?

To his wife, Konstanze Mozart (19 May 1789)

Oh, how glad I shall be to be with you again, my darling! But the first thing I shall do is to take you by your front curls; for how on earth could you think, or even imagine, that I had forgotten you? How could I possibly do so? For even supposing such a thing, you will get on the very first night a thorough spanking on your dear little kissable arse, and this you may count upon.

To his wife (2 May 1789)

On Thursday, the 28th, I shall leave for Dresden, where I shall spend the night. On June 1st I intend to sleep in Prague, and on the 4th – the 4th – with my darling little wife. Arrange your dear sweet nest very daintily, for my little fellow deserves it indeed, he has really behaved himself very well and is only longing to possess your sweetest... Just picture to yourself that rascal; as I write he crawls onto the table and looks at me questioningly. I, however, box his ears properly – but the rogue is simply... and now the knave burns only more fiercely and can hardly be restrained. Surely you will drive out to the first post stage to meet me? I shall get there at noon on the 4th.

To his wife (6 June 1791)

I have this moment received your dear letter and am delighted to hear that you are well and in good spirits. Madame Leutgeb has laundered my nightcap and neck-tie, but I should like you to see them! Good God! I kept on telling her, '*Do let me show you how she (my wife) does them!* – But it was no use. I am delighted that you have a good appetite – but whoever gorges a lot, must also shit a lot – no, walk a lot, I mean. But I should not like you to take *long walks* without me. I entreat you to follow my advice exactly, for it comes from my heart. Adieu – my love – my only one. Do catch them in the air – those 2999$^1/_2$ little kisses from me which are flying about, waiting for someone to snap them up. Listen, I want to whisper something in your ear – and you in mine – and now we open and close our mouths – again – again and again – at last we say: 'It is all about Plumpi – Strumpi –' Well, you can think what you like – that is just why it's so convenient. Adieu. A thousand tender kisses. Ever your

Mozart

WILLIAM COBBETT

IN 1792 THE ENGLISH WRITER WILLIAM COBBETT (1763–1835) emigrated to America, "Ambitious" as he said to a friend, "to become the citizen of a free state". He returned to England two years later.

To Rachel Smither (6 July 1794), sent from Philadelphia

This country is good for getting money, that is to say, if a person is industrious and enterprising. In every other respect the country is miserable. Exactly the contrary of what I expected. The land is bad, rocky: houses wretched: roads impassable after the least rain. Fruit in quantity, but good for nothing. One apple or peach in England or France is worth a bushel of them here. The seasons are detestable. All is burning or freezing. There is no spring or autumn. The weather is so very inconstant that you are never sure for an hour, a single hour at a time. Last night we made a fire to sit by, and to-day it is scorching hot. The whole month of March was so hot that we could hardly bear our clothes, and three parts of the month of June there was a frost every night, and so cold in the day-time that we were obliged to wear great-coats. The people are worthy of the country, a cheating, sly, roguish gang. Strangers make fortunes here in spite of all this, particularly the English. The natives are by nature idle, and seek to live by cheating, while foreigners, being industrious, seek no other means than those dictated by integrity and are sure to meet with encouragement even from the idle and roguish themselves; for, however roguish a man may be, he always loves to deal with an honest man. You have perhaps heard of the plague being at Philadelphia last year. It was no plague; it was a fever of the country, and is by no means extraordinary among the Americans. In the fall of the year almost every person, in every place, has a spell of fever that is called fall-fever. It is often fatal, and the only way to avoid it is to quit the country. But this fever is not all. Every month has its particular malady. In July, for example, everybody almost, or at least one half of the people, are taken with vomitings for several days at a time; they often carry off the patient, and almost always children. In short, the country is altogether detestable.

The greatest part of my acquaintance in this country are French merchants from St Domingo and Martinico. To one of those Islands I shall probably go in about eight or nine months; and in that case, if I live so long, I shall be in England in about three years. For I do not intend to stay much above a couple of years in the Islands. Take care of my trunk and box, if you please, till you see me or hear from me. My Nancy's kind love to you all, and accept of mine at the same time. Doctor Priestley is just arrived here from England. He has attacked our English laws and Constitution in print, and declared his sentiments in favour of those butchers in France. He has, however, been attacked in his turn by an Englishman here. I will send you one of these pieces by another ship. Accept my love, and God bless you.

Wm. Cobbett

Charles Lamb

For thirty years Charles Lamb (1775–1834) worked as a clerk at India House, combining this with care of his mentally ill sister (who, in a fit of insanity, had murdered their mother), and a career as a poet and essayist. For the human warmth and wit – he was an inveterate punner – of his correspondence Lamb is often held to be the doyen of English letterists.

To Samuel Taylor Coleridge (27 September 1796)

Coleridge (1772–1834), English poet, a friend of Lamb's since their schooldays at Christ's Hospital.

My Dearest Friend:

White or some my friends or the public papers by this time may have informed you of the terrible calamities that have fallen on our family. I will only give you the outlines. My poor dear dearest sister in a fit of insanity has been the death of her own mother. I was at hand only time enough to snatch the knife out of her grasp. She is at present in a mad house, from whence I fear she must be moved to an hospital. God has preserved to me my senses, – I eat and drink and sleep, and have my judgment I believe very sound. My poor father was slightly wounded, and I am left to take care of him and my aunt. Mr Norris of the Bluecoat school has been very kind to us, and we have no other friend, but thank God I am very calm and composed, and able to do the best that remains to do. Write, – as religious a letter as possible – but no mention of what is gone and done with – with me the former things are passed away, and I have something more to do that [than] to feel —

God almighty
            have us all in
            his keeping.—

                                                    C. *Lamb*

mention nothing of poetry. I have destroyed every vestige of past
vanities of that kind. Do as you please, but if you publish, publish
mine (I give free leave) without name or initial, and never send me
a book, I charge you, you [your] own judgment will convince you not
to take any notice of this yet to your dear wife. – You look after your
family, – have my reason and strength left to take care of mine. I
charge you don't think of coming to see me; Write. I will not see you
if you come. God almighty love you and all of us –

Coleridge to Lamb (28 September 1796)

Your letter, my friend, struck me with a mighty horror. It rushed
upon me and stupefied my feelings. You bid me write you a religious
letter; I am not a man who would attempt to insult the greatness of
your anguish by any other consolation. Heaven knows that in the
easiest fortunes there is much dissatisfaction and weariness of spirit;
much that calls for the exercise of patience and resignation; but in
storms, like these, that shake the dwelling and make the heart
tremble, there is no middle way between despair and the yielding up
of the whole spirit unto the guidance of faith. And surely it is a
matter of joy, that your faith in Jesus has been preserved; the
Comforter that should relieve you is not far from you. But as you are
a Christian, in the name of that Saviour, who was filled with
bitterness and made drunken with wormwood, I conjure you to have
recourse in frequent prayer to "his God and your God", the God of
mercies, and father of all comfort. Your poor father is, I hope, almost
senseless of the calamity; the unconscious instrument of Divine
Providence knows it not, and your mother is in heaven. It is sweet
to be roused from a frightful dream by the song of birds, and the

gladsome rays of the morning. Ah, how infinitely more sweet to be awakened from the blackness and amazement of a sudden horror, by the glories of God manifest, and the hallelujahs of angels.

As to what regards yourself, I approve altogether of your abandoning what you justly call vanities. I look upon you as a man, called by sorrow and anguish and a strange desolation of hopes into quietness, and a soul set apart and made peculiar to God; we cannot arrive at any portion of heavenly bliss without in some measure imitating Christ. And they arrive at the largest inheritance who imitate the most difficult parts of his character, and bowed down and crushed under foot, cry in fullness of faith, "Father, thy will be done."

I wish above measure to have you for a little while here – no visitants shall blow on the nakedness of your feelings – you shall be quiet, and your spirit may be healed. I see no possible objection, unless your father's helplessness prevent you, and unless you are necessary to him. If this be not the case, I charge you write me that you will come.

I charge you, my dearest friend, not to dare to encourage gloom or despair – you are a temporary sharer in human miseries, that you may be an eternal partaker of the Divine nature. I charge you, if by any means it be possible, come to me. I remain, your affectionate,

S. T. Coleridge

To Thomas Manning (16 October 1800)

Thomas Manning (1772–1840), traveller, the first Englishman to visit Lhasa in Tibet.

Dear Manning:

Had you written one week before you did, I certainly should have obeyed your injunction; you should have seen me before my letter. I will explain to you my situation. There are six of us in one department. Two of us (within these four days) are confined with severe fevers; and two more, who belong to the Tower Militia, expect to have marching orders on Friday. Now six are absolutely necessary. I have already asked and obtained two young hands to supply the loss of the *Feverites*; and, with the other prospect before me, you may believe I cannot decently ask leave of absence for myself. All I can promise (and I do promise with the sincerity of *Saint* Peter, and the contrition of *Sinner* Peter if I fail) that I will come the very first spare week, and go nowhere till I have been at Camb. No matter if you are in a state of pupilage when I come; for I can employ myself in Cambridge very pleasantly in the mornings. Are there not Libraries, Halls, Colleges, Books, Pictures, Statues?

I wish to God you had made London in your way. There is an exhibition quite uncommon in Europe, which could not have escaped *your genius*, – A LIVE RATTLESNAKE, 10 feet in length, and the thickness of a big leg. I went to see it last night by candle-light. We were ushered into a room very little bigger than ours at Pentonville. A man and woman and four boys live in this room, joint tenants with nine snakes, most of them such as no remedy has been discovered for their bite. We walked into the middle, which is formed by a half-moon of wired boxes, all mansions of *snakes*, – whip-snakes, thunder-snakes, pig-nose-snakes, American vipers, and *this monster*. He lies curled up in folds; and immediately a stranger enters (for he is used to the family, and sees them play at cards,) he set up a rattle like a watchman's in London, or near as loud, and reared up a head, from the midst of these folds, like a toad, and shook his head, and showed every sign a snake can show of irritation. I had the foolish curiosity to strike the wires with my finger, and the devil flew at me with his toad-mouth wide open: the inside of his mouth is quite white. I had got my finger away, nor could he well have bit me with his damn'd big mouth, which would have been certain death in five minutes. But it frightened me so much, that I did not recover my voice for a minute's space. I forgot, in my fear, that he was secured. You would have forgot too, for 'tis incredible how such a monster can be confined in small gauzy-looking wires. I dreamed of snakes in the night. I wish to heaven you could see it. He absolutely swelled with passion to the bigness of a large thigh. I could not retreat without infringing on another box, and just behind, a little devil not all inch from my back, had got his nose out, with some difficulty and pain, quite through the bars! He was soon taught better manners. All the snakes were curious, and objects of terror: but this monster, like Aaron's serpent, swallowed up the impression of the rest. He opened his damn'd mouth, when he made at me, as wide as his head was broad. I hallooed out quite loud, and felt pains all over my body with the fright...

Yours sincerely,
Philo-Snake, C. L.

~✲~

To Samuel Taylor Coleridge (9 March 1822)

Samuel Taylor Coleridge (1772–1834), poet.

Dear Coleridge, –

It gives me great satisfaction to hear that the pig turned out so well: they are interesting creatures at a certain age. What a pity such buds should blow out into the maturity of rank bacon! You had all some of the crackling and brain sauce. Did you remember to rub it with butter, and gently dredge it a little, just before the crisis? Did the eyes come away kindly with no OEdipean avulsion? Was the crackling the colour of the ripe pomegranate? Had you no complement of boiled neck of mutton before it, to blunt the edge of delicate desire? Did you flesh maiden teeth in it? Not that *I* sent the pig, or can form the remotest guess what part Owen could play in the business. I never knew him give any thing away in my life. He would not begin with strangers. I suspect the pig, after all, was meant for me; but at the unlucky juncture of time being absent, the present somehow went round to Highgate. To confess all honest truth, a pig is one of those things which I could never think of sending away. Teal, widgeon, snipes, barn-door fowls, ducks, geese – your tame villatic things – Welsh mutton, collars of brawn, sturgeon, fresh or pickled, your potted char, Swiss cheeses, French pies, early grapes, muscadines, I impart as freely unto my friends as to myself. They are but self-extended; but pardon me if I stop somewhere. Where the fine feeling of benevolence giveth a higher smack than the sensual rarity, there my friends (or any good man) may command me; but pigs are pigs, and I myself therein am nearest to myself. Nay, I should think it an affront, an undervaluing done to Nature who bestowed such a boon upon me, if in a churlish mood I parted with the precious gift. One of the bitterest pangs of remorse I ever felt was when a child – when my kind old aunt had strained her pocket-strings to bestow a sixpenny whole plum-cake upon me. In my way home through the Borough I met a venerable old man, not a mendicant, but thereabouts; a look-beggar, not a verbal petitionist; and in the coxcombry of taught charity I gave away the cake to him. I walked on a little in all the pride of an Evangelical peacock, when of a sudden my old aunt's kindness crossed me; the sum it was to her; the pleasure she had a right to expect that I – not the old imposter – should take in eating her cake; the ingratitude by which, under the colour of a Christian virtue, I had frustrated her cherished purpose. I sobbed, wept, and took it to heart so grievously, that I think I never suffered the like; and I was right. It was a piece of unfeeling hypocrisy, and it proved a lesson to me ever after. The cake has long been masticated, consigned to the dunghill with the ashes of that unseasonable pauper.

But when Providence, who is better to us all than our aunts, gives me a pig, remembering my temptation and my fall, I shall endeavour to act towards it more in the spirit of the donor's purpose.

Yours (short of pig) to command in every thing.

C.L.

To Leigh Hunt (1824)

James Henry Leigh Hunt (1784–1859), English essayist and editor; he was caricatured as Harold Skimpole by Dickens in Bleak House.

Illustrezzimo Signor, –

I have obeyed your mandate to a tittle. I accompany this with a volume; but what have you done with the first I sent you? Have you swapped it with some lazzaroni for macaroni, or pledged it with a gondolierer for a passage? Peradventuri the Cardinal Gonsalvi took a fancy to it: his Eminence has done my Nearness an honour. 'Tis but a step to the Vatican. As you judge, my works do not enrich the workman; but I get vat I can for 'em. They keep dragging me on, a poor, worn mill-horse in the eternal round of the damned magazine; but 'tis they are blind, not I. Colburn (where I recognize with delight the gay W. Honeycomb renovated) hath the ascendency. I was with the Novellos last week. They have a large, cheap house and garden, with a dainty library (magnificent) without books; but what will make you bless yourself, (I am too old for wonder,) something has touched the right organ in Vincentio at last. He attends a Wesleyan chapel on Kingsland Green. He at first tried to laugh it off; he only went for the singing; but the cloven foot – I retract – the lamb's trotters are at length apparent. Mary Isabella attributes it to a lightness induced by his headaches; but I think I see in it a less accidental influence. Mr Clark is at perfect staggers! the whole fabric of his infidelity is shaken. He has no one to join him in his horse-insults and indecent obstreperousnesses against Christianity; for Holmes (the bonny Holmes) is gone to Salisbury to be organist, and Isabella and the Clark make but a feeble quorum. The children have all neat little clasped pray-books; and I have laid out seven shillings and eight-pence in Watts's Hymns for Christmas presents for them. The eldest girl alone holds out. She has been at Boulogne, skirting upon the vast focus of Atheism, and imported bad principles in patois French. But the strongholds are crumbling. N. appears as yet to have but a confused notion of the Atonement. It makes him giddy, he says, to think much about it; but such giddiness is spiritual sobriety. Well, Byron is gone; and — is now the best poet in England. Fill up the gap to your fancy. Barry Cornwall has at last carried the pretty A[nne] S[kipper]. They are just in the treaclemoon. Hope it won't clog his wings (gaum, we used to say at school). Mary, my sister, has worn me out with eight weeks' cold and toothache, her average complement in the Winter; and it will not go away. She is otherwise well, and reads novels all day long. She has had an exempt year, a good year; for which forgetting the minor calamity, she and I are most thankful. Alsager is in a flourishing house, with wife and children about him, in Mecklenburg Square, – almost too fine to visit. Barron Field is come home from Sydney; but as yet I can hear no tidings of a pension. He is plump and friendly; his wife, really a very superior woman. He resumes the bar. I have got acquainted with Mr Irving, the Scotch preacher, whose fame must have reached you. He is an humble disciple at the foot of Gamaliel S. T. C. Judge how his own sectarists must stare, when I tell you he has dedicated a book to S. T. C., acknowledging to have learnt more of the nature of faith. Christianity, and Christian Church, from him than from all the men he ever conversed with! He is a most amiable, sincere, modest man in a room, this Boanerges in the temple. Mrs Montague told him the dedication would do him no good. "That shall be a reason for doing it," was his answer. Judge, now, whether this man be a quack. Dear H., take this imperfect notelet for a letter: it looks so much the more like conversing on nearer terms. Love to all the Hunts, old friend Thornton, and all.

Yours ever,
C. Lamb.

❧

To Bernard Barton (April 1825)

Barton (1784–1849) was a Quaker poet.

Dear B. B., –

My spirits are so tumultuary with the novelty of my recent emancipation, that I have scarce steadiness of hand, much more mind, to compose a letter.

I am free, B. B. – free as air.

> The little bird that wings the sky
> Knows no such Liberty!

I was set free on Tuesday in last week at four o'clock.

I came home for ever!

I have been describing my feelings as well as I can to Wordsworth in a long letter and don't care to repeat. Take it briefly that for a few days I was painfully oppressed by so mighty a change but it is becoming daily more natural to me.

I went and sat among 'em all at my old thirty-three years' desk yester morning; and deuce take me if I had not yearnings at leaving all my old pen-and-ink fellows, merry sociable lads, at leaving them in the Lurch, fag, fag, fag!

The comparison of my own superior felicity gave me any thing but pleasure.

B. B., I would not serve another seven years for seven hundred thousand pounds.

I have got £441 net for life, sanctioned by Act of Parliament, with a provision for Mary if she survives me.

I will live another 50 years, or if I live but 10, they will be thirty, reckoning the quantity of real time in them, i.e. the time that is a man's own.

Tell me how you like "Barbara S". Will it be received in atonement for the foolish vision, I mean by the Lady.

A-propos, I never saw Mrs Crawford in my life; nevertheless 'tis all true of Somebody.

Address me, in future, Colebrook Cottage, Islington. I am really nervous, (but that will wear off,) so take this brief announcement.

Yours truly,
C. L.

NAPOLEON BONAPARTE

BORN IN CORSICA, NAPOLEON BONAPARTE (1769–1821) studied at military schools in France and was commissioned a lieutenant of artillery in 1785. During the Revolution his "whiff of grapeshot" helped save Paris from counter-revolution, an act for which he was made commander of the army in Italy in 1796. In the same year he married Josephine, the widow of General Vicomte de Beauharnais. The relationship soon cooled. On Napoleon's crowning as Emperor of France – the reward for his military subjugation of half of Europe – he began to become desirous of an heir and accordingly divorced the childless Josephine in 1809, to marry Grand Duchess Marie Louise of Austria, who bore him a son. Napoleon would die in exile on St Helena, after defeat by a European coalition headed by Prussia and Britain.

❧

To Josephine Bonaparte (13 November 1796) sent from Verona, Italy

I don't love you, not at all; on the contrary, I detest you – You're a naughty, gawky, foolish Cinderella. You never write me; you don't love your husband; you know what pleasure your letters give him, and yet you haven't written him six lines, dashed off casually!

What do you do all day, Madam? What is the affair so important as to leave you no time to write to your devoted lover? What affection stifles and puts to one side the love, the tender and constant love you promised him? Of what sort can be that marvellous being, that new lover who absorbs every moment, tyrannizes over your days, and prevents your giving any attention to your husband? Josephine, take care! Some fine night, the doors will be broken open, and there I'll be.

Indeed, I am very uneasy, my love, at receiving no news of you; write me quickly four pages, pages full of agreeable things which shall fill my heart with the pleasantest feelings.

I hope before long to crush you in my arms and cover you with a million kisses burning as though beneath the equator.

Bonaparte

To Josephine Bonaparte (27 November 1796)

I arrive at Milan, I rush to your apartment, I have left everything to see you, to press you in my arms... You were not there: you run from town to town after the fêtes; you leave as I am about to arrive; you do not concern yourself about your dear Napoleon any more. It was a caprice that caused you to love him; inconstancy makes him indifferent to you. Accustomed to dangers, I know the remedy for the ennuis and evils of life. The ill-fortune I experience is beyond reckoning; I should have been exempt.

I shall be here until the evening of the 9th. Do not put yourself out; run the round of pleasures; happiness is made for you. The whole world is too happy if it can please you, and your husband alone is very, very unhappy.

Bonaparte

To Josephine Bonaparte (19 December 1805)

Great Empress, not a letter from you since your departure from Strassburg. You have been to Baden, to Stuttgart, to Munich, without writing us one word. That is not very amiable nor very tender. I am still at Brünn. The Russians have gone; I have made a truce. In a few days I shall see what I am going to be. Deign, from the height of your grandeur, to trouble yourself a little about your slaves.

Napoleon

Josephine to Napoleon Bonaparte (April 1810)

By the time of this letter, Napoleon had divorced Josephine; she, however, continued her affection to him.

A thousand thousand tender thanks for not having forgotten me. My son has just brought me your letter. With what ardour I read it and yet it has taken a deal of time, because there is not a word which has not made me weep; but those tears were very sweet! I have recovered my heart entirely, and such as it will always be; there are feelings which are life itself, and which may not end but with life.

I am in despair that my letter of the 19th should have displeased you; I do not entirely recall the wording; but I know what very painful feeling had dictated it, it was grief at not having a word from you.

I wrote you on leaving Malmaison; and how many times thereafter did I wish to write! But I felt the reason for your silence, and I feared to seem importunate, by writing. Your letter has been a balm to me. Be happy; be as happy as you deserve; it is my whole heart that speaks. You have given me my share, too, of happiness, and a share very keenly felt; nothing else can have for me the value of a token of remembrance.

Adieu, my friend; I thank you as tenderly as I shall love you always.

Josephine

WILLIAM WORDSWORTH

WILLIAM WORDSWORTH (1770–1850), ROMANTIC poet. In 1799 he moved, with his sister Dorothy, to Grasmere in the Lake District.

To Samuel Taylor Coleridge (27 December 1799) from Grasmere

We arrived here last Friday, and have now been four days in our new abode [Dove Cottage] without writing to you, a long time! but we have been in such confusion as not to have had a moment's leisure. We found two Letters from you one of which I had heard of at Sockburne. I do not think there is much cause to be uneasy about Cookes affair, but as he has not answered my Letter I cannot say but I am sorry I mentioned your name: feeling so forcibly as I did that, if any man had reason to suppose I could be of service to him, he would gain incalculably by the proposed change, I was betrayed into language not sufficiently considerate and reserved. If it is in my power to remedy any part of the evil by writing again to Cooke, or in any other way, pray mention it ...

I arrived at Sockburn the day after you quitted it, I scarcely knew whether to be sorry or no that you were no longer there. as it would have been a great pain to me to have parted from you. I was sadly disappointed in not finding Dorothy: Mary was a solitary housekeeper and overjoyed to see me. D. is now sitting by me racked with the tooth-ache. This is a grievous misfortune as she has so much work for her needle among the bed curtains etc that she is absolutely buried in it. We have both caught troublesome colds in our new and almost empty house, but we hope to make it a comfortable dwelling. Our first two days were days of fear as one of the rooms upstairs smoked like a furnace, we have since learned that it is uninhabitable as a sitting room on this account; the other room however which is fortunately the one we intended for our *living* room promises uncommonly well; that is, the chimney draws perfectly, and does not even smoke at the first lighting of the fire. In particular winds most likely we shall have *puffs* of *inconvenience*, but this I believe will be found a curable evil, by means of devils as they are called and other beneficent agents which we shall station at the top of the chimney if their services should be required. D is much pleased with the house and *appurtenances* the orchard especially; in imagination she has already built a seat with a summer shed on the highest platform in this our little domestic slip of mountain. The spot commands a view over the roof of our house, of the lake, the church, helm cragg, and two thirds of the vale. We mean also to enclose the two or three yards of ground between us and the road, this for the sake of a few flowers, and because it will make it more our own. Besides, am I fanciful when I would extend the obligation of gratitude to insensate things? May not a man have a salutary pleasure in doing something gratuitously for the sake of his house, as for an individual to which he owes so much. The manners of the neighbouring cottagers have far exceeded our expectations; They seem little adulterated; indeed as far as we have seen not at all. The people we have uniformly found kind-hearted frank and manly, prompt to serve without servility. This is but an experience of four days, but we have had dealings with persons of various occupations, and have had no reason whatever to complain. We do not think it will be necessary for us to keep a servant. We have agreed to give a woman who lives in one of the adjoining cottages two shillings a week for attending two or three hours a day to light the fires wash dishes etc etc In addition to this she is to have her victuals every Saturday when she will be employed in scouring, and to have her victuals likewise on other days if we should have visitors and she is wanted more than usual. We could have had this attendance for eighteen pence a week but we added the sixpence for the sake of the poor woman, who is made happy by it. The weather since our arrival has been a keen frost, one morning two thirds of the lake were covered with ice which continued all the day but to our great surprize the next morning, though there was no intermission of the frost had entirely disappeared. The ice had been so thin that the wind had broken it up, and most likely driven it to the outlet of the lake. Rydale is covered with ice, clear as polished steel, I have procured a pair of skates and tomorrow mean to give my body to the wind, – not however without reasonable caution. We are looking for John every day; it will [be] a pity, if he should come, that D. is so much engaged, she has scarcely been out since our arrival; one evening I tempted her forth; the planet Jupiter was on the top of the hugest of the Rydale mountains, but I had reason to repent of having seduced her from her work as she returned with a raging tooth-ache. We were highly pleased with your last short letter which we had confidently and eagerly expected at Sockburn. Stuarts conduct is liberal and I hope it will answer for him You make no mention of your health. I was uneasy on that account when you were with us: upon recollection it seemed to me that the fatigues, accidents, and exposures attendant upon our journey, took greater hold of you than they ought to have done had you[r] habit of body been such as not to render caution necessary for it. Your account of Pinney is not more than I should have expected as I know him to be an excellent man. I received a Letter from him enclosing a five pound note, and informing me he hoped soon to be able to render me more substantial assistance. I wrote to him requesting him to use all his interest to induce M. to repay the principal, etc. and, that if it was his intention to do anything to disentangle M. from his embarrassments, I recommended to him to consider my claim. We shall be glad to receive the German books though it will be at least 3 weeks before D. will have any leisure to begin. Your selection of names in your history of the eminent men with whom you dined entertained me much a wretched Painter, a worse Philosopher, and a respectable bonesetter. This last I mention merely for the sake of ekeing out my sentence, as I venerate the profession of a Surgeon, and deem it the only one which has anything that deserves the name of utility in it. I suspect that it may partly be owing to something like unconscious affectation, but in honest truth I feel little disposed to notice what you say of the Lyrical Ballads though the account when I first read it gave me pleasure. The said Mr G. I have often heard described as a puppy, one of the fawning, flattering kind in short, a polite liar, often perhaps without knowing himself to be so. Accordingly he would snatch at an opportunity of saying anything agreeable to your freind Fox ergo the account is smoke or something near it. You do not speak of your travelling conversations, I have begun the pastoral of *Bowman*: in my next letter I shall probably be able to send it to you. I am afraid it will have one fault that of being too long. As to the Tragedy and Peter Bell, D. will do all in her power to put them forward. Composition I find invariably pernicious to me, and even penmanship if continued for any length of time at one sitting. I shall therefore wish you good night my beloved friend, a wish, with a thousand others, in which D. joins me. I am afraid half of what I have written is illegible, farewell. Friday Ev: We have been overhead in confusion, painting the rooms, mending the doors, and heaven knows what! This however shall not prevent me from attempting to give you some account of our Journey hither. We left Sockburne tuesday before last early in the morning, D. on a double horse behind that good creature George, and I upon Lilly, or Violet as Cottle calls her. We cross'd the Tees in the Sockburn fields by moonlight. George accompanied us eight miles beyond Richmond and there we parted with sorrowful hearts. We were now in Wensley dale and D and I set off side by side to foot it as far as Kendal. A little before sunset we reached one of the waterfalls of which I read you a short description in Mr Taylor's tour I meant to have attempted to give you a picture of it but I feel myself too lazy to execute the task. Tis a singular scene; such a performance as you might have expected from some giant gardiner employed by one of Queen Elizabeth's Courtiers, if this same giant gardiner had consulted with Spenser and they two had finish'd the work together. By this you will understand that with something of vastness or grandeur it is at once formal and wild. We reach'd the town of Askrigg, 12 miles, about six in the evening, having walked the three last miles in the dark and two of them over hard-frozen road to the great annoyance of our feet and ancles. Next morning the earth was thinly covered with snow, enough to make the road soft and prevent its being slippery. On leaving Askrigg we turned aside to see another waterfall 'twas a beautiful morning with driving snow-showers that disappeared by fits, and unveiled the east which was all one delicious pale orange colour. After walking through two fields we came to a mill which we pass'd and in a moment a sweet little valley opened before us, with an area of grassy ground, and a stream dashing over various lamina of black rocks close under a bank covered with firs. The bank and stream on our left, another woody bank on our right, and the flat meadow in front from which, as at Buttermere, the stream had retired as it were to hide itself under the shade. As we walked up this delightful valley we were tempted to look back perpetually on the brook which reflected the orange light of the morning among the gloomy rocks with a brightness varying according to the agitation of the current. The steeple of Askrigg was between us and the east, at the bottom of the valley; it was not a quarter of a mile distant, but oh! how far we were from it. The two banks seemed to join before us with a facing of rock common to them both, when we reached this point the valley opened out again, two rocky banks on each side, which, hung with ivy and moss and fringed luxuriantly with brush-wood, ran directly parallel to each other and then approaching with a gentle curve, at their point of union presented a lofty waterfall, the termination of the valley. Twas a keen frosty morning, showers of snow threatening us but the sun bright and active; we had a task of twenty one miles to perform in a short winter's day, all this put our minds in such a state of excitation that we were no unworthy spectators of this delightful scene. On a nearer approach the water seemed to fall down a tall arch or rather nitch which had shaped itself by insensible moulderings in the wall of an old castle. We left this spot with reluctance but highly exhilarated. When we had walked about a mile and a half we overtook two men with a string of ponies and some empty carts. I recommended to D. to avail herself of this opportunity of husbanding her strength, we rode with them more than two miles, twas bitter cold, the wind driving the snow behind us in the best stile of a mountain storm. We soon reached an Inn at a place called Hardraw, and descending from our vehicles, after warming ourselves by the cottage fire we walked up the brook side to take a view of a *third* waterfall. We had not gone above a few hundred yards between two winding rocky banks before we came full upon it. It appeared to throw itself in a narrow line from a lofty wall of rock; the water which shot manifestly to some distance from the rock seeming from the extreme height of the fall to be dispersed before it reached the bason, into a thin shower of snow that was toss'd about like snow blown from the roof of a house. We were disappointed in the cascade though the introductory and accompanying banks were a noble mixture of grandeur and beauty. We walked up to the fall and what would I not give if I could convey to you the images and feelings which were then communicated to me. After cautiously sounding our way over stones of all colours and sizes encased in the clearest ice formed by the spray of the waterfall, we found the rock which before had seemed a perpendicular wall extending itself over us like the ceiling of a huge cave; from the summit of which the water shot directly over our heads into a bason and among fragments of rock wrinkled over with masses of ice, white as snow, or rather as D. says like congealed froth. The water fell at least ten yards from us and we stood directly behind it, the excavation not so deep in the rock as to impress any feeling of darkness, but lofty and magnificent, and in connection with the adjoining banks excluding as much of the sky as could well be spared from a scene so exquisitely beautiful. The spot where we stood was as dry as the chamber in which I am now sitting, and the incumbent rock of which the groundwork was limestone veined and dappled with colours which melted into each other in every possible variety. On the summit of the cave were three festoons or rather wrinkles in the rock which ran parallel to each other like the folds of a curtain when it is drawn up; each of them was hung with icicles of various length, and nearly in the middle of the festoons in the deepest valley made by their waving line the stream shot from between the rows of icicles in irregular fits of strength and with a body of water that momently varied. Sometimes it threw itself into the bason in one continued curve, sometimes it was interrupted almost midway in its fall and, being blown towards us, part of the water fell at no great distance from our feet like the heaviest thunder shower. In such a situation you have at every moment a feeling of the presence of the sky. Above the highest point of the waterfall large fleecy clouds drove over our heads and the sky appeared of a blue more than usually brilliant. The rocks on each side, which, joining with the sides of the cave, formed the vista of the brook were checquered with three diminutive waterfalls or rather veins of water each of which was a miniature of all that summer and winter can produce of delicate beauty. The rock in the centre of these falls where the water was most abundant, deep black, the adjoining parts yellow white purple violet and dove colour'd, or covered with water-plants of the most vivid green, and hung with streams and fountains of ice and icicles that in some places seemed to conceal the verdure of the plants and the variegated colours of the rocks and in some places to render their hues more splendid. I cannot express to you the enchanted effect produced by this Arabian scene of colour as the wind blew aside the great waterfall behind which we stood and hid and revealed each of these faery cataracts in irregular succession or displayed them with various gradations of distinctness, as the intervening spray was thickened or dispersed. In the luxury of our imaginations we could not help feeding on the pleasure which in the heat of a July noon this cavern would spread through a frame exquisitely sensible. That huge rock of ivy on the right! the bank winding round on the left with all its living foliage, and the breeze stealing up the valley and bedewing the cavern with the faintest imaginable spray. And then the murmur of the water, the quiet, the seclusions, and a long summer day to dream in! Have I not tired you? With difficulty we tore ourselves away, and on returning to the cottage we found we had been absent an hour. Twas a short one to us, we were in high spirits, and off we drove, and will you believe me when I tell you that we walked the next ten miles, by the watch over a high mountain road, thanks to the wind that drove behind us and the good road, in two hours and a quarter, a marvellous feat of which D. will long tell. Well! we rested in a tempting inn, close by Garsdale chapel, a lowly house of prayer in a charming little valley, here we stopp'd a quarter of an hour and then off to Sedbergh 7 miles farther in an hour and thirty five minutes, the wind was still at our backs and the road delightful. I must hurry on, next morning we walked to Kendal, 11 miles, a terrible up and down road, in 3 hours, and after buying and ordering furniture, the next day by half past four we reached Grasmere in a post chaise. So ends my long story. God bless you,

To Thomas De Quincey (29 July 1803)

At this time De Quincey (1785–1859) was an aspiring writer; he later wrote Confessions of an English Opium-Eater.

Dear Sir

Your Letter dated May 31 (owing I presume to the remissness of Messeurs Longman and Rees in forwarding it) I did not receive till the day before yesterday. I am much concerned at this as though I am sure you would not suppose me capable of neglecting such a Letter, yet still my silence must needs have caused you some uneasiness.

It is impossible not to be pleased when one is told that one has given so much pleasure: and It is to me a still higher gratification to find that my poems have impressed a stranger with such favorable ideas of my character as a man. Having said this which is easily said I find some difficulty in replying more particularly to your Letter.

It is needless to say that it would be out of nature were I not to have kind feelings towards one who expresses sentiments of such profound esteem and admiration of my writings as you have done. You can have no doubt but that these sentiments however conveyed to me must have been acceptable; and I assure you that they are still more welcome coming from yourself. You will then perceive that the main end which you proposed to yourself in writing to me is answered, viz. that I am already kindly disposed towards you. My friendship it is not in my power to give: this is a gift which no man can make, it is not in our own power: a sound and healthy friendship is the growth of time and circumstance, it will spring up and thrive like a wildflower when these favour, and when they do not, it is in vain to look for it.

I do not suppose that I am saying any thing which you do not know as well as myself. I am simply reminding you of a common place truth which your high admiration of me may have robbed perhaps of that weight which it ought to have with you. And this leads me to what gave me great concern, I mean the very unreasonable value which you set upon my writings, compared with those of others. You are young and ingenuous and I wrote with a hope of pleasing the young the ingenuous and the unworldly above all others, but sorry indeed should I be to stand in the way of the proper influence of other writers. You will know that I allude to the great names of past times, and above all to those of our own Country. I have taken the liberty of saying this much to hasten on the time, when you will value my poems not less, but those of others, more. That time I know would come of itself; and may come sooner for what I have said, which at all events I am sure you cannot take ill.

How many things are there in a mans character of which his writings however miscellaneous or voluminous will give no idea. How many thousand things which go to making up the value of a frank and moral man concerning not one of which any conclusion can be drawn from what he says of himself or of others in the Worlds Ear. You probably would never guess from any thing you know of me, that I am the most lazy and impatient Letter writer in the world. You will perhaps have observed that the first two or three Lines of this sheet are in a tolerably fair, legible hand, and, now every Letter, from A to Z, is in complete route, one upon the heals of the other. Indeed so difficult Do I find it to master this ill habit of idleness and impatience, that I have long ceased to write any Letters but upon business. In justice to myself and you I have found myself obliged to mention this, lest you should think me unkind if you find me a slovenly and sluggish Correspondent.

I am going with my friend Coleridge and my Sister upon a tour into Scotland for six weeks or two months. This will prevent me hearing from you as soon as I could wish, as most likely we shall set off in a few days. If however you write immediately I may have the pleasure of receiving your Letter before our departure; if we are gone, I shall order it to be sent after me. I need not add that it will give me great pleasure to see you at Grasmere if you should ever come this way. I am dear sir with great sincerity and esteem.

Yours sincerely,
W. Wordsworth

P.S. I have just looked my letter over, and find that towards the conclusion I have been in a most unwarrantable hurry, especially in what I have said on seeing you here. I seem to have expressed myself absolutely with coldness. This is not in my feelings I assure you. I shall indeed be very happy to see you at Grasmere; if you ever find it convenient to visit this delightful country. You speak of yourself as being very young; and therefore may have many engagements of great importance with respect to your wor[l]dly concerns and future happiness in life. Do not neglect these on any account; but if consistent with these and your other duties, you could find time to visit this country which is no great distance from your present residence I should, repeat it, be very happy to see you.

W.W.

SAMUEL TAYLOR COLERIDGE

SAMUEL TAYLOR COLERIDGE (1772–1834), POET AND pioneer, along with William Wordsworth, of English Romanticism.

❧

To William Godwin (3 March 1800)

William Godwin (1756–1836) was the author of the pamphlet Enquiry Concerning Political Justice, *the anarchist–atheist ideas of which, heavily influenced by the French Revolution, had captivated Coleridge, Wordsworth and Shelley, who was to marry his daughter Mary.*

8. Monday Morning

Dear Godwin

The Punch after the Wine made me tipsy last night – this I mention, not that my head aches, or that I felt after I quitted you, any unpleasantness, or titubancy – but because tipsiness has, and has always, one unpleasant effect – that of making me talk *very* extravagantly / & as when sober, I talk extravagantly enough for any *common* Tipsiness, it becomes a matter of nicety in discrimination to know when I am or am not affected. – An idea starts up in my hand [head?] – away I follow it thro' thick & thin, Wood & Marsh, Brake and Briar – with all the apparent Interest of a man who was defending one of his old and long-established Principles – Exactly of this kind was the Conversation, with which I quitted you / I do not believe it possible for a human Being to have a greater horror of the feelings that usually accompany such principles as I then supported, or a deeper Conviction of their irrationality than myself – but the whole Thinking of my Life will not bear me up against the accidental Press & Crowd of my mind, when it is elevated beyond it's natural Pitch / .–

167

We shall talk wiselier with the Ladies on Tuesday – God bless you, & give your dear little ones a kiss for me –

The Agnus Dei & the Virgin Mary desire their kind respects to you, you sad Atheist – !

> Your's with affectionate
> Esteem
> S. T. *Coleridge*

❧

To James West Tobin (25 July 1800)

> From the leads on the housetop of Greta Hall, Keswick, Cumberland at the present time in the occupancy and usufruct-possession of S T. Coleridge, Esq, Gentleman-poet and Philosopher in a mist.

Yes, my dear Tobin, here I am, with Skiddaw behind my back; the Lake of Bassenthwaite, with its simple and majestic *case* of mountains, on my right hand; on my left, and stretching far away into the fantastic mountains of Borrowdale, the Lake of Derwentwater: straight before me a whole camp of giants' tents,– or is it an ocean rushing in, in billows that, even in the serene sky, reach halfway to heaven? When I look at the feathery top of this scoundrel pen, with which I am making desperate attempts to write, I see (in that slant direction) the sun almost setting, – in ten minutes it will touch the top of the crag; the vale of Keswick lies between us, so much for the topography of the letter; as to the chronology, it is half past seven in the evening.

I left Wordsworth yesterday; he was tolerably well, and meditates more than his side permits him even to attempt. He has a bed for you; but I absolutely stipulate that you shall be half the time at Keswick. We have house-room enough, and I am sure I need say nothing of anything else. What should prevent you from coming and spending the next brace of months here? I will suppose you to set off in the second week of August, and Davy will be here in the first week of September at the farthest; and then, my dear fellow, for physiopathy and phileleutherism – sympathy lemonaded with a little argument – punning and green peas with bacon, or *very ham*; rowing and sailing on the lake (there is a nice boat obsequious to my purposes). Then, as to chemistry, there will be Davy with us. We shall be as rich with reflected light as yon cloud which the sun has taken to his very bosom!

When you come, I pray you do not forget to bring Bartram's *Travels* with you. Where is John Pinny? He talked of accompanying you. Wordsworth builds on his coming down this autumn; if I knew his present address, I would write to him. Wordworth remains at Grasmere till next summer (perhaps longer). His cottage is indeed in every respect so delightful a residence, the walks so dry after the longest rains, the heath and a silky kind of fern so luxurious a bedding on every hilltop, and the whole vicinity so tossed about on those little hills at the feet of the majestic mountains, that he moves in an eddy; he cannot get out of it.

In the way of books. we are extraordinarily well off for a country place. My landlord has a respectable library, full of dictionaries and useful modern things; *ex. gr.*, the Scotch Encyclopaedia, the authors of which may the devil scotch, for toothless serpents that poison with dribble! But there is at some distance Sir Wilfred Lawson's magnificent library, and Sir Wilfred talks of calling upon me, and of course I keep the man in good humor with me, and gain the use of his books.

Hartley [Coleridge's son] returns his love to you; he talks often about you. I hear his voice at this moment distinctly; he is below in the garden, shouting to some foxgloves and fern, which he has transplanted, and telling them what he will do for them if they grow like good boys! This afternoon I sent him naked into a shallow of the river Greta; he trembled with the novelty, yet you cannot conceive his raptures.

God bless you!

I remain, with affectionate esteem,
Yours sincerely,
S. T. *Coleridge*.

I open the letter, and make a new fold, to tell you that I have bit the wafer [seal] into the very shape of the young moon that is just above the opposite hill.

To Joseph Cottle (26 April 1814)

Joseph Cottle was the publisher of Coleridge and Wordsworth's Lyrical Ballads; *he had written to Coleridge imploring him to renounce his opium habit.*

You have poured oil in the raw and festering Wound of an old friend's Conscience, Cottle! but it is oil of Vitriol! I but barely glanced at the middle of the first page of your Letter, & have seen no more of it – not for resentment (God forbid!) but from the state of my bodily & mental sufferings that scarcely permitted human fortitude to let in a new Visitor of affliction. The object of my present reply is to state the case just as it is – first, that for years the anguish of my spirit has been indescribable, the sense of my danger *staring*, but the conscience of my GUILT worse, far far worse than all! – I have prayed with drops of agony on my Brow, trembling not only before the Justice of my Maker, but even before the Mercy of my Redeemer "I gave thee so many Talents. What hast thou done with them"? – Secondly – that it is false & cruel to say, (overwhelmed as I am with the sense of my direful Infirmity) that I attempt or ever have attempted to *disguise* or conceal the cause. On the contrary, not only to friends have I stated the whole Case with tears & the very bitterness of shame; but in two instances I have warned young men, mere aquaintances who had spoken of having taken Laudanum, of the direful Consequences, by an ample exposition of it's tremendous effects on myself – Thirdly, tho' before God I dare not lift up my eyelids, & only do not despair of his Mercy because to despair would be adding crime to crime; yet to my fellow-men I may say, that I was seduced into the ACCURSED Habit ignorantly. – I had been almost bed-ridden for many months with swellings in my knees – in a medical Journal I unhappily met with an account of a cure performed in a similar case (or what to me appeared so) by rubbing in of Laudanum, at the same time taking a given dose internally – It acted like a charm, like a miracle! I recovered the use of my Limbs, of my appetite, of my Spirits – & this continued for near a fortnight – At length, the unusual Stimulus subsided – the complaint returned – the supposed remedy was recurred to but I can not go thro' the dreary history – suffice it to say, that effects were produced, which acted on me by *Terror & Cowardice* of PAIN & sudden Death, not (so help me God!) by any temptation of Pleasure, or expectation or desire of exciting pleasurable Sensations. On the very contrary, Mrs Morgan & her Sister will bear witness so far, as to say that the longer I abstained, the higher my spirits were, the keener my enjoyments – till the moment, the direful moment, arrived, when my pulse began to fluctuate, my Heart to palpitate, & such a dreadful *falling-abroad*, as it were, of my whole frame, such intolerable Restlessness & incipient Bewilderment that in the last of my several attempts to abandon the dire poison, I exclaimed in agony, what I now repeat in seriousness & solemnity – I am too poor to hazard this! Had I but a few hundred Pounds, but 200£, half to send to Mrs Coleridge, & half to place myself in a private madhouse, where I could procure nothing but what a Physician thought proper, & where a medical attendant could be constantly with me for two or three months (in less than that time Life or Death would be determined) then there might be Hope. Now there is none – O God! how willingly would I place myself under Dr Fox in his Establishment – for my Case is a species of madness, only that it is a derangement, an utter impotence of the *Volition*, & not of the intellectual Faculties – You bid me rouse myself – go, bid a man paralytic in both arms rub them briskly together, & that will cure him. Alas! (he would reply) that I cannot move my arms is my Complaint & my misery. –

My friend, Wade, is not at home – & I sent off all the little money, I had – or I would with this have inclosed the 10£ received from you. –

May God bless you

&

Your affectionate &

most afflicted

S. T. *Coleridge*

Dr Estlin, I found, is raising the city against me, as far as he & his friends can, for having staged a mere matter of fact, . . . – viz – that Milton had represented Satan as a sceptical Socinian – which is the case, & I could not have explained the excellence of the sublimest single Passage in all his Writings had I not previously informed the Audience, that Milton had represented Satan as knowing the prophetic & Messianic Character of Christ, but sceptical as to any higher Claims – & what other definition could Dr E. himself give of a sceptical Socinian? – Now that M. has done so, please to consult *Par. Regained*, Book IV, from line 196. – & then the same Book from line 500. –

WILLIAM BLAKE

THE ENGLISH MYSTICAL POET AND ARTIST WILLIAM Blake (1757–1827) received little public approbation in his lifetime, but was supported in his endeavours by his unflagging religious devotion and a circle of admiring friends. Among them was the sculptor John Flaxman.

~❧~

To John Flaxman (21 September 1800, from Felpham)

Dear Sculptor of Eternity:

We are safe arrived at our cottage, which is more beautiful than I thought it, and more convenient. It is a perfect model for cottages, and I think for palaces of magnificence, only enlarging not altering its proportions and adding ornaments and not principles. Nothing can be more grand than its simplicity and usefulness. Simple without intricacy, it seems to be the spontaneous expression of humanity, congenial to the wants of man. No other formed house can ever please me so well, nor shall I ever be persuaded, I believe, that it can be improved either in beauty or use.

Mr Hayley received us with his usual brotherly affection. I have begun to work. Felpham is a sweet place for study, because it is more spiritual than London. Heaven opens here on all sides her golden gates: her windows are not obstructed by vapours; voices of celestial inhabitants are more distinctly heard and their forms more distinctly seen; and my cottage is also a shadow of their houses. My wife and sister are both well, courting Neptune for an embrace.

Our journey was very pleasant, and, though we had a great deal of luggage, no grumbling. All was cheerfulness and good humour on the road, and yet we could not arrive at our cottage before half-past eleven at night, owing to the necessary shifting of our luggage from one chaise to another, for we had seven different chaises and as many different drivers. We set out between six and seven in the morning of Thursday, with sixteen heavy boxes and portfolios full of prints.

And now begins a new life, because another covering of earth is shaken off. I am more famed in heaven for my works than I could well conceive. In my brain are studies and chambers filled with books and pictures of old, which I wrote and painted in ages of eternity before my mortal life; and those works are the delight and study of archangels. Why then should I be anxious about the riches and fame of mortality? The Lord our Father will do for us and with us according to His divine will.

You, O dear Flaxman, are a sublime archangel – my friend and companion from eternity. In the divine bosom is our dwelling place. I look back into the regions of reminiscence, and behold our ancient days before this earth appeared in its vegetative mortality to my mortal vegetated eyes. I see our houses of eternity which can never be separated, though our mortal vehicles should stand at the remotest corners of heaven from each other.

Farewell, my best Friend; – remember me and my wife in love and friendship to our dear Mrs Flaxman, whom we ardently desire to entertain beneath our thatched roof of rusted gold. And believe me for ever to remain your grateful and affectionate

William Blake

To George Cumberland (12 April 1827)

Dear Cumberland,

I have been very near the Gates of Death & have returned very weak & an Old Man feeble & tottering, but not in Spirit & Life, not in The Real Man The Imagination which Liveth for Ever. In that I am stronger & stronger as this Foolish Body decays. I thank you for the Pains you have taken with Poor Job. I know too well that a great majority of Englishmen are fond of The Indefinite which they Measure by Newton's Doctrine of the Fluxions of an Atom, A Thing that does not Exist. These are Politicians & think that Republican Art is Inimical to their Atom. For a Line or Lineament is not formed by Chance: a Line is a Line in its Minutest Subdivisions: Strait or Crooked It is Itself & Not Intermeasurable with or by any Thing Else. Such is Job, but since the French Revolution Englishmen are all Intermeasurable One by Another, Certainly a happy state of Agreement to which I for One do not Agree. God keep me from the Divinity of Yes & No too, The Yea Nay Creeping Jesus, from supposing Up & Down to be the same Thing as all Experimentalists must suppose.

You are desirous I know to dispose of some of my Works & to make them Pleasing. I am obliged to you & to all who do so. But having none remaining of all that I had Printed I cannot Print more Except at a great loss, for at the time I printed those things I had a whole House to range in: now I am shut up in a Corner therefore am forced to ask a Price for them that I scarce expect to get from a Stranger. I am now Printing a Set of the Songs of Innocence & Experience for a Friend at Ten Guineas which I cannot do under Six Months consistent with my other Work, so that I have little hope of doing any more of such things. The Last Work I produced is a Poem Entitled Jerusalem the Emanation of the Giant Albion, but find that to Print it will Cost my Time the amount of Twenty Guineas. One I have Finish'd. It contains 100 Plates but it is not likely that I shall get a Customer for it.

As you wish me to send you a list with the Prices of these things they are as follows

	£	s	D
America	6.	6.	0
Europe	6.	6.	0
Visions & c	5.	5.	0
Thel	3.	3.	0
Songs of Inn. & Exp.	10.	10.	0
Urizen	6.	6.	0

The Little Card I will do as soon as Possible but when you Consider that I have been reduced to a Skeleton from which I am slowly recovering you will I hope have Patience with me.

Flaxman is Gone & we must All soon follow, every one to his Own Eternal House, Leaving the Delusive Goddess Nature & her Laws to get into Freedom from all Law of the Members into The Mind, in which every one is King & Priest in his own House. God send it so on Earth as it is in Heaven.

I am, Dear Sir, Yours Affectionately
William Blake

12 April 1827
N 3 Fountain Court Strand

JANE AUSTEN

JANE AUSTEN (1775–1817), AUTHOR OF *SENSE AND Sensibility* (1811) and *Pride and Prejudice* (1813).

To her sister, Cassandra (20 November 1800)

My Dear Cassandra,

Your letter took me quite by surprise this morning; you are very welcome, however, and I am very much obliged to you. I believe I drank too much wine last night at Hurstbourne; I know not how else to account for the shaking of my hand today. You will kindly make allowance therefore for any indistinctness of writing, by attributing it to this venial error.

Naughty Charles did not come on Tuesday, but good Charles came yesterday morning. About two o'clock he walked in on a Gosport hack. His feeling equal to such a fatigue is a good sign, and his feeling no fatigue in it a still better. He walked down to Deane to dinner; he danced the whole evening, and today is no more tired than a gentleman ought to be.

Your desiring to hear from me on Sunday will, perhaps, bring you a more particular account of the ball than you may care for, because one is prone to think much more of such things the morning after they happen, than when time has entirely driven them out of one's recollection.

It was a pleasant evening; Charles found it remarkably so, but I cannot tell why, unless the absence of Miss Terry, towards whom his conscience reproaches him with being now perfectly indifferent, was a relief to him. There were only twelve dances, of which I danced nine, and was merely prevented from dancing the rest by the want of a partner. We began at ten, supped at one, and were at Deane before five. There were but fifty people in the room; very few families indeed from our side of the county, and not many more from the other. My partners were the two St. Johns, Hooper, Holder, and very prodigious Mr Mathew, with whom I called the last, and whom I liked the best of my little stock.

There were very few beauties, and such as there were were not very handsome. Miss Iremonger did not look well, and Mrs Blount was the only one much admired. She appeared exactly as she did in September, with the same broad face, diamond bandeau, white shoes, pink husband, and fat neck. The two Miss Coxes were there: I traced in one the remains of the vulgar, broad-featured girl who danced at Enham eight years ago; the other is refined into a nice, composed-looking girl, like Catherine Bigg. I looked at Sir Thomas Champneys and thought of poor Rosalie; I looked at his daughter; and thought her a queer animal with a white neck. Mrs Warren, I was constrained to think, a very fine young woman, which I much regret. She danced away with great activity. Her husband is ugly enough, uglier even than his cousin John; but he does not look so *very* old. The Miss Maitlands are both prettyish, very like Anne, with brown skins, large dark eyes, and a good deal of nose. The general has got the gout, and Mrs Maitland the jaundice. Miss Debary, Susan, and Sally, all in black, but without any stature, made their appearance, and I was as civil to them as circumstances would allow me.

They told me nothing new of Martha. I mean to go to her on Thursday, unless Charles should determine on coming over again with his friend Shipley for the Basingstoke ball, in which case I shall not go till Friday. I shall write to you again, however, before I set off, and I shall hope to hear from you in the meantime. If I do not stay for the ball, I would not on any account do so uncivil a thing by the neighbourhood as to set off at that very time for another place, and shall therefore make a point of not being later than Thursday *morning*.

Mary said that I looked very well last night. I wore my aunt's gown and handkerchief, and my hair was at least tidy, which was all my ambition. I will now have done with the ball, and I will moreover go and dress for dinner.

LORD NELSON

HORATIO NELSON (1758–1805), ENGLISH NAVAL COMmander. He began an affair with Emma Hamilton, the wife of Sir William, the British ambassador to Naples, in 1798. She later gave birth to their illegitimate daughter, Horatia.

To Lady Hamilton (17 February 1801)

Nelson was concerned at the Regent's interest in Emma Hamilton

I am so agitated that I can write nothing. I knew it would be so, and you can't help it. Why did you not tell Sir William? Your character will be gone. Good God! he will be next you, and telling you soft things. If he does, tell it out at table, and turn him out of the house. Do not sit long. If you sing a song, I know you cannot help it, do not let him set next you, but at dinner he will hob glasses with you. I cannot write to Sir Wm, but he ought to go to the Prince and not suffer your character to be ruined by him. O, God, that I was dead! But I do not, my dearest Emma, blame you, nor do I fear your inconstancy. I tremble, and God knows how I write. Can nothing be thought of? I am gone almost mad, but you cannot help it. It will be in all the newspapers with hints. Recollect what the villain said to Mr Nisbet, *how you hit his fancy*. I am mad, almost dead, but ever for ever yours to the last moment, your, only your, & c.

I could not write another line if I was to be made King. If I was in town nothing should make me dine with you that damned day, but my dear Emma, I do not blame you, only remember your poor miserable friend, that you must be singing and appear gay. I shall that day have no one to dinner; it shall be a fast day to me. He will put his foot near you. I pity you from my soul, as I feel confident you wish him in hell. Have plenty of people and do not say a word you can help to him. He wishes, I dare say, to have you alone. Don't let him touch, nor yet sit next you; if he comes, get up. God strike him blind if he looks at you – this is high treason, and you may get me hanged by revealing it. Oh, God! that I were. I have read your letter, your resolution never to go where the fellow is, but you must have him at home. Oh, God! but you cannot, I suppose, help it, and you cannot turn him out of your own house. He will stay and sup and sit up till 4 in the morning, and the fewer that stay the better. Oh, God! why do I live? But I do not blame you; it is my misfortune. I feel nobody uses me ill. I am only fit to be second, or third, or 4, or to black shoes. I want no better part than I have. I see your determination to be on your guard, and am as fixed as fate. If you'll believe me, don't scold me; I am more dead than alive, to the last breath yours. If you cannot get rid of this I hope you will tell Sir William never to bring the fellow again.

I send a note for Mrs T.

To Lady Hamilton (19 February 1801)

Forgive my letter wrote and sent last night, perhaps my head was a little affected. No wonder, it was such an unexpected, such a knock-down blow, such a death. But I will not go on, for I shall get out of my senses again. Will you sing for the fellow, *The Prince, unable to Conceal His Pain*, &c? No, you will not. I will say no more for fear of my head. It was so good of you to send to thank Mr Nisbet for his not asking you to meet the fellow, as he knew his vile interest, and yet, the same morning to let him come and dine with you en famille! – but I know it was not my Emma; Sir William always asks all partys to dinner. I forgive you. Forgive, I beseech, your old and dear friend! Tell me all, every word, that passes. He will propose if you – no, you will not try; he is Sir Wm's guest.

Thursday – I have just got your letter and I live again. DO NOT let the lyar come. I never saw him but once, the 4th day after I came to London, and he never mentioned your name. May God blast him! Be firm! Go and dine with Mrs Denis on Sunday. Do not, I beseech you, risk being at home. Does Sir William want you to be a whore to the rascal? Forgive all my letter; you will see what I feel, and have felt. I have eat not a morsel, except a little rice, since yesterday morning, and resolution, and thank you 1,000,000 of times. I write you a letter, which may be said as coming from me if you like, I will endeavour to word it properly. Did you sit alone with the villain for a moment? No, I will not believe it! O, God! keep my sences. Do not let the rascal in. Tell the Duke that you will never go to his house. Mr G must be a scoundrel; he treated you once ill enough, and cannot love you, or he would sooner die. Ever for ever, aye for ever, your, &c.

I have this moment got my orders to put myself under Sir Hyde Parker's orders, and suppose I shall be ordered to Portsmouth tomorrow or next day, & then I will try & get to London for 3 days. May Heaven bless us! but do not let that fellow dine with you. Don't write here after you receive this, I shall be gone. You can, in Sir Wm's name, write a note to Sir H. Parker, asking if the

St George is ordered to Spithead. If so, write to Portsmouth desiring my letters to be left at the Post Office till the ship's arrival.

Forgive every cross word, I now live.

To Lady Hamilton (1 March 1801)

Now, my dear wife, for such you are in my eyes and in the face of heaven, I can give full scope to my feelings, for I daresay Oliver will faithfully deliver this letter. You know, my dearest Emma, that there is nothing in this world that I would not do for us to live together, and to have our dear little child with us. I firmly believe that this campaign will give us peace, and then we will sett off for Bronte. In twelve hours we shall be across the water and freed from all the nonsense of his friends, or rather pretended ones. Nothing but an event happening to him could prevent my going, and I am sure you will think so, for unless all matters accord it would bring 100 of tongues and slanderous reports if I separated from her (which I would do with pleasure the moment we can be united; I want to see her [Nelson's wife] no more), therefore we must manage till we can quit this country or your uncle dies. I love, I never did love any one else. I never had a dear pledge of love till you gave me one, and you, thank my God, never gave one to any body else. I think before March is out you will either see us back, or so victorious that we shall insure a glorious issue to our toils. Think what my Emma will feel at seeing return safe, perhaps with a little more fame, her own dear loving Nelson. Never, if I can help it, will I dine out of my ship, or go on shore, except duty calls me. Let Sir Hyde have any glory he can catch – I envy him not. You, my beloved Emma, and my country, are the two dearest objects of my fond heart – a heart susceptible and true. Only place confidence in me and you never shall be disappointed. I burn all your dear letters, because it is right for your sake, and I wish you would burn all mine – they can do no good, and will do us both harm if any seizure of them, or the dropping even one of them, would fill the mouths of the world sooner than we intend.

(My longing for you, both person and conversation, you may readily imagine. What must be my sensations at the idea of sleeping with you! it setts me on fire, even the thoughts, much more would the reality. I am sure my love & desires are all to you, and if any woman naked were to come to me, even as I am this moment from thinking of you, I hope it might rot off if I would touch her even with my hand. No, my heart, person, and mind is in perfect union of love towards my own dear, beloved Emma – the real bosom friend of her, all hers, all Emma's, &c.

Oliver is gone to sleep, he is grown half foolish. I shall give him £10 in the morning, and I have wrote a letter recommending a friend of his to the Chairman of the East India Company, which he said you would be glad I should do for him. I have nothing to send my Ernma, it makes me sorry you & Sir Wm could not come to Yarmouth, that would be pleasant, but we shall not be there more than a week at farthest.) I had a letter this day from the Rev. Mr Holden, who we met on the Continent; he desired his kind compliments to you and Sir William: he sent me letters of my name, and recommended it as my motto – Honor est a Nilo – HORATIO NELSON. May the Heavens bless you. (My love, my darling angel, my heaven-given wife, the dearest only true wife of her own till death, &c. I know you will never let that fellow or any one come near you.)

Monday Morning. – Oliver is just going on shore; the time will ere long arrive when Nelson will land to fly to his Emma, to be for ever with her. Let that hope keep us up under our present difficulties. Kiss and bless *our* dear Horatia – think of that.

FANNY BURNEY

THE ENGLISH NOVELIST AND DIARIST FANNY BURNEY (1752–1840) was the daughter of the musicologist Dr Charles Burney. She was a keeper of robes to Queen Charlotte, before retiring, due to ill health, and marrying the French emigré, General Alexandre d'Arblay. It was while living with d'Arblay in Paris that she underwent a mastectomy performed by Napoleon's surgeon, M. Larrey, described here in a letter to her sister.

~❧~

To Esther Burney (22 March–June 1812)

... A formal consultation now was held, of Larrey, Ribe, & Moreau – &, in fine, I was formally condemned to an operation by all Three. I was as much astonished as disappointed – for the poor breast was no where discoloured, & not much larger than its healthy neighbour. Yet I felt the evil to be deep, so deep, that I often thought if it could not be dissolved, it could only with life be extirpated. I called up, however, all reason I possessed, or could assume, & told them – that if they saw no other alternative, I would not resist their opinion & experience: – the good Dr Larry [sic], who, during his long attendance had conceived for me the warmest friendship, had now tears in his Eyes; from my dread he had expected resistance. He proposed again calling in M. Dubois. No, I told him, if I could not by himself be saved. I had no sort of hope elsewhere, &, if it must be, what I wanted in courage should be supplied by Confidence. The good man was now dissatisfied with himself, and declared I ought to have the First & most eminent advice his Country could afford: "Vous êtes si considerée, Madame" said he, "ici, que le public même sera mécontent si vous n'avez pas tout le secours que nous avons à vous offrir" – Yet this modest man is premier chirugien de la Garde Imperiale, & had been lately created a Baron for his eminent services – M. Dubois, he added, from his super-skill & experience, might yet, perhaps, suggest some cure. This conquered me quickly, ah – Send for him! Send for him! I cried – & Dr Moreau received the commission to consult with him. – What an interval was this! Yet my poor M. d'A was more to be pitied than myself, though he knew not the terrible idea I had internally annexed to the trial – but Oh what he suffered!

– & with what exquisite tenderness he solaced all I had to bear! My poor Alex I kept as much as possible, and as long, ignorant of my situation. – M. Dubois behaved extremely well, no pique intervened with the interest he had professed in my well-doing, & his conduct was manly & generous. It was difficult still to see him, but he appointed the earliest day in his power for a general & final consultation. I was informed of it only on the Same day, to avoid useless agitation. He met here Drs Larrey, Ribe & Moreau. The case, I saw, offered uncommon difficulties, or presented eminent danger, but, the examination over, they desired to consult together. I left them – what an half an hour I passed alone! – M. d'A. was at his office. Dr Larrey then came to summon me. He did not speak, but looked very like my dear Brother James, to whom he has a personal resemblance that has struck M. d'A. as well as myself. I came back, & took my seat, with what calmness I was able. All were silent, & Dr Larrey, I saw, hid himself nearly behind my Sofa. My heart beat fast: I saw all hope was over. I called upon them to speak. M. Dubois then, after a long & unintelligible harangue, from his own disturbance, pronounced my doom. I now saw it was inevitable, and abstained from any further effort. They received my formal consent, & retired to fix a day.

All hope of escaping this evil being now at an end, I could only console or employ my mind in considering how to render it less dreadful to M. d'A. M. Dubois had pronounced "il faut s'attendre à souffrir. Je ne veux pas vous trompez – Vous Souffrirez – vous souffrirez *beaucoup*!" – M. Ribe had *charged* me to cry! to withhold or restrain myself might have seriously had consequences, he said. M. Moreau, in ecchoing this injunction, enquired whether I had cried or screamed at the birth of Alexander – Alas, I told him, it had not been possible to do otherwise; Oh then, he answered, there is no fear! – What terrible inferences were here to be drawn! I desired, therefore, that M. d'A. might be kept in ignorance of the day till the operation should be over. To this they agreed, except M. Larrey, with high approbation: M. Larrey looked dissentient, but was silent. M. Dubois protested he would not undertake to act, after what he had seen of the agitated spirits of M. d'A. if he were present: nor would he suffer me to know the time myself over night; I obtained with difficulty a promise of 4 hours warning, which were essential to me for sundry regulations.

From this time, I assumed the best spirits in my power, *to meet the coming blow*: – & support my too sympathising Partner. They would let me make no preparations, refusing to inform me what would be necessary; I have known since, that Mad^e de Tessé, an admirable old friend of M. d'A, now mine, equally, & one of the first of her sex, in any country, for uncommon abilities, & nearly universal knowledge, had insisted upon sending all that might be necessary, & of keeping me in ignorance. M. d'A filled a Closet with Charpie, compresses, & bandages – All that to *me* was owned, as wanting, was an arm Chair & some Towels. – Many things, however, joined to the depth of my pains, assured me the business was not without danger. I therefore made my Will – unknown, to this moment, to M. d'A, & entrusted it privately to M. La Tour Maubourg, without even letting my friend his Sister, Mad^e de Maisonneuve, share the secret. M. de M^g convened it for me to Maria's excellent M. Gillet, from whom M. de M^g brought me directions. As soon as I am able to go out I shall reveal this clandestine affair to M. d'A. – till then, it might still affect him. Mad^e de Maisonneuve desired to be present at the operation; – but I would not inflict such pain. Me de Chastel belle soeur to Mad^e de Boinville, would also have sustained the shock; but I secured two Guards, one of whom is known to my dear Charlottes. Made Soubiren, portière to l'Hotel Marengo: a very good Creature, who often amuses me by repeating "*ver, vell, Mawm*:" which she tells me she learnt of Charlotte the younger, whom she never names but with rapture, The other is a workwoman whom I have often employed. The kindnesses I received at this period would have made me for-ever love France, had I hitherto been hard enough of heart to hate it – but Mad^e d'Henin – the tenderness she shewed me surpasses all description. Twice she came to Paris from the Country, to see, watch & sit with me; there is nothing that can be suggested of use or comfort that she omitted. She loves me not only from her kind heart, but also from her love of Mrs Lock, often, often exclaiming "Ah! si votre angelique amie étoit ici!" – But I must force myself from these episodes, though my dearest Esther will not think them *de trop*.

After sentence thus passed, I was in hourly expectation of a summons to execution; judge, then, my surprise to be suffered to go on full 3 Weeks in the same state! M. Larrey from time to time visited me. but pronounced nothing, & was always melancholy. at length, M. d'A. was told that he waited himself for a Summons! & that, a formal one, & in writing! *I* could not give one, a *consent* was my utmost effort. But poor M. d'A. wrote a desire that the operation, if necessary, might take place without further delay. In my own mind. I had all this time been persuaded there were hopes of a cure: why else, I thought, let me know my doom thus long? But here I must account for this apparently useless, & therefore cruel measure, though I only learnt it myself 2 months afterwards. M. Dubois had given his opinion that the evil was too far advanced for any remedy; that the cancer was already internally declared: that I was inevitably destined to that most frightful of deaths, & that an operation would but accellerate my dissolution. Poor M. Larrey was so deeply affected by this sentence, that – as he has lately told me, – he regretted to his Soul ever having known me, & was upon the point of demanding a commission to the furthest end of France in order to force me into other hands. I had said, however he remembered, once, that I would far rather suffer a quick end without, than a lingering life with this dreadfullest of maladies: he finally therefore considered it might be possible to save me by the trial, but that without it my case was desperate, & resolved to make the attempt. Nevertheless, the responsibility was too great to rest upon his own head entirely: & therefore he waited the formal summons. – In fine, One morning – the last of September, 1811, while I was still in Bed, & M. d'A. was arranging some papers for his office, I received a Letter written by M. de Lally to a Journalist, in vindication of the honoured memory of his Father against the assertions of Mad^e du Deffand. I read it aloud to My Alexanders, with tears of admiration & sympathy, & then sent it by Alex: to its excellent Author, as I had promised the preceding evening. I then dressed, aided, as usual for many months, by my maid, my right arm being condemned to total inaction; but not yet was the grand business over, when another Letter was delivered to me – another, indeed! – was from M. Larrey, to acquaint me that at 10 o'clock he should be with me, properly accompanied, & to exhort me to rely as much upon his sensibility & his prudence, as upon his dexterity & his experience; he charged to secure the absence of M. d'A: & told me that the young Physician who would deliver me this *announce*, would prepare for the operation, in which he must lend his aid: & also that it had been the decision of the consultation to allow me but two hours notice, – judge, my Esther, if I read this unmoved! – yet I had to disguise my sensations & intentions from M. d'A! – Dr Aumont, the Messenger & terrible Herald, was in waiting: M. d'A stood by my bed side: I affected to be long reading the Note, to gain time for forming some plan, & such was my terror of involving M. d'A. in the unavailing wretchedness of witnessing what I must go through, that it conquered every other, & gave me the force to act as if I were directing some third person. The detail would be too *Wordy*, as James says, but the *wholesale* is – I called Alex to my Bed side, & sent him to inform M. Barbier Neuville, chef du division du Bureau de M. d'A. that *the moment was come*, & I entreated him to write a summons upon urgent business for M. d'A. & to detain him till all should be over. Speechless & appalled, off went Alex, &, as I have since heard, was forced to sit down & sob in executing his commission. I then, by the maid, sent word to the young Dr Aumont that I could not be ready till one o'clock: & I finished my breakfast, & – not with much appetite, you will believe! forced down a crust of bread, & hurried off, under various pretences, M. d'A. He was scarcely gone, when M. Du Bois arrived: I renewed my request for one o'clock: the rest came; all were fain to consent to the delay, for I had an apartment to prepare for my banished Mate. This arrangement & those for myself, occupied me completely. Two engaged nurses were out of the way – I had a bed, Curtains, & heaven knows what to prepare – but business was good for my nerves. I was obliged to quit my room to have it put in order: – Dr Aumont would not leave the house; he remained in the Sallon, folding linen – He had demanded 4 or 5 old & fine left off under Garments – I glided to our Book Cabinet: sundry necessary works & orders filled up my time entirely till One O'clock. When all was ready – but Dr Moreau then arrived, with news that M. Dubois could not attend till three. Dr Aumont went away – & the Coast was clear. This, indeed, was a dreadful interval. I had no longer any thing to do – I had only to think – two hours thus spent seemed never-ending. I would fain have written to my dearest Fath – to You, my Esther – to Charlotte James – Charles – Amelia Lock – but my arm prohibited me: I strolled to the Sallon – I saw it fitted with preparations, & I recoiled – But I soon returned: to what effect disguise from myself what I must so soon know? – yet the sight of the immense quantity of bandages, compresses, spunges, Lint – made me a little sick: – I walked backwards & forwards till I quieted all emotion, & became, by degrees, nearly stupid – torpid, without sentiment or consciousness – & thus I remained till the Clock struck three. A sudden spirit of exertion then returned, – I defied my poor arm, no longer worth sparing, & took my long banished pen to write a few words to M. D'A – & a few more for Alex, in case of a fatal result. These short billets I could only deposit safely, when the Cabriolets – one – two – three – four – succeeded rapidly to each other in stopping at the door. Dr Moreau instantly entered my room, to see if I were alive. He gave me a wine cordial, & went to the Sallon. I rang for my Maid & Nurses, – but before I could speak to them, my room, without previous message, was entered by 7 Men in black, Dr Larry, M. Dubois, Dr Moreau, Dr Aumont, Dr Ribe, & a pupil of Dr Larry, & another of M. Dubois. I was now awakened from my stupor – & by a sort of indignation – Why so many? & without leave? – But I could not utter a syllable. M. Dubois acted as Commander in Chief. Dr Larry kept out of sight; M. Dubois ordered a Bed stead into the middle of the room. Astonished, I turned to Dr Larry, who had promised that an Arm Chair would suffice; but he hung his head, & would not look at me. Two *old mattrasses* M. Dubois then demanded, & an old Sheet. I now began to tremble violently, more with distaste & horror of the preparations even than of the pain. These arranged to his liking, he desired me to mount the Bed stead. I stood suspended, for a moment, whether I should not abruptly escape – I looked at the door, the windows – I felt desperate – but it was only for a moment, my reason then took the command, & my fears &

feelings struggled vainly against it. I called to my maid – she was crying, & the two Nurses stood, transfixed, at the door. Let those women all go! cried M. Dubois. This order recovered me my Voice – No, I cried, let them stay! *qu'elles restent*! This occasioned a little dispute, that re-animated me – The maid, however, & one of the nurses ran off – I charged the other to approach, & she obeyed. M. Dubois now tried to issue his commands *en militaire*, but I resisted all that were resistable – I was compelled, however, to submit to taking off my long robe de Chambre, which I had meant to retain – Ah, then, how did I think of my Sisters! – not one, at so dreadful an instant, at hand, to protect – adjust – guard me – I regretted that I had refused Me de Maisonneuve – Me Chastel – no one upon whom I could rely – my departed Angel! – how did I think of her! – how did I long – long for my Esther – my Charlotte! – My distress was, I suppose, apparent, though not my Wishes, for M. Dubois himself now softened, & spoke soothingly. Can *You*, I cried, feel for an operation that, to *You*, must seem so trivial? – Trivial? he repeated – taking up a bit of paper, which he tore, unconsciously, into a million of pieces "*oui – c'est peu de chose – mais –*" he stammered, & could not go on. No one else attempted to speak, but I was softened myself, when I saw even M. Dubois grow agitated, while Dr Larry kept always aloof, yet a glance shewed me he was pale as ashes. I knew not, positively, then, the immediate danger, but every thing convinced me danger was hovering about me, & that this experiment could alone save me from its jaws. I mounted, therefore, unbidden, the Bed stead – & M. Dubois placed me upon the mattress, & spread a cambric handkerchief upon my face. It was transparent, however, & I saw, through it that the Bed stead was instantly surrounded by the 7 men & my nurse. I refused to be held; but when, Bright through the cambric, I saw the glitter of polished Steel – I closed my Eyes. I would not trust to convulsive fear the sight of the terrible incision. A silence the most profound ensued, which lasted for some minutes, during which, I imagine, they took their orders by signs, & made their examination – Oh what a horrible suspension! – I did not breathe – & M. Dubois tried vainly to find any pulse. This pause, at length, was broken by Dr Larry, who, in a voice of solemn melancholy, said Qui me tiendra ce sein? –

No one answered; at least not verbally; but this aroused me from my passively submissive state, for I feared they imagined the whole breast infected – feared it too justly, – for, again through the Cambric, I saw the hand of M. Dubois held up, while his fore finger first described a straight line from top to bottom of the breast, secondly a Cross, & thirdly a Circle: intimating that the WHOLE was to be taken off. Excited by this idea, I started up, threw off my veil, &, in answer to the demand "Qui me tiendra ce sein," "C'est moi, Monsieur!" & I held my hand under it, & explained the nature of my sufferings, which all sprang from one point, though they darted into every part. I was heard attentively, but in utter silence, & M. Dubois then replaced me as before, &, as before, spread my veil over my face. how vain, alas, my representation! immediately again I saw the fatal finger describe the Cross – & the circle – hopeless, then, desperate, & self-given up. I closed once more my Eyes, relinquishing all watching, all resistance, all interference, & sadly resolute to be wholly resigned.

My dearest Esther – & all my dears to whom she communicates this doleful ditty, will rejoice to hear that this resolution once taken, was firmly adhered to, in defiance of a terror that surpasses all description, & the most torturing pain. Yet – when the dreadful steel was plunged into the breast – cutting through the veins – arteries – flesh – nerves – I needed no injunctions not to restrain my cries. I began a scream that lasted unintermittingly during the whole time of the inclusion – & I almost marvel that it rings not in my Ears still! so excruciating was the agony. When the wound was made, & the instrument was withdrawn, the pain seemed undiminished, for the air that suddenly rushed into those delicate parts felt like a mass of minute but sharp & forked poniards, that were tearing the edges of the wound – but when again I felt the instrument – describing a curve – cutting against the grain, if I may so say, while the flesh resisted in a manner so forcible as to oppose & tire the hand of the operator, who was forced to change from the right to the left – then, indeed, I thought I must have expired. I attempted no more to open my Eyes, – they felt as if hermettically shut, & so firmly closed, that the Eyelids seemed indented into the Cheeks. The instrument this second time withdrawn, I concluded the operation over – Oh no! presently the terrible cutting was renewed – & worse than ever, to separate the bottom, the foundation of this dreadful gland from the parts to which it adhered – Again all description would be baffled – yet again all was not over, – Dr Larry rested but his own hand, & – Oh Heaven! – I then felt the Knife [rack]ling against the breast bone – scraping it! – This performed, while I yet remained in utterly speechless torture, I heard the Voice of Mr Larry, – (all the other guarded a dead silence) in a tone nearly tragic, desire every one present to pronounce if any thing more remained to be done; The general voice was Yes, – but the finger of Mr Dubois – which I literally *felt* elevated over the wound, though I saw nothing, so indescribably sensitive was the spot – pointed to some further requisition – & again began the scraping! – and, after this, Dr Moreau thought he discerned a peccant attom – and still, & still, M. Dubois demanded attom after attom – My dearest Esther, not for days, not for Weeks, but for Months I could not speak of this terrible business without nearly again going through it! I could not *think* of it with impunity! I was sick, I was disordered by a single question – even now, 9 months after it is over, I have a head ache from going on with the account! & this miserable account, which I began 3 Months ago, at least. I dare not revise, nor read, the recollection is still so painful.

To conclude, the evil was so profound, the case so delicate, & the precautions necessary for preventing a return so numerous, that the operation, including the treatment & the dressing, lasted 20 minutes! a time, for sufferings so acute, that was hardly supportable – However, I bore it with all the courage I could exert & never moved, nor stopt them, nor resisted, nor remonstrated, nor spoke – except once or twice, during the dressing, to say "Ah Messieurs! que je vous plains!–" for indeed I was sensible to the feeling concern with which they all saw what I endured, though my speech was principally – *very* principally meant for Dr Larry. Except this, I uttered not a syllable, save, when so often they re-commenced, calling out "Avertissez moi, Messieurs! avertissez moi!–" Twice, I believe, I fainted; at least, I have two total chasms in my memory of this transaction, that impede my tying together what passed. When all was done, & they lifted me up that I might be put to bed, my strength was so totally annihilated, that I was obliged to be carried, & could not even sustain my hands & arms, which hung as if I had been lifeless; while my face, as the Nurse has told me, was utterly colourless. This removal made me open my Eyes – & I then saw my good Dr Larry, pale nearly as myself, his face streaked with blood, & its expression depicting grief, apprehension, & almost horror.

When I was in bed, – my poor M. d'Arblay – who ought to write you himself his own history of this Morning – was called to me – & afterwards our Alex. –

[Here M. d'Arblay commented to a length of 13 lines:]

No! No my dearest & ever more dear friends. I shall not make a fruitless attempt. No language could convey what I felt in the deadly course of these seven hours. Nevertheless, every one of *you, my dearest dearest friends*, can guess, must even know it. Alexandre had no less feeling, but showed more fortitude. He, perhaps, will be more able to describe to you, nearly at least, the torturing state of my poor heart & soul. Besides, I must own, to you, that these details which were, till just now, quite unknown to me, have almost killed me, & I am only able to thank God that this more than half Angel has had the sublime courage to deny herself the comfort I might have offered her, to spare me, not the sharing of her excruciating pains, that was impossible, but the witnessing so terrific a scene, & perhaps the remorse to have rendered it more tragic, for I don't flatter myself I could have got through it – I must confess it.

Thank Heaven! She is now surprisingly well, & in good spirits, & we hope to have many many still happy days. May that of peace soon arrive, and enable me to embrace better than with my pen my beloved & ever ever more dear friends of the town & country. Amen. Amen!

WILLIAM GODWIN

AFTER TRAINING AS A PRESBYTERIAN MINISTER, William Godwin (1756–1836) became a "complete unbeliever" and a political radical. In 1793 he wrote the *Enquiry Concerning Political Justice*, which brought fame and admiration. Four years later he married the feminist Mary Wollstonecraft, who bore him a daughter, Mary. To Godwin's ire, his daughter eloped with the poet Shelley – who was married to Harriet Westbrook – in 1814.

To John Taylor (27 August 1814)

Dear Sir

I have a story to tell you of the deepest melancholy. I should not intrude this story at all upon you if I could help it: first, because it is my temper, as far as with convenience I can, to shut up my sorrows in my own bosom, & not disturb all my friends indiscriminately with matters in which they can afford me no aid; & secondly, because I am anxious to confine this story to the deepest secrecy, & not by any indiscretion of mine to allow a breath of it to escape to the world... You are already acquainted with the name of Shelley, the gentleman who more than twelve months ago undertook by his assistance to rescue me from my pecuniary difficulties. Not to keep you longer in suspense, he, a married man, has run away with my daughter. I cannot conceive of an event of more accumulated horror.

... He lodged at an inn in Fleet Street, & took his meals with me. I had the utmost confidence in him; I knew him susceptible of the noblest sentiments; he was a married man, who had lived happily with his wife for three years. Accordingly the first week of his visit passed in perfect innocence; ...

On Sunday, June 26, he accompanied Mary, & her sister, Jane

Clairmont, to the tomb of Mary's mother, one mile distant from London; & there, it seems, the impious idea first occurred to him of seducing her, playing the traitor to me, & deserting his wife. On Wednesday, the 6th of July, the transaction of the loan was completed; & on the evening of that very day he had the madness to disclose his plans to me, & to ask my consent. I expostulated with him with all the energy of which I was master, & with so much effect that for the moment he promised to give up his licentious love, & return to virtue. I applied all my diligence to waken up a sense of honour & natural affection in the mind of Mary, & I seemed to have succeeded. They both deceived me. In the night of the 27th Mary & her sister Jane escaped from my house; and the next morning when I rose, I found a letter on my dressing table, informing me what they done...

I had been of opinion from the first that Mary could only be withheld from ruin by her mind; & in that, by a series of the most consummate dissimulation, she made me believe I had succeeded. I formed the plan of sending her from home, knowing the violence of Shelley's temper, & far from certain what scenes he might be capable of acting: but I was well aware that in sending her from home I should be doing good, if she concurred with me, & concealed her retreat from her betrayer, but that if she were capable of an opposite conduct, I should be rather throwing her into his power.

You will imagine our distress. If anything could have added to it, it was this circumstance of Jane's having gone with her sister. Jane we were, & still are, most anxious to recover immediately; & therefore... it was agreed that Mrs G should set off after them by the evening mail. She overtook them at Calais. I had made it a condition in suffering her to depart, that she should avoid seeing Shelley, who had conceived a particular adversion to her as a dangerous foe to his views, & might be capable of any act of desperation. Mrs Godwin wrote to Jane... who... promised to return with her to England the next morning. But when morning arrived...all her resolutions were subverted...Mrs Godwin returned once more, alone.

At Mrs Godwin's request ...I forward to you a small parcel by this day's mail, containing the copies of two letters I wrote to Shelley, between the time of his disclosing his licentious passion to me & the catastrophe. From them you will perceive fully, what were my feelings, & how I conducted myself on the subject. You, I believe, are acquainted with my character on these points, & would, I doubt not, without such an explanation do me justice. But I have many enemies; & Mrs Godwin thinks I may stand in need of vindication. We are divided in this particular, between justification, & (what we infinitely prefer) the entire suppression of all knowledge of the affair. This, for the present at least, we owe to the poor girls, who may be brought back to the path of duty, time enough to prevent a stigma from being fastened on their characters. I had a thousand times rather remain unvindicated, than publish the tale to a single human creature to whom it might remain unknown ... These papers ... are the only copies I possess, & I request you therefore to return them with speed.

When I use the word stigma, I am sure it is wholly unnecessary to say that I apply it in a very different sense to the two girls. Jane has been guilty of indiscretion only, & has shown a want of these filial sentiments, which it would have been most desirable to us to have discovered in her: Mary has been guilty of a crime.

Yours
William Godwin

LORD BYRON

AFTER THE FAILURE OF HIS MARRIAGE TO ANNE Milbanke and amid suspicions of an incestuous relationship with his half-sister Augusta, the poet George Gordon, Lord Byron (1788–1824), left England for continental Europe, never to return. He died of marsh fever while aiding Greek insurrection against Turkish rule.

To Augusta Leigh (17 May 1819, from Venice)

The letter was censored after Byron's death; 'the infamous fiend' is Anne Milbanke.

My dearest Love –

I have been negligent in not writing, but what can I say[.] Three years absence – & the total change of scene and habit make such a difference – that we have now nothing in common but our affections & our relationship.—

But I have never ceased nor can cease to feel for a moment that perfect & boundless attachment which bound & binds me to You – which renders me utterly incapable of *real* love for any other human being – what could they be to me after *you*? My own XXXX [Short word crossed out] we may have been very wrong – but I repent of nothing except that cursed marriage – & your refusing to continue to love me as you had loved me – I can neither forget nor *quite forgive* you for that precious piece of reformation. – but I can never be other than I have been – and whenever I love anything it is because it reminds me in some way or other of yourself – for instance I not long ago attached myself to a Venetian for no earthly reason (although a pretty woman) but because she was called XXXX [short word crossed out] and she often remarked (without knowing the reason) how fond I was of the name. – It is heart-breaking to think of our long Separation – and I am sure more than punishment enough for all our sins – Dante is more humane in his "Hell" for he places his unfortunate lovers (Francesca of Rimini & Paolo whose case fell a good deal short of *ours* – though sufficiently naughty) in company – and though they suffer – it is at least together. ⚘ If ever I return to England – it will be to see you – and recollect that in all time – & place – and feelings – I have never ceased to be the same to you in heart – Circumstances may have ruffled my manner – & hardened my spirit – you may have seen me harsh & exasperated with all things around me; grieved & tortured with *your new resolution*, – & the soon after persecution of that infamous fiend who drove me from my Country & conspired against my life – by endeavouring to deprive me of all that could render it precious – but remember that even then *you* were the sole object that cost me a tear? and *what tears*! do you remember *our* parting? I have not spirits now to write to you upon other subjects – I am well in health – and have no cause of grief but the reflection that we are not together – When you write to me speak to me of yourself – & say that you love me – never mind common-place people & topics – which can be in no degree interesting – to me who see nothing in England but the country which holds *you* – or around it but the sea which divides us. – They say absence destroys weak passions – & confirms strong ones – Alas! *mine* for you is the union of all passions & of all affections – Has strengthened itself but will destroy me – I do not speak of *physical* destruction – for I have endured & can endure much – but of the annihilation of all thoughts feelings or hopes – which haven't more or less a reference to you & to *our recollections* –

Ever dearest
[Signature erased]

To John Murray (1 August 1819, from Venice)

Murray was Byron's publisher. The Countess Guiccioli was the poet's Venetian mistress.

Dear Sir,

Don't be alarmed. – You will see me defend myself gaily – that is – if I happen to be in Spirits – and by *Spirits* I don't mean your meaning of the word – but the spirit of a bull-dog when pinched – or a bull when pinned – it is then that they make best sport – and as my Sensations under an attack are probably a happy compound of the united energies of those amiable animals – you may perhaps see what Marrall calls "rare sport" – and some good tossing and goring in the course of the controversy. – But I must be in the right cue first – and I doubt I am almost too far off to be in a sufficient fury for the purpose

– and then I have effeminated and enervated myself with love and the summer in these last two months. – I wrote to Mr Hobhouse the other day – and foretold that Juan would either fall entirely or succeed completely – there will be no medium – appearances are not favourable – but as you write the day after publication – it can hardly be decided what opinion will predominate. – You seem in a fright – and doubtless with cause. – Come what may – I never will flatter the Million's canting in any shape – circumstances may or may not have placed me at times in a situation to lead the public opinion – but the public opinion – never led nor ever shall lead me. – I will not sit on "a degraded throne" so pray put Messrs Southey – or Sotheby – or Tom Moore – or Horace Twiss upon it – they will all of them be transported with their coronation.

You have bought Harlow's drawings of Margarita and me rather dear methinks – but since you desire the story of Margarita Cogni – you shall be told it – though it may be lengthy.

Her face is of the fine Venetian cast of the old Time – and her figure though perhaps too tall not less fine – taken altogether in the national dress.

In the summer of 1817, Hobhouse and myself were sauntering on horseback along the Brenta one evening – when amongst a group of peasants we remarked two girls as the prettiest we had seen for some time. – About this period there had been great distress in the country and I had a little relieved some of the people. – Generosity makes a great figure at very little cost in Venetian lives – and mine had probably been exaggerated – as an Englishman's.

Whether they remarked us looking at them or no – I know not – but one of them called out to me in Venetian – "Why do not you who relieve others – think of us also?" – I turned round and answered her – "Cara – tu sei troppo bella e giovane per aver' bisogno del' soccorso mio" – she answered – ["]if you saw my hut and my food – you would not say so["] – All this passed half jestingly – and I saw no more of her for some days – A few evenings after – we met with these two girls again – and they addressed us more seriously – assuring us of the truth of their statement. – They were cousins – Margarita married – the other single. – As I doubted still of the circumstance

– I took the business up in a different light – and made an appointment with them for the next evening. – Hobhouse had taken a fancy to the single lady – who was much shorter – in stature – but a very pretty girl also.

They came attended by a third woman – who was cursedly in the way – and Hobhouse's charmer took fright (I don't mean at Hobhouse but at not being married – for here no woman will do anything under adultery), and flew off – and mine made some bother – at the propositions – and wished to consider of them. – I told her "if you really are in want I will relieve you without any conditions whatever – and you may make love with me or no just as you please – *that* shall make no difference – but if you are not in absolute necessity – this is naturally a rendezvous – and I presumed that you understood this – when you made the appointment."

She said that she had no objection to make love with me – as she was married – and all married women did it – but that her husband (a baker) was somewhat ferocious – and would do her a mischief. – In short – in a few evenings we arranged our affair – and for two years – in the course of which I had [almost two] more women than I can count or recount – she was the only one who preserved over me an ascendancy – which was often disputed & never impaired. – As she herself used to say publicly – "It don't matter – he may have five hundred – but he will always come back to me."

The reasons of this were firstly – her person – very dark – tall – the Venetian face – very fine black eyes – and certain other qualities which need not be mentioned. – She was two & twenty years old – and never having had children – had not spoilt her figure – or anything else – which is I assure you – a great desideration in a hot climate where they grow relaxed and doughy and *flumpity* in a short time after breeding.

She was besides a thorough Venetian in her dialect – in her thoughts – in her countenance – in every thing – with all their naïveté and Pantaloon humour. – Besides she could neither read nor write – and could not plague me with letters – except twice that she paid sixpence to a public scribe under the piazza – to make a letter for her – upon some occasion when I was ill and could not see her.

In other respects she was somewhat fierce and "prepotente" that is – overbearing – and used to walk in whenever it suited her – with no very great regard to time, place, nor persons – and if she found any women in her way she knocked them down. – Then I first knew her I was in "relazione" (liaison) with la Signora Segati – who was silly enough one evening at Dolo – accompanied by some of her female friends – to threaten her – for the Gossips of the Villeggiatura – had already found out by the neighing of my horse one evening – that I used to "ride late in the night" to meet the Fornarina.

Margarita threw back her veil (fazziolo) and replied in very explicit Venetian – "*You* are *not* his wife: I am *not* his *wife* – *you* are his Donna – and *I* am his *donna* – *your* husband is a cuckold – and mine is another; – for the rest, what right have you to reproach me? – if he prefers what is mine – to what is yours – is it my fault? if you wish to secure him – tie him to your petticoat-string – but do not think to speak to me without a reply because you happen to be richer than I am."

Having delivered this pretty piece of eloquence (which I translate as it was related to me by a byestander) she went on her way – leaving a numerous audience with Madame Segati – to ponder at her leisure on the dialogue between them. – When I came to Venice for the Winter she followed: – I never had any regular liaison with her – but whenever she came I never allowed any other connection to interfere with her – and as she found herself out to be a favourite she came pretty often. – But She had inordinate Self-love – and was not tolerant of other women – except of the Segati – who was as she said my regular "Amica" – so that I being at that time somewhat promiscuous – there was great confusion – and demolition of head dresses and handkerchiefs – and sometimes my servants in "redding the fray" between her and other feminine persons – received more knocks than acknowledgements for their peaceful endeavours.

At the "Cavalchina" the masqued ball on the last night of the Carnival – where all the World goes – she snatched off the mask of Madame Contarini – a lady noble by birth – and decent in conduct – for no other reason but because she happened to be leaning on my arm – You may suppose what a cursed noise this made – but this is

only one of her pranks – At last she quarrelled with her husband –
and one evening ran away to my house. – I told her this would not
do – she said she would lie in the street but not go back to him – that
he beat her (the gentle tigress) spent her money – and scandalously
neglected his Oven. As it was Midnight – I let her stay – and next
day there was no moving her at all. – Her husband came roaring &
crying – & entreating her to come back, *not* She! – He then applied
to the Police – and they applied to me – I told them and her husband
to *take* her – I did not want her – she had come and I could not fling
her out of the window – but they might conduct her through that or
the door if they chose.

She went before the Commissary – but was obliged to return with
that "becco Ettico" (consumptive cuckold), as she called the *poor*
man who had a Ptisick. – In a few days she ran away again. – After
a precious piece of work she fixed herself in my house – really & truly
without my consent – but owing to my indolence – and not being
able to keep my countenance – for if I began in a rage she always
finished by making me laugh with some Venetian pantaloonery or
other – and the Gipsy knew this well enough – as well as her other
powers of persuasion – and exerted them with the usual tact and
success of all She-things – high and low – they are all alike for that.
– Madame Benzone also took her under her protection – and then
her head turned. – She was always in extremes either crying or
laughing – and so fierce when angered that she was the terror of men
women and children – for she had the strength of an Amazon with
the temper of Medea. She was a fine animal – but quite untameable.
I was the only person that could at all keep her in any order – and
when she saw me really angry – (which they tell me is rather a savage
sight), she subsided. – But she had a thousand fooleries in her faziolo
– the dress of the lower orders – she looked beautiful – but alas! she
longed for a hat and feathers and all I could say or do (and I said
much) could not prevent this travestie. – I put the first into the fire
– but I got tired of burning them before she did of buying them – so
that she made herself a figure – for they did not at all become her. –
Then she would have her gowns with a *tail* – like a lady forsooth –
nothing would serve her – but "l'abito colla *coua*", or *cua*, (that is the

Venetian for "la *Coda*" the tail or train) and as her cursed pronunciation of the word made me laugh – there was an end of all controversy – and she dragged this diabolical tail after her every where.

In the mean time she beat the women – and stopped my letters. – I found her one day pondering over one – she used to try to find out by their shape whether they were feminine or no – and she used to lament her ignorance – and actually studied her Alphabet – on purpose (as she declared) to open all letters addressed to me and read their contents.

I must not omit to do justice to her housekeeping qualities – after she came into my house as "donna di governo" the expences were reduced to less than half – and every body did their duty better – the apartments were, kept in order – and every thing and every body else except herself.

That she had a sufficient regard for me in her wild way I had many reasons to believe – I will mention one.

In the autumn one day going to the Lido with my Gondoliers – we were overtaken by a heavy Squall and the Gondola put in peril – hats blown away – boat filling – oar lost – tumbling sea – thunder – rain in torrents – night coming – & wind increasing. – On our return – after a tight struggle: I found her on the open steps of the Mocenigo palace on the Grand Canal – with her great black eyes flashing though her tears and the long dark hair which was streaming drenched with rain over her brows & breast, – she was perfectly exposed to the storm – and the wind blowing her hair & dress about her tall thin figure – and the lightning flashing round her – with the waves rolling at her feet – made her look like Medea alighted from her chariot – or the Sibyl of the tempest that was rolling around her – the only living thing within hail at that moment except ourselves. – On seeing me safe – she did not wait to greet me as might be expected – but calling out to me – "Ah! Can' della Madonna xe esto ii tempo per andar' al' Lido?" (ah! Dog of the Virgin! – is this a time to go to Lido?) ran into the house – and solaced herself with scolding the boatmen for not foreseeing the "temporale". – I was told by the servants that she had only been prevented from coming in a boat to look after me – by the refusal of all the Gondoliers of the Canal to put out into the harbour in such a moment and that then she sate down on the steps in all the thickest of the Squall – and would neither be removed nor comforted. Her joy at seeing me again – was moderately mixed with ferocity – and gave me the idea of a tigress over her recovered Cubs. – But her reign drew near a close. – She became quite ungovernable some months after – and a concurrence of complaints some true and many false – "a favourite has no friend" – determined me to part with her. – I told her quietly that she must return home – (she had acquired a sufficient provision for herself and mother, &c. in my service,) and She refused to quit the house – I was firm – and she went – threatening knives and revenge. – I told her – that I had seen knives drawn before her time – and that if she chose to begin – there was a knife – and fork also at her service on the table and that intimidation would not do. – The next day while I was at dinner – she walked in, (having broke open a glass door that led from the hall below to the staircase by way of prologue) and advancing strait up to the table snatched the knife from my hand – cutting me slightly in the thumb in the operation. – Whether she meant to use this against herself or me I know not – probably against neither – but Fletcher seized her by the arms – and disarmed her. – I then called my boatmen – and desired them to get the Gondola ready and conduct her to her own house again – seeing carefully that she did herself no mischief by the way. – She seemed quite quiet and walked down stairs. – I resumed my dinner. – We heard a great noise – I went out – and met them on the staircase – carrying her up stairs. – She had thrown herself into the Canal. – That she intended to destroy herself I do not believe – but when we consider the fear women and men who can't swim have of deep or even of shallow water – (and the Venetians in particular though they live on the waves) and that it was also night – and dark – & very cold – it shows that she had a devilish spirit of some sort within her. – They had got her out without much difficulty or damage except the salt water she had swallowed and the wetting she had undergone. – I foresaw her intention to refix herself, and sent for a Surgeon – enquiring how many hours it would require to restore her from her agitation, and he named the time. – I then said – "I give you that time – and more if you require it – but at the expiration of the prescribed period – if She does not leave the house – *I* will".

All my people were consternated – they had always been frightened at her – and were now paralyzed – they wanted me to apply to the police – to guard myself – &c. &c. – like a pack of sniveling servile boobies as they were.

I did nothing of the kind – thinking that I might as well end that way as another – besides – I had been used to savage women and knew their ways. – I had her sent home quietly after her recovery – and never saw her since except twice at the opera – at a distance amongst the audience. – She made many attempts to return – but no more violent ones. – And this is the story of Margharita Cogni – as far as it belongs to me. – I forgot to mention that she was very devout – and would cross herself if she heard the prayer-time strike – sometimes – when that ceremony did not appear to be much in unison with what she was then about. – She was quick in reply – as for instance – one day when she had made me very angry with beating somebody or other – I called her a Cow (*Cow* in Italian is a sad affront and tantamount to the feminine of dog in English) I called her "Vacca" she turned round – curtsied – and answered "Vacca *tua* – 'Celenza" (i.e. Eccclenza) *your* Cow – please your Excellency. – In short – she was – as I said before – a very fine Animal of considerable beauty and energy – with many good & several amusing qualities – but wild as a witch – and fierce as a demon. – She used to boast publicly of her ascendancy over me – contrasting it with that of other women – and assigning for it sundry lessons physical and moral which did more credit to her person than her modesty. –

True it was that they all tried to get her away – and no one succeeded – till her own absurdity helped them. – Whenever there was a competition, and sometimes – one would be shut in one room and one in another – to prevent battle – she had generally the preference. –

yrs. very truly and affectly

B

P.S. The Countess G[uiccioli] is much better than she was. – I sent you before leaving Venice – a letter containing the real original sketch – which gave rise to the "Vampire" &c. did you get it?

✤

To The Honourable Douglas Kinnaird
(26 October 1819)

The first two cantos of Don Juan (written in the new metre of ottava rima) had been published earlier in the year; the "M.S" was Byron's the manuscript memoirs, destroyed on his death.

My dear Douglas –

My late expenditure has arisen from living at a distance from Venice and being obliged to keep up two establishments from frequent journeys – and buying some furniture and books as well as a horse or two – and not from any renewal of the EPICUREAN system as you suspect. I have been faithful to my honest liaison with Countess Guiccioli – and I can assure you that *She* has never cost me directly or indirectly a sixpence – indeed the circumstances of herself and family render this no merit. – I never offered her but one present – a broach of brilliants – and she sent it back to me with her own *hair* in it (I shall *not* say of *what* part but *that* is an Italian custom) and a note to say that she was not in the habit of receiving presents of that value – but hoped that I would not consider her sending it back as an affront – nor the value diminished by the enclosure. – I have not had a whore this half-year – confining myself to the strictest adultery.

Why should you prevent Hanson from making a *peer* if he likes it – I think the "*Garretting*" would be by far the best parliamentary privilege – I know of.

Damn your delicacy – It is a low commercial quality – and very unworthy a man who prefixes 'honourable"to his nomenclature. If you say that I must sign the bonds – I suppose that I must – but it is very iniquitous to make me pay my debts – you have no idea of the pain it gives one. – Pray do three things – get my property out of the *funds* – get Rochdale sold – get me some information from Perry about *South America* – and 4thly. ask Lady Noel not to live so very long.

As to Subscribing to Manchester – if I do that – I will write a letter to Burdett – for publication – to accompany the Subscription – which shall be more radical than anything yet rooted – but I feel lazy. – I have thought of this for some time – but alas! the air of this cursed Italy enervates – and disfranchises the thoughts of a man after nearly four years of respiration – to say nothing of emission. – As to "Don Juan" – I confess – confess – you dog – and be candid – that it is the sublime of *that there* sort of writing – it may be bawdy – but is it not good English? – it may be profligate – but is it not *life*. is it not *the thing*? – Could any man have written it – who has not lived in the world? – and tooled in a post-chaise? in a hackney coach? in a Gondola? against a wall? in a court carriage? in a vis a vis? – on a table? – and under it? – I have written about a hundred stanzas of a third Canto – but it is damned modest – the outcry has frightened me. – I had such projects for the Don – but the *Cant* is so much stronger than *Cunt* – now a days, – that the benefit of experience in a man who had well weighed the worth of both monosyllables – must be lost to despairing posterity. – After all what stuff this outcry is – Lalla Rookh and Little – are more dangerous than my burlesque poem can be – Moore has been here – we got tipsy together – and were very amicable – he is gone on to Rome – I put my life (in M.S.) into his hands – (*not* for publication) you – or any body else may see it – at his return – only comes up to 1816.

He is a noble fellow – and looks quite fresh and poetical – nine years (the age of a poem's education) my Senior – he looks younger – this comes of marriage and being settled in the Country. I want to go to South America – I have written to Hobhouse all about it. – I wrote to my wife – three months ago – under care to Murray – has she got the letter – or is the letter got into Blackwood's magazine?

You ask after my Christmas pye – Remit it any how – *Circulars* is the best – you are right about *income* – I must have it all – how the devil do I know that I may live a year or a month? – I wish I knew that I might regulate my spending in more ways than one. – As it is one always thinks that there is but a span. – A man may as well break or be damned for a large sum as a small one – I should be loth to pay the devil or any other creditor more than sixpence in the pound.

[scrawl for signature]

P.S. I recollect nothing of "Davies's landlord" – but what ever Davies says – I will *swear* to – and *that's* more than *he* would. – So pray pay – has he a landlady too? perhaps I may owe her something. With regard to the bonds I will sign them but – it goes against the grain.

As to the rest – you *can't* err – so long as you *don't* pay.

Paying is executor's or executioner's work.

You may write somewhat oftener – Mr Galignani's messenger gives the outline of your public affairs – but I see no results – you have no man yet – (always excepting Burdett – & you & H[obhouse] and the Gentlemanly leaven of your two-penny loaf of rebellion) don't forget however my charge of horse – and commission for the Midland Counties and by the holies. – You shall have your account in decimals. – Love to Hobby – but why leave the Whigs?

JOHN KEATS

JOHN KEATS (1795–1821), ENGLISH POET. IN 1818 HE fell in love with Fanny Brawne, but their affair was always shadowed by his worsening tuberculosis. After preparing his greatest work, *Lamia and Other Poems*, for press in 1820, Keats sailed to Italy, where he suffered a final attack of consumption and died attended only by his friend Joseph Severn.

To Fanny Brawne (5[?] July 1820)

My dearest Girl,

I have been a walk this morning with a book in my hand, but as usual I have been occupied with nothing but you I wish I could say in an agreeable manner. I am tormented day and night. They talk of my going to Italy. 'Tis certain I shall never recover if I am to be so long separate from you yet with all this devotion to you I cannot persuade myself into any confidence of you. Past experience connected with the fact of my long separation from you gives me agonies which are scarcely to be talked of. When your mother comes I shall be very sudden and expert in asking her whether you have been to Mʳˢ Dilke's, for she might say no to make me easy. I am literally worn to death, which seems my only recourse. I cannot forget what has pass'd. What? nothing with a man of the world but to me deathful. I will get rid of this as much as possible. When you were in the habit of flirting with Brown you would have left off, could your own heart have felt one half of one pang mine did. Brown is a good sort of Man – he did not know he was doing me to death by inches. I feel the effect of every one of those hours in my side now; and for that cause, though he has done me many services though I know his love and friendship for me, though at this moment I should be without pence were it not for his assistance, I will never see or speak to him until we are both old men, if we are to be. I *will* resent my heart having been made a football. You will call this madness. I have heard you say that it was not unpleasant to wait a few years – you have amusements – your mind is away – you have not brooded over one idea as I have, and how should you? You are to me an object intensely desireable – the air I breathe in a room empty of you is unhealthy. I am not the same to you – no – you can wait – you have a thousand activities – you can be happy without me. Any part, any thing to fill up the day has been enough. How have you pass'd this month? Who have you smil'd with? All this may seem savage in me. You do not feel as I do – you do not know what it is to love – one day you may – your time is not come. Ask yourself how many unhappy hours Keats has caused you in Loneliness. For myself I have been a Martyr the whole time, and for this reason I speak; the confession is forc'd from me by the torture. I appeal to you by the blood of that Christ you believe in: Do not write to me if you have done anything this month which it would have pained me to have seen. You may have altered – if you have not – if you still behave in dancing rooms and other societies as I have seen you – I do not want to live – if you have done so I wish this coming night may be my last. I cannot live without you, and not only you but *chaste you; virtuous you*. The Sun rises and sets, the day passes, and you follow the bent of your inclination to a certain extent – you have no conception of the quantity of miserable feeling that passes through me in a day. – Be serious! Love is not a plaything – and again do not write unless you can do it with a crystal conscience. I would sooner die for want of you than –

> Yours for ever
> J . Keats

To Percy Bysshe Shelley (16 August 1820)

Shelley (1792–1822), Romantic poet. Shelley had written to Keats inviting him to Pisa.

My dear Shelley,

I am very much gratified that you, in a foreign country, and with a mind almost over occupied, should write to me in the strain of the Letter beside me. If I do not take advantage of your invitation it will be prevented by a circumstance I have very much at heart to prophesy – There is no doubt that an english winter would put an end to me, and do so in a lingering hateful manner, therefore I must either voyage or journey to Italy as a soldier marches up to a battery. My nerves at present are the worst part of me, yet they feel soothed when I think that come what extreme may, I shall not be destined to remain in one spot long enough to take a hatred of any four particular bed-posts. I am glad you take any pleasure in my poor Poem; – which I would willingly take the trouble to unwrite, if possible, did I care so much as I have done about Reputation. I received a copy of the Cenci, as from yourself from Hunt. There is only one part of it I am judge of; the Poetry, and dramatic effect, which by many spirits now a days is considered the mammon. A modern work it is said must have a purpose, which may be the God – *an artist* must serve Mammon – he must have "self concentration" selfishness perhaps. You I am sure will forgive me for sincerely remarking that you might curb your magnanimity and be more of an artist, and "load every rift" of your subject with ore. The thought of such discipline must fall like cold chains upon you, who perhaps never sat with your wings furl'd for six Months together. And is not this extraordina[r]y talk for the writer of Endymion? whose mind was like a pack of scattered cards – I am pick'd up and sorted to a pip. My Imagination is a Monastry and I am its Monk – you must explain my metaphysics to yourself. I am in expectation of Prometheus every day. Could I have my own wish for its interest effected you would have it still in manuscript – or be but now putting an end to the second act. I remember you advising me not to publish my first-blights, on Hampstead heath – I am returning advice upon your hands. Most of the Poems in the volume I send you have been written above two years, and would never have been publish'd but from a hope of gain; so you see I am inclined enough to take your advice now. I must exp[r]ess once more my deep sense of your kindness, adding my sincere thanks and respects for Mrs Shelley. In the hope of soon seeing you [I] remain

most sincerely yours,
John Keats

To Fanny Brawne (August 1820)

My dearest Girl,

I wish you could invent some means to make me at all happy without you. Every hour I am more and more concentrated in you;

every thing else tastes like chaff in my Mouth. I feel it almost Impossible to go to Italy – the fact is I cannot leave you, and shall never taste one minute's content until it pleases chance to let me live with you for good. But I will not go on at this rate. A person in health as you are can have no conception of the horror that nerves and a temper like mine go through. What Island do your friends propose retiring to? I should be happy to go with you there alone, but in company I should object to it; the backbitings and jealousies of new colonists who have nothing else to amuse themselves, is unbearable. Mr Dilke came to see me yesterday, and gave me a very great deal more pain than pleasure. I shall never be able any more to endure to [for the] society of any of those who used to meet at Elm Cottage and Wentworth Place. The last two years taste like brass upon my Palate. If I cannot live with you I will live alone. I do not think my health will improve much while I am separated from you. For all this I am averse to seeing you – I cannot bear flashes of light and return into my glooms again. I am not so unhappy now as I should be if I had seen you yesterday. To be happy with you seems such an impossibility! it requires a luckier Star than mine! it will never be. I enclose a passage from one of your Letters which I want you to alter a little – I want (if you will have it so) the matter express'd less coldly to me. If my health would bear it, I could write a Poem which I have in my head, which would be a consolation for people in such a situation as mine. I would show some one in Love as I am, with a person living in such Liberty as you do. Shakspeare always sums up matters in the most sovereign manner. Hamlet's heart was full of such Misery as mine is when he said to Ophelia "Go to a Nunnery, go, go!" Indeed I should like to give up the matter at once – I should like to die. I am sickened at the brute world which you are smiling with. I hate men and women more. I see nothing but thorns for the future – wherever I may be next winter in Italy or nowhere Brown will be living near you with his indecencies – I see no prospect of any rest. Suppose me in Rome – well, I should there see you as in a magic glass going to and from town at all hours. I wish you could infuse a little confidence in human nature into my heart. I cannot muster any – the world is too brutal for me – I am glad there is such a thing as the grave – I am sure I shall never have any rest till I get there. At any rate I will indulge myself by never seeing any more Dilke or Brown or any of their Friends. I wish I was either in your arms full of faith or that a Thunder bolt would strike me.

God bless you.
J.K.

❧

To Charles Brown (1 November 1820, written in Naples)

My dear Brown,

Yesterday we were let out of Quarantine, during which my health suffered more from bad air and a stifled cabin than it had done the whole voyage. The fresh air revived me a little, and I hope I am well enough this morning to write to you a short calm letter; – if that can be called one, in which I am afraid to speak of what I would the fainest dwell upon. As I have gone thus far into it, I must go on a little; – perhaps it may relieve the load of WRETCHEDNESS which presses upon me. The persuasion that I shall see her no more will kill me. I cannot q— My dear Brown, I should have had her when I was in health, and I should have remained well. I can bear to die – I cannot bear to leave her. Oh, God! God! God! Every thing I have in my trunks that reminds me of her goes through me like a spear. The silk lining she put in my travelling cap scalds my head. My imagination is horribly vivid about her – I see her – I hear her. There is nothing in the world of sufficient interest to divert me from her a moment. This was the case when I was in England: I cannot recollect, without shuddering, the Time that I was prisoner at Hunt's, and used to keep my eyes fixed on Hampstead all day. Then there was a good hope of seeing her again – Now! – O that I could be buried near where she lives! I am afraid to write to her – to receive a letter from her – to see her hand writing would break my heart – even to hear of her any how, to see her name written would be more than I can bear. My dear Brown, what am I to do? Where can I look for consolation or ease? If I had any chance of recovery, this passion would kill me. Indeed through the whole of my illness, both at your house and at Kentish Town, this fever has never ceased wearing me out. When you write to me, which you will do immediately, write to Rome (poste restante) – if she is well and happy, put a mark thus +. – if – Remember me to all. I will endeavour to bear my miseries patiently. A person in my state of health should not have such miseries to bear. Write a short note to my sister, saying you have heard from me. Severn is very well. If I were in better health I should urge your coming to Rome. I fear there is no one can give me any comfort. Is there any news of George? O, that something fortunate had ever happened to me or my brothers! – then I might hope, – but despair is forced upon me as a habit. My dear Brown, for my sake, be her advocate for ever. I cannot say a word about Naples; I do not feel at all concerned in the thousand novelties around me. I am afraid to write to her. I should like her to know that I do not forget her. Oh, Brown, I have coals of fire in my breast. It surprised me that the human heart is capable of containing and bearing so much misery. Was I born for this end? God bless her, and her mother, and my sister, and George, and his wife, and you, and all!

Your ever affectionate friend,
John Keats.

WILLIAM HAZLITT

IN 1819 THE ENGLISH ESSAYIST WILLIAM HAZLITT (1778–1830) became infatuated with Sarah Walker, the daughter of a tailor. At first she encouraged his obsession, then tired of it. He wrote numerous letters about the affair to his friend Peter Patmore, eventually collecting these into the volume *Liber Amoris* (1823).

To Peter Patmore (31 May 1822)

A letter written from Edinburgh, where Hazlitt had gone to finalize his divorce.

My dear friend,

I wrote yesterday by Scarborough to say that the iron had entered my soul – forever. I have since thought more profoundly about it than ever before, & am convinced beyond a doubt that she is a regular lodging-house decoy, who leads a sporting life with every one who comes in succession, & goes different lengths according as she is urged or inclined. This is why she will not marry, because she hankers after this sort of thing. She has an itch for being slabbered & felt, & this she is determined to gratify upon system, & has a pride in making fools of the different men she indulges herself with & at the same time can stop short from the habit of running the gauntlet with so many. The impudent whore to taunt me, that "she had always told me she had no affection for me," as a salve for her new lewdness – and how did she tell me this, sitting in my lap, twining herself round me, [letting me enjoy her through her petticoats] looking as if she would faint with tenderness & modesty, admitting all sorts of indecent liberties & declaring "however she might agree to her own ruin, she would never consent to bring disgrace upon her family," as if this last circumstance only prevented her, & all this without any affection – is it not to write whore, hardened, impudent, heartless whore after her name? Her look is exactly this. It is that of suppressed lewdness & conscious & refined hypocrisy, instead of innocence or timidity or real feeling. She never looks at you, nor has a single involuntary emotion. For any one to suffer what she has done from me, without feeling it, is unnatural & monstrous. A common whore would take a liking to a man who had shewn the same love of her & to whom she had granted the same incessant intimate favours. But her heart is seared, as her eyes gloat, with habitual hypocrisy & *lech* for the mere act of physical contact with the other sex. "Do you let any one else do so," I said to her when I was kissing her. "No, not now," was her answer, that is, because there was nobody in the house to do it with her. While the coast was clear, I had it all my own way: but the instant Tomkins came, she made a dead set at him, ran breathless upstairs before him, blushed when his foot was heard, watched for him in the passage, & he going away either tired of her or without taking the hint, she has taken up in my absence with this quackdoctor, a tall stiff-backed able bodied half blackguard that she can make use of & get rid of when she pleases. The bitch wants a *stallion*, & hates a lover, that is, any one who talks of affection & is prevented by fondness or regard for her from going or attempting to go all lengths. I at present think she liked me to a certain extent as a friend but still I was not good enough for her. She wanted to be courted not as a bride, but as a common wench. "Why, could we not go on as we were, & never mind about the word, *forever?*" She would not agree to "a tie," because she would leave herself open to any new pretender that answered her purpose better, & *bitch* me without ceremony or mercy, & then say – "She had always told me she had no regard for me" – as a rea[son for] transferring her obscenities (for such they were without [doubt) from] me to her next favourite. Her addicting herself to Tomkins was endurable, because he was a gentlemanly sort of man. but her putting up with this prick of a fellow, merely for bore & measurement & gross manners, sets me low indeed. The monster of lust & duplicity! I that have spared her so often because I hoped better things of her & to make her my future wife, & to be refused in order that she may be the trull of an itinerant apothecary, a fellow that she made a jest of & despised, till she had nobody else in the way to pamper her body & supply her morning's meal of studied wantonness. "That way madness lies." I do not feel as if I can ever get the better of it: I have sucked in the poison of her seeming modesty & tenderness too long. I thought she was dreaming of her only love & worshipped her equivocal face, when she wanted only a codpiece & I ought to have pulled up her petticoats & felt her. But I could not insult the adored of my heart, & find out her real character; & you see what has become of me. I was wrong at first in fancy[ing] a wench at a lodging house to be a Vestal, merely for her demure looks. The only chance I had was the first day: after that my hands were tied & I became the fool of love. Do you know the only thing that soothes or melts me is the idea of taking my little boy whom I can no longer support & wandering through the country as beggars, not through the wide world, for I cannot leave the country where she is. Oh God! Oh God! The slimy, varnished, marble fiend to bring me to this when three kind words would have saved me! Yet if I only knew she was a whore, *flagrante delicto*, it would wean me from her, & burst my chain. Could you ascertain this fact for me, by any means or through any person (E. for example) who might try her as a lodger? I should not like her to be seduced by elaborate means, but if she gave up as a matter of course, I should then be no longer the wretch I am or the God I might have been, but what I was before [poor] plain,

W. H.

MARY SHELLEY

MARY SHELLEY (1791–1851) WAS THE DAUGHTER OF William Godwin and Mary Wollstonecraft. She married Percy Bysshe Shelley in 1816, moving with him to Italy. She was the author of *Frankenstein*. Here she writes of Shelley's death by drowning.

❧

To Maria Gisborne (15 August 1822)

I said in a letter to Peacock, my dear Mrs Gisborne, that I would send you some account of the last miserable months of my disastrous life. From day to day I have put this off, but I will now endeavour to fulfill my design. The scene of my existence is closed & though there be no pleasure in retracing the scenes that have preceded the event which has crushed my hopes yet there seems to be a necessity in doing so, and I obey the impulse that urges me. I wrote to you either at the end of May or the beginning of June. I described to you the place we were living in – Our desolate house, the beauty yet strangeness of the scenery and the delight Shelley took in all this – he never was in better health or spirits than during this time. I was not well in body or mind. My nerves were wound up to the utmost irritation, and the sense of misfortune hung over my spirits. No words can tell you how I hated our house & the country about it. Shelley reproached me for this – his health was good & the place was quite after his own heart – What could I answer – that the people were wild & hateful, that though the country was beautiful yet I liked a more *countryfied* place, that there was great difficulty in living – that all our Tuscans would leave us, & that the very jargon of these *Genovese* was disgusting – This was all I had to say but no words could describe my feelings – the beauty of the woods made me weep & shudder – so vehement was my feeling of dislike that I used to rejoice when the winds & waves permitted me to go out in the boat so that I was not obliged to take my usual walk among tree shaded paths, allies of vine festooned trees – all that before I doated on – & that now weighed on me. My only moments of peace were on board that unhappy boat, when lying down with my head on his knee I shut my eyes & felt the wind & our swift motion alone. My ill health might account for much of this – bathing in the sea somewhat relieved me – but on the 8th of June (I think it was) I was threatened with a miscarriage, & after a week of great ill health on sunday the 16th this took place at eight in the morning. I was so ill that for seven hours I lay nearly lifeless – kept from fainting by brandy, vinegar eau de Cologne & – at length ice was brought to our solitude – it came before the doctor so Claire & Jane were afraid of using it but Shelley overruled them & by an unsparing application of it I was restored. They all thought & so did I at one time that I was about to die – I hardly wish that I had, my own Shelley could never have lived without me, the sense of eternal misfortune would have pressed to heavily upon him, & what would have become of my poor babe? My convalescence was slow and during it a strange occurence happened to retard it...

As I said Shelley was at first in perfect health but having over fatigued himself one day, & then the fright my illness gave him caused a return of nervous sensations & visions as bad as in his worst times. I think it was the saturday after my illness while yet unable to walk I was confined to my bed – in the middle of the night I was awoke by hearing him scream & come rushing into my room; I was sure that he was asleep & tried to waken him by calling on him, but he continued to scream which inspired me with such a panic that I jumped out of bed & ran across the hall to Mʳˢ W's room where I fell through weakness, though I was so frightened that I got up again immediately – she let me in & Williams went to S. who had been wakened by my getting out of bed – he said that he had not been asleep & that it was a vision that he saw that had frightened him – But as he declared that he had not screamed it was certainly a dream & no waking vision – What had frightened him was this – He dreamt that lying as he did in bed Edward & Jane came into him, they were in the most horrible condition, their bodies lacerated – their bones starting through their skin, the faces pale yet stained with blood, they could hardly walk, but Edward was the weakest & Jane was supporting him – Edward said – "Get up, Shelley, the sea is flooding the house & it is all coming down." S. got up, he thought, & went to his window that looked on the terrace & the sea & thought he saw the sea rushing in. Suddenly his vision changed & he saw the figure of himself strangling me, that had made him rush into my room, yet fearful of frightening me he dared not approach the bed, when my jumping out awoke him, or as he phrased it caused his vision to vanish. All this was frightful enough, & talking it over the next morning he told me that he had had many visions lately – he had seen the figure of himself which met him as he walked on the terrace & said to him – "How long do you mean to be content" – No very terrific words & certainly not prophetic of what has occurred. But Shelley had often seen these figures when ill; but the strangest thing is that Mʳˢ W. saw him. Now Jane though a woman of sensibility, has not much imagination & is not in the slightest degree nervous – neither in dreams or otherwise. She was standing one day, the day before I was taken ill, at a window that looked on the Terrace with Trelawny – it was day – she saw as she thought Shelley pass by the window, as he often was then, without a coat or jacket – he passed again – now as he passed both times the same way – and as from the side towards which he went each time there was no way to get back except past the window again (except over a wall twenty feet from the ground) she was struck at seeing him pass twice thus & looked out & seeing him no more she cried – "Good God can Shelley have leapt from the wall? Where can he be gone?" Shelley, said Trelawny – "No Shelley has past – What do you mean?" Trelawny says that she trembled exceedingly when she heard this & it proved indeed that Shelley had never been on the terrace & was far off at the time she saw him. Well we thought [no] more of these things & I slowly got better. Having heard from Hunt that he had sailed from Genoa, on Monday July 1st S., Edward & Captain Roberts (the Gent. who built our boat) departed in our boat for Leghorn to receive him – I was then just better, had begun to crawl from my bedroom to the terrace; but bad spirits succeeded to ill health, and this departure of Shelley's seemed to add insuferably to my misery. I could not endure that he should go – I called him back two or three times, & told him that if I did not see him soon I would go to Pisa with the child – I cried bitterly when he went away. They went & Jane, Claire & I remained alone with the children – I could not walk out, & though I gradually gathered strength it was slowly & my ill spirits encreased; in my letters to him I entreated him to return – "the feeling that some misfortune would happen," I said, "haunted me". I feared for the child, for the idea of danger connected with him never struck me – When Jane & Claire took their evening walk I used to patrole the terrace, oppressed with wretchedness, yet gazing on the most beautiful scene in the world. This Gulph of Spezia is subdivided into many small bays of which ours was far the most beautiful – the two horns of the bay (so to express myself) were wood covered promontories crowned with castles – at the foot of these on the furthest was Lerici on the nearest San Arenzo – Lerici being above a mile by land from us & San Arenzo about a hundred or two yards – trees covered the hills that enclosed this bay & then beautiful groups were picturesquely contrasted with the rocks the castle on [and] the town – the sea lay far extended in front while to the west we saw the promontory & islands which formed one of the extreme boundarys of the Gulph – to see the sun set upon this scene, the stars shine & the moon rise was a light of wondrous beauty, but to me it added only to my wretchedness – I repeated to myself all that another would have said to console me, & told myself the tale of love peace & competence which I enjoyed – but I answered myself by tears – did not my William die? & did I hold my Percy by a firmer tenure? – Yet I thought when he, when my Shelley returns I shall be happy – he will comfort me, if my boy be ill he will restore him & encourage me. I had a letter or two from Shelley mentioning the difficulties he had in establishing the Hunts, & that he was unable to fix the time of his return. Thus a week past. On Monday 8th June had a letter from Edward, dated saturday, he said that he waited at Leghorn for S. who was at Pisa That S's return was certain, "but" he continued, "if he should not come by monday I will come in a felucca, & you may expect me tuesday evening at furthest." This was monday, the fatal monday, but with us it was stormy all day & we did not at all suppose that they could put to sea. At twelve at night we had a thunderstorm; Tuesday it rained all day & was calm – the sky wept on their graves – on Wednesday – the wind was fair from Leghorn & in the evening several felucca's arrived thence – one brought word that they had sailed monday, but we did not believe them – thursday was another day of fair wind & when twelve at night came & we did not see the tall sails of the little boat double the promontory before us we began to fear not the truth, but some illness – some disagreeable news for their detention. Jane got so uneasy that she determined to proceed the next day to Leghorn in a boat to see what was the matter – friday came & with it a heavy sea & bad wind – Jane however resolved to be rowed to Leghorn (since no boat could sail) and busied herself in preparations – I wished her to wait for letters, since friday was letter day – she would not – but the sea detained her, the swell rose so that no boat would venture out – At 12 at noon our letters came – there was one from Hunt to Shelley, it said – "pray write to tell us how you got home, for they say that you had bad weather after you sailed monday & we are anxious" – the paper fell from me – I trembled all over – Jane read it – "Then

219

it is all over!" she said."No, my dear Jane," I cried, "it is not all over, but this suspense is dreadful – come with me, we will go to Leghorn, we will post to be swift & learn our fate." We crossed to Lerici, despair in our hearts; they raised our spirits there by telling us that no accident had been heard of & that it must have been known &c – but still our fear was great – & without resting we posted to Pisa. It must have been fearful to see us – two poor, wild, aghast creatures – driving (like Matilda) towards the *sea* to learn if we were to be for ever doomed to misery. I knew that Hunt was at Pisa at Lord Byrons' house but I thought that L.B. was at Leghorn. I settled that we should drive to Casa Lanfranchi that I should get out & ask the fearful question of Hunt "do you know any thing of Shelley?" On entering Pisa the idea of seeing Hunt for the first time for four years under such circumstances, & asking him such a question was so terrific to me that it was with difficulty that I prevented myself from going into convulsions – my struggles were dreadful – they knocked at the door & some one called out "Chi è?" it was the Guiccioli's maid L.B. was in Pisa – Hunt was in bed, so I was to see LB. instead of him – This was a great relief to me; I staggered up stairs – the Guiccioli came to meet me smiling while I could hardly say – "Where is he – Sapete alcuna cosa di Shelley" – They knew nothing – he had left Pisa on sunday – on Monday he had sailed – there had been bad weather monday afternoon – more they knew not. Both LB & the lady have told me since – that on that terrific evening I looked more like a ghost than a woman – light seemed to emanate from my features, my face was very white. I looked like marble – Alas. I had risen almost from a bed of sickness for this journey – I had travelled all day – it was now 12 at night – & we, refusing to rest, proceeded to Leghorn – not in despair – no, for then we must have died; but with sufficient hope to keep up the agitation of the spirits which was all my life. It was past two in the morning when we arrived – They took us to the wrong inn – neither Trelawny or Cap^n Roberts were there nor did we exactly know where they were so we were obliged to wait until daylight. We threw ourselves drest on our beds & slept a little but at 6 o'clock we went to one or two inns to ask for one or the other of these gentlemen. We found Roberts at the

Globe. He came down to us with a face which seemed to tell us that the worst was true, and here we learned all that had occurred during the week they had been absent from us, & under what circumstances they had departed on their return.

Shelley had past most of the time a[t] Pisa – arranging the affairs of the Hunts – & skrewing LB's mind to the sticking place about the journal. He had found this a difficult task at first but at length he had succeeded to his heart's content with both points. Mrs Mason said that she saw him in better health and spirits than she had ever known him, when he took leave of her sunday July 7th his face burnt by the sun, & his heart light that he had succeeded in rendering the Hunts' tolerably comfortable. Edward had remained at Leghorn. On Monday July 8th during the morning they were employed in buying many things – eatables &c for our solitude. There had been a thunderstorm early but about noon the weather was fine & the wind right fair for Lerici – They were impatient to be gone. Roberts said, "Stay until tomorrow to see if the weather is settled", & S. might have staid but Edward was in so great an anxiety to reach home – saying they would get there in seven hours with that wind – that they sailed! S. being in one of those extravagant fits of good spirits in which you have sometimes seen him. Roberts went out to the end of the mole & watched them out of sight – they sailed at one & went off at the rate of about 7 knots – About three – Roberts, who was still on the mole – saw wind coming from the Gulph – or rather what the Italians call a temporale, anxious to know how the boat w^d weather the storm, he got leave to go up the tower & with the glass discovered them about ten miles out at sea, off Via Reggio, they were taking in their topsails – "The haze of the storm," he said, "hid them from me & I saw them no more – when the storm cleared I looked again fancying that I should see them on their return to us – but there was no boat on the sea." – This then was all we knew, yet we did not despair – they might have been driven over to Corsica & not knowing the coast & Gone god knows where. Reports favoured this belief. – it was even said that they had been seen in the Gulph – We resolved to return with all possible speed – We sent a courier to go from tower to tower along the coast to know if any thing had been seen or found, & at 9 AM. we quitted Leghorn – stopped but one moment at Pisa & proceeded towards Lerici. When at 2 miles from Via Reggio we rode down to that town to know if they knew any thing – here our calamity first began to break on us – a little boat & a water cask had been found five miles off – they had manufactured a *piccolissima lancia* of thin planks stitched by a shoemaker just to let them run on shore without wetting themselves as our boat drew 4 feet water. – the description of that found tallied with this – but then this boat was very cumbersome & in bad weather they might have been easily led to throw it overboard – the cask frightened me most – but the same reason might in some sort be given for that. I must tell you that Jane & I were not now alone – Trelawny accompanied us back to our home. We journied on & reached the Magra about ¹/₂ past ten P.M. I cannot describe to you what I felt in the first moment when, fording this river, I felt the water splash about our wheels – I was suffocated – I gasped for breath – I thought I should have gone into convulsions, & I struggled violently that Jane might not perceive it – looking down the river I saw the two great lights burning at the *foce* – A voice from within me seemed to cry aloud that is his grave. After passing the river I gradually recovered. Arriving at Lerici we [were] obliged to cross our little bay in a boat – San Arenzo was illuminated for a festa – what a scene – the roaring sea – the scirocco wind – the lights of the town towards which we rowed – & our own desolate hearts – that coloured all with a shroud – we landed; nothing had been heard of them. This was saturday July 13. & thus we waited until Thursday July 25ᵗʰ thrown about by hope & fear. We sent messengers along the coast towards Genoa & to Via Reggio – nothing had been found more than the *lancetta*; reports were brought us – we hoped – & yet to tell you all the agony we endured during those 12 days would be to make you conceive a universe of pain – each moment intolerable & giving place to one still worse. The people of the country too added to one's discomfort – they are like wild savages – on festa's the men & women & children in different bands – the sexes always separate –

pass the whole night in dancing on the sands close to our door running into the sea then back again & screaming all the time one perpetuel air – the most detestable in the world – then the scirocco perpetually blew & the sea for ever moaned their dirge. On thursday 25th Trelawny left us to go to Leghorn to see what was doing or what could be done. On friday I was very ill but as evening came on I said to Jane – "If any thing had been found on the coast Trelawny would have returned to let us know. He has not returned so I hope." About 7 o'clock P.M. he did return – all was over – all was quiet now, they had been found washed on shore – Well all this was to be endured.

Well what more have I to say? The next day we returned to Pisa And here we are still – days pass away – one after another – & we live thus. We are all together – we shall quit Italy together. Jane must proceed to London – if letters do not alter my views I shall remain in Paris. – Thus we live – Seeing the Hunts now & then. Poor Hunt has suffered terribly as you may guess. Lord Byron is very kind to me & comes with the Guiccioli to see me often.

Today – this day – the sun shining in the sky – they are gone to the desolate sea coast to perform the last offices to their earthly remains. Hunt, LB. & Trelawny. The quarantine laws would not permit us to remove them sooner – & now only on condition that we burn them to ashes. That I do not dislike – His rest shall be at Rome beside my child – where one day I also shall join them – Adonais is not Keats's it is his own elegy – he bids you there go to Rome. – I have seen the spot where he now lies – the sticks that mark the spot where the sands cover him – the shall not be there it is too nea[r] Via Reggio – They are now about this fearful office – & I live!

One more circumstance I will mention. As I said he took leave of Mrs Mason in high spirits on sunday – "Never," said she, "did I see him look happier than the last glance I had of his countenance." On Monday he was lost – on monday night she dreamt – that she was somewhere – she knew not where & he came looking very pale & fearfully melancholy – she said to him – "You look ill, you are tired, sit down & eat." "No," he replied, "I shall never eat more; I have not a *soldo* left in the world." – "Nonsense," said she, "this is no inn – you need not pay –" – "Perhaps," he answered, "it is the worse for that." Then she awoke & going to sleep again she dreamt that my Percy was dead & she awoke crying bitterly (so bitterly th) & felt so miserable – that she said to herself – "why if the little boy should die I should not feel it in this manner." She [was] so struck with these dreams that she mentioned them to her servant the next day saying she hoped all was well with us.

Well here is my story – the last story I shall have to tell – all that might have been bright in my life is now despoiled – I shall live to improve myself, to take care of my child, & render myself worthy to join him. Soon my weary pilgrimage will begin – I rest now – but soon I must leave Italy – & then – there is an end of all despair. Adieu I hope you are well & happy. I have an idea that while he was at Pisa that he received a letter from you that I have never seen – so not knowing where to direct I shall send this letter to Peacock – I shall send it open – he may be glad to read it –

Your's ever truly,
Mary WS

THOMAS CARLYLE AND JANE BAILLIE WELSH

THOMAS CARLYLE (1795–1881), SCOTTISH HISTORIAN. He married Jane Baillie Welsh, a minor heiress, in 1826. She wrote nothing for publication, despite Carlyle's promptings and the talent evidenced in her letters.

❦

Jane Baillie Welsh to Eliza Stodart (8 March 1823)
Well! my beloved Cousin, here I am once more at the bottom of the

pit of dullness, hemmed in all round, straining my eyeballs, and stretching my neck to no purpose. Was ever Starling in a more desperate plight? but *I will "get out"* – by the wife of Job I *will*. Here is no sojourn for me! I must dwell in the open world, live amid life; but *here* is no life, no motion, no variety. It is the dimest, deadest spot (I verily believe) in the Creators universe: to look round in it, one might imagine that time had made a stand: the shopkeepers are to be seen standing at the doors of their shops, in the very same postures in which they have stood there ever since I was born; "*the thing that hath been is that also which shall be*" everything is *the same*, every thing is stupid; the very air one breathes is impregnated with stupidity. Alas my native place! the Goddess of dullness has strewed it with all her poppies!

But it is my native place still! and after all there is much in it that I love. I love the bleaching-green, where I used to caper, and roll, and tumble, and make gowan necklaces, and chains of dandelion stalks, in the days of my "*wee existence*", and the schoolhouse where I carried away prizes, and signalized myself not more for the quickness of my parts, than for the valour of my arm, above all the boys of the community; and the mill-dam too where I performed feats of agility which it was easier to extol than to imitate, and which gained me at the time the reputation of a sticket callant (un garçon assasiné) which I believe I have maintained with credit up to the present hour; and above all I feel an affection for a field by the side of the river, where corn is growing now, and where a hayrick once stood – you remember it? For my part I shall never forget that summer's day; but cherish it "*within the secret cell of the heart*" as long as I live – the sky was so bright the air so balmy, the whole universe so beautiful I was happy then! all my little world lay glittering in tinsel at my feet! but years have passed over it since; and storm after storm has stript it of much of its finery – Allons ma chere! – let us talk of the "*goosish*" man, my quondam lover.

He came; arrived at the George Inn, at eleven o'clock at night, twelve hours after he received my answer to his letter; slept there "*more soundly*", according to his own statement, "*than was to have been expected, all the circumstances of the case considered*"; and in the morning sent a few nonsensical lines to announce his nonsensical arrival. Mother and I received him more politely "than was to have been expected, all the circumstances of the case considered" and we proceeded to walk, and play at battledoor; and talk inanities, about new novels, and new belles, and what had gone on at a splendid party, the night before, where he had been (he told us) for half an hour *with his arm under his hat*; and there he corrected himself, and said, *with his head under his arm*! it was of very little consequence where his head was; it is not much worth; but the Lord defend me from visitors so equipped, when I come to give parties! Before dinner he retired to his Inn, and vapoured back, in the course of an hour of so, in all the pride of two waistcoats (one of figured velvet, another of sky-blue satin) gossamer silk stockings and morocco leather slippers – "*these little things are great to little men*" – I should not like to pay his Tailor's bill however – Craigenputtock could not stand it. Next morning he took himself away, leaving us more impressed with the idea of his imbecillity than ever. In a day or two after his return to town, there came a huge parcel from him, containing a letter for Mother, expressed with a still greater command of absurdity than any of the preceeding ones, and a quantity of music for me; (*pour parenthèse*, I shall send you a sheet of it, having another copy of "*Home sweet home*" beside) and in two days more another letter, and another supply of music. Hitherto there had been nothing of hope, nothing more of love or marriage; but now my Gentleman presumed to flatter himself, in the expansion of the folly of his heart, that I *might possibly change my mind*. Ass! I change my mind indeed! and for him! Upon my word, to be an imbécille as he is, he has a monstrous stock of modest assurance! However I very speedily relieved him of any doubts which he might have upon the matter. I told him "*ce que j'ai fait je le ferais encore*" in so many words as must (I think) have brought him to his senses – if he has any. He has since written to Mother begging of her to deprecate my displeasure – there the transaction rests and peace be with it!

I have neither heard nor seen anything of "*Doctor Fieff*" – The Lord be praised! He not only wasted a very unreasonable proportion of my time; but his *fuffs* and explosions were very hurtful to my nervous system.

Talking of nerves, we got a horrible fright in church on Saturday. An old Lady dropt down in the adjoining seat and was carried out as dead. Mother screamed out "Oh" so stoutly, that Mr Gordon was obliged to stop in his prayer, and sit down: She seems destined to make a distinguished figure in all church hub bubs. Witness the scene of the repenting stool! The old Lady has got better –

What of *Wull*? is he coming out soon? a visit from any man with brains in his head would really be an act of mercy to us here.

There is a long letter for you! now will you write to me soon? I cannot recollect your excuse without some feeling of displeasure. "*You cannot write letters that I will care about*" surely this compliment to my understanding (if it was meant as such) is at the expense of my heart. It is not for the sake of grammar or rhetorick (I should think) that friends, like you and I, write to one another. When your letters cease to interest me, credit me, I will not ask them. My Mother has quite got rid of her cold. It was as bad as need be after we came home. For myself I am quite well, still suffering a little from the *maladie des adieux*; but that is all. Both of us unite in kindest love to your Uncle and yourself. *Will* you kiss him for me?

Ever most affectionately yours
Jane Baillie Welsh

~❧~

Jane Baillie Welsh to Thomas Carlyle (20 May 1824)

In the name of Heaven why don't you write to me? I have waited day after day in the utmost impatience; and hope deferred has not only made my heart sick, but is like to drive me out of my judgement.

For Godsake write the instant this reaches you, if you have not done it before. I shall learn no lesson, settle no occupation, till I have your Letter. Wretch! You cannot conceive what anxiety I am in about you. One moment I imagine you ill or in trouble of some sort, the next tired of me; the next something else as bad. In short there is no end to my imaginings.

I do not think that in the whole course of our correspondence so long an interval has ever elapsed before: never but when we quarrelled – and this time there is no quarrel! To add to my perplexities, there have I had a Letter from that stupendous Ass the Orator, telling me such nonsensical things; and among the rest, that he is full of joy because Thomas Carlyle is to be with him this month! Can he mean you? This month! and twenty days of it already past and gone! The man must have been delirious when he wrote such an impossible story. You can never, never mean to be in London this month! You promised to be here before you went, in words that it would be impiety to doubt. I have looked forward to your coming for weeks. You cannot dream of disappointing me!

What I would give to be assured this moment that excessive occupation is the sole cause of your present neglectfulness: that 'devils' are dunning you for the rest of your book, and that you are merely giving yourself all to *Meister* just now that you may the sooner be all for me. Is it not hard? This is the only comfortable conjecture I can form to explain your silence; and yet I can never believe in it for more than a minute at a time. Were I but certain that all is really well, what a Devil of a rage I would be in with you! Write, write – I will tell you about my *visit to London*, then; I have no heart for it now. What an idiot I was ever to think that man so estimable! But I am done with his Preachership now and forever.

And Byron is dead! I was told it all at once in a roomful of people. My God, if they had said that the sun or the moon had gone out of the heavens, it could not have struck me with the idea of a more awful and dreary blank in the creation than the words, "Byron is dead!" I have felt quite cold and dejected ever since: all my thoughts have been fearful and dismal. I wish you was come.

Yours forever affectionately,
Jane Welsh

Thomas Carlyle to Jane Baillie Welsh
(26 February 1826)

... Jane, Jane! your half-jesting enumeration of your wooers does any
thing but make me laugh. A thousand and a thousand times have I
thought the same thing in deepest earnest. That you have the power
of making many good matches is no secret to me; nay it would be a
piece of news for me to learn that I am not the very worst you ever
thought of. And you add with the same tearful smile: "Alas! we are
married already." Let me now cut off the interjection, and say simply
what is true that we are *not* married already; and do you hereb[y]
receive farther my distinct and deliberate declaration that it depends
on yourself, and shall [al]ways depend on yourself whether ever we
be married or not. God knows I do not say this in a vulgar spirit of
defiance; which in our present relation were coarse and cruel; but I
say it in the spirit of disinterested affection for you, and of fear for
the reproaches of my own conscience should your fair destiny be
marred by me, and you wounded in the house of your friends. Can
you believe it with the good nature which I declare it deserves? It
would absolutely give me satisfaction to know that you thought
yourself entirely free of all ties to me, but those, such as they might
be, of your own still-renewed election. It is reasonable and right that
you should be concerned for your future establishment: Look round
with calm eyes on the persons you mention or may hereafter so
mention; and if there is any one among them whose wife you had
rather be – I do not mean whom you love better than me – but
whose wife, *all* things considered, you had rather be than mine, then
I call upon you, I your brother and husband and friend thro' every
fortune, to accept that man and leave me to my destiny. But if on the
contrary my heart and my hand with the barren and perplexed
destiny which promises to attend them shall after all appear the *best*
that this poor world can offer you, then take me and be content with
me, and do not vex yourself with struggling to alter what is
unalterable, to make a man who is poor and sick suddenly become
rich and healthy. You tell me that you often weep when you think
what is to become of us. It is unwise in you to weep: if you are

reconciled to be *my* wife (not the wife of an ideal *me*, but the simple actual prosaic *me*), there is nothing frightful in the future. I look into it now with more and more confidence and composure. Alas! Jane you do not know me: it is not the poor, unknown, rejected Thomas Carlyle that you know, but the prospective rich known and admired. I am reconciled to my fate as it stands or promises to stand ere long: I have pronounced the word *unpraised* in all its cases and numbers; and find nothing terrific in it, even when it means *unmonied*, and by the mass of his Majesty's subjects *neglected* or even partially *contemned*. I thank Heaven I have other objects in my eye than either *their* pudding or their breath. This comes of the circumstance that my Apprenticeship is ending, and yours still going on. O Jane! Jane! I could weep too; for I love you in my deepest heart...

T. Carlyle

Jane Baillie Welsh to Thomas Carlyle
(4 March 1826)

...But surely, surely Mr Carlyle, you must know me better, than to have supposed it possible I should ever make a new choice! To say nothing of the sentiments I entertain towards *you*, which would make a marriage with another worse than death; is there no spark of honour, think you, in this heart, that I should not blush at the bare idea of such shame? Give myself to another, after having given myself with such unreservedness to you! Take another to my arms, with your image on my heart, your kisses on my lips! Oh be honest, and say you knew this would never be, – knew I could never sink so low! Let me not have room to suppose, that possessing your love, I am unfortunate enough to be without your respect! For how light must my open fondness have seemed; if you doubted of its being sanctified by a marriage-vow – a vow spoken, indeed, before no Minister, but before a presence, surely as awful God and my Conscience – And yet, it is so unlike *you*, the sworn enemy of cant, to make high-sounding offers, in the firm confidence of their being rejected! and unless I lay this to your charge in the present instance how can I help concluding that there is some virtue m me, which you have yet to learn? – for it is in no jesting, or yet "half-jesting" manner that you tell me my hand is free – "If there be any other – *you do not mean whom I love more* – but whose wife all things considered I would rather be; you call upon me as my Husband – (as my Husband!) to accept that man." Were these words really Thomas Carlyle's, and addressed to *me*? Ah! ich kenne dich nicht mehr! Dearest! Dearest! it will take many caresses to atone for these words! . . .

You say you are "the very worst *match* I ever thought of"; that "it is reasonable and right I should be concerned for my future *establishment*" and that I do not know you as the poor, unknown, rejected Thomas Carlyle; but "ask the prospe[c]tive rich, known, and admired" – Alas! my brother, you were wont to call me "generous," "devoted," "noble-minded": how comes it you address me now as a vulgar creature whose first object is "*a good settlement*"? Such sayings from another would have found with me no gentle hearing; and probably called forth an indignant exposition of my mind: but when the man I have loved with a love so pure from all worldliness, – for whom I am ready to sacrifice every thing on earth but my sense of right, – when *he* talks to me of matches, and establishments, and riches and honours, it is the thrust of a Brother which it would be ignominy to resist . . .

One thing more; and I am done. Look cross at me, reproach me, even whip me if you have the heart; your next kiss will make amends for all: but if you love me, cease I beseech you to make me offers of freedom; for this is an outrage which I find it not easy to forgive. If made with any idea that it is in the nature of things I should take you at your word; they do a wrong to my love, my truth, my modesty, that is, to my whole character as a Woman; if not, they are a mocking better spared; since you know my answer must be still: "permit me O Shinvarig, to wear out my days in prison, for its walls are to me more pleasing than the most splendid palace!" – but ohe jam satis! Farewell my Beloved! I am still yours

Jane Baillie Welsh

Carlyle to Ralph Waldo Emerson (27 January 1867)

*Carlyle had met the American poet Emerson in 1833, beginning a friend-
ship – conducted through letters – until Carlyle's death. Jane Carlyle died
in 1866, causing Carlyle to withdraw from public life.*

My dear Emerson,

It is a long time since I last wrote to you; and a long distance in
space and in fortune, – from the shores of the Solway in summer 1865,
to this niche of the Alps and Mediterranean to-day, after what has
befallen me in the interim. A longer interval, I think, and surely by
far a sadder, than ever occurred between us before, since we first met
in the Scotch moors, some five and thirty years ago. You have written
me various Notes, too, and Letters, all good and cheering to me –
almost the only truly *human* speech I have heard from anybody living
– and still my stony silence could not be broken; not till now, though
often looking forward to it, could I resolve on such a thing. You will
think me far gone, and much bankrupt in hope and heart – and
indeed I am; as good as without hope and without fear; a gloomily
serious, silent, and sad old man; gazing into the final chasm of things,
in mute dialogue with "Death, Judgment, and Eternity" (dialogue
mute on *both* sides!), not caring to discourse with poor articulate-
speaking fellow-creatures on *their* sorts of topics. It is right of me; and
yet also it is not right. I often feel that I had better be dead than thus
indifferent, contemptuous, disgusted with the world and its roaring
nonsense, which I have no thought farther of lifting a finger to help,
and only try to keep out of the way of, and shut my door against. But
the truth is, I was nearly killed by that hideous Book on Friedrich, –
twelve years in continuous wrestle with the nightmares and the
subterranean hydras; – nearly *killed*, and had often thought I should
be altogether, and must die leaving the monster not so much as
finished! This is one truth, not so evident to any friend or onlooker
as it is to myself: and then there is another, known to myself alone, as
it were; and of which I am best not to speak to others, or to speak to
them no farther. By the calamity of April last, I lost my little all in this
world; and have no soul left who can make any corner of this world

into a *home* for me any more. Bright, heroic, tender, true and noble was that lost treasure of my heart, who faithfully accompanied me in all the rocky ways and climbings; and I am forever poor without her. She was snatched from me in a moment, – as by a death from the gods. Very beautiful her death was; radiantly beautiful (to those who understand it) had all her life been: quid plura? I should be among the dullest and stupidest, if I were not among the saddest of all men. But not a word more on all this.

All summer last, my one solacement in the form of work was writing, and sorting of old documents and recollections; summoning out again into clearness old scenes that had now closed on me without return. Sad, and in a sense sacred; it was like a kind of *worship*; the only *devout* time I had had for a great while past. These things I have half or wholly the intention to burn out of the way before I myself die: – but such continues still mainly my employment, – so many hours every forenoon; what I call the "work" of my day; – to me, if to no other, it is useful; to reduce matters to writing means that you shall know them, see them in their origins and sequences, in their essential lineaments, considerably better than you ever did before. To set about writing my own *Life* would be no less than horrible to me; and shall of a certainty never be done. The common impious vulgar of this earth, what has it to do with my life or me? Let dignified oblivion, silence, and the vacant azure of Eternity swallow *me*; for my share of it, that, verily, is the handsomest, or one handsome way, of settling my poor account with the *canaille* of mankind extant and to come. "Immortal glory", is not that a beautiful thing, in the Shakespeare Clubs and Literary Gazettes of our improved Epoch? – I did not leave London, except for fourteen days in August, to a fine and high old Lady-friend's in Kent; where riding about the woods and by the sea-beaches and chalk cliffs, in utter silence, I felt sadder than ever, though a little less *miserably* so, than in the intrusive babblements of London, which I could not quite lock out of doors. We read, at first, Tennyson's *Idyls*, with profound recognition of the finely elaborated execution, and also of the inward perfection of *vacancy*, – and, to say truth, with considerable impatience at being treated so very like infants, though the lollipops were so superlative.

We gladly changed for one Emerson's *English Traits*; and read that, with increasing and ever increasing satisfaction every evening; blessing Heaven that there were still Books for grown-up people too! That truly is a Book all full of thoughts like winged arrows (thanks to the Bowyer from us both): – my Ladyfriend's name is Miss Davenport Bromley; it was at Wooton, in her Grandfather's House, in Staffordshire, that Rousseau took shelter in 1760; and one hundred and six years later she was reading Emerson to me with a recognition that would have pleased the man, had he seen it.

About that same time my health and humors being evidently so, the Dowager Lady Ashburton (*not* the high Lady you saw, but a Successor of Mackenzie-Highland type), who wanders mostly about the Continent since her widowhood, for the sake of a child's health, began pressing and inviting me to spend the blade months of Winter here in her Villa with her; – all friends warmly seconding and urging; by one of whom I was at last snatched off, as if by the hair of the head, (in spite of my violent No, no!) on the eve of Christmas last, and have been here ever since, – really with improved omens. The place is beautiful as a very picture, the climate superlative (today a sun and sky like very June); the *hospitality* of usage beyond example. It is likely I shall be here another six weeks, or longer. If you please to write me, the address is on the margin; and I will answer.

Adieu.
T. *Carlyle*

JOEY GRIMALDI

JOSEPH GRIMALDI (1799–1837), CLOWN; HIS LAST PUBLIC performance was at Drury Lane, London, in 1828.

To unknown (20 December 1829)

Dear Sir

It is with sorrow I am unable to do as you wish. Christmas is near – but I shall be unable to accept your invite. I am extremely ill and hardly able to stand with the cursed gout – no grinning *now* for poor old Joey – none! I shall be with you in spirit dear Friend and as such shall think of all your enjoyments & amusements. I do not think I shall see many more Christmases – but Providence willing, next year I will if alive be with you. Accept my hearty wishes for happiness and believe me

Your true old
Friend
Joey Grimaldi
(now grin all day!).

CHARLOTTE BRONTË

CHARLOTTE BRONTË (1816–55), ENGLISH NOVELIST, the author of *Jane Eyre* (1847).

To Robert Southey (16 March 1837)

Sir,

I cannot rest till I have answered your letter, even though by addressing you a second time I should appear a little intrusive; but I must thank you for the kind and wise advice you have condescended to give me. I had not ventured to hope for such a reply; so considerate in its tone, so noble in its spirit. I must suppress what I feel, or you will think me foolishly enthusiastic.

At the first perusal of your letter I felt only shame and regret that

I had ever ventured to trouble you with my crude rhapsody; I felt a painful heat rise to my face when I thought of the quires of paper I had covered with what once gave me so much delight, but which now was only a source of confusion; but after I had thought a little, and read it again and again, the prospect seemed to clear. You do not forbid me to write; you do not say that what I write is utterly destitute of merit. You only warn me against the folly of neglecting real duties for the sake of imaginative pleasures; of writing for the love of fame; for the selfish excitement of emulation. You kindly allow me to write poetry for its own sake, provided I leave undone nothing which I ought to do, in order to pursue that single, absorbing, exquisite gratification. I am afraid, sir, you think me very foolish. I know the first letter I wrote to you was all senseless trash from beginning to end; but I am not altogether the idle, dreaming being it would seem to denote.

My father is a clergyman of limited though competent income, and I am the eldest of his children. He expended quite as much in my education as he could afford in justice to the rest. I thought it therefore my duty, when I left school, to become a governess. In that capacity I find enough to occupy my thoughts all day long, and my head and hands too, without having a moment's time for one dream of the imagination. In the evenings, I confess, I do think, but I never trouble any one else with my thoughts. I carefully avoid any appearance of preoccupation and eccentricity, which might lead those I live amongst to suspect the nature of my pursuits. Following my father's advice – who from my childhood has counselled me, just in the wise and friendly tone of your letter – I have endeavoured not only attentively to observe all the duties a woman ought to fulfil, but to feel deeply interested in them. I don't always succeed, for sometimes when I'm teaching or sewing I would rather be reading or writing; but I try to deny myself; and my father's approbation amply rewarded me for the privation. Once more allow me to thank you with sincere gratitude. I trust I shall never more feel ambitious to see my name in print; if the wish should rise, I'll look at Southey's letter, and suppress it. It is honour enough for me that I have written to him, and received an answer. That letter is consecrated; no one shall ever see it but papa and my brother and sisters. Again I thank you. This incident, I suppose, will be renewed no more; if I live to be an old woman, I shall remember it thirty years hence as a bright dream. The signature which you suspected of being fictitious is my real name. Again, therefore, I must sign myself

C. Brontë

P.S. – Pray, sir, excuse me for writing to you a second time; I could not help writing, partly to tell you how thankful I am for your kindness, and partly to let you know that your advice shall not be wasted, however sorrowfully and reluctantly it may at first be followed.

C. B.

To W. S. Williams (2 October 1846)

Williams was a publisher's reader, and instrumental in publishing Jane Eyre. *Branwell Brontë, the Brontë sisters' dissolute brother, had died on 24 September.*

My Dear Sir,

"We have buried our dead out of sight." A lull begins to succeed the gloomy tumult of last week. It is not permitted us to grieve for him who is gone as others grieve for those they lose. The removal of our only brother must necessarily be regarded by us rather in the light of a mercy than a chastisement. Branwell was his father's and his sisters' pride and hope in boyhood, but since manhood the case has been otherwise. It has been our lot to see him take a wrong bent; to hope, expect, wait his return to the right path; to know the sickness of hope deferred, the dismay of prayer baffled; to experience despair at last – and now to behold the sudden early obscure close of what might have been a noble career.

I do not weep from a sense of bereavement – there is no prop withdrawn, no consolation torn away, no dear companion lost – but for the wreck of talent, the ruin of promise, the untimely dreary extinction of what might have been a burning and a shining light. My brother was a year my junior. I had aspirations and ambitions for him once, long ago – they have perished mournfully. Nothing remains of him but a memory of errors and sufferings. There is such a bitterness of pity for his life and death, such a yearning for the emptiness of his whole existence as I cannot describe. I trust time will allay these feelings.

ABRAHAM LINCOLN

LINCOLN (1809–65), A FORMER LAWYER, WAS THE 16TH President of the USA and led the country during the Civil War of 1861–5.

To Mrs Orville Browning (1 April 1838)

Browning was the wife of a Whig member of the Illinois legislature, a friend of Lincoln's. The fiancé Lincoln despairs of was Mary S. Owens; he later married Mary Todd.

Dear Madam:

Without apologizing for being egotistical, I shall make the history of so much of my own life as has elapsed since I saw you the subject of this letter. And by the way, I now discover that in order to give a full and intelligible account of the things I have done and suffered *since* I saw you, I shall necessarily have to relate some that happened *before*.

It was, then, in the autumn of 1836, that a married lady of my acquaintance, and who was a great friend of mine, being about to pay a visit to her father and other relatives residing in Kentucky, proposed to me, that on her return she would bring a sister of hers with her, upon condition that I would engage to become her brother-in-law with all convenient dispatch. I, of course, accepted the proposal; for you know I could not have done otherwise, had I really been averse to it; but privately between you and me, I was most confoundedly well pleased with the project. I had seen the said sister some three years before, thought her intelligent and agreeable, and saw no good objection to plodding life through hand in hand with her. Time passed on, the lady took her journey and in due time returned, sister in company sure enough. This stomached me a little; for it appeared to me that her coming so readily showed that she was a trifle too willing; but on reflection it occurred to me that she might have been prevailed on by her married sister to come without anything concerning me ever having been mentioned to her, and so I concluded that if no other objection presented itself I would consent to waive this. All this occurred upon my *hearing* of her arrival in the neighbourhood; for, be it remembered, I had not yet *seen* her, except about three years previous, as before mentioned.

In a few days we had an interview, and although I had seen her before, she did not look; as my imagination had pictured her. I knew she was oversize, but she now appeared a fair match for Falstaff; I knew she was called an "old maid," and I felt no doubt of the truth of at least half of the appellation; but now, when I beheld her, I could not for my life avoid thinking of my mother; and this, not from withered features, for her skin was too full of fat to permit its contracting into wrinkles; but from her want of teeth, weather-beaten appearance in general, and from a kind of notion that ran in my head that *nothing* could have commenced at the size of infancy and reached her present bulk in less than thirty-five or forty years; and, in short, I was not [at] all pleased with her. But what could I do? I had told her sister that I would take her for better or for worse; and I made a point of honor and conscience in all things to stick to my word, especially if others had been induced to act on it, which in this case I doubted not they had, for I was now fairly convinced that no other man on earth would have her, and hence the conclusion that they were bent on holding me to my bargain. Well, thought I, I have said it, and, be consequences what they may, it shall not be my fault if I fail to do it. At once I determined to consider her my wife; and this done, all my powers of discovery were put to the rack in search of perfections in her, which might be fairly set off against her defects. I tried to imagine she was handsome, which, but for her unfortunate corpulency, was actually true. Exclusive of this, no woman that I have seen has a finer face. I also tried to convince myself that the mind was much more to be valued than the person; and in this she was not inferior, as I could discover, to any with whom I had been acquainted.

Shortly after this, without attempting to come to any positive understanding with her, I set out for Vandalia, where and when you first saw me. During my stay there I had letters from her which did not change my opinion of either her intellect or intention but on the contrary, confirmed it in both.

All this while, although I was fixed "firm as the surge repelling rock" in my resolution, I found I was continually repenting the rashness which had led me to make it. Through life I have been in no bondage, either real or imaginary, from the thraldom of which I so much desired to be free.

After my return home I saw nothing to change my opinion of her in any particular. She was the same and so was I. I now spent my time between planning how I might get along through life after my contemplated change of circumstances should have taken place; and how I might procrastinate the evil day for a time, which I really dreaded as much – perhaps more – than an Irishman does the halter.

After all my suffering upon this deeply interesting subject, here I am, wholly unexpectedly, completely out of the "scrape", and I now want to know if you can guess how I got out of it. Out clear in every sense of the term; no violation of word, honor, or conscience. I don't believe you can guess, and so I may as well tell you at once. As the lawyers say, it was done in the manner following, to wit. After I had delayed the matter as long as I thought I could in honor do, which by the way had brought me round into the last fall, I concluded I might as well bring it to a consummation without further delay; and so I mustered my resolution, and made the proposal to her direct; but, shocking to relate, she answered,

No. At first I supposed she did it through an affectation of modesty, which I thought but ill became her, under the peculiar circumstances of her case; but on my renewal of the charge, I found she repelled it with greater firmness than before. I tried it again and again, but with the same success, or rather with the same want of success. I finally was forced to give it up, at which I very unexpectedly found myself mortified almost beyond endurance. I was mortified, it seemed to me, in a hundred different ways. My vanity was deeply wounded by the reflection that I had so long been too stupid to discover her intentions, and at the same time never doubting that I understood them perfectly; and also, that she whom I had taught myself to believe nobody else would have, had actually rejected me with all my fancied greatness; and to cap the whole, I then, for the first time, began to suspect that I was really a little in love with her. But let it all go. I'll try and outlive it. Others have been made fools of by the girls; but this can never be with truth said of me. I most emphatically, in this instance, made a fool of myself. I have now come to the conclusion never again to think of marrying; and for this reason: I can never be satisfied with anyone who would be blockhead enough to have me.

When you receive this, write me a long yarn about something to amuse me. Give my respects to Mr Browning. Your sincere friend

To John D. Johnston (December 1848)

Johnston was Lincoln's stepbrother.

Dear Johnston:

Your request for eighty dollars, I do not think it best to comply with now. At the various times when I have helped you a little, you have said to me "We can get along very well now" but in a very short time I find you in the same difficulty again. Now this can only happen by some defect in your *conduct*. What that defect is, I think I know. You are not *lazy*, and still you *are* an *idler*. I doubt whether since I saw you,

you have done a good whole day's work, in any one day. You do not very much dislike to work; and still you do not work much, merely because it does not seem to you that you could get much for it. This habit of uselessly wasting time is the whole difficulty; and it is vastly important to you, and still more so to your children, that you should break this habit. It is more important to them, because they have longer to live, and can keep out of an idle habit before they are in it, easier than they can get out after they are in.

You are now in need of some ready money; and what I propose is, that you shall go to work "tooth and nails" for somebody who will give you money for it. Let father and your boys take charge of things at home – prepare for a crop, and make the crop; and you go to work for the best money wages, or in discharge of any debt you owe, that you can get. And to secure you a fair reward for your labor, I now promise you that for every dollar you will, between this and the first of next May, get for your own labor, either in money or in your own indebtedness, I will then give you one other dollar. By this, if you hire yourself at ten dollars a month, from me you will get ten more, making twenty dollars a month for your work. In this I do not mean you shall go off to St Louis, or the lead mines, or the gold mines, in California, but I mean for you to go at it for the best wages you can get close to home in Coles county. Now if you will do this, you will soon be out of debt, and what is better, you will have a habit that will keep you from getting in debt again. But if I should now clear you out, next year you will be just as deep in as ever. You say you would almost give your place in heaven for $70 or $80. Then you value your place in heaven very cheaply for I am sure you can with the offer I make you get the seventy or eighty dollars for four or five months' work. You say if I furnish you the money you will deed me the land, and, if you don't pay the money back, you will deliver possession. Nonsense! If you can't now live *with* the land, how will you then live without it? You have always been kind to me, and I do not now mean to be unkind to you. On the contrary, if you will but follow my advice, you will find it worth more than eight times eighty dollars to you. Affectionately your brother

242

To General Joseph Hooker (January 1863)

Joseph "Fighting Joe" Hooker (1814–79) replaced Ambrose Burnside as commander of the Army of the Potomac; he himself was superseded by G.G. Meade.

I have placed you at the head of the Army of the Potomac. Of course I have done this upon what appear to me to be sufficient reasons. And yet I think it best for you to know that there are some things in regard to which, I am not quite satisfied with you. I believe you to be a brave and a skilful soldier, which, of course, I like. I also believe you do not mix politics with your profession, in which you are right. You have confidence in yourself, which is a valuable, if not an indispensable quality. You are ambitious, which, within reasonable bounds, does good rather than harm. But I think that during Gen. Burnside's command of the Army, you have taken counsel of your ambition, and thwarted him as much as you could, in which you did a great wrong to the country, and to a most meritorious and honorable brother officer. I have heard, in such way as to believe it, of your recently saying that both the Army and the government needed a dictator. Of course it was not *for* this, but in spite of it, that I have given you the command. Only those generals who gain successes, can set up dictators. What I now ask of you is military success, and I will risk the dictatorship. The government will support you to the utmost of its ability, which is neither more nor less than it has done and will do for all commanders. I much fear that the spirit which you have aided to infuse into the Army, of criticizing their commander, and withholding confidence from him, will now turn upon you. I shall assist you as far as I can, to put it down. Neither you, nor Napoleon, if he were alive again, could get any good out of an army, while such a spirit prevails in it.

And now, beware of rashness. Beware of rashness, but with energy, and sleepless vigilance, go forward, and give us victories.

Yours very truly

QUEEN VICTORIA

ALEXANDRINA VICTORIA (1819–1901), QUEEN OF THE United Kingdom, empress of India. She ascended the throne in 1837, on the death of her uncle, William IV.

To Prince Albert of Saxe-Cobourg and Gotha (31 January 1840)

Written shortly before Victoria's marriage to Albert.

...You have written to me in one of your letters about our stay at Windsor, but, dear Albert, you have not at all understood the matter. *You forget, my dearest Love, that I am the Sovereign, and that business can stop and wait for nothing. Parliament is sitting, and something occurs almost every day, for which I may be required, and it is quite impossible for me to be absent from London; therefore two or three days is already a long time to be absent. I am never easy a moment, if I am not on the spot, and see and hear what is going on, and everybody, including all my Aunts (who are very knowing in all these things), says I must come out after the second day, for, as I must be surrounded by my Court, I cannot keep alone. This is also my own wish in every way.*

Now as to the Arms: *as an English Prince you have no right, and Uncle Leopold had no right to quarter the English Arms, but the Sovereign has the power to allow it by Royal Command; this was done for Uncle Leopold by the Prince Regent, and I will do it again for you. But it can only be done by Royal Command...*

Farewell, dearest Albert, and think often of thy faithful

Victoria R.

To Leopold, King of the Belgians (29 November, 1841)

Leopold I (1790–1865), elected king of the Belgians in 1831. He was uncle to Victoria, and her constant correspondent. The "little boy" of the letter was later to ascend the throne as Edward VII; "Pussy" was Victoria Adelaide, Queen Victoria's first-born.

My dearest Uncle,

I would have written sooner, had I not been a little bilious, which made me very low, and not in spirits to write. The weather has been so exceedingly relaxing, that it made me at the end of the fortnight quite bilious, and this, you know, affects the spirits. I am much better, but they think that I shall not get my appetite and spirits back till I can get out of town; we are therefore going in a week at latest. I am going for a drive this morning, and am certain it will do me good. Our little boy is a wonderfully strong and large child, with very large dark-blue eyes, a finely formed but somewhat large nose, and a pretty little mouth; I *hope* and *pray* he may be like his dearest Papa. He is to be called *Albert*, and Edward is to be his second name. Pussy, dear child, is still *the* great pet amongst us all, and is getting so fat and strong again... I beg you to forgive this letter being so badly written, but my feet are being rubbed, and as I have got the box on which I am writing on my knee, it is not easy to write quite straight – but you must not think my hand trembles.

Ever your devoted Niece,
Victoria R.

Pussy is not at all pleased with her brother.

To Leopold, King of the Belgians (December 1861)

Prince Albert had died of typhoid on 14 December.

My *own* Dearest, Kindest *Father*,

For as such have I *ever* loved you. The poor fatherless baby of eight months is now the utterly broken-hearted and crushed widow of forty-two! My *life* as a *happy* one is *ended*! the world is gone for *me*! If I *must live* on (and I will do nothing to make me worse than I am), it is henceforth for our poor fatherless children – for my unhappy country, which has lost *all* in losing him – and in *only* doing what I know and feel he would wish, for he is near me – his spirit will guide and inspire me! But oh! to be cut off in the prime of life – to see our pure, happy, quiet domestic life, which *alone* enabled me to bear my *much* disliked position, CUT OFF at forty-two – when I *had* hoped with such instinctive certainty that God *would never* part us, and would let us grow old together (though *he* always talked of the shortness of life) – is *too awful*, too cruel! And yet it *must* be for *his* good, his happiness! His purity was too great, his aspiration *too high* for this poor, *miserable* world! His great soul is *now only* enjoying that for which it *was* worthy! And I will *not* envy him – only pray that mine may be perfected by it and for to be with him eternally, for which blessed moment I earnestly long. Dearest, dearest Uncle, *how* kind of you to come! It will be an unspeakable *comfort*, and you *can do* much to tell people to do what they ought to do. As for my *own good*, *personal* servants – poor Phipps in particular – nothing can be more devoted, heartbroken as they are, and anxious only to live as *he* wished!

> Ever your devoted, wretched Child,
> *Victoria R.*

HENRY DAVID THOREAU

HENRY DAVID THOREAU (1817–62) WAS THE AUTHOR of the American classic, *Walden, or Life in the Woods* (1845), describing his reclusive life in a shack by the side of Walden Pond.

To Ralph Waldo Emerson (11 March 1842)

Thoreau first met the poet and essayist Emerson (1803–82) in 1842, and later lived in his household.

Dear Friend,

I see so many "carvells ticht; fast tending throw the sea" to your El Dorado, that I am in haste to plant my flag in season on that distant beach, in the name of God and king Henry. There seems to be no occasion why I who have so little to say to you here at home should take pains to send you any of my silence in a letter – Yet since no correspondence can hope to rise above the level of those homely speechless hours, as no spring ever bursts above the level of the still mountain tarn whence it issued – I will not delay to send a venture. As if I were to send you a piece of the house-sill – or a loose casement rather. Do not neighbors sometimes halloo with good will across a field, who yet never chat over a fence?

The sun has just burst through the fog, and I hear blue-birds, song-sparrows, larks, and robins, down in the meadow. The other day I walked in the woods, but found myself rather denaturalized by late habits. Yet it is the same nature that Burns and Wordsworth loved – the same life that Shakspeare and Milton lived. The wind still roars in the wood, as if nothing had happened out of the course of nature. The sound of the waterfall is not interrupted more than if a feather had fallen.

Nature is not ruffled by the rudest blast – The hurricane only snaps a few twigs in some nook of the forest. The snow attains its average depth each winter, and the chic-adee lisps the same notes. The old laws prevail in spite of pestilence and famine. No genius or virtue so rare & revolutionary appears in town or village, that the pine ceases to exude resin in the wood, or beast or bird lays aside its habits.

How plain that death is only the phenomenon of the individual or class. Nature does not recognize it, She finds her own again under new forms without loss. Yet death is beautiful when seen to be a law, and not an accident – It is as common as life. Men die in Tartary – in Ethiopia – in England – in Wisconsin. And after all what portion of this so serene and living nature can be said to be alive? Do this year's grasses and foliage outnumber all the past.

Every blade in the field – every leaf in the forest – lays down its life in its season as beautifully as it was taken up. It is the pastime of a full quarter of the year. Dead trees – sere leaves – dried grass and herbs – are not these a good part of our life? And what is that pride of our autumnal scenery but the hectic flush – the sallow and cadaverous countenance of vegetation – its painted throes – with the November air for canvas –

When we look over the fields we are not saddened because these particular flowers or grasses will wither – for the law of their death is the law of new life. Will not the land be in good heart *because* the crops die down from year to year? The herbage cheerfully consents to bloom, and wither, and give place to a new.

So it is with the human plant. We are partial and selfish when we lament the death of the individual, unless our plaint be a paean to the departed soul, and we sigh as the wind sighs over the fields, which no shrub interprets into its private grief.

One might as well go into mourning for every sere leaf – but the more innocent and wiser soul will snuff a fragrance in the gales of autumn, and congratulate Nature upon her health.

After I have imagined thus much will not the Gods feel under obligations to make me realize something as good?

I have just read some good verse by the Scotch poet John Bellenden—

> "The fynest gold or silver that we se,
> May nocht be wrocht to our utilitie,
> Bot flammis kein & bitter violence;
> The more distress, the more intelligence.
> Quhay sailis lang in hie prosperitie,
> Ar sone oureset be stormis without defence."

From your friend
Henry D. Thoreau

248

To Ellen Emerson (31 July 1849)

Ellen Emerson was the daughter (then aged ten) of Ralph Waldo Emerson.

Dear Ellen,

I think that we are pretty well acquainted, though we never had any very long talks. We have had a good many short talks, at any rate Dont you remember how we used to despatch our breakfast two winters ago, as soon as Eddy could get on his feeding tire, which was not always remembered, before the rest of the household had come down? Dont you remember our wise criticisms on the pictures in the portfolio and the Turkish book with Eddy and Edith looking on, – how almost any pictures answered our purpose, and we went through the Penny Magazine, first from beginning to end, and then from end to beginning, and Eddy stared just as much the second time as the first, and Edith thought that we turned over too soon, and that there were some things which she had not seen – ? I can guess pretty well what interests you, and what you think about. Indeed I am interested in pretty much the same things myself. I suppose you think that persons who are as old as your father and myself are always thinking about very grave things, but I know that we are meditating the same old themes that we did when we were ten years old, only we go more gravely about it. You love to write or to read a fairy story and that is what you will always like to do, in some form or other. By and by you will discover that you want what are called the necessaries of life only that you may realize some such dream.

Eddy has got him a fish-pole and line with a pin-hook at the end, which he flourishes over the dry ground and the carpet at the risk of tearing out our eyes; but when I told him that he must have a cork and a sinker, his mother took off the pin and tied on a cork instead; but he doubts whether that will catch fish as well. He tells me that he is five years old. Indeed I was present at the celebration of his birthday lately, and supplied the company with onion and squash pipes, and rhubarb whistles, which is the most I can do on such occasions. Little Sammy Hoar blowed them most successfully, and made the loudest noise, though it almost strained his eyes out to do it. Edith is full of spirits. When she comes home from school, she goes hop skip and jump down into the field to pick berries, currants, gooseberries, raspberries, and thimbleberries; if there is one of these that has thoughts of changing its hue by to-morrow morning, I guess that Edith knows something about it and will consign it to her basket for Grandmama.

Children may now be seen going a-berrying in all directions. The white-lillies are in blossom, and the john's wort and goldenrod are beginning to come out. Old people say that we have not had so warm a summer for thirty years. Several persons have died in consequence of the heat, – Mr Kendal, perhaps, for one. The Irishmen on the railroad were obliged to leave off their work for several days, and the farmers left their fields and sought the shade. William Brown of the poor house is dead, – the one who used to ask for a cent – "Give me a cent?" I wonder who will have his cents now!

I found a nice penknife on the bank of the river this afternoon, which was probably lost by some villager who went there to bathe lately. Yesterday I found a nice arrowhead. which was lost some time before by an Indian who was hunting there. The knife was a very little rusted; the arrowhead was not rusted at all.

You must see the sun rise out of the ocean before you come home. I think that Long Island will not be in the way, if you climb to the top of the hill – at least, no more than Bolster Island, and Pillow Hill and even the Lowlands of Never-get-up are elsewhere.

Do not think that you must write to me because I have written to you. It does not follow at all. You would not naturally make so long a speech to me here in a month as a letter would be. Yet if sometime it should be perfectly easy, and pleasant to you, I shall be glad to have a sentence.

Your old acquaintance
Henry Thoreau.

SYDNEY SMITH

ACLERGYMAN BY TRAINING, SYDNEY SMITH (1771–1845) developed a reputation as a wit and was a leading member of the political and literary circle centred on Holland House, the London home of Lord and Lady Holland.

To Lady Holland (13 September 1842)

The Allen referred to was John Allen, a physician and philosopher.

My dear Lady Holland,

I am sorry to hear Allen is not well; but the reduction of his legs is a pure and unmixed good; they are enormous, – they are clerical! He has the creed of a philosopher and the legs of a clergyman; I never saw such legs, – at least, belonging to a layman.

Read *A Life in the Forest*, skipping nimbly; but there is much of good in it.

It is a bore, I admit, to be past seventy, for you are left for execution, and are daily expecting the death-warrant; but, as you say, it is not anything very capital we quit. We are, at the close of life, only hurried away from stomach-aches, pains in the joints, from sleepless nights and unamusing days, from weakness, ugliness, and nervous tremors; but we shall all meet again in another planet, cured of all defects. Rogers will be less irritable; Macaulay more silent; Hallam will assent; Jeffrey will speak slower; Bobus will be just as he is; I shall be more respectful to the upper clergy; but I shall have as lively a sense as I now have of all your kindness and affection for me.

Sydney Smith

To his Grandchild (1843)

The recipient had sent Smith an overweight letter.

Oh, you little wretch! your letter cost me fourpence. I will pull all the plums out of your puddings; I will undress your dolls and steal their under petticoats; you shall have no currant-jelly to your rice; I will kiss you till you cannot see out of your eyes; when nobody else whips you, I will do so; I will fill you so full of sugar-plums that they shall run out of your nose and ears; lastly, your frocks shall be so short that they shall not come below your knees.

Your loving grandfather
Sydney Smith

KARL MARX AND FRIEDRICH ENGELS

THE FOUNDER OF MODERN COMMUNISM, KARL MARX (1818–83) was born in Trier, Germany. After completing a doctorate in philosophy at Berlin University he worked for the newspaper *Rheinische Zeitung*, before emigrating to Paris, then London, living there with his family in some poverty while pursuing the researches that eventually produced his magnum opus, *Das Kapital* (vol. 1, 1867). He was supported by his collaborator Friedrich Engels (1820–95), the scion of a prominent German manufacturer, who followed Marx to England, where he ran the family's Manchester cotton factory. Marx sometimes signed himself in letters, and was addressed by Engels as, "Moor" or "El Moro", a nickname acknowledging his swarthy complexion.

Friedrich Engels to Karl Marx
(17 March 1845 from Barmen, Germany)

Dear Marx

...Let me tell you I'm leading a real dog's life. What with all the meetings and the "debauchery" of several of our local communists, whom I naturally meet, the whole religious fanaticism of my old man has been awakened again, further intensified by my declaration that I will definitively give up being a filthy businessman – and my public appearance as a communist has moreover given rise to a splendid bourgeois fanaticism in him. Just picture my position. Since I'm leaving in a fortnight or so I don't wish to start a row; I submit to everything, and that they are not used to and so they grow bolder. When I get a letter it is sniffed at from all sides before I receive it myself. Since they know they are all letters from communists they invariably put on pious long-suffering faces – enough to drive you round the bend. If I leave the house – the same faces. If I stay in my room and work, naturally on communism, they know that – the same faces. I cannot eat, drink, sleep or let out a single fart without those self-same confounded pious faces before my eyes. No matter whether I go out or stay at home, whether I keep silent or speak, whether I read or write, whether I laugh or not, no matter what I do – immediately my old man puts on that infamous mug. At the same time my old man is so stupid that he throws communism and liberalism into the same pot as "revolutionary" and thus, for example, in spite of all my protestations, keeps holding me responsible for the insanities of the British *bourgeoisie* in parliament! And now the pious season has started at home here anyway. A week ago today two of my siblings were confirmed, today the whole kith and kin are trotting off to Holy Communion – the body of the Lord has done its work, the long faces this morning surpassed everything. To make misfortune complete I spent last night with Hess in Elberfeld, where we learnedly talked communism until 2 am. Needless to say, long faces today about my late return, hints that I was probably in clink. Eventually they summoned the courage to ask where I had been. With Hess. "With Hess! Good Heavens!" A pause, an intensification of Christian despair in their faces."The people you've chosen to consort with!" Sighs, etc. It's enough to drive you insane. You've no idea of the malice of this Christian chase after my "soul". All my old man now needs is to discover that *Critical Critique* exists and he may well kick me out of the house. And there is this continuing annoyance of seeing that you just cannot get anywhere with those people, that they positively *want* to torment and torture themselves with their visions of hell, and that one cannot even make them understand the most ordinary principles of fairness. If it weren't for my mother, who has a fine fund of humanity and only lacks all independence *vis-a-vis* my father, and whom I genuinely love, I would not for a moment consider making even the minutest concession to my fanatical and despotic old man. But as it is, my mother worries herself sick every moment of the day and each time she is specifically annoyed with me has a headache for a week – it's just no longer bearable, I've got to get away and I scarcely know how to hang on for these few weeks that I'm still here. But I'll manage somehow.

[. . .]

Yours, E.

❧

Karl Marx to Friedrich Engels in Manchester (8 September 1852, from London)

Dear Engels!

Your letter today dropped into a very disturbed atmosphere. My wife is ill, little Jenny is ill, little Lene has a kind of nervous fever. I could not and cannot call the doctor because I have no money for medicine. For 8–10 days I have kept the family going on bread and potatoes, and it is even doubtful whether I can get these today. That diet of course was not conducive to health in the present climatic conditions. I've written no articles for Dana because I did not have the penny to go to read newspapers. Incidentally, as soon as you've sent No. xix I'll send you a letter with my opinion on xx, a summary of this present shit.

When I was with you and you told me you'd be able to obtain for me a somewhat larger sum by the end of August I wrote and told my wife to put her mind at rest. Your letter 3–4 weeks ago indicated that there was not much hope but nevertheless some. Thus I put off all creditors until the beginning of September, who, as you know, are always only paid small fragments. Now the storm is universal.

I have tried everything but in vain. First that dog Weydemeyer cheats me of 15£. I write to Germany to Streit (because he had written to Dronke in Switzerland). The pig doesn't even reply. I turn to Brockhaus and offer him articles for *Gegenwart*, of harmless content. He declined in a very polite letter. Finally throughout last week I've been running around with an Englishman all day long because he wanted to obtain from me the discount for the bills on Dana. In vain.

The best and most desirable thing that could happen would be for my landlady to throw me out of the house. At least I would save the sum of 22£ then. But I can hardly expect her to be so obliging. Then there are the baker, the milkman, the tea fellow, the greengrocer, and an old butcher's bill. How am I to cope with all this diabolical mess? In the end, during the past 8–10 days I borrowed a few shillings and pence from Knoten, which was the last thing I wanted to do but it was necessary in order not to croak.

You will have observed from my letters that, as usual when I am in it myself and do not just hear about it from afar, I am wading through the shit with great indifference. But what's to be done? My house is a hospital, and the crisis is getting so disruptive that it compels me to give it my all-highest attention. What's to be done?

[…]

Yours, K. M.

❧

Friedrich Engels to Karl Marx (11 February 1858)

Dear Moor,

[…]

Unfortunately I can't send you anything today. I allowed myself to

be persuaded to go to a coursing meeting, when hares are chased by hounds, and had 7 hours in the saddle. Although this has generally done me a great deal of good, it prevented me from working.[...]
[...]

Incidentally, so you should not get any false ideas about my physical condition I will also tell you that yesterday on my mount I jumped over an embankment and hedge 5 foot and a few inches high, the highest jump I've ever made. Such exertions, if they are to be made in comfort, presuppose fairly sound limbs. Altogether we'll give the Prussian cavalry a riding lesson or two when we get back to Germany. Those gentry shall find it difficult to keep up with me, I now have a lot of practice and am improving every day; my reputation is also gradually being established. But I am only now beginning to realize the real problems of riding in difficult terrain, that is a most complicated business.

[...]

Yours, F. E.

Friedrich Engels to Karl Marx (27 April 1867)

Dear Moor,
[...]
I have always felt that this damned book [*Das Kapital*] over which you have gestated such a long time, was the basic core of all your misfortunes and that you would and could never get out of them until you had shaken it off. This eternally unfinished thing weighed you down physically, mentally and financially, and I can very well understand that, having shaken off this nightmare, you now feel an entirely different person, especially as the world, once you enter it again, no longer looks as gloomy as before. [...] I am enormously pleased about this whole turn the matter has taken, first for its own sake, secondly for you especially and your wife, and thirdly because it really is about time that this should improve. In

2 years my contract with the Gottfried* pig expires and, the way things are shaping here, it is hardly likely that either of us will wish to extend it; indeed it is not impossible that a separation may occur even sooner. If that is the case I shall have to *get out completely* from commerce, because to start a business of my own now would mean 5–6 years' terribly hard work without appreciable results and then another 5–6 years' hard work in order to glean the fruits of the first 5 years. But that would finish me. There's nothing I long for more than release from this filthy commerce which is totally demoralizing me with its waste of time. So long as I am in it I'm incapable of anything, and since I've been Principal things have become much worse because of the greater responsibility. If it were not for the higher income I would truly prefer to be a clerk again. At any rate, my life as a businessman will come to an end in a few years, and then the income, too, will flow very, very much more sparingly, and that's what I've always racked my brains about, how we shall then arrange matters with you. However, if things continue as they are now beginning then we'll find a way of arranging that too, even if the Revolution does not intervene to put an end to all financial projects. But if that does not come about I reserve the right to treat myself to a huge frolic on my release and to write an entertaining book: *Woes and Joys of the English Bourgeoisie...*

That Bismarck would knock at your door is something I expected, though not in such a hurry. It is significant for the thinking and the horizon of that fellow that he judges everybody by himself. Well may the bourgeoisie admire the great men of today: it sees itself reflected in them. All the qualities which enabled Bonaparte and Bismarck to achieve successes are mercantile qualities: the pursuit of a definite objective through waiting and experimenting until the right moment has been found, the diplomacy of the ever-open back door, compromise and arrangements, the swallowing of insults when one's interest demands it, the "we don't wish to be thieves", in short the

---

*Gottfried Ermen, Engels senior's business partner.

merchant in all things. Gottfried Ermen in his way is as great a statesman as Bismarck, and if one follows the manipulations of these great men one feels transported time and again to the Manchester Exchange. Bismarck thinks: if only I keep knocking at Marx's door I shall eventually find the right amount, and we'll then do a little business together. Gottfried Ermen to a T.

[...]

Yours, F. E.

❧

Karl Marx to Friedrich Engels (22 July 1869)

Dear Fred,

For about 6 days I've had a fierce carbuncle on my left arm, which is not pleasant in "this heat".

I had yet another "familiar" unpleasantness. The point is that for some time I've noticed that my wife is not managing with the money I give her each week, even though our expenses have in no way increased. As I certainly don't wish to get into debt again, and as the money that I gave her last Monday was again all "gone" yesterday, I asked for an explanation. And then the folly of women emerged. In the list of debts which I made her compile for you she had suppressed approximately 75£ which she was now trying to pay off bit by bit from the housekeeping money. I asked her why? Answer: She was afraid to come out with the big overall total! Women evidently always need some guardianship! ...

Yours, Moor

NAPOLEON DANA

LIEUTENANT DANA OF THE US 7TH CAVALRY WAS A professional soldier. The letter here was written on the banks of the Nueces as he waited for war with Mexico.

To his wife Sue (11 October 1845)

When I come home... I shall want to kiss you all over, and won't you let me do it? I know you will, for you told me on the steamboat you would do everything I want. May I kiss you over and over again on your lips, titties, belly, legs, and between them too? Yes, I must. Tell me, dear one, if I may.

You don't know how anxious I am lest you are in a delicate situation. Tell me all about it, Sue. It is possible that nursing may make your courses irregular, and they may come yet, but it was after the time when you last wrote me? I really hope you are not so. It appears too much to lose. You will have all the pain and trouble, without our having all the enjoyment. If you are so, we are losing a deal of fun in bed.

Say, darling, don't you like for me to talk to you in this way? Do you ever think of me in that way? So you have not put my miniature in my place yet? Are you not going to do it? I am just as big a rascal as ever, am I not? It is my love for you which prompts it all, dearest one. I never think of anyone else in that way and when I used to talk to you of others it was only to laugh at you. A brute beast will lick the dirt from its own young but will only bite those of another. So with me, darling wife. Your parts inspire me with love and excite my desires. Other women would disgust me. Conversations which, before I was married, I would sit and listen to and join in now fill me with the deepest disgust. Will you really send me the measure of your leg right high up?

Well, no paymaster came by the *Alabama* and I am sure you will want money. Captain Sanders of the engineers very kindly volunteered to lend me a check, which he has, and I will get that and send it to you. It is not a large one but it will do for you until I can send you more. You shall have just as much as you want, and I want you to tell me always how much you stand in need of. I would send you a pay account of seventy-five dollars but I owe these men so much that I am anxious to keep by me all you have not use for.

ELIZABETH BARRETT AND ROBERT BROWNING

ELIZABETH BARRETT (1806–61) FIRST MET ROBERT Browning (1812–89) in 1845. Within a year he freed her from her sickroom in Wimpole Street, London, and the prison of her possessive father and eloped with her to Italy. There they formed the nucleus of a literary circle, and a son, Robert "Penn" Browning, was born to them.

Elizabeth Barrett to Robert Browning (September 1846, from her father's house in Wimpole Street)

Dearest take this word, as if it were many. I am so tired – and then it shall be the right word.

Sunday and Friday are impossible. On Saturday I will go to you, if you like – with half done, – nothing done – scarcely. Will you come for me to Hodgson's? or shall I meet you at the station? At what o'clock should I set out, to be there at the hour you mention?

Also, for the boxes, – we cannot carry them out of the house, you know, Wilson and I. They must be sent on Friday evening to the Vauxhall station, "to be taken care of." Will the people keep them carefully? Ought someone to be spoken to beforehand? If we sent them to New Cross, they would not reach you in time.

Hold me my beloved – with your love. It is very hard – But Saturday seems the only day for us. Tell me if you think so indeed.

Your very own *BA*

Robert Browning to Elizabeth Barrett (12 September 1846)

Browning and Barrett had married in secret earlier that day.

You will only expect a few words – what will those be? When the heart is full it may run over, but the real fulness stays within.

You asked me yesterday "if I should repent?" Yes – my own Ba, – I could wish all the past were to do over again, that in it I might somewhat more, – never so little more, conform in the outward homage to the inward feeling. What I have professed... (for I have performed nothing) seems to fall short of what my first love required ever and when I think of *this* moment's love... I could repent, as I say.

Words can never tell you, however, – form them, transform them anyway, – how perfectly dear you are to me – perfectly dear to my heart and soul.

I look back, and in every one point, every word and gesture, *every* letter, every silence – you have been entirely perfect to me – I would not change one word, one look.

My hope and aim are to preserve this love, not to fall from it – for which I trust to God who procured it for me, and doubtlessly can preserve it.

Enough now, my dearest, dearest, own Ba! You have given me the highest, completest proof of love that ever one human being gave another. I am all gratitude – and all pride (under the proper feeling which ascribes pride to the right source) all pride that my life has been so crowned by you.

God bless you prays your very own R.

I will write to-morrow of course. Take every care of *my life* which is in that dearest little hand; try and be composed, my beloved.

Remember to thank Wilson for me.

Elizabeth Barrett to Robert Browning (14 September 1846)

My Own Beloved, if ever you should have reason to complain of me in things voluntary and possible, all other women would have a right to tread me underfoot, I should be so vile and utterly unworthy. There is my answer to what you wrote yesterday of wishing to be better to me ... you! What could be better than lifting me from the ground and carrying me into life and the sunshine? I was yours rather by right than by gift (yet by gift also, my beloved!); for what you have saved and renewed is surely yours. All that I am, I owe you – if I enjoy anything now and henceforth, it is through you. You know this well. Even as *I*, from the beginning, knew that I had no power against you ... or that, if I *had* it was for your sake.

Dearest, in the emotion and confusion of yesterday morning, there was yet room in me for one thought which was not a feeling – for I thought that, of the many, many women who have stood where I stood, and to the same end, not one of them all perhaps, not one perhaps, since that building was a church, has had reasons strong as mine, for an absolute trust and devotion towards the man she married, – not one! And then I both thought and felt, that it was only just, for them ... those women who were less happy, ... to have that affectionate sympathy and support and presence of their nearest relations, parent or sister... which failed to *me*, ... needing it less through being happier!

All my brothers have been here this morning, laughing and talking, and discussing this matter of the leaving town, – and in the room, at the same time, were two or three female friends of ours, from Herefordshire – and I did not dare to cry out against the noise, though my head seemed splitting in two (one-half for each shoulder), I had such a morbid fear of exciting a suspicion. Treppy too being one of them, I promised to go to see her tomorrow and dine in her drawing-room if she would give me, for dinner, some bread and butter. It was like having a sort of fever. And all in the midst, the bells began to ring. "What bells are those?" asked one of the provincials. "Marylebone Church bells," said Henrietta, standing behind my chair.

And now... while I write, having escaped from the great din, and sit here quietly, – comes... who do you think? – Mr Kenyon.

He came with his spectacles, looking as if his eyes reached to their rim all the way round; and one of the first words was, "*When did you see Browning?*" And I think I shall make a pretension to presence of mind henceforward; for, though *certainly* I changed colour and he saw it, I yet answered with a tolerably quick evasion,... "He was here on Friday" – and leapt straight into another subject, and left him gazing fixedly on my face. Dearest, he saw something, but not all. So we talked, talked. He told me that the "Fawn of Sertorius" (which I refused to cut open the other day) was ascribed to Landor and he told me that he meant to leave town again on Wednesday, and would see me once more before then. On rising to go away, he mentioned your name a second time... "When do you see Browning again?" To which I answered that I did not know.

Is not *that* pleasant? The worst is that all these combinations of things make me feel so bewildered that I cannot make the necessary arrangements, as far as the letters go. But I must break from the dream-stupor which falls on me when left to myself a little, and set about what remains to be done.

A house near Watford is thought of now but, as none is concluded on, the removal is not likely to take place in the middle of the week even, perhaps.

I sit in a dream, when left to myself I cannot believe, or understand Oh! but in all this difficult, embarrassing and painful situation. I look over the palms to Troy –I feel happy and exulting to belong to you, past every opposition, out of sight of every will of man – none can put us asunder, now at least I have a right now openly to love you, and to hear other people call it a *duty*, when I do, knowing that if it were a sin, it would be done equally. Ah – I shall not be the first to leave off *that* – see if I shall! May God bless you, ever and ever dearest! Beseech for me the indulgence of your father and mother, and ask your sister to love me. I feel so as if I had slipped down over the wall into somebody's garden – I feel ashamed. To be grateful and affectionate to them all, while I live; is all that I can do, and it is too much a matter of course to need to be promised. Promise it however for your very own Ba whom you made so happy with the dear letter last night. But say in the next how you are – and how your mother is.

I did hate so, to have to take off the ring. You will have to take the trouble of putting it on again, some day.

GUSTAVE FLAUBERT

GUSTAVE FLAUBERT (1821–80) WAS THE AUTHOR OF *Madame Bovary*. Throughout his life he was affected by a nervous disease, leading to fits of morbidity and pessimism.

To Louise Colet (11 August 1846)

The poet Louise Colet was Flaubert's lover between 1846 and 1854.

You could kindle love in a dead man. How can I help loving you? You have a power of seduction such that stones rise up at the sound of your voice. Your letters stir me to my very entrails. Have no fear that I shall forget you! You must know that beings such as you are never forsaken, beings so moved, so moving, so profound. I reproach myself, I could kick myself for having hurt you. Forget everything I said in the letter I wrote on Sunday. I was addressing myself to your virile intelligence, thinking that you would be able to set aside your feelings and understand me without emotion. You saw so many things that were not there at all, you exaggerated everything I said to you. Perhaps you thought I was *posing*, trying to pass myself off as a plebeian Antony. You regard me as a Voltairean and a materialist. Yet God knows if I am one! You also mention my exclusive tastes in literature, which ought to have indicated what kind of lover I am. I try in vain to work out what that means. It baffles me. On the contrary I admire the world with all my heart, and if I am worth anything it is because of this pantheistic faculty and also that *asperity* which wounded your feelings. Come on, let it drop. I was wrong, I was stupid. With you I have only done what I always do with people I love best: I let the cat right out of the bag, and the sour dust that leaks out catches in everyone's throats. How many times, without wishing it, did I reduce my father to tears, a man of such intelligence and finesse. But he understood not one word of my idiom, just like you, just like everyone else. It is my infirmity to have been born speaking a special language to which only I have the key. I am not at all unhappy; I'm not in the least blasé; everyone thinks my character very cheerful and never once do I complain, for I am entirely free of envy and yearning. Go on, I shall torment you no longer; I shall touch you gently as if you were a child I feared to hurt, I shall draw in my spines. With a little goodwill the porcupine doesn't always lash out. You say that I analyse myself too much; personally I don't think I know myself well enough; every day I discover something new within. In myself I travel as in a strange land, even though I have passed that way a thousand times before. You do not give me credit for my frankness (women want to be deceived; they force you to do it to them and, if you resist, they reproach you). You say that that was not how I showed myself at first; but look into your memory. I began by displaying my sores. Remember everything I told you the first time we had dinner together; you even exclaimed: "You condone everything! You have no sense of good and evil!" No, I never told you lies; I loved you instinctively, and I didn't try to please you intentionally. It all happened because it had to happen. Scoff at my fatalism, and then tell me I'm behind the times playing at being Turkish. Fatalism is the Providence of evil; the kind you actually see, the one I believe in.

The tears that I see upon the pages of your letters, tears caused by me, I should like to atone for them with so many cups of blood. I reproach myself; they add to my self-disgust. If I didn't think you liked me, I should loathe myself. Besides, that's always the way it is:

you bring suffering upon those you love, or they bring suffering upon you. How can you possibly reproach me for the phrase: "I wish I had never known you!" I cannot think of anything more affectionate. Shall I tell you what I would consider to be the equivalent? Something I said the day before my sister died, it slipped out and shocked everyone. We were talking about my mother: "If only she could die!" I said. And as they cried shame upon me, I said: "Yes, if she wanted to throw herself out of the window I would open it for her without a second thought." I get the impression that one is not supposed to say such things, they sound strange or heartless. What the hell.do you say when your heart is bursting? Ask yourself if there are many men who would have written that letter that hurt you so much. Few, I believe, would have had the courage and the gratuitous self-abnegation. That letter, my love, is to be torn up, don't think of it again, or read it sometimes when you are feeling strong.

Talking of letters, when you write to me on Sundays post it early; you know the offices close at two o'clock. Yesterday I didn't get one. I was full of vague worries. But both of them arrived today and the little flower as well. Thank you for the idea of the mitten: if only you could send yourself with it. If I could hide you in the drawer of my little cabinet, the one that stands just here by me, I'd certainly keep you under lock and key!

Come on, laugh! I'm feeling cheerful today, I don't know why. The sweetness of your letters this morning has passed into my blood. But you mustn't vent any more cliches upon me, such as: money is what has made me unhappy; or, if I had worked I'd have been better off. As if you only had to be an apothecary's boy, a baker or a wine-merchant to escape being bored in this life. That sort of thing has been said to me all too often by a flock of bourgeois for me to want to hear it on your lips; it spoils them, they were never made for that. But I am grateful that you approve of my literary silence. If it is my task to say something new, when the time comes it will out by itself. How I should like to write great works so as to please you! How I should like to see you quiver at my style! I who have no desire for fame (more naïve than the fox in the fable), I want it because of you, to throw it to you like a bouquet, like another caress, or a soft couch for your spirit to lounge upon and dream of me. You think me handsome; I wish I were handsome; I wish I had long black curly hair hanging down to ivory shoulders, like some Greek youth; I wish I were strong and pure. But when I look at myself in the mirror and I consider that you love me, I do find myself revoltingly commonplace. I have rough hands, knock-knees and a narrow chest. If only I had a voice, if I could sing, ah, how I would make music from those deep breaths that disappear in merely sighing! If you had known me ten years ago, I was fresh, sweet-smelling, I breathed out life and love; these days I sense that my maturity is edging towards decay. Why were you not the first woman in my life? Why was it not in your arms that I felt for the first time the intoxications of the body and the divine spasms that bring us to ecstasy?

I feel regret for all my past; I think I ought to have held myself in reserve, waiting for something, to give it all to you when the day came. But I had no idea that anyone could love me; even now it still seems a thing against nature. Love for me! how peculiar! And, like a wastrel who is out to ruin himself in just one day, I have given away all my riches, great and small. Things unspeakable I have loved with a ferocious passion. I have idolized vile women, sacrificed at every altar and drunk from every barrel. Ah, my moral capital! The silver pieces that I flung out of the window to anyone passing by, and the gold I used up playing ducks and drakes. This comparison, not really a comparison at all but a pure equivalent, will give you a notion of the man I am. When I was living in Paris I used to spend six or seven thousand francs a year and I often went without dinner three times a week. I'm just the same when it comes to feelings: with enough for an army regiment to guzzle themselves on, here I am starving to death. It is in my nature to be needy; though do not think me dejected and worn out. I used to be, but I'm not any more. There was a time when I was unhappy. The reproaches you send me today might have been fair then. I shall write to Phidias, but I'm not sure how to phrase it to convey the idea that he is to summon me to Patis urgently. – What if he is out of town? – Where exactly? – When will he be back? I shall arrive one evening, stay the night and the next day until seven, that's agreed. As from Thursday, address your letters to me like this Monsieur Du Camp, c/o Monsieur Flaubert, because the letters I receive every day from you are supposed to be from him and, once he's here, it would look odd if I kept on getting them just the same. Questions might be asked, and so on. However, if you feel the slightest distaste for this, don't do it, I don't mind; I'm bashful on account of you; I know that I'd blush if I even spoke your name and then it would all come out.

I read your stories, *Saintes et folles*, and nearly all of your poetry. [...] I have reread a hundred times the one called *A une amie*, to you, in other words, the one you recited to me on my bed, with my arms round you, looking into my eyes. You wanted me to send something about us. So, here is a page written about this time two years ago, (it is a piece of a letter to a friend): "from her eyes there flowed a liquid light that made them look bigger, her gaze was fired and motionless. Her naked shoulders (for she wore no lace shawl and her dress seemed loose upon her body), her naked shoulders were silvery pale, smooth and firm as weathered marble. Blue veins were pulsing in her excited flesh. Her heaving breast rose and fell, swelling with a sobbing breath that I breathed down in turn. It lasted for a hundred years. The whole earth had disappeared. I could see only the black centre of her eye which dilated more and more. In that deep silence I could hear only the sound of her breathing.

"I moved closer, I kissed her eyes, they were moist and soft. She looked at me in great astonishment. She said: 'Will you love me? will you really love me?' I let her speak, saying nothing, holding her in my arms and feeling the beating of her heart.

"She pulled away from me. 'I'll come back tonight... let me go... let me go, until tonight!' She vanished.

"At dinner, her foot rested upon mine, and every so often she touched my elbow, looking away the while." How's that?

You want me to teach you Latin? What would be the point? And anyway I'd need to know it myself. You are over-indulgent when you regard me as a man with a profound knowledge of ancient languages. In a few years' time I hope to be able to read them almost fluently. I think it would be difficult, by letter, to achieve anything worthwhile, however we can talk it over. I have no heart for work. I do nothing; I walk up and down my study, I lie on my green leather couch and I think about you. The afternoons in particular seem tediously long. I'm bored with the things of the mind; I'd like to be completely simple so as to love you like a child, or else be a Goethe or a Byron. As soon as I get a letter from Phidias, I shall leave my friend (even though he's coming here especially to see me) and I'll come running. You can see I no longer have a heart, a will of my own, anything. I am a flaccid, sensitive thing, moving at your command. I live dreamily in among the folds of your dress, in the delicate curls of your hair. I have some here. How sweet it smells! If you knew how I think of your dear voice, of your shoulders that smell so good! I meant to do some work, not to write to you until this evening. I couldn't do it. I had to give in.

Farewell now. Upon your lips I leave this great lingering kiss.

Midnight. I have just read your letters again, gazed at everything again. I send you a final kiss for the night. I have just written to Phidias. I think I have managed to convey to him that I want to come to Paris at once. I shall put the letter in the post in Rouen tomorrow, along with this one. I hope to be there in time for this to reach you tomorrow evening.

Farewell, a thousand kisses, never-ending. Before too long, my darling, before too long.

GEORGE SAND

GEORGE SAND WAS THE PEN NAME OF THE NOVELIST Amandine Aurore Lucie Dupin, Baronne Dudevant (1804–76).

To *Gustave Flaubert, 15 March 1873*

Well, my old troubadour, we can hope for you very soon, I was worried about you. I am always worried about you. To tell the truth, I am not happy over your ill tempers, and your *prejudices*. They last too long, and in effect they are like an illness, you recognize it yourself. Now, forget; don't you know how to forget? You live too much in yourself and you get to consider everything in relation to yourself. If you were an egoist, and a conceited person, I would say that it was a normal condition; but with you who are so good and so generous it is an anomaly, an evil that must be combatted. Rest assured that life is badly arranged, painful, irritating for everyone; but do not neglect the immense compensations which it is ungrateful to forget.

That you get angry with this or that person, is of little importance if it is a comfort to you; but that you remain furious, indignant for weeks, months, almost years, is unjust and cruel to those who love you, and who would like to spare you all anxiety and all deception.

You see that I am scolding you; but while embracing you, I shall think only of the joy and the hope of seeing you flourishing again. We are waiting for you with impatience, and we are counting on Turgeneff [to visit] whom we adore also.

I have been suffering a good deal lately with a series of very painful hemorrhages; but they have nor prevented me from amusing myself writing tales and from playing with my *little children*. They are so dear, and my big children are so good to me, that I shall die, I believe, smiling at them. What difference does it make whether one has a hundred thousand enemies if one is loved by two or three good souls? Don't you love me too, and wouldn't you reproach me for thinking that of no account? When I lost Rollinat, didn't you write to me to love the more those who were left? Come, so that I may *overwhelm* you with reproaches; for you are not doing what you told me to do.

We are expecting you, we are preparing a mid-Lent fantasy; try to take part. Laughter is a splendid medicine. We shall give you a costume; they tell me that you were very good as a pastry cook at Pauline's! If you are better, be certain it is because you have gotten out of your rut and have distracted yourself a little. Paris is good for you, you are too much alone yonder in your lovely house. Come and work, at our house; how perfectly easy to send on a box of books!

CHARLES DICKENS

CHARLES DICKENS (1812–70), ENGLISH AUTHOR.

~❧~

To John Forster (Autumn 1846)

After finding literary success, Dickens became a regular traveller to Europe and America.

And now, sir, I will describe, modestly, tamely, literally, the visit to the small select circle which I promised should make your hair stand on end. In our hotel were a Mother and a Daughter, who came to the Peschiere shortly before we left it, and who have a deep admiration for your humble servant the inimitable B. They are both very clever. Daughter, extremely well-informed in languages living and dead, books, and gossip; very pretty; with two little children, and not yet five and twenty. Mother, plump, fresh, and rosy; matronly, but full of spirits and good looks. Nothing would serve them but we *must* dine with them; and accordingly, on Friday at six, we went down to their room. I knew them to be rather odd. For instance, I have known the Mother, *full dressed*, walk alone through the streets of Genoa, the squalid Italian bye streets, to the Governor's soirée; and announce herself at the palace of state, by knocking at the door. I have also met the Daughter full dressed, without any cap or bonnet, walking a mile to the opera, with all sorts of jingling jewels about her, beside a sedan chair in which sat enthroned her mama. Consequently, I was not surprised at such little sparkles in the conversation (from the lady) as "Oh God what a sermon we had here, last Sunday!" "And did you ever read such infernal trash as Mrs Gore's?" – and the like. Still, but for Kate and Georgy (who were decidedly in the way, as we agreed afterwards), I should have thought it all very funny; and, as it was, I threw the ball back again, was mighty free and easy, made some rather broad jokes, and was highly applauded. "You smoke, don't you?" said the young lady, in a pause of this kind of conversation. "Yes," I said, "I generally take a cigar after dinner when I am alone." "I'll give you a good 'un," said she, "when we go up-stairs." Well, sir, in due course we went up-stairs, and there we were joined by an American lady residing in the same hotel, who looked like what we call in old England "a regular Bunter" – fluffy face (rouged); considerable development of figure; one groggy eye; blue satin dress made low with short sleeves, and shoes of the same. Also a daughter; face likewise fluffy; figure likewise developed; dress likewise low, with short sleeves, and shoes of the same; and one eye not yet actually groggy, but going to be. American lady married at sixteen; American daughter sixteen now, often mistaken for sisters, &c. &c. &c. When that was over, the younger of our entertainers brought out a cigar box, and gave me a cigar, made of negrohead she said, which would quell an elephant in six whiffs. The box was full of cigarettes – good large ones, made of pretty strong tobacco; I always smoke them here, and used to smoke them at Genoa, and I knew them well. When I lighted my cigar, Daughter lighted hers, at mine; leaned against the mantelpiece, in conversation with me; put out her stomach, folded her arms, and with her pretty face cocked up sideways and her cigarette smoking away like a Manchester cotton mill, laughed, and talked, and smoked, in the most gentlemanly manner I ever beheld. Mother immediately lighted her cigar; American lady immediately lighted hers; and in five minutes the room was a cloud of smoke, with us four in the centre pulling away bravely, while American lady related stories of her "Hookah" up-stairs, and described different kinds of pipes. But even this was not all. For presently two Frenchmen came in, with whom, and the American lady, Daughter sat down to whist. The Frenchmen smoked of course (they were really modest gentlemen and seemed dismayed) and Daughter played for the next hour or two with a cigar continually in her mouth – never out of it. She certainly smoked six or eight. Mother gave in soon – I think she only did it out of vanity. American lady had been smoking all the morning. I took no more; and Daughter and the Frenchmen had it all to themselves.

Conceive this in a great hotel, with only their own servants, but half a dozen waiters coming constantly in and out! I showed no atom of surprise, but I never was so surprised, so ridiculously taken aback, in my life; for in all my experience of 'ladies' of one kind and another, I never saw a woman – not a basket woman or a gypsy – smoke before!

❦

To Mrs Winter (10 February 1855)

Maria Winter (née Beadnell) had been Dickens's first love. After a renewed correspondence in 1855, Dickens and Maria Winter met again; to his horror he found that her self-description of herself as having become "toothless, fat, old and ugly" was correct.

My dear Mrs Winter, –

I constantly receive hundreds of letters in great varieties of writing, all perfectly strange to me, and (as you may suppose) have no particular interest in the faces of such general epistles. As I was reading by my fire last night, a handful of notes was laid down on my table. I looked them over, and recognising the writing of no private friend, let them lie there and went back to my book. But I found my mind curiously disturbed, and wandering away through so many years to such early times of my life, that I was quite perplexed to account for it. There was nothing in what I had been reading, orimmediately thinking about, to awaken such a train of thought, and at last it came into my head that it must have been suggested by something in the look of one of those letters. So I turned them over again – and suddenly the remembrance of your hand came upon me with an influence that I cannot express to you. Three or four and twenty years vanished like a dream, and I opened it with the touch of my young friend David Copperfield when he was in love.

There was something so busy and so pleasant in your letter – so true and cheerful and frank and affectionate that I read on with perfect delight until I came to your mention of your two little girls. In the unsettled state of my thoughts, the existence of these dear children appeared such a prodigious phenomenon, that I was inclined to suspect myself of being out of my mind, until it occurred to me, that perhaps I had nine children of my own! Then the three or four and twenty years began to rearrange themselves in a long procession between me and the changeless Past, and I could not help considering what strange stuff all our little stories are made of.

Believe me, you cannot more tenderly remember our old days and our old friends than I do. I hardly ever go into the City but I walk up an odd little court at the back of the Mansion House and come out by the corner of Lombard Street. Hundreds of times as I have passed the church there – on my way to and from the Sea, the Continent, and where not – I invariably associate it with somebody (God knows who) having told me that poor Anne* was buried there. If you would like to examine me in the name of a good-looking Cornish servant you used to have (I suppose she has twenty-nine great grandchildren now, and walks with a stick), you will find my knowledge on the point, correct, though it was a monstrous name too. I forget nothing of those times. They are just as still and plain and clear as if I had never been in a crowd since, and had never seen or heard my own name out of my own house. What should I be worth, or what would labour and success be worth, if it were otherwise!

Your letter is more touching to me from its good and gentle associations with the state of Spring in which I was either much more wise or much more foolish than I am now – I never know which to think it—than I could tell you if I tried for a week. I will not try at all. I heartily respond to it, and shall be charmed to have a long talk with you, and most cordially glad to see you after all this length of time. I am going to Paris to-morrow morning, but I propose being back within a fortnight. When I return, Mrs Dickens will come to you, to arrange a day for our seeing you and Mr Winter (to whom I beg to be remembered) quietly to dinner. We will have no intruder or foreign creature on any pretence whatever, in order that we may set in without any restraint for a tremendous gossip.

*Maria Winter's sister.

Mary Anne Leigh we saw at Broadstairs about fifty years ago. Mrs Dickens and her sister, who read all the marriages in the papers shrieked to me when the announcement of hers appeared, what did I think of *that*? I calmly replied that I thought it was time. I should have been more excited if I had known of the old gentleman with seven thousand a year, uncountable grown-up children, and no English grammar.

My mother has a strong objection to being considered in the least old, and usually appears here on Christmas Day in a juvenile cap which takes an immense time in the putting on. The Fates seem to have made up their minds that I shall never see your Father when he comes this way. David Lloyd is altogether an imposter – not having in the least changed (that I could make out when I saw him at the London Tavern) since what I suppose to have been the year 1770, when I found you three on Cornhill, with your poor mother, going to St Mary Axe to order mysterious dresses – which afterwards turned out to be wedding garments. That was in the remote period when you all wore green cloaks, cut (in my remembrance) very round, and which I am resolved to believe were made of Merino. I escorted you with native gallantry to the Dress Maker's door, and your mother, seized with an apprehension – groundless upon my honor – that I might come in, said emphatically: "And now, Mr Dickin" – which she always used to call me— "We'll wish *you* good morning."

When I was writing the word Paris just now, I remembered that my existence was once entirely uprooted and my whole Being blighted by the Angel of my soul being sent there to finish her education! If I can discharge any little commission for you, or bring home anything for the darlings, whom I cannot yet believe to be anything but a delusion of yours, pray employ me. I shall be at the Hotel Meurice – locked up when within, as my only defence against my country and the United States – but a most punctual and reliable functionary, if you will give me any employment.

My Dear Mrs Winter, I have been much moved by your letter; and the pleasure it has given me has some little sorrowful ingredient in it. In the strife and struggle of this great world where most of us lose each other so strangely, it is impossible to be spoken to out of the old times without a softened emotion. You so belong to the days when the qualities that have done me most good since, were growing in my boyish heart that I cannot end my answer to you lightly. The associations my memory has with you made your letter more – I want a word – invest it with a more immediate address to me than such a letter could have from anybody else. Mr Winter will not mind that. We are all sailing away to the sea, and have a pleasure in thinking of the river we are upon, when it was very narrow and little. – Faithfully your friend.

FREDERICK DOUGLASS

BORN INTO SLAVERY, FREDERICK DOUGLASS (1817–95) escaped bondage to become a self-taught writer. His *Narrative of the Life of Frederick Douglass* introduced many Americans to the agonies of the slave system. A lecture tour of Britain raised £150, enough to buy his freedom.

❧

To Captain Thomas Auld (8 September 1848)

Auld was Douglass' former master. The letter was published openly in the North Star.

Sir –

The long and intimate, though by no means friendly, relation which unhappily subsisted between you and myself, leads me to hope that you will easily account for the great liberty which I now take in address you in this open and public manner. The same fact may possibly remove any disagreeable surprise which you may experience on again finding your name coupled with mine, in any other way than in an advertisement, accurately describing my person, and offering a large sum for my arrest. In thus dragging you again before the public, I am aware that I shall subject myself to no inconsiderable amount of censure. I shall probably be charged with an unwarrantable, if not a wanton and reckless disregard of the rights and properties of private life. There are those north as well as south who entertain a much higher respect for rights which are merely conventional, than they do for rights which are personal and essential. Not a few there are in our country, who, while they have no scruples against robbing the laborer of the hard earned results of his patient industry, will be shocked by the extremely indelicate manner of bringing your name before the public. Believing this to be the case, and wishing to meet every reasonable or plausible objection to my conduct, I will frankly state the ground upon which I justify myself in this instance, as well as on former occasions when I have thought proper to mention your name in public. All will agree that a man guilt of theft, robbery, or murder, has forfeited the right to concealment and private life; that the community have a right to subject such persons to the most complete exposure. However much they may desire retirement, and aim to conceal themselves and their movements from the popular gaze, the public have a right to ferret them out, and bring their conduct before the proper tribunals of the country for investigation. Sir, you will undoubtedly make the proper application of these generally admitted principles, and will easily see the light in which you are regarded by me; I will not therefore manifest ill temper, by calling you hard names. I know you to be a man of some intelligence, and can readily determine the precise estimate which I entertain of your character. I may therefore indulge in language which may seem to others indirect and ambiguous, and yet be quite well understood by yourself.

I have selected this day on which to address you, because it is the anniversary of my emancipation; and knowing no better way, I am led to this as the best mode of celebrating that truly important event. Just ten years ago this beautiful September morning, yon bright sun beheld me a slave – a poor degraded chattel – trembling at the sound of your voice, lamenting that I was a man, and wishing myself a brute. The hopes which I had treasured up for weeks of a safe and successful escape from your grasp, were powerfully confronted at this last hour by dark clouds of doubt and fear, making my person shake and my bosom to heave with the heavy contest between hope and fear. I have no words to describe to you the deep agony of soul which I experienced on that never-to-be-forgotten morning – for I left by daylight. I was making a leap in the dark. The probabilities, so far as I could by reason determine them, were stoutly against the undertaking. The preliminaries and precautions I had adopted previously, all worked badly. I was like one going to war without weapons – ten chances of defeat to one of victory. One in whom I had confided, and one who had promised me assistance, appalled by fear at the trial hour, deserted me, thus leaving the responsibility of success or failure solely with myself. You, sir, can never know my feelings. As I look back to them, I can scarcely realize that I have passed through a scene so trying. Trying, however, as they were, and gloomy as was the prospect, thanks be to the Most High, who is ever the God of the oppressed, at the moment which was to determine my whole earthly career, His grace was sufficient; my mind was made up. I embraced the golden opportunity, took the morning tide at the flood, and a free man, young, active, and strong is the result.

I have often thought I should like to explain to you the grounds upon which I have justified myself in running away from you. I am almost ashamed to do so now, for by this time you may have discovered them yourself. I will, however, glance at them. When yet but a child about six years old, I imbibed the determination to run away. The very first mental effort that I now remember on my part, was an attempt to solve the mystery – why am I a slave? and with this question my youthful mind was troubled for many days, pressing upon me more heavily at times than others. When I saw the slave-driver whip a slave-woman, cut the blood out of her neck, and heard her piteous cries, I went away into the corner of the fence, wept and pondered over the mystery. I had, through some medium, I know not what, got some idea of God, the Creator of all mankind, the black and the white, and that he had made the blacks to serve the whites as slaves. How he could do this and be *good*, I could not tell. I was not satisfied with this theory, which made God responsible for slavery, for it pained me greatly, and I have wept over it long and often. At one time, your first wife, Mrs Lucretia, heard me singing and saw me shedding tears, and asked of me the matter, but I was afraid to tell her. I was puzzled with this question, till one night while sitting in the kitchen, I heard some of the old slaves talking of their parents having been stolen from Africa by white men, and were sold here as slaves. The whole mystery was solved at once. Very soon after this, my Aunt Jinny and Uncle Noah ran away, and the great noise made about it by your father-in-law, made me for the first time acquainted with the fact, that there were free states as well as slave states. From that time, I resolved that I would some day run away. The morality of the act I dispose of as follows: I am myself; you are yourself; we are two distinct persons, equal persons. What you are, I am. You are a man, and so am I. God created both, and made us separate beings. I am not by nature bond to you, or you to me. Nature does not make your existence depend upon me, or mine to depend upon yours. I cannot walk upon your legs, or you upon mine. I cannot breathe for you, or you for me; I must breathe for myself, and you for yourself. We are distinct persons, and are each equally provided with faculties necessary to our individual existence. In leaving you, I took nothing but what belonged to me, and in no way lessened your means for obtaining an honest living. Your faculties remained yours, and mine became useful to their rightful owner. I therefore see no wrong in any part of the transaction. It is true, I went off secretly; but that was more your fault than mine. Had I let you into the secret, you would have defeated the enterprise entirely; but for this, I should have been really glad to have made you acquainted with my intentions to leave.

You may perhaps want to know how I like my present condition. I am free to say, I greatly prefer it to that which I occupied in Maryland. I am, however, by no means prejudiced against the state as such. Its geography, climate, fertility, and products, are such as to make it a very desirable abode for any man; and but for the existence of slavery there, it is not impossible that I might again take up my abode in that state. It is not that I love Maryland less, but freedom more. You will be surprised to learn that people at the north labor under the strange delusion that if the slaves were emancipated at the south, they would flock to the north. So far from this being the case, in that event, you would see many old and familiar faces back again to the south. The fact is, there are few here who would not return to the south in the event of emancipation. We want to live in the land of our birth, and to lay our bones by the side of our fathers; and nothing short of an intense love of personal freedom keeps us from the south. For the sake of this most of us would live on a crust of bread and a cup of cold water.

Since I left you, I have had a rich experience. I have occupied stations which I never dreamed of when a slave. Three out of the ten years since I left you, I spent as a common laborer on the wharves of New Bedford, Massachusetts. It was there I earned my first free dollar. It was mine. I could spend it as I pleased. I could buy hams or herring with it, without asking any odds of anybody. That was a precious dollar to me. You remember when I used to make seven or eight, or even nine dollars a week in Baltimore, you would take every cent of it from me every Saturday night, saying that I belonged to you, and my earnings also. I never liked this conduct on your part – to say the best, I thought it a little mean. I would not have served you so. But let that pass. I was a little awkward about counting money in New England fashion when I first landed in New Bedford. I came near betraying myself several times. I caught myself saying phip, for fourpence; and at one time a man actually charged me with being a runaway, whereupon I was silly enough to become one by running away from him, for I was greatly afraid he might adopt measures to get me again into slavery, a condition I then dreaded more than death.

I soon learned, however, to count money, as well as to make it, and got on swimmingly. I married soon after leaving you; in fact, I was engaged to be married before I left you; and instead of finding my companion a burden, she was truly a helpmate. She went to live at service, and I to work on the wharf, and though we toiled hard the first winter, we never lived more happily. After remaining in New Bedford for three years, I met with William Lloyd Garrison, a person of whom you have *possibly* heard, as he is pretty generally known among slaveholders. He put it into my head that I might make myself serviceable to the cause of the slave, by devoting a portion of my time to telling my own sorrows, and those of other slaves, which had come under my observation. This was the commencement of a higher state of existence than any to which I had ever aspired. I was thrown into society the most pure, enlightened, and benevolent, that the country affords. Among these I have never forgotten you, but have invariably made you the topic of conversation – thus giving you all the notoriety I could do. I need not tell you that the opinion formed of you in these circles is far from being favorable. They have little respect for your honesty, and less for your religion.

But I was going on to relate to you something of my interesting experience. I had not long enjoyed the excellent society to which I have referred, before the light of its excellence exerted a beneficial influence on my mind and heart. Much of my early dislike of white persons was removed, and their manners, habits, and customs, so entirely unlike what I had been used to in the kitchen-quarters on the plantations of the south, fairly charmed me, and gave me a strong disrelish for the coarse and degrading customs of my former condition. I therefore made an effort so to improve my mind and deportment, as to be somewhat fitted to the station to which I seemed almost providentially called. The transition from degradation to respectability was indeed great, and to get from one to the other without carrying some marks of one's former condition, is truly a difficult matter. I would not have you think that I am now entirely clear of all plantation peculiarities, but my friends here, while they entertained the strongest dislike of them, regard me with that charity to which my past life somewhat entitles me, so that my condition in this respect is exceedingly pleasant. So far as my domestic affairs are concerned, I can boast of as comfortable a dwelling as your own. I have an industrious and neat companion, and four dear children – the oldest a girl of nine years, and three fine boys, the oldest eight, the next six, and the youngest four years old. The three oldest are now going regularly to school – two can read and write, and the other can spell, with tolerable correctness, words of two syllables. Dear fellows! they are all in comfortable beds. and are sound asleep, perfectly secure under my own roof. There are no slaveholders here to rend my heart by snatching them from my arms, or blast a mother's dearest hopes by tearing them from her bosom. These dear children are ours – not to work up into rice, sugar, and tobacco, but to watch over, regard, and protect, and to rear them to the paths of wisdom and virtue, and, as far as we can, to make them useful to the world and to themselves. Oh! sir, a slaveholder never appears to me so completely an agent of hell as when I think of and look upon my dear children. It is then that my feelings rise above my control. I meant to have said more with respect to my own prosperity and happiness, but thoughts and feelings which this recital has quickened, unfits me to proceed further in that direction. The grim horrors of slavery rise in all their ghastly terror before me; the wails of millions pierce my heart and chill my blood. I remember the chain, the gag, the bloody whip; the death-like gloom overshadowing the broken spirit of the fettered bondman; the appalling liability of his being torn away from wife and children, and sold like a beast in the market. Say not that this is a picture of fancy. You well know that I wear stripes on my back, inflicted by your direction; and that you, while we were brothers in the same church, caused this right hand, with which I am now penning this letter, to be closely tied to my left, and my person dragged at the pistol's mouth, fifteen miles, from the Bay side to Easton, to be sold like a beast in the market, for the alleged crime of intending to escape from your possession. All this, and more, you remember, and know to be perfectly true, not only of yourself, but of nearly all of the slaveholders around you.

At this moment, you are probably the guilty holder of at least three of my own dear sisters, and my only brother, in bondage. These you regard as your property. They are recorded on your ledger. or perhaps have been sold to human flesh-mongers, with a view to filling your own ever-hungry purse. Sir, I desire to know how and where these dear sisters are. Have you sold them? or are they still in your possession? What has become of them? are they living or dead? And my dear old grandmother, whom you turned out like an old horse to die in the woods – is she still alive? Write and let me know all about them. If my grandmother be still alive, she is of no service to you, for by this time she must be nearly eighty years old – too old to be cared for by one to whom she has ceased to be of service; send her to me at Rochester, or bring her to Philadelphia, and it shall be the crowning happiness of my life to take care of her in her old age. Oh! she was to me a mother and a father, so far as hard toil for my comfort could make her such. Send me my grandmother! that I may watch over and take care of her in her old age. And my sisters – let me know all about them. I would write to them, and learn all I want to know of them, without disturbing you in any way, but that, through your unrighteous conduct, they have been entirely deprived of the power to read and write. You have kept them in utter ignorance, and have therefore robbed them of the sweet enjoyments of writing or receiving letters from absent friends and relatives. Your wickedness and cruelty, committed in this respect on your fellow-creatures, are greater than all the stripes you have laid upon my back or theirs. It is an outrage upon the soul, a war upon the immortal spirit, and one for which you must give account at the bar of our common Father and Creator.

The responsibility which you have assumed in this regard is truly awful, and how you could stagger under it these many years is marvelous. Your mind must have become darkened, your heart hardened, your conscience seared and petrified, or you would have long since thrown off the accursed load, and sought relief at the hands of a sin-forgiving God. How, let me ask, would you look upon me, were I, some dark night, in company with a band of hardened villains, to enter the precincts of your elegant dwelling, and seize the person of your own lovely daughter, Amanda, and carry her off from your family, friends, and all the loved ones of her youth – make her my slave – compel her to work, and I take her wages – place her name on my ledger as property – disregard her personal rights – fetter the powers of her immortal soul by denying her the right and privilege of learning to read and writ – feed her coarsely – clothe her scantily, and whip her on the naked back occasionally; more, and still more horrible, leave her unprotected – a degraded victim to the brutal lust of fiendish overseers, who would pollute, blight, and blast her fair soul – rob her of all dignity – destroy her virtue, and annihilate in her person all the graces that adorn the character of virtuous womanhood? I ask, how would you regard me, if such were my conduct? Oh! the vocabulary of the damned would not afford a word sufficiently infernal to express your idea of my God-provoking wickedness. Yet, sir, your treatment of my beloved sisters is in all essential points precisely like the case I have now supposed. Damning as would be such a deed on my part, it would be no more so than that which you have committed against me and my sisters.

I will now bring this letter to a close; you shall hear from me again unless you let me hear from you. I intend to make use of you as a weapon with which to assail the system of slavery – as a means of concentrating public attention on the system, and deepening the horror of trafficking in the souls and bodies of men. I shall make use of you as a means of exposing the character of the American church and clergy – and as a means of bringing this guilty nation, with yourself, to repentance. In doing this, I entertain no malice toward you personally. There is no roof under which you would be more safe than mine, and there is nothing in my house which you might need for your comfort, which I would not readily grant. Indeed, I should esteem it a privilege to set you an example as to how mankind ought to treat each other.

> I am your fellow-man, but not your slave.
> *Frederick Douglass*

JOHN CLARE

THE ENGLISH PASTORAL POET JOHN CLARE (1793–1864) spent his life in poverty, and eventually went insane. He was committed to Northampton Asylum in 1837, where he died.

To Patty Clare (c. 1849)

My dear Wife

I have wrote some few times to enquire about yourself & the Family & thought about yourself & them a thousand othe[r] things that I use to think of the childern – Freddy when I led him by the hand in his childhood – I see him now in his little pink frock – sealskin cap – & gold band – with his little face as round as a apple & as red as a rose – & now a stout Man both strangers to each other the father a prisoner under a bad government so bad in fact that its no government at all but prison discipline where every body is forced to act contrary to their own wishes "the mother against the daughter in law & the daughter against the mother in law" "the father against the son & the son against the Father" – in fact I am in Prison because I wont leave my family & tell a falsehood – this is the English Bastile a government Prison where harmless people are trapped & tortured till they die – English priestcraft & english bondage more severe then the slavery of Egypt & Africa while the son is tyed up in his manhood from all the best thoughts of his childhood bye lying & falsehood – not dareing to show love or remembrance for Home or home affections living in the world as a prison estranged from all his friends still Truth is the best companion for it levels all distinctions in pretentions Truth wether it enters the Ring or the Hall of Justice shows a plain Man that is not to be scared at shadows or big words full of fury & meaning nothing when done & said with them truth is truth & the rights of man – age of reason & common sense are sentences full of meaning & the best comment of its truth is themselves – an honest man makes priestcraft an odious lyar & coward & a filthy disgrace to Christianity – that coward I hate & detest – the Revelations has a placard in capitals about "The Whore of Babylon & the mother of Harlots" does it mean Priestcraft I think it must – this rubbish of cant must soon die – like all other – I began a letter & ended a Sermon – & the paper too

I am dear Wife yours ever *John Clare*

To Mary Collingwood (1850)

The letter was written in code; a translation is given beneath.

M Drst Mr Cllngwd

  M nrl wrn t & wnt thr frm Nbd wll wn M r hv m t n prc & wht hv dn D knw wht r n m Dbt – kss's fr tn yrs & lngr stll & lngr thn tht whn ppl mk sch mstks s t cll m Gds bstrd & whrs p m b shttng m p frm Gds ppl t f th w f cmmn snse & thn tk m hd ff bcs th cnt fnd m t t hrds hrd

  Drst Mr r fthfll r d thnk f m knw wht w sd tgth – ldd vst m n hll sm tm bck bt dnt cm hr gn fr t s ntrs bd plc wrs nd wrs nd w r ll trnd Frnchmn flsh ppl tll m hv gt n hm n this wrld nd s dnt believe n th thr nrt t mk mslf hvn wth m drst Mr nd sbscrb mslf rs fr vr & vr

Jhn Clr

My Dearest Mary Collingwood

  I am nearly worn out & want to hear from you Nobody will own me or have me at any price & what have I done Do you know what you are in my Debt – kisses for ten years & longer still & longer than that when people make such mistakes as to call me Gods bastard & whores pay me by shutting me up from Gods people out of the way of common sense & then take my head because they cant find me ii out herods herod

  Dearest Mary are you faithfull or do you think of me you know what we said together – you did visit me in hell some time back but dont come here again for it is a notorious bad place worse and worse and we are all turned Frenchmen foolish people tell me I have got no home in this world and as I dont believe in the other [? any rate] to make myself heaven with my dearest Mary and subscribe myself yours for ever & ever

John Clare

To James Hipkins (8 March 1860)

Dear Sir

I am in a Madhouse & quite forget your Name or who you are you must excuse me for I have nothing to commu[n]incate or tell of & why I am shut up I don't know I have nothing to say so I conclude

yours respectfully *John Clare*

Mr J Hipkins

FYODOR DOSTOYEVSKY

IN 1849 DOSTOYEVSKY (1821–81) WAS ARRESTED BY THE Czar's police for participation in the socialist "Petrashevsky circle" and sentenced to death. In this letter he describes to his brother his reprieve, given almost at the moment of execution. He was afterwards confined in a convict prison at Omsk, an experience that became the basis for his novel *The House of the Dead* (1860). His other novels include *Crime and Punishment* (1866) and *The Brothers Karamazov* (1880).

To his brother (22 December 1849), from the Peter and Paul Fortress, St Petersburg

Brother, my precious friend! all is settled! I am sentenced to four years' hard labour in the fortress (I believe, of Orenburg), and after that to serve as a private. To-day, the 22nd of December, we were taken to the Semionov Drill Ground. There the sentence of death was read to all of us, we were told to kiss the Cross, our swords were broken over our heads, and our last toilet was made (white shirts). Then three were tied to the pillar for execution. I was the sixth. Three at a time were called out; consequently, I was in the second batch and no more than a minute was left me to live.

I remembered you, brother, and all yours; during the last minute you, you alone, were in my mind, only then I realized how I love you, dear brother mine! I also managed to embrace Plescheyev and Durov who stood close to me, and to say good-bye to them. Finally the retreat was sounded, and those tied to the pillar were led back, and it was announced to us that His Imperial Majesty granted us our lives. Then followed the present sentences. Palm alone has been pardoned, and returns with his old rank to the army.

I was just told, dear brother, that to-day or to-morrow we are to be sent off. I asked to see you. But I was told that this was impossible; I may only write you this letter: make haste and give me a reply as soon as you can.

I am afraid that you may somehow have got to know of our death sentence. From the windows of the prison van, when we were taken to the Semionov Drill Ground, I saw a multitude of people; perhaps the news reached you, and you suffered for me. Now you will be easier on my account.

Brother! I have not become down-hearted or low-spirited. Life is everywhere life, life in ourselves, not in what is outside us. There will be people near me, and to be a *man* among people and remain a man for ever, not to be down-hearted nor to fall in whatever misfortunes may befall me – this is life; this is the task of life. I have realized this. This idea has entered into my flesh and into my blood.

Yes, it's true. The head which was creating, living with the highest life of art, which had realized and grown used to the highest needs of the spirit, that head has already been cut off from my shoulders. There remain the memory and the images created but not yet incarnated by me. They will lacerate me, it is true! But there remains in me my heart and the same flesh and blood which can also love, and suffer, and desire, and remember, and this, after all, is life. *On voit le soleil*! Now, good-bye, brother! Don't grieve for me!

Now about material things: my books (I have the Bible still) and several sheets of my manuscript, the rough plan of the play and the novel (and the finished story A *Child's Tale*) have been taken away from me, and in all probability will be got by you. I also leave my overcoat and old clothes, if you send to fetch them. Now, brother, I may perhaps have to march a long distance. Money is needed. My dear brother, when you receive this letter, and if there is any possibility of getting some money, send it to me at once. Money I need now more than air (for one particular purpose). Send me also a few lines. Then if the money from Moscow comes – remember me and do not desert me. Well, that is all! I have debts, but what can I do?...

Kiss your wife and children. Remind them of me continually; see that they do not forget me. Perhaps we shall yet meet some time! Brother, take care of yourself and of your family, live quietly and carefully. Think of the future of your children...

Live positively. There has never yet been working in me such a healthy abundance of spiritual life as now. But will my body endure? I do not know. I am going away sick. I suffer from scrofula. But never mind! Brother, I have already gone through so much in life that now hardly anything can frighten me. Let come what may!

At the first opportunity I shall let you know about myself. Give the Maikovs my farewell and last greetings. Tell them that I thank them all for their constant interest in my fate. Say a few words for me, as warm as possible, as your heart only prompt you, to Eugenia Petrovna. I wish her much happiness and shall ever remember her with grateful respect. Press the hands of Nikolay Apollonovich, and Apollon Maikov, and also of all the others. Find Yanovsky. Press his hand, thank him. Finally, press the hands of all who have not forgotten me. And those who have forgotten me – remember me to them also. Kiss our brother Kolya. Write a letter to our brother Andrey and let him know about me. Write also to Uncle and Aunt. This I ask you in my own name, and greet them for me. Write to our sisters: I wish them happiness.

And maybe, we shall meet again some time, brother! Take care of yourself, go on living, for the love of God, until we meet. Perhaps some time we shall embrace each other and recall our youth, our golden time that was, our youth and our hopes, which at this very instant I am tearing out from my heart with my blood, to bury them.

Can it indeed be that I shall never take a pen into my hands? I think that after the four years there may be a possibility. I shall send you everything that I may write, if I write anything, my God! How many imaginations, lived through by me, created by me anew, will perish, will be extinguished in my brain or will be spilt as poison in my blood! Yes, if I am not allowed to write, I shall perish. Better fifteen years of prison with a pen in my hands!

Write to me more often, write more details, more, more facts. In every letter write about all kinds of family details, of trifles, don't forget. This will give me hope and life. If you knew how your letters revived me here in the fortress! These last two months and a half, when it was forbidden to write or receive a letter, have been very hard on me. I was ill. The fact that you did not send me money now and then worried me on your account; it meant you yourself were in great need! Kiss the children once again; their lovely little faces do not leave my mind. Ah, that they may be happy! Be happy yourself too, brother, be happy!

But do not grieve, for the love of God, do not grieve for me! Do believe that I am not down-hearted, do remember that hope has not deserted me. In four years there will be a mitigation of my fate. I shall be a private soldier – no longer a prisoner, and remember that some time I shall embrace you. I was to-day in the grip of death for three quarters of an hour; I have lived it through with that idea; I was at the last instant and now I live again!

If anyone has bad memories of me, if I have quarrelled with anyone, if I have created in anyone an unpleasant impression – tell them they should forget it, if you manage to meet them. There is no gall or spite in my soul; I should dearly love to embrace any one of my former friends at this moment. It is a comfort, I experienced it to-day when saying good-bye to my dear ones before death. I thought at that moment that the news of the execution would kill you. But now be easy, I am still alive and shall live in the future with the thought that some time I shall embrace you. Only this is now in my mind.

What are you doing? What have you been thinking to-day? Do

you know about us? How cold it was to-day!

Ah, if only my letter reaches you soon! Otherwise I shall be for four months without news of you. I saw the envelopes in which you sent money during the last two months; the address was written in your hand, and I was glad that you were well.

When I look back at the past and think how much time has been wasted in vain, how much time was lost in delusions, in errors, in idleness, in ignorance of how to live, how I did not value time, how often I sinned against my heart and spirit – my heart bleeds. Life is a gift, life is happiness, each minute might have been an age of happiness. *Si jeunesse savait!* Now, changing my life, I am being reborn into a new form. Brother! I swear to you that I shall not lose hope and shall preserve my spirit and heart in purity. I shall be reborn to a better thing. That is my whole hope, my whole comfort!

The life in prison has already sufficiently killed in me the demands of the flesh which were not wholly pure; I took little heed of myself before. Now privations are nothing to me, and, therefore, do not fear that any material hardship will kill me. This cannot be! Ah! To have health!

Good-bye, good-bye, my brother! When shall I write you again? You will receive from me as detailed an account as possible of my journey. If I can only preserve my health, then everything will be right!

Well, good-bye, good-bye, brother! I embrace you closely, I kiss you closely. Remember me without pain in your heart. Do not grieve, I pray you, do not grieve for me! In the next letter I shall tell you of how I go on. Remember then what I have told you: plan out your life, do not waste it, arrange your destiny, think of your children. Oh, to see you, to see you! Good-bye! Now I tear myself away from everything that was dear; it is painful to leave it! It is painful to break oneself in two, to cut the heart in two. Good-bye! Good-bye! But I shall see you, I am convinced – I hope; do not change, love me, do not let your memory grow cold, and the thought of your love will be the best part of my life. Good-bye, good-bye, once more! Good-bye to all! Your brother

Fiodor Dostoevsky

22 Dec. 1849

At my arrest several books were taken away from me. Only two of them were prohibited books. Won't you get the rest for yourself? But there is this request: one of the books was *The Work of Valerian Maikov*: his critical essays – Eugenia Petrovna's copy. It was her treasure, and she lent it to me. At my arrest I asked the police officer to return that book to her, and gave him the address. I do not know if he returned it to her. Make inquiries! I do not want to take this memory away from her. Good-bye, good-bye, once more! – Your

F. Dostoevsky

[*In the margins*]

I do not know if I shall have to march or go on horses. I believe I shall go on horses. Perhaps!

Once again press Emily Fiodorova's hand, kiss the little ones. Remember me to Krayevsky: perhaps...

Write me more particularly about your arrest, confinement, and liberation.

HARRIET BEECHER STOWE

HARRIET BEECHER STOWE (1811–96) WAS THE AUTHOR of *Uncle Tom's Cabin*, published in 1852.

To Mrs George Beecher (December 1850)

Mrs Beecher was her sister-in-law.

My dear Sister,

Is it really true that snow is on the ground and Christmas coming, and I have not written unto thee, most dear sister? No, I don't believe it! I haven't been so naughty – it's all a mistake – yes, written

I must have – and written I have, too – in the night-watches as I lay on my bed – such beautiful letters – I wish you had only received them; but by day it has been hurry, hurry, hurry, and drive, drive, drive! or else the calm of a sick-room, ever since last spring.

I put off writing when your letter first came, because I meant to write you a long letter – a full and complete one; and so days slid by, – and became weeks, – and my little Charley came ... etc. and etc.!!! Sarah, when I look back, I wonder at myself, not that I forget any one thing that I should remember, but that I have remembered anything. From the time that I left Cincinnati with my children to come forth to a country that I knew not of almost to the present time, it has seemed as if I could scarcely breathe, I was so pressed with care. My head dizzy with the whirl of railroads and steamboats; then ten days' sojourn in Boston, and a constant toil and hurry in buying my furniture and equipments; and then landing in Brunswick in the midst of a drizzly, inexorable north-east storm, and beginning the work of getting in order a deserted, dreary, damp old house. All day long running from one thing to another, as, for example, thus:–

"Mrs Stowe, how shall I make this lounge, and what shall I cover the back with first?"

Mrs Stowe. "With the coarse cotton in the closet."

Woman. "Mrs Stowe, there isn't any more soap to clean the windows."

Mrs Stowe. "Where shall I get soap?"

"Here, H., run up to the store and get two bars."

"There is a man below wants to see Mrs Stowe about the cistern. Before you go down, Mrs Stowe, just show me how to cover this round end of the lounge."

"There's a man up from the depot, and he says that a box has come for Mrs Stowe, and it's coming up to the house; will you come down and see about it?"

"Mrs Stowe, don't go till you have shown the man how to nail that carpet in the corner. He's nailed it all crooked; what shall he do? The black thread is all used up, and what shall I do about putting gimp on the back of that sofa? Mrs Stowe, there is a man come with a lot of pails and tinware from Furbish; will you settle the bill now?"

"Mrs Stowe, here is a letter just come from Boston inclosing that bill of lading; the man wants to know what he shall do with the goods. If you will tell me what to say, I will answer the letter for you."

"Mrs Stowe, the meat-man is at the door. Hadn't we better get a little beefsteak, or something, for dinner?"

"Shall Hatty go to Boardman's for some more black thread?"

"Mrs Stowe, this cushion is an inch too wide for the frame. What shall we do now?"

"Mrs Stowe, where are the screws of the black walnut bedstead?"

"Here's a man has brought in these bills for freight. Will you settle them now?" "

"Mrs Stowe, I don't understand using this great needle. I can't make it go through the cushion; it sticks in the cotton."

Then comes a letter from my husband, saying he is sick abed, and all but dead; don't ever expect to see his family again; wants to know how I shall manage, in case I am left a widow; knows we shall get in debt and never get out; wonders at my courage; thinks I am very sanguine; warns me to be prudent, as there won't be much to live on in case of his death, etc., etc., etc. I read the letter and poke it into the stove, and proceed...

Some of my adventures were quite funny; as for example: I had in my kitchen-elect no sink, cistern, or any other water privileges, so I bought at the cotton factory two of the great hogsheads they bring oil in, which here in Brunswick are often used for cisterns, and had them brought up in triumph to my yard, and was congratulating myself on my energy, when to and behold! it was discovered that there was no cellar door except one in the kitchen, which was truly a strait and narrow way, down a long pair of stairs. Hereupon, as saith John Bunyan, I fell into a muse, – how to get my cisterns into my cellar. In days of chivalry I might have got a knight to make me a breach through the foundation walls, but that was not to be thought of now, and my oil hogsheads, standing disconsolately in the yard, seemed to reflect no great credit on my foresight. In this strait I fell upon a real honest Yankee cooper, whom I besought, for the reputation of his craft and mine, to take my hogsheads to pieces, carry them down in staves, and set them up again, which the worthy man actually accomplished one fair summer forenoon, to the great astonishment of "us Yankees." When my man came to put up the pump, he stared very hard to see my hogsheads thus translated and standing as innocent and quiet as could be in the cellar, and then I told him, in a very mild, quiet way, that I got 'em taken to pieces and put together, – just as if I had been always in the habit of doing such things. Professor Smith came down and looked very hard at them and then said, "Well, nothing can beat a willful woman." Then followed divers negotiations with a very clever, but (with reverence) somewhat lazy gentleman of jobs, who occupieth a carpenter's shop opposite to mine. This same John Titcomb, my very good friend, is a character peculiar to Yankeedom. He is part owner and landlord of the house I rent, and connected by birth with all the best families in town; a man of real intelligence, and good education, a great reader, and quite a thinker. Being of an ingenious turn, he does painting, gilding, staining, upholstery jobs, varnishing; all in addition to his primary trade of carpentry. But he is a man studious of ease, and fully possessed with the idea that man wants but little here below; so he boards himself in his workshop on crackers and herring, washed down with cold water, and spends his time working, musing, reading new publications, and taking his comfort. In his shop you shall see a joiner's bench, hammers, planes, saws, gimlets, varnish, paint, picture frames, fence posts, rare old china, one or two fine portraits of his ancestry, a bookcase full of books, the tooth of a whale, an old spinning-wheel and spindle, a lady's parasol frame, a church lamp to be mended, in short, Henry says Mr Titcomb's shop is like the ocean; there is no end to the curiosities in it.

In all my moving and fussing Mr Titcomb has been my right-hand man. Whenever a screw was loose, a nail to be driven, a lock mended, a pane of glass set – and these cases were manifold, – he was always on hand. But my sink was no fancy job, and I believe nothing but a very particular friendship would have moved him to undertake it. So this same sink lingered in a precarious state for some weeks, and when I had *nothing else to do*, I used to call and do what I could in the way of enlisting the good man's sympathies in its behalf.

How many times I have been in and seated myself in one of the old rocking-chairs, and talked first of the news of the day, the railroad, the last proceedings in Congress, the probabilities about the millennium, and thus brought the conversation by little and little round to my sink!... because, till the sink was done, the pump could not be put up, and we couldn't have any rain-water. Sometimes my courage would quite fail me to introduce the subject, and I would talk of everything else, turn and get out of the shop, and then turn back as if a thought had just struck my mind, and say:—

"Oh, Mr Titcomb! about that sink?"

"Yes, ma'am, I was thinking about going down street this afternoon to look out stuff for it."

"Yes, sir, if you would be good enough to get it done as soon as possible; we are in great need of it."

"I think there's no hurry. I believe we are going to have a dry time now, so that you could not catch any water, and you won't need a pump at present."

These negotiations extended from the first of June to the first of July, and at last my sink was completed, and so also was a new house spout, concerning which I had had divers communings with Deacon Dunning of the Baptist church. Also during this time good Mrs Mitchell and myself made two sofas, or lounges, a barrel chair, divers bedspreads, pillow cases, pillows, bolsters, mattresses; we painted rooms; we revarnished furniture; we – what *didn't* we do?

Then came on Mr Stowe; and then came the eighth of July and my little Charley. I was really glad for an excuse to lie in bed, for I was full tired, I can assure you. Well, I was what folks call very comfortable for two weeks when my nurse had to leave me...

During this time I have employed my leisure hours in making up my engagements with newspaper editors. I have written more than anybody, or I myself, would have thought. I have taught an hour a day in our school, and I have read two hours every evening to the children. The children study English history in school, and I am reading Scott's historic novels in their order. To-night I finish the *Abbot*; shall begin *Kenilworth* next week; yet I am constantly pursued and haunted by the idea that I don't do anything. Since I began this note I have been called off at least a dozen times; once for the fishman, to buy a codfish; once to see a man who had brought me some barrels of apples; once to see a book-man; then to Mrs Upham, to see about a drawing I promised to make for her; then to nurse the baby; then into the kitchen to make a chowder for dinner; and now I am at it again, for nothing but deadly determination enables me ever to write; it is rowing against wind and tide.

I suppose you think now I have begun, I am never going to stop, and, in truth, it looks like it; but the spirit moves now and I must obey.

Christmas is coming, and our little household is all alive with preparations; every one collecting their little gifts with wonderful mystery and secrecy...

To tell the truth, dear, I am getting tired; my neck and back ache, and I must come to a close.

Your ready kindness to me in the spring I felt very much; and *why* I did not have the sense to have sent you one line just by way of acknowledgment, I'm sure I don't know; I felt just as if I had, till I awoke, and behold! I had not. But, my dear, if my wits are somewhat wool-gathering and unsettled, my heart is as true as a star. I love you, and have thought of you often.

This fall I have felt often *sad*, lonesome, both very unusual feelings with me in these busy days; but the breaking away from my old home, and leaving father and mother, and coming to a strange place affected me naturally. In those sad hours my thoughts have often turned to George; I have thought with encouragement of his blessed state, and hoped that I should soon be there, too. I have many warm and kind friends here, and have been treated with great attention and kindness. Brunswick is a delightful residence, and if you come East next summer, you must come to my new home. George would delight to go a-fishing with the children, and see the ships, and sail in the sailboats, and all that.

Give Aunt Harriet's love to him, and tell him when he gets to be a painter to send me a picture.

Affectionately yours,
H. *Stowe*

To Mrs Follen (16 February 1853)

Follen, an English writer, had written to Stowe asking about her life.

My Dear Madam:

I hasten to reply to your letter, to me the more interesting that I have long been acquainted with you, and during all the nursery part of my life made daily use of your poems for children.

I used to think sometimes in those days that I would write to you, and tell you how much I was obliged to you for the pleasure which they gave us all.

So you want to know something about what sort of a woman I am! Well, if this is any object, you shall have statistics free of charge. To begin, then, I am a little bit of a woman, – somewhat more than forty, about as thin and dry as a pinch of snuff; never very much to look at in my best days, and looking like a used-up article now.

I was married when I was twenty-five years old to a man rich in Greek and Hebrew, Latin and Arabic, and, alas! rich in nothing else. When I went to housekeeping, my entire stock of china for parlor and kitchen was bought for eleven dollars. That lasted very well for two years, till my brother was married and brought his bride to visit me. I then found, on review, that I had neither plates nor tea-cups to set a table for my father's family; wherefore I thought it best to reinforce the establishment by getting me a tea-set that cost ten dollars more, and this, I believe, formed my whole stock-in-trade for some years.

But then I was abundantly enriched with wealth of another sort.

I had two little curly-headed twin daughters to begin with, and my stock in this line was gradually increased, till I have been the mother of seven children, the most beautiful and the most loved of whom lies buried near my Cincinnati residence. It was at his dying bed and at his grave that I learned what a poor slave mother may feel when her child is torn away from her. In those depths of sorrow which seemed to me immeasurable, it was my only prayer to God that such anguish might not be suffered in vain. There were circumstances about his death of such peculiar bitterness, of what seemed almost cruel suffering, that I felt that I could never be consoled for it unless this crushing of my own heart might enable me to work out some great good to others...

I allude to this here because I have often felt that much that is in that book (*Uncle Tom*) had its root in the awful scenes and bitter sorrows of that summer. It has left now, I trust, no trace on my mind except a deep compassion for the sorrowful, especially for mothers who are separated from their children. During long years of struggling with poverty and sickness, and a hot, debilitating climate, my children grew up around me. The nursery and the kitchen were my principal fields of labor. Some of my friends, pitying my trials, copied and sent a number of little sketches from my pen to certain liberally paying "Annuals" with my name. With the first money that I earned in this way I bought a feather-bed! for as I had married into poverty and without a dowry, and as my husband had only a large library of books and a great deal of learning, the bed and pillows were thought the most profitable investment. After this I thought that I had discovered the philosopher's stone. So when a new carpet or mattress was going to be needed, or when, at the close of the year it began to be evident that my family accounts, like poor Dora's "wouldn't add up", then I used to say to my faithful friend and factotum Anna, who shared all my joys and sorrovrs, "Now, if you will keep the babies and attend to the things in the house for one day, I'll write a piece, and then we shall be out of the scrape." So I became an author – very modest at first, I do assure you, and remonstrating very seriously with the friends who had thought it best to put my name to the pieces by way of getting up a reputation; and if you ever see a woodcut of me, with an immoderately long nose, on the cover of all the U.S. Almanacs, I wish you to take notice that I have been forced into it contrary to my natural modesty by the imperative solicitations of my dear five thousand friends and the public generally. One thing I must say with regard to my life at the West, which you will understand better than many English women could.

I lived two miles from the city of Cincinnati, in the country, and domestic service, not always you know to be found in the city, is next to an impossibility to obtain in the country, even by those who are willing to give the highest wages; so what was to be expected for poor me, who had very little of this world's goods to offer?

Had it not been for my inseparable friend Anna, a noble-hearted English girl, who landed on our shores in destitution and sorrow, and clave to me as Ruth to Naomi, I had never lived through all the trials which this uncertainty and want of domestic service imposed on both; you may imagine, therefore, how glad I was when, our seminary property being divided out into small lots which were rented at a low price, a number of poor families settled in our vicinity, from whom we could occasionally obtain domestic service. About a dozen families of liberated slaves were among the number, and they became my favourite resort in cases of emergency. If anybody wishes to have a black face look handsome, let them be left, as I have been, in feeble health in oppressive hot weather, with a sick baby in arms, and two or three other little ones in the nursery, and not a servant in the whole house to do a single turn. Then, if they could see my good old Aunt Frankie coming with her honest, bluff, black face, her long, strong arms, her chest as big and stout as a barrel, and her hilarious, hearty laugh, perfectly delighted to take one's washing and do it at a fair price, they would appreciate the beauty of black people.

My cook, poor Eliza Buck, – how she would stare to think of her name going to England! – was a regular epitome of slave life in herself; fat, gentle, easy, loving and lovable, always calling my very modest house and dooryard "The Place", as if it had been a plantation with seven hundred hands on it. She had lived through the whole sad story of a Virginia-raised slave's life. In her youth she must have been a very handsome mulatto girl. Her voice was sweet, and her manners refined and agreeable. She was raised in a good family as a nurse and seamstress. When the family became embarrassed, she was suddenly sold on to a plantation in Louisiana. She has often told me how, without any warning, she was suddenly forced into a carriage, and saw her little mistress screaming and stretching her arms from the window towards her as she was driven away. She has told me of scenes on the Louisiana plantation, and she has often been out at night by stealth ministering to poor slaves who had been mangled and lacerated by the lash. Hence she was sold into Kentucky, and her last master was the father of all her children. On this point she ever maintained a delicacy and reserve that always appeared to me remarkable. She always called him her husband; and it was not till after she had lived with me some years that I discovered the real nature of the connection. I shall never forget how sorry I felt for her, nor my feelings at her humble apology, "You know, Mrs. Stowe, slave women cannot help themselves." She had two very pretty quadroon daughters, with her beautiful hair and eyes, interesting children, whom I had instructed in the family school with my children. Time would fail to tell you all that I learned incidentally of the slave system in the history of various slaves who came into my family, and of the underground railroad which, I may say, ran through our house. But the letter is already too long.

You ask with regard to the remuneration which I have received for my work here in America. Having been poor all my life and expecting to be poor the rest of it, the idea of making money by a book which I wrote just because I could not help it never occurred to me. It was therefore an agreeable surprise to receive ten thousand dollars as the first-fruits of three months' sale. I presume as much more is now due...

I have very much at heart a design to erect in some of the Northern States a normal school for the education of coloured teachers in the United States and in Canada. I have very much wished that some permanent memorial of good to the coloured race might be created out of the proceeds of a work which promised to have so unprecedented a sale. My own share of the profits will be less than that of the publishers, either English or American; but I am willing to give largely for this purpose, and I have no doubt that the publishers, both American and English, will unite with me; for nothing tends more immediately to the emancipation of the slave than the education and elevation of the free.

I am now writing a work which will contain, perhaps, an equal amount of matter with *Uncle Tom's Cabin*. It will contain all the facts and documents on which that story was founded, and an immense body of facts, reports of trials, legal documents, and testimony of people now living South, which will more than confirm every statement in *Uncle Tom's Cabin*.

I must confess that till I began the examination of facts in order to write this book, much as I thought I knew before, I had not begun to measure the depth of the abyss. The law records of courts and judicial proceedings are so incredible as to fill me with amazement whenever I think of them. It seems to me that the book cannot but be felt, and, coming upon the sensibility awaked by the other, do something.

I suffer exquisitely in writing these things. It may be truly said that I write with my heart's blood. Many times in writing *Uncle Tom's Cabin* I thought my health would fail utterly; but I prayed earnestly that God would help me till I got through, and still I am pressed beyond measure and above strength.

This horror, this nightmare abomination! can it be in my country! It lies like lead on my heart, it shadows my life with sorrow; the more so that I feel, as for my own brothers, for the South, and am pained by every horror I am obliged to write, as one who is forced by some awful oath to disclose in court some family disgrace. Many times I have thought that I must die, and yet I pray God that I may live to see something done. I shall in all probability be in London in May: shall I see you?

It seems to me so odd and dream-like that so many persons desire to see me, and now I cannot help thinking that they will think, when they do, that God hath chosen "the weak things of this world." If I live till spring I shall hope to see Shakespeare's grave, and Milton's mulberry-tree, and the good land of my fathers, – old, old England! May that day come!

Yours affectionately,
H. B. *Stowe*

CAMILLE COROT

J EAN BAPTISTE CAMILLE COROT (1796–1875), FRENCH landscape painter.

To unknown (1857), written at Gruyère

You know, a landscape painter's day is delightful. You get up early, at three o'clock in the morning, before sunrise; you go and sit under a tree; you watch and wait. At first there is nothing much to be seen. Nature looks like a whitish canvas with a few broad outlines faintly sketched in, all is misty, everything quivers in the cool dawn breeze. The sky lights up. The sun has not yet burst through the gauze veil that hides the meadow, the little valley, the hills on the horizon. The nocturnal vapours are still creeping in silvery flakes over the frozen green of the grass. Ah! a first ray of sunshine! The tiny flowers seem to wake up happily. Each has its tremulous dewdrop. The leaves shiver with cold in the morning breeze. Invisible birds are singing beneath the leaves. It seems as though the flowers were saying their prayers. Little butterfly-winged cupids frolic over the meadow, making the tall grass ripple. One sees nothing. Everything is there! The whole landscape lies behind the transparent gauze of the fog that now rises, drawn upwards by the sun, and, as it rises, reveals the silver-spangled river, the fields, the trees, the cottages, the further scene. At last one can discern all that one could only guess at before.

The sun is up! There is a peasant at the end of the field, with his waggon drawn by a yoke of oxen. You can hear the little bell round the neck of the ram, the leader of the flock. Everything is bursting into life, sparkling in the full light – light which as yet is still soft and golden. The background, simple in line and harmonious in colour, melts into the infinite expanse of sky, through the bluish, misty atmosphere. The flowers raise their heads, the birds flutter hither and thither. A countryman on a white horse rides away down the steep-banked lane. The little rounded willows on the bank of the stream look like birds spreading their tails. It's adorable! and one paints! and paints!...

FRIEDRICH NIETZSCHE

FRIEDRICH NIETZSCHE (1844–1900), GERMAN PHILO-sopher. His views, particularly his celebration of "superman" and detestation of democracy, were later taken up in a perverted form by the Nazis. His own life was blighted by mental illness, and he was nursed for many years by his widowed mother and sister.

To his mother (April 1863)

Written while Nietzsche was a student.

Dear Mother,

If I write to you to-day it is certainly about the saddest and most unpleasant business that it has ever been my lot to relate. For I have been very wicked and do not know whether you will or can forgive me. It is with a heavy heart and most unwillingly that I take up my pen to write to you, more particularly when I think of our pleasant and absolutely unruffled time together during the Easter holidays. Well, last Sunday I got drunk and have no excuse but this, that I did not know how much I could stand and that I happened to be somewhat excited that afternoon. When I returned, Herr Kern, one of the masters, came across me in that condition. He had called me before the Synod on Tuesday, when I was degraded to third of my division and one hour of my Sunday walk was cancelled. You can imagine how depressed and miserable

I feel about it, and especially at having to cause you so much sorrow over such a disgraceful affair, the like of which has never occurred in my life before... Through this one lapse I have completely spoilt the fairly good position I succeeded in winning for myself last term. I am so much annoyed with myself that I can't even get on with my work or settle down at all. Write to me soon and write severely, for I deserve it; and no one knows better than I do how much I deserve it.

There is no need for me to give you any further assurances as to how seriously I shall pull myself together, for now a great deal depends upon it. I had once again grown too cocksure of myself, and this self-confidence has now, at all events, been completely shaken, and in a very unpleasant manner.

I shall go and see the Rev. Kletschke to-day and have a talk with him. By-the-bye, do not tell anyone anything about it if it is not already known. Also, please send me my muffler as soon as possible, for I am constantly suffering from hoarseness and pains in my chest. Send me the comb too that I have spoken about. Now, good-bye and write to me very soon, and do not be too cross with me, mother dear.

Your very sorrowful,
Fritz

LOUISA MAY ALCOTT

LOUISA MAY ALCOTT (1832–88) WAS THE AUTHOR OF the children's classic *Little Women*. During the American Civil War she worked as a nurse in a Union hospital.

To Alfred Whitman (1863)

Whitman was a childhood friend from Concord, called by Alcott "Dolphus" after a character in her juvenile play The Haunted Man; *she sometimes styled herself Sophy Tetterby, another character from the same play.*

My dear old Dolphus.

Carrie sent me word the other day that you felt badly because we none of us wrote, & you wanted to hear. Of course all the times I'd planned to write you & didn't, immediately rose up before me & in a great state of remorse I rush at my pen here at six oclock in the morning & scribble a line to my beloved Tetterby.

My only excuse is I've been to Washington a nursing in the army, got typhoid fever & came bundling home to rave, & ramp, & get my head shaved & almost retire into the tombs in consequence, not to mention picking up again, & appearing before the eyes of my grateful country in a wig & no particular flesh on my bones, also the writing some Hospital Sketches & when folks said put em in a book, doing the same & being drove wild with proof, & printers, & such matters, besides keeping house, seeing company, adoring my nephew, & furnishing literary gems for sundry papers – Thus you see I have not been idle though I've seemed to neglect my old boy.

How do you come on? What are you doing? & when are you coming East to be clutched at & kissed by all the "girls you left behind you"? Annie says Carrie showed her a fine picture of your father & self & writes me that Dolphus has gone & growed up in the most appalling manner. Now I wish to know what you mean by that? I'm not changed a bit, barring the wig, & I dont wish my boys to be men folks in this rapid manner. Wilkie James has gone & been made Adjutant in the 54th, got smashed at Fort Wagner & blossomed into a hero; his brother, a sixteen year older, has put on a Lieutenant's shoulder straps & pranced off with the 55th. Julian Hawthorne has set up a manly whisker & got into college, so all my boys are gone & I'm a love lorn old Sophy.

Among my hospital fellows was a jolly little Sergeant who had lost his right arm at Fredricksburg – he learned to write with his left hand & sends me the funniest letters you ever saw. He has got a false arm, shouldered his rifle & is going back to his regiment for "another dig at those thundering rebs" as he says

Dont you feel inclined to give them a slap? or are [you] helping in the peaceful & perhaps more sensible ways?

Carrie probably has told all the news about her family so I will mention what my own is up to just now, though we go on pretty much as usual. Father writes & sees to his schools; mother sings "Glory Hallelujah" over the papers & makes berry pies; Ab has been at Clarke's Island with a party of young people from New York & Concord. Rowing, dancing, sailing, flirting & singing are the amusements in which they spend their shining hours. She says she is as brown as a berry & as plump as a partridge, so her trip has done her good. Annie & her John brood over the infant Freddy who is the one perfect & divine brat in the world though his nose turns straight up & he has n't half a dozen hairs on his head.

I live in my inkstand scribble, scribble from morning till night & am more peckish than ever if disturbed.

There we are & I hope you recognize the picture.

Our Concord company is to return tonight & the town is in as wild a state of excitement as it is possible for such a dozy old place to be without dying of brain fever. Flags are flapping every where, wreaths & "Welcome home" are stuck on every stickable place & our drum corps, consisting of eight small boys with eight large drums, keep a continual rub-a-dubbing.

Now my son drop me a line & send me one of your new "picters" that I may behold your manly charms. I have no photographs now & must wait till my plumage is renewed when I will return the favor as I believe that is ettiquette .

Bless your buttons & "adoo".

Yours Ever *Sophy Tetterby*

To an unknown recipient
(29 December 1870), from Rome

Possibly to Daniel Noyes Haskell, editor of the Transcript.

My Dear Mr —

As we are having very exciting times just now, I will send you a little account of the two last "sensations," though I dare say the news will be rather old by the time you receive it.

Yesterday morning at breakfast our maid, Lavinia, came flying in from market with the news that the Tiber had overflowed its banks and inundated the lower part of the city; that people just outside the walls were drowned, others in the Ghetto were washed out of their houses, the Corso was under water, and the world generally coming to an end. We instantly went out to see how things stood, or rather floated, and found that Lavinia's story was true. The heavy rains and warm winds had swelled the river and melted the snow on the mountains, till the Tiber rose higher than at any time since 1805, and had done much damage in a few hours.

When we reached the Piazza di Spagna it seemed as if we were in Venice, for all the long streets leading up to it from the lower part of the city were under water, and rafts and boats were already floating about. The Piazza del Popolo was a lake, with the four stone lions just above the surface, still faithfully spouting water, though it was a drug in the market. Garrett's great stables were flooded, and his horses and carriages were standing disconsolately on the banks about the Piazza. In at the open gates rolled a muddy stream bearing haystacks and brushwood from the country along the Corso. People stood on their balconies, wondering what they should do, many breakfastless; for meals are sent in, and how were the trattoria boys to reach them with the coffee-pots across such canals of water? Carriages splashed about in the shallower pans with agitated loads of people hurrying to safer quarters; many were coming down ladders into boats, and flocks stood waiting their turn with little bundles of valuables in their hands

The soldiers were out in full force, working gallantly to save life and property; making rafts, carrying people on their backs, and later, going through the inundated streets with boatloads of food for the hungry, shut up in their ill-provided houses. It has since been said that usually at such times the priests have done this work; but now, they stand looking on and smile maliciously, saying it is a judgment on the people for their treatment of the Pope. The people are troubled because the priests refuse to pray for them; but otherwise they snap their fingers at the sullen old gentleman in the Vatican, and the brisk, brave troops work for the city quite as well (we heretics think better) than the snuffy priests. Some of the saintly young Jesuits amused themselves by throwing stones at the soldiers while they were working during the flood; for which cowardly trick the aforesaid heretics feel a strong desire to box the long-coated boys' ears and cast their shovel-hats in the mud. By the way, I heard that one whole college of lads left in a body and went to the free school the King has opened, demanding to be taken in and taught something, being disgusted with their Jesuitical masters; a sure sign that young Italy is waking up. Three cheers for the boys!

To return to the flood. In the Ghetto, the disaster was really terrible, for the flood came so suddenly that the whole quarter was under water in an hour. At five no one dreamed of such a danger; at seven all the lower part of the city was covered, up to the first story in many places. A friend who promptly went to the rescue of the Jews, told us that the scene was pitiful; for the poor souls live in cellars, packed like sardines in a box, and being washed out all of a sudden were utterly destitute. In one street he saw a man and woman pushing a mattress before them as they waded nearly to their waists in water, and on the mattress were their little children – all they could save. Later in the day, as the boats of provisions came along, women and children swarmed at the windows, crying "Bread! bread!" and their wants could not be supplied, in spite of the generosity and care of the city authorities. One old woman who had lost everything but her life besought the rescuers to bring her a little snuff for the love of heaven; which was very characteristic of the Italian race. One poor man, in trying to save his wife and children in a cart, upset them, and the little ones were drowned at their own door. Tragedy and comedy, side by side.

Outside the city houses were carried away, and people saved with difficulty, so sudden and rapid was the overflow. A bridge near the Ghetto was destroyed, and a boatful of soldiers upset in the current and several men drowned. In the Corso several shops were spoilt, and many people were ruined by the mishap. Friends of ours from Boston were cut off from supplies for two days, and lived on bread and water till help came. A pleasant little experience for the Christmas holidays.

We fared better, for our piazza is on the hill and our Lavinia, forseeing a famine, laid in stores; among them live fowls, who roost in the kitchen with the cats and L's relatives, who infest that region in swarms. If the heavy rains continue we may come to want; for the woodyards are under water, the railroads down in all directions, and the peasants from outside cannot get in to bring supplies, unless the donkeys swim. So far we enjoy the excitement; for the sleepy old city is all astir, and we drive about seeing unexpected sights in every direction. Being a Goth and a Vandal, I enjoy it more than chilly galleries or mouldy pictures. It thrills me more to see one live man work like a Trojan to save suffering women and babies, than to sit hours before a Dying Gladiator who has been gasping for centuries in immortal marble. It's sad, but I can't help it.

Last night the gas went out in many parts of the city, and people were ordered to put lamps at their windows – for thieves abound. We prepared our arms, consisting of one pistol, two daggers, and a heavy umbrella, and slept peacefully, although it was possible that we might wake to find ourselves floating gently out at the Porta Pia. My last idea was a naughty hope that the Pope might get his pontifical petticoats very wet, be a little drowned, and terribly scared by the flood; for he deserves it.

Today the water is abating, and we are becoming accustomed to the sight of boats in the market-place, gentlemen paying visits on the backs of stout soldiers, and family dinners being hoisted in at two-story windows. All the world is up on the Pincio looking at the flood; and a sad sight it is. Outside the Popolo Gate a wide sea stretches down the valley, with roofs and trees sticking up dismally from the muddy water. A raging river foams between us and the Vatican, and the Corso is a grand canal where unhappy shopkeepers float lamenting. The Pantheon is under water over the railing, the Post Office has ceased to work, the people have become amphibious, and Rome is what Grandmother Rigglesty would call "a wash..."

⊱❦⊰

To Miss Churchill (Christmas Day 1878)

My Dear Miss Churchill.

I can only say to you as I do to the many young writers who ask for advice – There is no easy road to successful authorship; it has to be earned by long & patient labor, many disappointments, uncertainties & trials. Success is often a lucky accident, coming to those who may not deserve it, while others who do have to wait & hope till they have *earned* it. That is the best sort & the most enduring.

I worked for twenty years poorly paid, little known, & quite without any ambition but to eke out a living, as I chose to support myself & began to do it at sixteen. This long drill was of use, & when I wrote *Hospital Sketches* by the beds of my soldier boys in the shape of letters home I had no idea that I was taking the first step toward what is called fame. It nearly cost my life but I discovered the secret of winning the ear & touching the heart of the public by simply telling the comic & pathetic incidents of life.

Little Women was written when I was ill, & to prove that I could *not* write books for girls. The publisher thought it *flat*, so did I, & neither hoped much for or from it. We found out our mistake, & since then, though I do not enjoy writing "moral tales" for the young, I do it because it pays well.

But the success I value most was making my dear mother happy in her last years & taking care of my family. The rest soon grows wearisome & seems very poor beside the comfort of being an earthly Providence to those we love.

I hope you will win this joy at least, & think you *will*, for you seem to have got on well so far, & the stories are better than many sent me. I like the short one best. Lively tales of home-life or children go

well, & the *Youth's Companion* is a good paying paper. I do not like
Loring as he is neither honest nor polite. I have had dealings with
him & know. Try Roberts Brothers 299 Washington St. They are
very kind & just & if the book suits will give it a fair chance. With
best wishes for a prosperous & happy New Year I am your friend

L. M. A.

LEWIS CARROLL

LEWIS CARROLL WAS THE PSEUDONYM OF CHARLES
Dodgson (1832–98), Oxford mathematician, photo-
grapher, and author of the children's books *Alice's
Adventures in Wonderland* (1865) and *Through the Looking
Glass and What Alice Found There* (1871).

୶୶

To Mary MacDonald (23 May 1864)

*Mary MacDonald was the daughter of the poet George MacDonald and
his wife, and one of Carroll's "child-friends", of which there were many,
leading to suggestions that Carroll may have been inclined to paedophilia.*

My dear Child,

It's been so frightfully hot here that I've been almost too weak to
hold a pen, and even if I had been able, there was no ink – it had all
evaporated into a cloud of black steam, and in that state it has been
floating about the room, inking the walls and ceiling till they're
hardly fit to be seen: today it is cooler, and a little has come back into
the ink-bottle in the form of black snow – there will soon be enough
for me to write and order those photographs your Mamma wants.

This hot weather makes me very sad and sulky: I can hardly keep my temper sometimes. For instance, just now the Bishop of Oxford came in to see me – it was a civil thing to do, and he meant no harm, poor man: but I was so provoked at his coming in that I threw a book at his head, which I am afraid hurt him a good deal (Mem: this isn't quite true, so you needn't believe it. Don't be in such a hurry to believe next time – I'll tell you why. If you set to work to believe everything, you will tire out the believing-muscles of your mind, and then you'll be so weak you won't be able to believe the simplest true things. Only last week a friend of mine set to work to believe Jack-the-giant-killer. He managed to do it, but he was so exhausted by it that when I told him it was raining (which was true) he *couldn't* believe it, but rushed out into the street without his hat or umbrella, the consequence of which was his hair got seriously damp, and one curl didn't recover its right shape for nearly 2 days. (Mem: some of that is not quite true, I'm afraid.)) Will you tell Greville I am getting on with his picture (to go into the oval frame, you know) and I hope to send it in a day or two. Also tell your Mamma that I'm sorry to say none of my sisters are coming to London this summer.

With my kind regards to your Papa and Mamma, and love to you and the other infants, I remain

Your affectionate Friend,
Charles L. Dodgson

The only unlucky thing that happened to me last Friday was *your* writing to me. There!

❧

To Mary Talbot (8 January 1872)

Talbot was another child-friend. Through the Looking Glass had been published the month previously.

My dear Mary
    Thanks for your nice little note, though I am sorry to hear you find

Through the Looking-Glass so uninteresting. You see I have done my best, so that it really isn't really *my* fault if you think Tweedledum & Tweedledee stupid and wish that I had left out all about the train and the gnat. You see, if *all* the book is stupid, and if I leave out *all* the stupid parts, there really will be so *very* little left.

Please remember that you are *not* one of the "dear children I have made friends with whose faces I shall never see." I consider that we *have* made friends, but you may tell your uncle I shall be seriously angry with him, if he doesn't soon invite you to Keble College. and then bring you to see me at Christ Ch[urch].

Your affectionate friend,
Lewis Carroll

~❧~

To the Lowrie children (18 August 1884)

My dear Children,

It was a real pleasure to me to get your letter; but, before I answer it, I have two humble requests to make: One is, please don't make it generally known that I have written to you, so as to bring on me a flood of letters from all the American children who have read *Alice*, and who would all expect answers! I *don't* want to spend all the rest of my life (being close on the age when Dr O. W. Holmes says "old age" begins) in writing letters! (I wonder if you know his *Autocrat of the Breakfast Table?* I delight in it.) And my other request is, please never again *praise* me at all, as if any powers I may have, in writing books for children, were my own doing. I just feel myself a trustee, that is all – you would not take much credit to yourselves, I suppose, if a sum of money had been put into your hands and you had been told "spend all this for the good of the little ones"? And besides *praise* isn't good for any of us; love is, and it would be a good thing if all the world were full of it: I like my books to be loved, and I like to think some children love me for the books, but I don't like them *praised*. I'll tell you what I like to think of best, about the *Alice* books. I've had a lot printed on cheaper paper, in plain bindings, and given them to hospitals and Convalescent Homes – for poor, sick children: and it's ever so much pleasanter to think of one child being saved some weary hours, than if all the town followed at my heels crying, "How clever he is!" I'm sure you would think so too.

Some rather droll things happened about those hospitals: I sent round a printed letter, to offer the books, with a list of the Hospitals, and asking people to add to the list any I had left out. And one manager wrote that he knew of a place where there were a number of sick children, but he was afraid I wouldn't like to give them any books – and why, do you think? "Because they are Jews!" I wrote to say, of course I would give them some: why in the world shouldn't little Israelites read *Alice's Adventures* as well as other children!

Another – a "Lady Superior" – wrote to ask to see a copy of *Alice* before accepting it: for she had to be very careful, all the children being Roman Catholics, as to what "religious reading" they got! I wrote to say, "You shall certainly see it first, if you like: but I can guarantee that the books have no religious teaching whatever in them – in fact, they do not teach anything at all." She said she was quite satisfied, and would accept the books.

But, while I am running on in this way, I'm leaving your letter unanswered. As to the meaning of the Snark? I'm very much afraid I didn't mean anything but nonsense! Still, you know, words mean more than we mean to express when we use them: so a whole book ought to mean a great deal more than the writer meant. So, whatever good meanings are in the book, I'm very glad to accept as the meaning of the book. The best that I've seen is by a lady (she published it in a letter to a newspaper) – that the whole book is an allegory on the search after happiness. I think this fits beautifully in many ways – particularly, about the bathing-machines: when the people get weary of life, and can't find happiness in town or in books, then they rush off to the seaside, to see what bathing-machines will do for them.

Would you mind giving me a more definite idea of who I am writing to, by sending me your names and your ages? I feel as if we were kind of friends already, but the one idea of "The Lowrie Children" is too shadowy to get hold of fairly. It is like making friends with a will-o'-the-wisp. I believe nobody ever succeeded in making an intimate friend of one of those things. Read up your ancient history, and you won't find a single instance of it. I would have added, to "names and ages" "and your cartes," only I'm afraid you'd then expect mine, and that I never give away (my reason is that I want to be personally unknown: to be known by sight, by strangers, would be intolerable to me), so I'm afraid I can't, with a good grace, ask for yours.

I'm very fond of inventing games; and I enclose you the rules of one, *Mischmasch*: see how you like it. One advantage is that it needs no counters or anything: so you can play it out walking, or up in a balloon, or down in a diving-bell, or anywhere!

Your loving friend,
Lewis Carroll

After posting the letter, I remembered I had never said a word about Jabberwocky and *Der Tyroler und sein Kind*. Thank you very much for it: it is one of the loveliest airs I know – and oh, so much too good for such words! Once more, your loving friend (your twopenny-halfpenny friend this time),

Lewis Carroll

To Alice Hargreaves (1 March 1885)

Alice Hargreaves (née Liddell) was the model for Carroll's fictional Alice, a book born out of a boat trip made with Alice and her sisters in the "golden afternoon" of 4 July 1862.

My dear Mrs Hargreaves,

I fancy this will come to you almost like a voice from the dead, after so many years of silence – and yet those years have made no difference, that I can perceive, in *my* clearness of memory of the days when we *did* correspond. I am getting to feel what an old man's failing memory is, as to recent events and new friends (for instance, I made friends, only a few weeks ago, with a very nice little maid of about 12, and had a walk with her – and now I can't recall either of her names!) but my mental picture is as vivid as ever, of one who was, through so many years, my ideal child-friend. I have had scores of child-friends since your time: but they have been quite a different thing.

However, I did not begin this letter to say all *that*. What I want to ask is – would you have any objection to the original MS book of *Alice's Adventures* (which I suppose you still possess) being published in facsimile? The idea of doing so occurred to me only the other day. If, on consideration, you come to the conclusion that you would rather *not* have it done, there is an end of the matter. If, however, you give a favorable reply, I would be much obliged if you would lend it me (registered post I should think would be safest) that I may consider the possibilities. I have not seen it for about 20 years: so am by no means sure that the illustrations may not prove to be so awfully bad, that to reproduce them would be absurd.

There can be no doubt that I should incur the charge of gross egoism in publishing it. But I don't care for that in the least: knowing that I have no such motive: only I think, considering the extraordinary popularity the books have had (we have sold more than 120,000 of the two) there must be many who would like to see the original form.

Always your friend,
C. L. Dodgson

~❧~

To May Mileham (6 September 1885)

Dearest May,

Thank you very much indeed for the peaches. They were delicious. Eating one was almost as nice as kissing you: of course not quite: I think, if I had to give the exact measurement, I should say "three-quarters as nice." We are having such a lovely time here; and the sands are beautiful. I only wish I could some day come across you, washing your pocket-handkerchief in a pool among the rocks! But I wander on the beach, and look for you, in vain: and then I say, "Where is May?" And the stupid boatmen reply, "It isn't May, sir! It's September!" But it doesn't comfort me.

Always your loving
C. L. D

CARDINAL NEWMAN

JOHN HENRY NEWMAN (1801–90) WAS ORIGINATOR OF the "Oxford Movement" and converted to Roman Catholicism in 1845. Two years later he founded the Birmingham Oratory.

To Monsignor Talbot (25 July 1864)

Talbot was a prelate at the Vatican.

Dear Monsignor Talbot

I have received your letter, inviting me to preach next Lent in your Church at Rome, to "an audience of Protestants more educated than could ever be the case in England."

However, Birmingham people have souls; and I have neither taste nor talent for the sort of work, which you cut out for me: and I beg to decline your offer.

I am &c *J H N*

MARK TWAIN

MARK TWAIN (1835–1910), AMERICAN HUMORIST and writer. Born Samuel Langhorne Clemens, Twain – who took his pseudonym from the Mississippi riverboatman's call for marking two fathoms – made his reputation with a short story "Jim Smiley and His Jumping Frog".

❧

To Jane Clemens and Pamela Moffett (20 January 1866), from San Francisco

My dear Mother and Sister,

I do not know what to write, my life is so uneventful. I wish I was back there piloting up and down the river again. Verily all is vanity and little worth – save piloting.

To think that after writing many an article a man might be excused for thinking tolerably good, those New York people should single out a villainous backwoods sketch to compliment me on! – "Jim Smiley and His Jumping Frog" – a squib which would never have been written but to please Artemus Ward, and then it reached New York too late to appear in his book.

But no matter. His book was a wretchedly poor one, generally speaking, and it could be no credit to either of us to appear between its covers.

This paragraph is from the New York correspondence of the San Francisco *Alta*:

[*Clipping pasted in*]

Mark Twain's story in the Saturday Press of November 18th, called "Jim Smiley and His Jumping Frog," has set all New York in a roar, and he may be said to have made his mark. I have been asked fifty times about it and its author, and the papers are copying it far and near. It is voted the best thing of the day. Cannot the *Californian* afford to keep Mark all to itself? It should not let him scintillate so widely without first being filtered through the California press.

The New York publishing house of Carleton & Co. gave the sketch to the *Saturday Press* when they found it was too late for the book.

Though I am generally placed at the head of my breed of scribblers in this part of the country, the place properly belongs to Bret Harte, I think, though he denies it, along with the rest. He wants me to club a lot of old sketches together with a lot of his and publish a book. I wouldn't do it, only he agrees to take all the trouble. But I want to know whether we are going to make anything out of it, first. However, he has written to a New York publisher, and if we are offered a bargain that will pay for a month's labor we will go to work and prepare the volume for the press.

Yours affy,
Sam

To a gas and electricity company, Hartford (n.d.)

Gentlemen,

There are but two places in our whole street where lights could be of any value, by any accident, and you have measured and appointed your intervals so ingeniously as to leave each of those places in the center of a couple of hundred yards of solid darkness. When I noticed that you were setting one of your lights in such a way that I could almost see how to get into my gate at night, I suspected that it was a piece of carelessness on the part of the workmen and would be corrected as soon as you should go around inspecting and find it out.

My judgment was right. It is always right when you are concerned. For fifteen years, in spite of my prayers and tears, you persistently kept a gas lamp exactly half-way between my gates so that I couldn't find either of them after dark, and then furnished such execrable gas that I had to hang a danger signal on the lamp post to keep teams from running into it, nights. Now I suppose your present idea is to leave us a little more in the dark.

Don't mind us – out our way. We possess but one vote apiece, and no rights which you are in any way bound to respect. Please take your electric light and go to – but never mind, it is not for me to suggest. You will probably find the way. And anyway you can reasonably count on divine assistance if you lose your bearings.

S. L. Clemens

~❧~

To William Dean Howells (15 June 1872)

Howells, author and journalist, was one of Twain's closest friends.

Friend Howells,

Could you tell me how I could get a copy of your portrait as published in *Hearth and Home*? I hear so much talk about it as being among the finest works of art which have yet appeared in that journal that I feel a strong desire to see it. Is it suitable for framing? I have written the publishers of H & H time and again but they say that the demand for the portrait immediately exhausted the edition and now a copy cannot be had even for the European demand, which has now begun. Bret Harte has been here and says his family would not be without that portrait for any consideration. He says his children get up in the night and yell for it. I would give anything for a copy of that portrait to put up in my parlor. I have Oliver Wendell Holmes's and Bret Harte's as published in *Every Saturday*, and of all the swarms that come every day to gaze upon them none go away that are not softened and humbled and made more resigned to the will of God. If I had yours to put up alongside of them I believe the combination would bring more souls to earnest reflection and ultimate conviction of their lost condition than any other kind of warning would.

Where in the nation can I get that portrait? Here are heaps of people that want it, that *need* it. There is my uncle. *He* wants a copy. He is lying at the point of death. He has *been* lying at the point of death for two years. He wants a copy, and I want him to *have* a copy. And I want you to send a copy to the man that shot my dog. I want to see if he is dead to every human instinct.

Now you send me that portrait. I am sending you mine in this letter, and am glad to do it, for it has been greatly admired. People who are judges of art find in the execution a grandeur which has not been equalled in this country, and an expression which has not been approached in *any*.

Yrs truly,
S. L. *Clemens*

P. S. 62,000 copies of *Roughing It* sold and delivered in 4 months.

GERARD MANLEY HOPKINS

GERARD MANLEY HOPKINS (1844–89), ENGLISH POET and classicist.

လွှဲ့

To his sister Kate Manley Hopkins (25 April 1871)
At this time Manley Hopkins was a Jesuit novice.

My dear Katie:
Many thanks for your letter, which I was delighted to get. When it

first came to hand I stood balancing in my mind who it could be from, there was such a youngladyship and grownupdom about the address, until I remembered that you were older than you used to be. As for me I will say no more than this, that I have prescribed myself twenty-four hourglasses a day (which I take even during sleep, such is the force of habit) and that even this does not stop the ravages of time.

What month in the year it may be at Hampstead I will not be sure; with us it is a whity-greeny January. What with east winds, cloud, and rain I think it will never be spring. If we have a bright afternoon the next morning it is winter again.

We were all vaccinated the other day. The next day a young Portug[u]ese came up to me and said "Oh misther Opkins, do *you* feel the cows in *yewer* arm?" I told him I felt the horns coming through. I do I am sure. I cannot remember now whether one ought to say the calf of the arm or the calf of the leg. My shoulder is like a shoulder of beef. I dare not speak above a whisper for fear of bellowing – there now, I was going to say I am obliged to speak low for fear of lowing. I dream at night that I have only two of my legs in bed. I think there is a split coming in both my slippers. Yesterday I could not think why it was that I would wander about on a wet grass-plot: I see now. I chew my pen a great deal. The long and short of it is that my left forequarter is swollen and painful (I meant to have written arm but I could not). Besides the doctor has given us medicine, so that I am in a miserable way just now.

From cows I will turn to lambs. Our fields are full of them. When they were a little younger and nicer and sillier they wd. come gambolling up to one as if one were their mother. One of them sucked my finger and my companion took another up in his arms. The ewes then came up and walked around us making suspicious sheep's eyes at us, as people say. Now, when they are not sucking the breast (to do which they make such terrific butts and digs at the old dam that two of them together will sometimes lift her off her hind legs) they spend their time in bounding and spinning round as if they were tumblers. The same thing is I daresay to be seen (and earlier than this) about Hampstead: still as many of these lambs are ours I cannot pass it by and must tell you of it in black and white.

One thing made me very sad the day we were vaccinated. I was coming away: I left a number of my companions in a room in the infirmary – some had come from the doctor and others were waiting for their turn – all laughing and chatting. As I came down one of the galleries from the room I saw one of our young men standing there looking at a picture. I wondered why he stayed by himself and did not join the rest and then afterwards I remembered that he had had the smallpox and was deeply marked with it and all his good looks gone which he would have had and he did not want to face the others at that time when they were having their fun taking safe precautions against catching what it was too late for him to take any precautions against.

I want to know two things by the next person who writes – first some particulars from Arthur about the American yacht Sappho which seems to have had such great successes last year and next whether it is true that the cuckoo has come unusually early this year, as I heard said. It has not come here yet and I do not know if it will.

With best love to all believe me your loving brother

Gerard M. Hopkins

CLAUDE MONET

CLAUDE MONET (1840–1926), FRENCH IMPRESSIONIST painter.

To George Charpentier (1878)

Charpentier was a publisher and art collector.

I am literally penniless here, obliged to petition people, almost to beg for my keep, not having a penny to buy canvas and paints...

I had called on you this morning in the hope of arranging some small deal, no matter how small, so as not to go home with no money. I was unable to see you, and greatly regret it. I will send you a painting I think you will like. I ask you 150 francs for it, or, if that price seems to you too high, 100 francs, which I should be extremely grateful if you would send to me at Vétheuil, Seine-et-Oise. If the picture is not what you want, I will change it for another when I come back.

Thanking you in anticipation, your devoted

Claude Monet

P.S. I felt I could ask you this because for a long time you had led me to hope you would buy something from me.

I want to ask if you would be good enough to lend me or send me five or ten louis, I am in terrible difficulties at the moment.

I have been ten days in Paris without being able to raise a penny, and I cannot go back to the country, where my wife is very ill.

You would do me a very great service by giving that sum to the bearer and as soon as I return to Paris for good I will call on you and repay you either in painting or in money.

I hope you will not refuse me.

ELIZA SAVAGE

E LIZA SAVAGE (1840–88), ENGLISH GOVERNESS, WIT and assistant secretary of the Society of Lady Artists.

To Samuel Butler (15 September 1880)

Butler was the author of the Utopian satire Erewhon *(1872). The correspondence between Savage and Butler lasted for fourteen years.*

Dear Mr Butler,

... I am glad you are so well; if you have not quite got rid of the spleen you must go and see *The World* at Drury Lane. I went last week; it is a wonderful play. The hero is a delightful man; who could help being charmed with a young man, who, for the sake of making the voyage with the girl he loves, starts from the Cape of Good Hope at a moment's notice, without any other baggage than a bouquet of artificial flowers?

But he is a man of astonishing resources, for in the second scene he appears dressed in a beautiful suit of flannels, which he could not have borrowed as the passengers and crew are all undersized, meagre, little men, whereas the hero is a fine fellow, standing about 5 ft. 11 in. and measuring at least 45 in. round the waist. Later on he escapes from a lunatic asylum, knocking down a dozen or so of keepers, as if they were rag dolls. The asylum is indeed admirably planned for escaping from – the principal entrance being about two feet from the river's brink, and there is a punt kept quite handy into which the hero springs.

This scene is greatly applauded, and well it may be, for I never before saw a punt going at the rate of 20 miles per hour, and it is a sight I am glad to have seen. In the last scene but one the hero shows himself to be of exceeding subtlety, for he goes to the three archvillains who are carousing together and makes them confess, having taken the precaution to bring two shorthand writers with him. They are hidden behind the door, and the audience see them taking notes of all the villains say.

The third scene is rather an uncomfortable one. Four men on a raft in mid ocean – one of them dies of starvation and sticks out his arms and legs, in a really ghastly manner. The survivors fall to fighting, and every minute we expect the portly hero to go plump upon the dead man, who will of course jump up with a yell, and spoil the tragedy of the scene, for the raft is only ten feet square, if that. However they keep clear of the corpse in the most skilful manner; and it is like dancing on eggs. Do go and see this play; there are ever so many more scenes all equally good...

Yours very truly,
E. M. A. *Savage*

To Samuel Butler (18 November 1884)

Dear Mr Butler,

...Are you not glad that Mr and Mrs Carlyle were married to one another, and not to other people? They certainly were justly formed to meet by nature. I was provoked last night by the nonsense some people were talking about him, and as they went on to excuse his bad temper on account of his bad digestion, I said that probably his bad digestion should be excused on account of his bad temper, as probably he had been born with a bad temper, but that bad digestions were generally made (I remember *Erewhon* you see)...

Yours very truly,
E. M. A. Savage

❧

Samuel Butler to Eliza Savage (21 November 1884)

Dear Miss Savage,

...Yes it was very good of God to let Carlyle and Mrs Carlyle marry one another and so make only two people miserable instead of four.

Believe me, Yours very truly,
S. Butler

GENERAL CHARLES GORDON

IN EARLY 1884 GENERAL GORDON (1833–85) WAS ASKED by the British government to relieve Egyptian garrisons threatened by the jihad of the Mahdi. A month after he reached Khartoum it was invested by enemy troops; a relief force, belatedly organized, made slow progress not reaching Khartoum until 28 January 1885. The town had fallen two days before, with Gordon murdered on the palace steps.

To Major Watson
(14 December 1884, from Khartoum)

My dear Watson,

I think the game is up and send Mrs Watson, you & Graham my adieux. We may expect a catastrophe in the town, on or after 10 days time. This would not have happened (if it does happen) if our people had taken better precautions as to informing us, of their movements, but this is "spilt milk". Good bye, Mind & let my brother (68 Elm Park Road, Chelsea) know what I owe you.

Yours sincerely
C. G. *Gordon*.

WINSTON CHURCHILL

SIR WINSTON LEONARD SPENCER CHURCHILL (1874–1965), British soldier and statesman, prime minister 1940–5, 1951–5.

To his mother, Lady Randolph Churchill (7 November 1888)

Written while Churchill was a pupil at Harrow.

Dearest Mamma,

I am going to write you a proper epistle, hoping you will forgive my former negligence. On Saturday we had a lecture on the

"Phonograph"

By "Col Gouraud". It was very amusing he astonished all sober-minded People by singing into the Phonograph

"John Brown Body lies – Mouldy in the grave
And is soul goes marching on
Glory, glory, glory Halleluja"

And the Phonograph spoke it back in a voice that was clearly audible in the "Speech Room"

He shewed us it in private on Monday. We went in 3 or 4 at a time.
His boys are at Harrow.
He fought at Gettysburg.
His wife was at school with you.
Papa gave him letter of introduction to India.
He told me to ask Papa if he remembered the "tall Yankee".
I want to be allowed to join the Harrow work shop for they then supply you wood and I want to make some scenery for the nursery if we have any Party. 3 or 4 scenes cost about $1/2$ a sovereign and the man who is in charge thoroughly understands scenery making.

With love & kisses I remain
Winston S. Churchill

P.S. Will you write to say whether I may join as I have no imployment for odd half hours. W. C.

JOSEPH CONRAD

J OSEPH CONRAD (1857–1924), POLISH-BORN NOVELIST,
originally Jozef Teodor Konrad Nalecz Korzeniowski.
He spent many years as a merchant sailor, gaining a
master's certificate in 1884, including a spell in the
Belgian Congo which provided the basis for *Heart of
Darkness*.

To his aunt, Marguerite Poradowska (26 September 1890), from Kinshasa

Dearest and best of Aunts!

I received your three letters together on my return from Stanley
Falls, where I went as a supernumerary on board the vessel *Roi des
Belges* in order to learn about the river. I learn with joy of your
success at the Academy, which, of course, I never doubted. I cannot
find words sufficiently strong to make you understand the pleasure
your charming (and above all kind) letters have given me. They
were as a ray of sunshine piercing through the grey clouds of a dreary
winter day; for my days here are dreary. No use deluding oneself!
Decidedly I regret having come here. I even regret it bitterly. With
all of a man's egoism, I am going to speak of myself. I cannot stop
myself. Before whom can I ease my heart if not before you?! In
speaking to you, I am certain of being understood down to the
merest hint. Your heart will divine my thoughts more quickly than I
can express them.

Everything here is repellent to me. Men and things, but men
above all. And I am repellent to them, also. From the manager in
Africa who has taken the trouble to tell one and all that I offend him
supremely, down to the lowest mechanic, they all have the gift of
irritating my nerves – so that I am not as agreeable to them perhaps

as I should be. The manager is a common ivory dealer with base instincts who considers himself a merchant although he is only a kind of African shop-keeper. His name is Delcommune. He detests the English, and out here I am naturally regarded as such. I cannot hope for either promotion or salary increases while he is here. Besides, he has said that promises made in Europe carry no weight here if they are not in the contract. Those made to me by M. Wauters are not. In addition, I cannot look forward to anything because I don't have a ship to command. The new boat will not be completed until June of next year, perhaps. Meanwhile, my position here is unclear and I am troubled by that. So there you are! As crowning joy, my health is far from good. *Keep it a secret for me* – but the truth is that in going up the river I suffered from fever four times in two months, and then at the Falls (which is its home territory), I suffered an attack of dysentery lasting five days. I feel somewhat weak physically and not a little demoralized; and then, really, I believe that I feel homesick for the sea, the desire to look again on the level expanse of salt water which has so often lulled me, which has smiled at me so frequently under the sparkling sunshine of a lovely day, which many times too has hurled the threat of death in my face with a swirl of white foam whipped by the wind under the dark December sky. I regret all that. But what I regret even more is having tied myself down for three years. The truth is that it is scarcely probable I shall see them through. Either someone in authority will pick a groundless quarrel in order to send me back (and, really, I sometimes find myself wishing for it), or I shall be sent back to Europe by a new attack of dysentery, unless it consigns me to the other world, which would be a final solution to all my distress! And for four pages I have been speaking of myself! I have not told you with what pleasure I have read your descriptions of men and things at home. Indeed, while reading your dear letters I have forgotten Africa, the Congo, the black savages and the white slaves (of whom I am one) who inhabit it. For one hour I have been happy. Know that it is not a small thing (nor an easy thing) to make a human being happy for an *entire hour*. You can be proud of having succeeded. And so my heart goes out to you with a burst of gratitude and the most sincere and most profound affection. When will we meet again? Alas, meeting leads to parting – and the more one meets, the more painful the separations become. Such is Fate.

Seeking a practical remedy to the disagreeable situation which I have made for myself, I conceived of a little plan – still up in the air – in which you could perhaps help me. It appears that this company, or another affiliated with it, will have some ocean-going vessels (or even has one already). Probably that great (or fat?) banker who rules the roost where we are concerned will have a large interest in the other company. If someone could submit my name for the command of one of their ships (whose home port will be Antwerp) I would be able to get away for a day or two in Brussels when you are there. That would be ideal! If they wanted to call me home to take command, I would naturally pay the cost of coming back myself. This is perhaps not a very practicable idea, but if you return to Brussels in the winter, you could learn through M. Wauters what the chances are. Isn't that so, dear little Aunt?

I am going to send this care of the Princess (whom I love because she loves you). Soon, probably, you will see poor, dear Aunt Gaba, and that dear and good Charles Zagórski family with their charming little daughters. I envy you! Tell them that I love them all and that I ask a little something in return. Mlle Marysiénka has probably forgotten the promise she made me about her photograph. I am ever her devoted cousin and servant. I dare not say "admirer" for fear of my Aunt Oldakowska, to whom I wish to be remembered with affection. I urge you by all the gods to keep secret from *everybody* the state of my health, or else my uncle will certainly hear of it. I must finish. I leave within an hour for Bamou, by canoe, to select trees and have them felled for building operations at the station here. I shall remain encamped in the forest for two or three weeks, unless ill. I like the prospect well enough. I can doubtless have a shot or two at some buffaloes or elephants. I embrace you most warmly. I shall write a long letter by the next mail.

Your affectionate nephew
J.C.K.

Oscar Wilde

Oscar Fingall O'Flahertie Wills Wilde (1854–1900), playwright and wit. In May 1895 Wilde was imprisoned for homosexuality, serving two years with hard labour.

❧

To Lord Alfred Douglas (January 1893)

Lord Alfred Douglas, nicknamed "Bosie", was Wilde's lover.

My Own Boy,

Your sonnet is quite lovely, and it is a marvel that those red rose-leaf lips of yours should have been made no less for music of song than for madness of kisses. Your slim gilt soul walks between passion and poetry. I know Hyacinthus, whom Apollo loved so madly, was you in Greek days.

Why are you alone in London, and when do you go to Salisbury? Do go there to cool your hands in the grey twilight of Gothic things, and come here whenever you like. It is a lovely place – only it lacks you; but go to Salisbury first. Always, with undying love, yours

Oscar

❧

To Lord Alfred Douglas (March 1893)

Dearest of all Boys,

Your letter was delightful, red and yellow wine to me; but I am sad and out of sorts. Bosie, you must not make scenes with me. They kill me, they wreck the loveliness of life. I cannot see you, so Greek and gracious, distorted with passion. I cannot listen to your curved lips saying hideous things to me. I would sooner (be blackmailed by every renter in London) than have you bitter, unjust, hating. I must see you soon. You are the divine thing I want, the thing of grace and beauty; but I don't know how to do it. Shall I come to Salisbury? My bill here is £49 for a week. I have also got a new sitting-room over the Thames. Why are you not here, my dear, my wonderful boy? I fear I must leave; no money, no credit, and a heart of lead.

Your own *Oscar*

To Lord Alfred Douglas (20 May 1895)

My child,

Today it was asked to have the verdicts rendered separately. Taylor* is probably being judged at this moment, so that I have been able to come back here. My sweet rose, my delicate flower, my lily of lilies, it is perhaps in prison that I am going to test the power of love. I am going to see if I cannot make the bitter waters sweet by the intensity of the love I bear you. I have had moments when I thought it would be wiser to separate. Ah! moments of weakness and madness! Now I see that that would have mutilated my life, ruined my art, broken the musical chords which make a perfect soul. Even covered with mud I shall praise you, from the deepest abysses I shall cry to you. In my solitude you will be with me. I am determined not to revolt but to accept every outrage through devotion to love, to let my body be dishonoured so long as my soul may always keep the image of you. From your silken hair to your delicate feet you are perfection to me. Pleasure hides love from us but pain reveals it in its essence. O dearest of created things, if someone wounded by silence and solitude comes to you, dishonoured, a laughing-stock to men, oh! you can close his wounds by touching them and restore his

---

*Alfred Waterhouse Somerset Taylor, a prominent London homosexual, was indicted and tried alongside Wilde after refusing to turn Queen's evidence.

soul which unhappiness had for a moment smothered. Nothing will be difficult for you then, and remember, it is that hope which makes me live, and that hope alone. What wisdom is to the philosopher, what God is to his saint, you are to me. To keep you in my soul, such is the goal of this pain which men call life. O my love, you whom I cherish above all things, white narcissus in an unmown field, think of the burden which falls to you, a burden which love alone can make light. But be not saddened by that, rather be happy to have filled with an immortal love the soul of a man who now weeps in hell, and yet carries heaven in his heart. I love you, I love you, my heart is a rose which your love has brought to bloom, my life is a desert fanned by the delicious breeze of your breath, and whose cool springs are your eyes; the imprint of your little feet makes valleys of shade for me, the odour of your hair is like myrrh, and wherever you go you exhale the perfumes of the cassia tree.

Love me always, love me always. You have been the supreme the perfect love of my life; there can be no other.

I decided that it was nobler and more beautiful to stay. We could not have been together. I did not want to be called a coward or a deserter. A false name, a disguise, a hunted life, all that is not for me, to whom you have been revealed on that high hill where beautiful things are transfigured. O sweetest of all boys, most loved of all loves, my soul clings to your soul, my life is your life, and in all the worlds of pain and pleasure you arc my ideal of admiration and joy.

Oscar

❧

To Major J.O. Nelson (28 May 1897)

Wilde's letter to Nelson, the governor of Reading Gaol, was written shortly after his release and his emigration to France.

Dear Major Nelson,

I had of course intended to write to you as soon as I had safely reached French soil, to express, however inadequately, my real feelings of what you must let me term, not merely sincere, but *affectionate* gratitude to you for your kindness and gentleness to me in prison, and for the real care that you took of me at the end, when I was mentally upset and in a state of very terrible nervous excitement. You must not mind my using the word "gratitude." I used to think gratitude a burden to carry. Now I know that it is something that makes the heart lighter. The ungrateful man is one who walks slowly with feet and heart of lead. But when one knows the strange joy of gratitude to God and man the earth becomes lovelier to one, and it is a pleasure to count up, not one's wealth but one's debts, not the little that one possesses, but the much that one owes.

I abstained from writing, however, because I was haunted by the memory of the little children, & the wretched half witted lad who was flogged by the Doctor's orders. I could not have kept them out of my letter, and to have mentioned them to you might have put *you* in a difficult position. In your reply you *might* have expressed sympathy with my views – I think you would have – and then on the appearance of my public letter you might have felt as if I had, in some almost ungenerous or thoughtless way, procured your private opinion on official things, for use as corroboration.

I longed to speak to you about these things on the evening of my departure, but I felt that in my position as a prisoner it would have been wrong of me to do so, and that it would, or might have put you in a difficult position afterwards, as well as at the time. I only hear of my letter being published by a telegram from Mr Ross, but I hope they have printed it in full, as I tried to express in it my appreciation and admiration of your own humane spirit and affectionate interest in *all* the prisoners under your charge. I did not wish people to think that any exception had been specially made for me. Such exceptional treatment as I received was by order of the Commissioners. You gave me the same kindness as you gave to everyone. Of course I made more demands, but then I think I had really more needs than others – and I lacked often their cheerful acquiescence –

Of course I side with the prisoners – I was one, and I belong to their class now – I am not a scrap ashamed of having been in prison. I am horribly ashamed of the materialism of the life that brought me there. It was quite unworthy of an artist.

Of Martin, and the subjects of my letter I of course say nothing at all, except that the man who could change the system – if any one man can do so – is yourself. At present I write to ask you to allow me to sign myself, once at any rate in life,

your sincere and grateful friend
Oscar Wilde.

EMILE ZOLA

BORN IN PARIS OF AN ITALIAN ENGINEER FATHER, ZOLA (1840–1902) was the author of the Naturalist novels *L'Assommoir*, *La Terre* and *Germinal*. In 1898 Zola espoused the cause of the French Jewish officer Alfred Dreyfus, who was unjustly convicted of passing national defence material to a foreign government. Zola's open letter to President Félix Faure was published in the liberal newspaper *L'Aurore*. For writing the letter, known henceforth by the celebrated title of "*J'accuse...*", Zola was found guilty, in a rigged case, of criminal libel but avoided imprisonment by escaping to England. He later returned to France a national hero.

❧

To President Félix Faure of France (January 1898)

Mr President,
   Permit me, I beg you, in return for the gracious favours you once

accorded me, to be concerned with regard to your just glory and to tell you that your record, so fair and fortunate thus far, is now threatened with the most shameful, the most ineffaceable blot.

You escaped safe and sane from the basest calumnies; you conquered all hearts. You seem radiant in the glory of a patriotic celebration... and are preparing to preside over the solemn triumph of our Universal Exposition, which is to crown our great century of work, truth and liberty. But what a clod of mud is flung upon your name – I was about to say your reign – through this abominable Dreyfus affair. A court martial has but recently, by order, dared to acquit one Esterhazy – a supreme slap at all truth, all justice! And it is done; France has this brand upon her visage; history will relate that it was during your administration that such a social crime could be committed.

Since, they have dared, I too shall dare. I shall tell the truth because I pledged myself to tell it if justice, regularly empowered, did not do so, fully, unmitigatedly. My duty is to speak; I have no wish to be an accomplice. My nights would be haunted by the spectre of the innocent being, expiating under the most frightful torture, a crime he never committed.

And it is to you, Mr President, that I shall out this truth, with the force of my revolt as an honest man. To your honour, I am convinced that you are ignorant of the crime. And to whom, then, shall I denounce the malignant rabble of true culprits, if not to you, the highest magistrate in the country?...

I accuse Colonel du Paty de Clam of having been the diabolical agent of the judicial error, unconsciously, I prefer to believe, and of having continued to defend his deadly work during the past three years through the most absurd and revolting machinations.

I accuse General Mercier of having made himself an accomplice in one of the greatest crimes of history, probably through weak-mindedness.

I accuse General Billot of having had in his hands the decisive proofs of the innocence of Dreyfus and of having concealed them, and of having rendered himself guilty of the crime of lèse humanity and lèse justice, out of political motives and to save the face of the

General Staff.

I accuse General Boisdeffre and General Gonse of being accomplices in the same crime, the former no doubt through religious prejudice, the latter out of *esprit de corps*.

I accuse General de Pellieux and Major Ravary of having made a scoundrelly inquest, I mean an inquest of the most monstrous partiality, the complete report of which composes for us an imperishable monument of naïve effrontery.

I accuse the three handwriting experts, MM. Belhomme, Varinard and Couard, of having made lying and fraudulent reports, unless a medical examination will certify them to be deficient of sight and judgment.

I accuse the War Office of having led a vile campaign in the press, particularly in *l'Éclair* and *l'Écho de Paris*, in order to misdirect public opinion and cover up its sins.

I accuse, lastly, the first court martial of having violated all human right in condemning a prisoner on testimony kept secret from him, and I accuse the second court martial of having covered up this illegality by order, committing in turn the judicial crime of acquitting a guilty man with full knowledge of his guilt.

In making these accusations I am aware that I render myself liable to articles 30 and 31 of Libel Laws of 29 July 1881, which punish acts of defamation. I expose myself voluntarily.

As to the men I accuse, I do not know them, I have never seen them, I feel neither resentment nor hatred against them. For me they are only entities, emblems of social malfeasance. The action I take here is simply a revolutionary step designed to hasten the explosion of truth and justice.

I have one passion only, for light, in the name of humanity which has borne so much and has a right to happiness. My burning protest is only the cry of my soul. Let them dare, then, to carry me to the court of appeals, and let there be an inquest in the full light of the day!

I am waiting.

Mr President, I beg you to accept the assurances of my deepest respect.

Emile Zola

ERIK SATIE

E RIK SATIE (1866–1967), FRENCH COMPOSER.

To his brother, Conrad Satie (1900)

I am overcome with ennui to the extent of dying of a broken heart. Everything I quietly begin to undertake fails in the most spectacular fashion.

I am beginning to turn on God Himself and have got to the state of wondering whether He is not more unfortunate than all powerful.

What news have you?... Your future will not be like mine, fortunately for you. You will have a horse, a big carriage, open in summer, closed in winter; and you will go wherever you wish, like the people of leisure.

I take you into my poor arms.

EDITH WHARTON

E DITH WHARTON (c.1861–1937), AMERICAN NOVELIST and short-story writer. She married Edward Wharton in 1885, but the marriage was a disaster, partly because of his lack of interest in her work and literary friends. In 1907 she began an affair with the journalist W. Morton Fullerton, seven years her junior, but he gradually withdrew from her, to her despair.

To W. Morton Fullerton (26 August 1908)

Dear, won't you tell me soon the meaning of this silence?

At first I thought it might mean that your sentimental mood had cooled, & that you feared to let me see the change; & I wrote, nearly a month ago, to tell you how natural I should think such a change on your part, & how I hoped that our friendship – so dear to me! – might survive it. – It would have been easy, after that letter, to send a friendly: "Yes, chere amie – " surely, having known me so well all those months, you could have trusted to my understanding it?

But the silence continues! It was not *that* you wanted? For a time I fancied you were too busy & happy to think of writing – perhaps even to glance at my letters when they came. But even so – there are degrees in the lapse from such intimacy as ours into complete silence & oblivion; & if the inclination to write had died out, must not you, who are so sensitive & imaginative, have asked yourself to what conjectures you were leaving me, & how I should suffer at being so abruptly & inexplicably cut off from all news of you?

I re-read your letters the other day, & I will not believe that the man who wrote them did not feel them, & did not know enough of the woman to whom they were written to trust to her love & courage, rather than to leave her to this aching uncertainty.

What has brought about such a change? Oh, no matter what it is – *only tell me!* I could take my life up again courageously if I only understood; for whatever those months were to you, to me they were a great gift, a wonderful enrichment; & still I rejoice thanks for them! You woke me from a long lethargy, a dull acquiescence in conventional restrictions, a needless self-effacement. If I was awkward & inarticulate it was because, literally, all one side of me was asleep.

I remember, that night we went to the *Figlia di Iorio*, that in the scene in the cave, where the Figlia sends him back to his mother (I forget all their names), & as he goes he turns & kisses her, & *then she can't let him go* – I remember you turned to me & said laughing: "That's something you don't know anything about."

Well! I *did* know, soon afterward; & if I still remained inexpressive, unwilling, "always drawing away," as you said, it was because I discovered in myself such possibilities of feeling on that side that I feared, if I let you love me too much, I might lose courage when the time came to go away! – Surely you saw this, & understood how I dreaded to be to you, *even for an instant*, the "donna non più giovane" who clings & encumbers – how, situated as I was, I thought I could best show my love by refraining – & abstaining? You saw it was all because I loved you?

And when you spoke of your uncertain future, your longing to break away & do the work you really like, didn't you see how my heart *broke* with the thought that, if I had been younger & prettier, everything might have been different – that we might have had together, at least for a short time, a life of exquisite collaborations – a life in which your gifts would have had full scope, & you would have been able to do the distinguished & beautiful things that you ought to do. – Now, I hope, your future has after all arranged itself happily, just as you despaired, – but remember that *those were my thoughts* when you were calling me "conventional"...

I never expected to tell you this; but under the weight of this silence I don't know what to say or leave unsaid. After nearly a month my frank tender of friendship remains unanswered. If that was not what you wished, what is then your feeling for me? My reason rejects the idea that a man like you, who has felt a warm sympathy for a woman like me, can suddenly, from one day to another, without any act or word on her part, lose even a friendly regard for her, & discard the mere outward signs of consideration by which friendship speaks. And so I am almost driven to conclude that your silence has another meaning, which I have not guessed. If any feeling subsists under it, may these words reach it, & tell you what I felt in silence when we were together!

Yes, dear, I loved you then, & I love you now, as you then wished me to; only I have learned that one must put all happiness one can into each moment, & I will never again love you "sadly," since that displeases you.

You see I am once more assuming that you *do* care what I feel, in spite of this mystery! How can it be that the sympathy between two people like ourselves, so many-sided, so steeped in imagination, should end from one day to another like a mere "passade" – end by my passing, within a few weeks, utterly out of your memory? By all that I know you are, by all I am myself conscious of being, I declare that I am unable to believe it!

You told me once I should write better for this experience of loving. I felt it to be so, & I came home so fired by the desire that my work should please you! But this incomprehensible silence, the sense of your utter indifference to everything that concerns me, has stunned me. It has come so suddenly...

This is the last time I will write you, dear, unless the strange spell is broken. And my last word is one of tenderness for the friend I love – for the lover I worshipped.

Goodbye, dear.

Oh, I don't want my letters back, dearest! I said that in my other letter only to make it easier for you if you were seeking a transition –

Do you suppose I care what becomes of them if you don't care?

Is it really to my dear friend – to *Henry's friend* – to "dearest Morton" – that I have written this?

ALBAN BERG

ALBAN BERG (1885–1935), PIONEER OF ATONALITY, was the composer of the opera *Wozzeck*. He married Helene Nahowski in 1911. After Berg died, she wrote: "For twenty-eight years I lived in the Paradise of his love. His death was a catastrophe I only had the strength to survive because our souls were long ago joined in a union beyond space and time, a union through all eternity".

To Helene Nahowski (Autumn, 1907), from Vienna

This beautiful paper is all I can find in my bedroom, to make the most of the few minutes before midnight, the first free moments I can give completely to you; because things have been somewhat hectic the last twenty-four hours and I feel quite done up.

After we left you last night. I had a quick dinner and drove to the Schoenbergs'.* Conversation there very serious and lofty at first, but later quite light-hearted. Around midnight some of us walked into town, and went to the *Fledermaus*. Rather boring at first, and afterwards we five (Smaragda, Loos, La Bruckner, Klimt** and myself) went to the "Z-Keller am Hof" where things became fairly confused for the next few hours. In fact, Helene – well, how can I put it? Should I say the left side of my body, where the heart beats only for you, didn't know what the right side was doing? Because that was the side where La B. was sitting, and – oh, forgive me, Helene – that side was unfaithful to you. She has wonderful hands, which I can't help being attracted by, I confess it, and they made me behave in a stupid way, though I'm sure at any other time of day I could have resisted!

Afterwards we went on to the "Casa piccola", and home at dawn. To Schoenberg in the afternoon, then into town. Home at half past four, drank some tea to revive myself, and in the evening to the concert, where I thought a lot of you and Anna. Among other things they played Charpentier's *Impressions d'Italie*, with its glorious finale commonly called "Napoli". When I got back at night, I found the sad news of your not being well, which cast a dark shadow over the joys and fevers of the last hours. So I decided not to go to bed before writing to you. (To bring relief to myself, as it were, and help you pass a few minutes lying in bed.)

One glimpse into the near future – what about Saturday ? Will you come? It would be very dull without you.

That's all for now. I'm exhausted, and there's my bed, waiting enticingly to receive me. I want to dream of you, Helene – goodnight!

Alban

---

*Arnold Schoenberg, composer, and wife
**Adolf Loos, architect; Gustav Klimt, artist

To Helen Nahowski (8 November 1907)
"The day was almost frightening in its splendour, The day of the chrysanthemums white..."

Truly, Helene, my dearest and most beloved, I found the splendour of yesterday's joy almost frightening. I have kissed you! I had to join my lips with yours, I was driven, irresistibly, by some inner force I would not escape. So much ecstasy all at once, my eyes were wet with tears, all my body and soul swamped in one great flood of emotion. This is how much I love you.

Dazed with delight, I staggered homewards, feeling only your sweet hand caressing my soul. I was rocked in bliss, bearing home on my lips the most glorious of kisses.

"...You came; like fairy music faintly pealing
Soft rang the night."

To Helene Nahowski (Autumn 1907)

...When I came into my bedroom last night I felt a fragrance which made my heart tremble. At once I found myself thinking of you, and then I saw the three dark red roses amidst the green laurel leaves.

They are from you, that was my first thought – no, my first and only hope, my most solemn wish. Only you could have somehow produced from your heart this symbol – the three roses which, like my three songs, are comparable to gifts of love. Oh, leave me with the lovely dream, if dream it be, that these roses, their colour glowing with love, conceal the sparks of love within them. This thought went round and round in my mind for a long time, and it was very late in the night – or early morning – before I could get to sleep.

My first moment awake, I was already thinking of you again, my one and only love. Then I learnt that my fond hope was no dream, the laurel leaves and roses *were* from you. I can't describe how overjoyed I was at that moment, I could have hugged the pillow and kissed it in my utter bliss. And then, to crown everything, they told me you would be coming today with Smaragda. How am I going to thank you in words, I wondered, when all my thanks are revealed only in the beating of my heart? Could I thank you in front of everybody, or would you be embarrassed, would you even deny having sent the roses?

Alas, I was spared the answer to these questions, for you did not come. And now I am dying of desire for you. I plunge my face into the cool laurel leaves and soothe my sweet sorrow in the fragrance of the roses. But all too soon the blossoms will fade, and I shall have nothing left but the memory of the few moments, I was loved. That makes me unutterably sad.

"What a baby!"

D. H. LAWRENCE

THE SON OF A NOTTINGHAMSHIRE MINER, D. H. Lawrence (1885–1930) published his first novel *The White Peacock*, in 1911, the success of which allowed him to live by writing. *Women in Love*, *The Rainbow* and *Lady Chatterley's Lover* followed.

❧

To Rachel Annand Taylor (3 December 1910)

Rachel Taylor (1876–1960), poet.

Dear Mrs Taylor,

I did not know where you were. I am glad you wrote to me.

I have been at home now ten days. My mother is very near the end. Today I have been to Leicester. I did not get home till half past nine. Then I ran upstairs. Oh she was very bad. The pains had been again.

"Oh my dear" I said, "is it the pains?"

"Not pain now – Oh the weariness" she moaned, so that I could hardly hear her. I wish she could die tonight.

My sister and I do all the nursing. My sister is only 22. I sit upstairs hours and hours, till I wonder if ever it were true that I was at London. I seem to have died since, and that is an old life, dreamy.

I will tell you. My mother was a clever, ironical delicately moulded woman, of good, old burgher descent. She married below her. My father was dark, ruddy, with a fine laugh. He is a coal miner. He was one of the sanguine temperament, warm and hearty, but unstable: he lacked principle, as my mother would have said. He deceived her and lied to her. She despised him – he drank.

Their marriage life has been one carnal, bloody fight. I was born hating my father: as early as ever I can remember, I shivered with horror when he touched me. He was very bad before I was born.

This has been a kind of bond between me and my mother. We have loved each other, almost with a husband and wife love, as well as filial and maternal. We knew each other by instinct. She said to my aunt – about me:

"But it has been different with him. He has seemed to be part of me." – and that is the real case. We have been like one, so sensitive to each other that we never needed words. It has been rather terrible, and has made me, in some respects, abnormal.

I think this peculiar fusion of soul (don't think me high-falutin) never comes twice in a life-time – it doesn't seem natural. When it comes it seems to distribute one's consciousness far abroad from oneself, and one "understands" I think no one has got "Understanding" except through love. Now my mother is nearly dead, and I don't quite know how I am.

I have been to Leicester today, I have met a girl who has always been warm for me – like a sunny happy day – and I've gone and asked her to marry me: in the train, quite unpremeditated, between Rothley and Quorn – she lives at Quorn. When I think of her I feel happy with a sort of warm radiation – she is big and dark and handsome. There were five other people in the carriage. Then when I think of my mother: – if you've ever put your hand round the bowl of a champagne glass and squeezed it and wondered how near it is to crushing-in and the wine all going through your fingers – that's how my heart feels – like the champagne glass. There is no hostility between the warm happiness and the crush of misery: but one is concentrated in my chest, and one is diffuse – a suffusion, vague.

Muriel is the girl I have broken with. She loves me to madness, and demands the soul of me. I have been cruel to her, and wronged her, but I did not know.

Nobody can have the soul of me. My mother has had it, and nobody can have it again. Nobody can come into my very self again, and breathe me like an atmosphere. Don't say I am hasty this time – I know. Louie – whom I wish I could marry the day after the funeral – she would never demand to drink me up and have me. She loves me – but it is a fine, warm, healthy, natural love – not like Jane Eyre, who is Muriel, but like – say Rhoda Fleming or a commoner Anna Karénin. She will never plunge her hands through my blood and feel for my soul, and make me set my teeth and shiver and fight away. Ugh – I have done well – and cruelly – tonight.

I look at my father – he is like a cinder. It is very terrible, mismarriage.

They sent me yesterday one copy of the *Peacock* for my mother. She just looked at it. It will not be out till spring.

I will tell you next time about that meeting when I gave a paper on you. It was *most* exciting. I worked my audience up to red heat – and I laughed.

Are you any better? – you don't say so. Tell me you are getting strong, and then you and I will not re-act so alarmingly – at least, you on me.

Goodnight
D. H. Lawrence

D. H. LAWRENCE

To Bertrand Russell (19 February 1916)

*Bertrand Russell (1872–1970), philosopher, the author – with Alfred
North Whitehead – of Principia Mathematica which allowed that the
whole of mathematics could be derived from logic.*

My dear Russell,

I didn't like your letter. What's the good of living as you do, anyway.
I don't believe your lectures are good. One must be an outlaw these
days, not a teacher or preacher. One must retire out of the herd and
then fire bombs into it. You said in your lecture on education that you
didn't set much count by the unconscious. That is sheer perversity. The
whole of the consciousness and the conscious content is old hat – the
millstone round your neck. Even your mathematics are only dead truth:
and no matter how fine you grind the dead meat, you'll not bring it to
life again. Do stop working and writing altogether and become a
creature instead of a mechanical instrument. Do clear out of the social
ship. Do for your very pride's sake become a mere nothing, a mole, a
creature that feels its way and doesn't think. Do for heavens sake be a
baby, and not a savant any more. Don't do anything any more – but for
heavens sake begin to be – start at the very beginning and be a perfect
baby: in the name of courage. Soon I shall be penniless, and they'll
shove me into munitions, and I shall tell 'em what I think of 'em, and
end my days in prison or a madhouse. But I don't care. One can still
write bombs. But I don't want to be penniless and at their mercy. Life is
very good of itself, and I am terrified lest they should get me into their
power. They seem to me like an innumerable host of rats, and once they
get the scent, one is lost. My love to you. Stop working and being an
ego, and have the courage to be a creature.

❦

To a friend (1928), written from Germany

We are going back to Paris to-morrow, so this is the last moment to
write a letter from Germany. Only from the fringe of Germany, too.

It is a miserable journey from Paris to Nancy, through that Marne country, where the country still seems to have had the soul blasted out of it, though the dreary fields are ploughed and level, and the pale wire trees stand up. But it is all void and null. And in the villages, the smashed houses in the street rows, like rotten teeth between good teeth.

You come to Strasbourg, and the people still talk Alsatian German, as ever, in spite of French shop-signs. The place feels dead. And full of cotton goods, white goods, from Mülhausen, from the factories that once were German. Such cheap white cotton goods, in a glut.

The cathedral front rearing up high and flat and fanciful, a sort of darkness in the dark, with round rose windows and long, long prisons of stone. Queer that men should have ever wanted to put stone upon faithful stone to such a height without having it fall down. The gothic! I was always glad when my card-castle fell. But these goths and alemans seemed to have a craze for peaky heights.

The Rhine is still the Rhine, the great divider. You feel it as you cross. The flat, frozen, watery places. Then the cold and curving river. Then the other side, seeming so cold, so empty, so frozen, so forsaken. The train stands and steams fiercely. Then it draws through the flat Rhine plain, past frozen pools of flood-water, and frozen fields, in the emptiness of this bit of occupied territory.

Immediately you are over the Rhine, the spirit of place has changed. There is no more attempt at the bluff of geniality. The marshy places are frozen. The fields are vacant. There seems nobody in the world.

It is as if the life had retreated eastwards. As if the Germanic life were slowly ebbing away from contact with western Europe, ebbing to the deserts of the east. And there stand the heavy, ponderous round hills of the Black Forest, black with an inky blackness of Germanic trees, and patched with a whiteness of snow. They are like a series of huge, involved black mounds, obstructing the vision eastwards. You look at them from the Rhine plain, and know that you stand on an actual border, up against something.

The moment you are in Germany, you know. It feels empty, and, somehow, menacing. So must the Roman soldiers have watched

350

those black, massive round hills: with a certain fear, and with the knowledge that they were at their own limit. A fear of the invisible natives. A fear of the invisible life lurking among the woods. A fear of their own opposite.

So it is with the French: this almost mystic fear. But one should not insult even one's fears.

Germany, this bit of Germany, is very different from what it was two and a half years ago, when I was here. Then it was still open to Europe. Then it still looked to western Europe for a reunion, for a sort of reconciliation. Now that is over. The inevitable, mysterious barrier has fallen again, and the great leaning of the Germanic spirit is once more eastwards, towards Russia, towards Tartary. The strange vortex of Tartary has become the positive centre again, the positivity of western Europe is broken. The positivity of our civilisation has broken. The influences that come, come invisibly out of Tartary. So that all Germany reads *Men, Beasts and Gods* with a kind of fascination. Returning again to the fascination of the destructive East, that produced Attila.

So it is at night. Baden-Baden is a little quiet place, all its guests gone. No more Turgenevs or Dostoevskys or Grand Dukes or King Edwards coming to drink the waters. All the outward effect of a world-famous watering-place. But empty now, a mere Black Forest village with the wagon-loads of timber going through, to the French.

The Rentenmark, the new gold Mark of Germany, is abominably dear. Prices are high in England, but English money buys less in Baden than it buys in London, by a long chalk. And there is no work — consequently no money. Nobody buys anything, except absolute necessities. The shopkeepers are in despair. And there is less and less work.

Everybody gives up the telephone — can't afford it. The tramcars don't run, except about three times a day to the station. Up to the Annaberg, the suburb, the lines are rusty, no trams ever go. The people can't afford the ten pfennigs for the fare. Ten pfennigs is an important sum now: one penny. It is really a hundred Milliards of Marks.

Money becomes insane, and people with it.

At night the place is almost dark, economising light. Economy,

economy, economy – that, too, becomes an insanity. Luckily the government keeps bread fairly cheap.

But at night you feel strange things stirring in the darkness, strange feelings stirring out of this still-unconquered Black Forest. You stiffen your backbone and you listen to the night. There is a sense of danger. It is not the people. They don't seem dangerous. Out of the very air comes a sense of danger, a queer, bristling feeling of uncanny danger.

Something has happened. Something has happened which has not yet eventuated. The old spell of the old world has broken, and the old, bristling, savage spirit has set in. The war did not break the old peace-and-production hope of the world, though it gave it a severe wrench. Yet the old peace-and-production hope still governs, at least the consciousness. Even in Germany it has not quite gone.

But it feels as if, virtually, it were gone. The last two years have done it. The hope in peace-and-production is broken. The old flow, the old adherence is ruptured. And a still older flow has set in. Back, back to the savage polarity of Tartary, and away from the polarity of civilised Christian Europe. This, it seems to me, has already happened. And it is a happening of far more profound import than any actual event. It is the father of the next phase of events.

And the feeling never relaxes. As you travel up the Rhine valley, still the same latent sense of danger, of silence, of suspension. Not that the people are actually planning or plotting or preparing. I don't believe it for a minute. But something has happened to the human soul, beyond all hope. The human soil recoiling now from unison, and making itself strong elsewhere. The ancient spirit of prehistoric Germany coming back, at the end of history.

The same in Heidelberg. Heidelberg full, full, full of people. Students the same, youth with rucksacks the same, boys and maidens in gangs come down from the hills. The same, and not the same. These queer gangs of *Young Socialists*, youths and girls, with their non-materialistic professions, their half-mystic assertions, they strike one as strange. Something primitive, like loose, roving gangs of broken, scattered tribes, so they affect one. And the swarms of people, somehow produce an impression of silence, of secrecy, of stealth. It is as if everything and everybody recoiled away from the old unison, as barbarians lurking in a wood recoil out of sight. The old habits remain. But the bulk of the people have not money. And the whole stream of feeling is reversed.

And it all looks as if the years were wheeling swiftly backwards, no more onwards. Like a spring that is broken and whirls swiftly back, so time seems to be whirling with mysterious swiftness to a sort of death. Whirling to the ghost of the old Middle Ages of Germany, then to the Roman days, then to the days of the silent forest and the dangerous, lurking barbarians.

Something about the Germanic races is unalterable. White-skinned, elemental, and dangerous. Our civilisation has come from the fusion of the dark-eyed with the blue. The meeting and mixing and mingling of the two races has been the joy of our ages. And the Celt has been there, alien, but necessary as some chemical reagent to the fusion. So the civilisation of Europe rose up. So these cathedrals and these thoughts.

But now the Celt is the disintegrating agent. And the Latin and southern races are falling out of association with the northern races, the northern Germanic impulse is recoiling towards Tartary, the destructive vortex of Tartary.

It is a fate; nobody can alter it. It is a fate. The very blood changes. Within the last three years, the very constituency of the blood has changed, in European veins. But particularly in Germanic veins.

At the same time, we have brought it about ourselves – by a Ruhr occupation, by an English nullity, and by a German false will. We have done it ourselves. But apparently it was not to be helped.

Quos vult perdere Deus, dementat prius.

ROBERT FALCON SCOTT

THE ANTARCTIC EXPLORER SCOTT (1868–1912) LED the British attempt on the South Pole, to discover he had been preceded by the Norwegian Roald Amundsen.

The British team perished on their return leg, at the end of March 1912, near the vicinity of One Ton Depot. Their bodies, letters and diaries were found by a search party eight months later.

❧

To J. M. Barrie (c. 28 March 1912)

Barrie was a playwright and author of Peter Pan.

My dear Barrie,

We are pegging out in a very comfortless spot. Hoping this letter may be found and sent to you, I write a word of farewell... More practically I want you to help my widow and my boy – your godson. We are showing that Englishmen can still die with a bold spirit, fighting it out to the end. It will be known that we have accomplished our object in reaching the Pole, and that we have done everything possible, even to sacrificing ourselves in order to save sick companions. I think this makes an example for Englishmen of the future, and that the country ought to help those who are left behind to mourn us. I leave my poor girl and your godson, Wilson leaves a widow, and Edgar Evans also a widow in humble circumstances. Do what you can to get their claims recognized. Goodbye. I am not at all afraid of the end, but sad to miss many a humble pleasure which I had planned for the future on our long marches. I may not have proved a great explorer, but we have done the greatest march ever made and come very near to great success. Goodbye, my dear friend.

Yours ever, R. Scott

Later... As a dying man, my dear friend, be good to my wife and child. Give the boy a chance in life if the State won't do it. He ought to have good stuff in him... I never met a man in my life whom I admired and loved more than you, but I never could show you how much your friendship meant to me, for you had much to give and I nothing.

VIRGINIA WOOLF

VIRGINIA WOOLF (1882–1941), ENGLISH NOVELIST. She married Leonard Woolf in 1912; the marriage was never consummated. Long prone to depression, she committed suicide by drowning.

❧

To Leonard Woolf (Summer 1912)

Dearest Leonard,

To deal with the facts first (my fingers are so cold I can hardly write) I shall be back about 7 tomorrow, so there will be time to discuss – but what does it mean? You can't take the leave, I suppose, if you are going to resign certainly at the end of it. Anyhow, it shows what a career you're ruining!

Well then, as to the rest. It seems to me that I am giving you a great deal of pain – some in the most casual way – & therefore I ought to be as plain with you as I can. Of course I can't explain what I feel – these are some of the things that strike me. The obvious advantages of marriage stand in my way... I will not look upon marriage as a profession... Then, of course, I feel angry sometimes at the strength of your desire... And then I am fearfully unstable... I pass from hot to cold in an instant, without any reason... in spite of these feelings, which go chasing each other all day long, when I am with you, there is some feeling which is permanent, and growing. You want to know of course whether it will ever make me marry you. How can I say? I think it will... But I don't know what the future will bring. I'm half afraid of myself...I sometimes think that if I married you, I could have everything – & then – is it the sexual side of it that comes between us? As I told you brutally the other day, I feel no physical attraction in you... But you have made me very happy too. We both of us want a marriage that is a tremendous living thing, always alive, always hot, not dead and easy in parts as most marriages are. We ask a great deal of life, don't we? Perhaps we shall get it; then, how splendid!

Yrs

To Vanessa Bell (1 October 1938)

Bell, an artist, was Woolf's sister.

Your letter has just come. I scrambled off a very hurried letter to you last Wednesday, half thinking you'd be marooned somewhere, and thus not get it. Now still in a hurry and therefore typing to save your old eyes I will continue the narrative. I daresay its an old story now; but no doubt you will excuse repetitions. Never never has there been such a time. Last week end we were at Charleston and very gloomy. Gloom increased on Monday. It was pouring. Then in the morning Kingsley Martin rang up to insist that L. must come to London at once and make a desperate attempt to unite labour and liberals – to do what was not obvious. But he seemed desperate, and so we flung a nightgown into a bag and started. In London it was hectic and gloomy and at the same time despairing and yet cynical and calm. The streets were crowded. People were everywhere talking loudly about war. There were heaps of sandbags in the streets, also men digging trenches, lorries delivering planks, loud speakers slowly driving and solemnly exhorting the citizens of Westminster Go and fit your gas masks. There was a long queue of people waiting outside the Mary Ward settlement to be fitted. L. went off at once to see K.M. I discussed matters with Mabel. We agreed that she had better go to Bristol – whether she has or not I dont yet know. Then L came back and said Kingsley was in despair; they had talked for two hours; everybody came into the N. S [New Statesman] office and talked; telephones rang incessantly. They all said war was certain; also that there would be no war. Kingsley came to dinner. He had smudges of black charcoal round his eyes and was more melodramatic and histrionic than ever. Hitler was going to make his speech at 8. We had no wireless, but he said he would ring up the BBC after it was over and find out the truth. Then we sat and discussed the inevitable end of civilisation. He strode up and down the room, hinting that he meant to kill himself. He said the war would last our life time; also we should very likely be beaten. Anyhow Hitler meant to bombard London, probably with no warning; the plan was to drop bombs on London with twenty minutes intervals for forty eight hours. Also he meant to destroy all roads and railways; therefore Rodmell would be about as dangerous as Bloomsbury. Then he broke off; rang up Clark, the news man at The BBC; "Ah – so its hopeless..." Then to us, "Hitler is bawling; the crowds howling like wild beasts." More conversation of a lugubrious kind. Now I think I'll ring up Clark again... Ah so it couldn't be worse... To us. No Hitler is more mad than ever... Have some Whiskey Kingsley, said L. Well, it dont much matter either way, said K. At last he went: What are you going to do? I asked. Walk the streets. Its no good – I cant sleep. So we clasped hands, as I understood for the last time.

Next morning Tuesday every one was certain it was war. Everyone, except one poor little boy in a shop who had lost his head and was half crying when I asked for a packet of envelopes (and he may have been in some sort of row) was perfectly calm; and also without hope. It was quite different from 1914. Every one said Probably we shall win but it'll be just as bad if we do. I went to the London Library to look up some papers about Roger. I sat in the basement with the Times open of the year 1910. An old man was dusting. He went away; then came back and said very kindly, "They're telling us to put on our gas masks, Madam" I thought the raid had begun. However, he explained that it was the loudspeaker once more addressing the citizens of Westminster. Then he asked if he could dust under my chair; and said they had laid in a supply of sand bags, but if a bomb dropped there wouldnt be many books left over. After that I walked to the National Gallery, and a voice again urged me to fit my gas mask at once. The Nat Gallery was fuller than usual; a nice old man was lecturing to an attentive crowd on Watteau. I suppose they were all having a last look.

I went home, and found that L. had arranged that the Press was to go on; but the clerks to go away into the country if they liked. Then Miss Hepworth the traveller said the shops were mostly refusing to buy at all, and were mostly going to close. So it seemed we should have to shut down. The clerks wanted to go on, as they had no place in the country; and of course no money. We arranged to pay wages as long as we could – but plans were vague. Mrs Nicholls said she should prefer to lie in the trench that was being dug in the square; Miss Perkins preferred to sit in the stock room, which she had partly prepared with mattresses etc. Then, after lunch, an American editor arrived to ask me to write an article upon Culture in the United States. We agreed however that culture was in danger. In fact she said most English authors were either in Suffolk, or starting for America. In Suffolk they were already billeting children from the East end in cottages. Then Rosinsky came; he thought he had a visa for America and was going to try to go at once. Then Mrs Woolf rang up to say she was going to Maidenhead if she could get rooms. Then an express arrived from Victoria Ocampo who had just landed from South America, wished to see me at once, was trying to fly to America and what could she do with a sister who was ill – could we advise a safe retreat? Also Phil Baker and others rang up Leonard. With it all we were rather harassed; what should we need if we were marooned in Rodmell, without petrol, or bicycles? L. took his mackintosh and a thick coat; I Rogers letters to you, and a packet of stamped envelopes. Then we had to say good bye to the press, and I felt rather a coward, as clearly they were nervous although very sensible; and they had no garden. But the Govt; asked all who could to leave London and there was John in command. So off we went.

It was pouring terrific torrents; the roads packed; men nailing up shutters in shop windows; sandbags being piled; and a general feeling of flight and hurry. Also it was very dark; and we took about three hours to get back. At ten oclock Mr Perkins knocked and entered with a box of gas bags which he fitted on us. No sooner had he gone than Mr Jansen came with another box. He said that children were arriving from the East End next morning. Sure enough, next day, – but I wrote to you and told you how we had the news of the Prime Ministers sensational statement – we thought it meant anyhow a pause – well, after that, Mr Perkins came and said the children were coming – 9,000 had to be billeted in Sussex; fifty in Rodmell; how many could we put up? We arranged to take two. By that time, the nightmare feeling was becoming more nightmarish; more and more absurd; for no one knew what was happening; and yet everyone was behaving as if the war had begun. Mr Hartman had turned his barn into a hospital and so on. Of course we thought it was ridiculous; yet still they went on broadcasting messages about leaving London; about post cards with stamps being given to refugees who would be deposited safely, but they must not ask where. At any moment the fifty children might arrive. Also the Archbishop would offer up prayers; and at one moment the Pope's voice was heard… But I will shorten; and skip to Sissinghurst; where we went on Thursday; and heard that the Italian King had saved the situation by threatening to abdicate. Harold had seen the PM grow visibly ten years younger as he read the message which was handed him. It was all over. And I must play bowls. Leonard sends a message to Q; in his opinion we have peace without honour for six months.

I'll write again. Maynard comes tomorrow. Plans vague; but we write here, where we shall probably stay at present. No time to read this through.

Post going,
B.

To Leonard Woolf (March 1941)

This is Woolf's suicide letter.

I have the feeling that I shall go mad and cannot go on any longer in these terrible times. I hear voices and cannot concentrate on my work. I have fought against it, but cannot fight any longer. I owe all my happiness in life to you. You have been so perfectly good. I cannot go on and spoil your life.

RUPERT BROOKE

RUPERT BROOKE (1887–1915), ENGLISH POET. BEFORE the First World War – in which he died – Brooke travelled widely in Germany, the USA and the South Seas.

❦

To Edward Marsh (15 November 1913), from Fiji

Dear Eddie,

I'm conscious I haven't written to you for a long time: – though, indeed, my last letter was *posted* only a short time ago. When it, or when this, will get to you, God knows. About Christmas, I suppose, though it seems incredible. My *reason* tells me that you'll be slurring through London mud in a taxi, with a heavy drizzle falling, and a chilly dampness in the air, and the theatres glaring in the Strand, and crowds of white faces. But I can't help *thinking* of you trotting through crisp snow to a country church, holly-decorated, with, little robins picking crumbs all around, and the church-bells playing our brother Tennyson's In *Memoriam* brightly through the clear air. It may not be: it never has been: – that picture-postcard Christmas. But I shall think of you so.

You think of me, in a loin-cloth, brown and wild in the fair chocolate arms of a Tahitian beauty, reclining beneath a bread-fruit tree, on white sand, with the breakers roaring against the reefs a mile out, and strange brilliant fish darting through the pellucid hyaline of the sun-saturated sea.

Oh, Eddie, it's all true about the South Seas! I get a little tired of it at moments, because I am just too old for Romance. But there it is: there it wonderfully is: heaven on earth, the ideal life, little work, dancing and singing and eating, naked people of incredible loveliness, perfect manners, and immense kindliness, a divine tropic climate, and intoxicating beauty of scenery.

I came aboard and left Samoa two days ago. Before that I had been wandering with an "interpreter" – entirely genial and quite incapable of English – through Samoan villages. The last few days I stopped in one, where a big marriage-feast was going on. I lived in a Samoan house (the coolest in the world) with a man and his wife, nine children, ranging from a proud beauty of 18 to a round object of 1 year, a dog, a cat, a proud hysterical hen, and a gaudy scarlet and green parrot, who roved the roof and beams with a wicked eye, choosing a place whence to—, twice a day, with humorous precision, on my hat and clothes.

The Samoan girls have extraordinarily beautiful bodies, and walk like goddesses. They're a lovely brown colour, without any black Melanesian admixture, their necks and shoulders would be the wild envy of any European beauty; and in carriage and face they remind me continually and vividly of my incomparable heartless and ever-loved X. Fancy moving among a tribe of X's! Can't you imagine how shattered and fragmentary a heart I'm bearing away to Fiji and Tahiti? And, oh dear! I'm afraid they'll be just as bad.

And Eddie, it's all True about, for instance, Coconuts. You tramp through a strange vast dripping tropical forest for hours, listening to weird liquid hootings from birds and demons in the branches above. Then you feel thirsty, so you send your boy up a great perpendicular palm. He runs up with utter ease and grace, cuts off a couple of vast nuts and comes down and makes holes in them. And they are chock-full of the best drink in the world.

Romance! Romance! I walked 15 miles through mud and up and down mountains, and swam three rivers, to get this boat. But if ever you miss me, suddenly, one day, from lecture-room B. in King's, or from the Moulin d'Or at lunch, you'll know that I've got sick for the full moon on these little thatched roofs, and the palms against the morning, and the Samoan boys and girls diving thirty feet into a green sea or a deep mountain pool under a waterfall – and that I've gone back.

Romance? That's half my time. The rest is Life – Life, Eddie, is what you get in the bars of the hotels in 'Frisco, or Honolulu, or Suva, or Apia, and in the smoking-rooms in these steamers. It is incredibly like a Kipling story, and all the people are very self-consciously Kiplingesque. Yesterday, for instance, I sat in the Chief Engineer's cabin, with the first officer and a successful beach-comber lawyer from the white-man's town in Samoa, drinking Australian champagne from breakfast to lunch. "To-day I am not well." The beach-comber matriculated at Wadham, and was sent down. Also, he rode with the Pytchley, quotes you Virgil, and discusses the ins and outs of the Peninsular campaign. And his repertoire of smut is enormous. Mere Kipling, you see, but one gets some good stories. Verses, of a school-boy kind, too... *Sehr primitiv*. The whole thing makes a funny world.

I may pick up some mail, and hear from you, when I get to New Zealand. I'm afraid your post as my honorary literary agent, or grass-executor, is something of a sinecure. I *can't* write on the trail.

There's one thing I wanted to consult you about, and I can't remember if I mentioned it. I want some club to take an occasional stranger into, for a drink, and to read the papers in, and, sometimes, to have a quiet meal in. Where do you think I should go?... I want somewhere I needn't always be spick and span in, and somewhere I don't have to pay a vast sum.

There's nothing else in the way of my European existence, I think. That part of it which is left, out here, reads Ben Jonson. Kindly turn up his "New Inn" (which is sheer Meredith) and read Lovel's Song in Act IV. The second verse will dispel the impression of the first, that it is by Robert Browning. The whole thing is pure beauty.

No more. My love to everyone from Jackson down to — if you've made her acquaintance yet – Helena Darwin Cornford. And to such as Wilfred [Gibson] and Denis [Browne] and yourself and a few more poor, pale-skinned stay-at-homes, a double measure. I have a growing vision of next summer term spent between King's and Raymond Buildings: a lovely vision. May it be.

Manina! Tofa!
Thy
Rupert

PAUL CLAUDEL

PAUL CLAUDEL (1868–1955), THE CATHOLIC ESSAYIST and poet. In 1914 Claudel belatedly realized that his friend André Gide was homosexual.

∂❦৯

To André Gide (2 March 1914)

In the name of heaven, Gide, how could you write the passage which I find on page 478 of the last issue of the *N.R.F.*? Don't you know that after *Saül* and *L'Immoraliste* you cannot commit any further imprudence? Must I quite make up my mind, as I have wished to do, that you are yourself a participant in these hideous practices? Answer me. You owe me an answer. If you remain silent, or if you don't make yourself absolutely clear, I shall know where I stand. If you are not a pederast, why have you so strange a predilection for this sort of subject? And if you are one, cure yourself, you unhappy man, and do not make a show of these abominations. Consult Madame Gide; consult the better part of your own heart. Don't you see that you will be lost – you yourself and all those who are nearest to you? Don't you realize the effect which your books may have upon some unfortunate young people? It pains me to say these things, but I feel obliged to do so.

Your distressed friend,
P. Claudel

ANDRÉ GIDE

ANDRÉ GIDE (1869–1951) WAS THE AUTHOR OF *THE Immoralist* (1930) and a founder of the magazine *La Nouvelle Revue Française*. Although he married his cousin in 1892, he was homosexual.

ɔ❦ɔ

To Paul Claudel (7 March 1914)

What right have you to issue this summons? In what name do you put these questions? If it is in the name of friendship, can you suppose for an instant that I should evade them?

It pains me very much that there should be any misapprehension between us; but your letter has already done much to create a new one – for, no matter how I take it, and whether I answer or whether I don't, I foresee that you are going to misjudge me. I therefore beg you to consider this only: that I love my wife more than life itself, and I could not forgive any word or action on your part which might endanger her happiness. Now that has been said, I can tell you that for months, for years, I have longed to talk to you – although the tone of your letter makes me despair of receiving any advice from you to-day.

I am speaking now to a friend, as I should speak to a priest, whose binding duty it is to keep my secret before God. I have never felt any desire in the presence of a woman; and the great sadness of my life is that the most constant, the most enduring, and the keenest of my loves has never been accompanied by any of the things which normally precede love. It seemed, on the contrary, that in my case love prevented me from desiring...

As for the evil which, you say, is done by my books, I can't believe in it, for I know how many others are stifled, as I am, by lying conventions. And do not infer from this that I commend any particular habits, or even any particular desires; but I loathe the hypocrisy, and I know that some hypocrisies are mortal. I cannot believe that religion leaves on one side all those who are like myself...

GEORGE BERNARD SHAW

GEORGE BERNARD SHAW (1856–1950), IRISH-BORN dramatist and critic, winner of the 1925 Nobel Prize for Literature.

❦

To Mrs Patrick Campbell (22 February 1913)

Shaw was in love with the actress Stella Campbell for many years, and she was one of the main recipients of his fecund correspondence.

What a day! I must write to you about it, because there is no one else who didnt hate her mother, and even who doesnt hate her children. Whether you are an Italian peasant or a Superwoman I cannot yet find out; but anyhow your mother was not the Enemy. Why does a funeral always sharpen one's sense of humor and rouse one's spirits? This one was a complete success. No burial horrors. No mourners in black, snivelling and wallowing in induced grief. Nobody knew except myself, Barker & the undertaker. Since I could not have a splendid procession with lovely colors and flashing life and triumphant music, it was best with us three. I particularly mention the undertaker because the humor of the occasion began with him. I went down in the tube to Golders Green with Barker, and walked to the crematorium; and there came also the undertaker presently with his hearse, which had walked (the horse did) conscientiously at a funeral pace through the cold; though my mother would have preferred an invigorating trot. The undertaker approached me in the character of a man shattered with grief; and I, hard as nails and in loyally high spirits (rejoicing irrepressibly in my mother's memory), tried to convey to him that this professional chicanery, as I took it to be, was quite unnecessary. And lo! it wasnt professional chicanery at all. He had done all sorts of work for her for years, and was actually and really in a state about losing her, not merely as a customer, but as a person he liked and was accustomed to. And the coffin was covered with violet cloth – no black.

I must rewrite that burial service; for there are things in it that are deader than anyone it has ever been read over; but I had it read not only because the parson must live by his fees, but because with all its drawbacks it is the most beautiful thing that can be read as yet. And the parson did not gabble and hurry in the horrible manner common on such occasions. With Barker & myself for his congregation (and Mamma) he did it with his utmost feeling and sincerity. We could have made him perfect technically in two rehearsals; but he was excellent as it was; and I shook his hand with unaffected gratitude in my best manner.

At the passage "earth to earth, ashes to ashes, dust to dust," there was a little alteration of the words to suit the process. A door opened in the wall; and the violet coffin mysteriously passed out through it and vanished as it closed. People think that door the door of the furnace; but it isnt. I went behind the scenes at the end of the service and saw the real thing. People are afraid to see it; but it is wonderful. I found there the violet coffin opposite another door, a real unmistakeable furnace door. When it lifted there was a plain little chamber of cement and firebrick. No heat. No noise. No roaring draught. No flame. No fuel. It looked cool, clean, sunny, though no sun could get there. You would have walked in or put your hand in without misgiving. Then the violet coffin moved again and went in, feet first. And behold! The feet burst miraculously into streaming ribbons of garnet colored lovely flame, smokeless and eager, like pentecostal tongues, and as the whole coffin passed in it sprang into flame all over; and my mother became that beautiful fire.

The door fell; and they said that if we wanted to see it all through, we should come back in an hour and a half. I remembered the wasted little figure with the wonderful face, and said "Too long" to myself; but we went off and looked at the Hampstead Garden Suburb (in which I have shares), and telephoned messages to the theatre, and bought books, and enjoyed ourselves generally.

By the way I forgot one incident. Hayden Coffin suddenly appeared in the chapel. *His* mother also.

The end was wildly funny: she would have enjoyed it enormously. When we returned we looked down through an opening in the floor to a lower floor close below. There we saw a roomy kitchen, with a big cement table and two cooks busy at it. They had little tongs in their hands, and they were deftly and busily picking nails and scraps of coffin handles out of Mamma's dainty little heap of ashes and samples of bone. Mamma herself being at that moment leaning over beside me, shaking with laughter. Then they swept her up into a sieve, and shook her out; so that there was a heap of dust and a heap of calcined bone scraps. And Mamma said in my ear, "Which of the two heaps is me, I wonder!"

And that merry episode was the end, except for making dust of the bone scraps and scattering them on a flower bed.

O grave, where is thy victory?

In the afternoon I drove down to Oxford, where I write this. The car was in a merry mood, and in Notting Hill Gate accomplished a most amazing skid, swivelling right round across the road one way and then back the other, but fortunately not hitting anything...

And so goodnight, friend who understands about one's mother, and other things.

GBS

To Mrs Patrick Campbell (7 January 1918)

Campbell's son was killed on the Western Front at the end of December 1917. She wanted to send Shaw the letter of condolence from the company padre.

Never saw it or heard about it until your letter came. It is no use: I cant be sympathetic: these things simply make me furious. I want to swear. I do swear. Killed just because people are blasted fools. A chaplain, too, to say nice things about it. It is not his business to say nice things about it, but to shout that "the voice of thy son's blood crieth unto God from the ground."

To hell with your chaplain and his tragic gentleness! The next shell will perhaps blow *him* to bits; and some other chaplain will write such a nice letter to *his* mother. Such nice letters! Such nice little notices in papers!

Gratifying, isnt it. Consoling. It only needs a letter from the king to make me feel that the shell was a blessing in disguise.

No: dont show me the letter. But I should very much like to have a nice talk with that dear chaplain, that sweet sky pilot, that –

No use going on like this, Stella. Wait for a week; and then I shall be very clever and broadminded again, and have forgotten all about him. I shall be quite as nice as the chaplain.

Oh damn, damn, damn, damn, damn, damn, damn, damn,

DAMN DAMN!

And oh, dear, dear, dear, dear, dear, dearest!
G.B.S.

To Sylvia Beach (10 October 1921)

Beach was the owner of the Shakespeare & Co. Bookshop in Paris, the publisher of James Joyce's Ulysses *(February 1921).*

Dear Madam,

I have read several fragments of *Ulysses* in its serial form. It is a revolting record of a disgusting phase of civilisation; but it is a truthful one; and I should like to put a cordon round Dublin; round up every male person in it between the ages of 15 and 30; force them to read it; and ask them whether on reflection they could see anything amusing in all that foul mouthed, foul minded derision and obscenity. To you, possibly, it may appeal as art: you are probably (you see I don't know you) a young barbarian beglamoured by the excitements and enthusiasms that art stirs up in passionate material; but to me it is all hideously real: I have walked those streets and known those shops and have heard and taken part in those conversations. I escaped from them to England at the age of twenty; and forty years later have learnt from the books of Mr Joyce that Dublin is still what it was, and young men are still drivelling in slackjawed blackguardism just as they were in 1870. It is, however, some consolation to find that at last somebody has felt deeply enough about it to face the horror of writing it all down and using his literary genius to force people to face it. In Ireland they try to make a cat cleanly by rubbing its nose in its own filth. Mr Joyce has tried the same treatment' on the human subject. I hope it may prove successful.

I am aware that there are other qualities and other passages in *Ulysses*: but they do not call for any special comment from me.

I must add, as the prospectus implies an invitation to purchase, that I am an elderly Irish gentleman, and that if you imagine that any Irishman, much less an elderly one, would pay 150 francs for a book, you little know my countrymen.

Faithfully,
G. Bernard Shaw

KATHERINE MANSFIELD

KATHERINE MANSFIELD (1888–1923), SHORT-STORY writer, born in New Zealand as Katherine Mansfield Beauchamp.

❧

To John Middleton Murry
(19–20 March 1915), from Paris

Mansfield met the British critic and writer John Middleton Murry in 1911, beginning a stormy relationship that lasted until her premature death from tuberculosis.

[Paris]

Darling

I went to Chartier [Restaurant] to lunch and had a maquereau grillé et epinards à la creme. It was very strange to be there alone – I felt that I was a tiny little girl and standing on a chair looking into an aquarium. It was not a sad feeling, only strange and a bit "femme seuleish" – As I came out it began to snow. A wind like a carving knife cut through the streets – and everybody began to run – so did I into a café and there I sat and drank a cup of hot black coffee. Then for the first time I felt in Paris. It was a little café & hideous – with a black marble top to the counter garni with lozenges of white and orange. Chauffeurs and their wives & fat men with immense photographic apparatus sat in it – and a white fox terrier bitch – thin and eager ran among the tables. Against the window beat a dirty french flag, fraying out in the wind and then flapping on the glass. Does black coffee make you drunk – do you think? I felt quite enivrée (Oh Jack I *wont* do this. It's like George Moore. Don't be cross) and could have sat there years, smoking & sipping and thinking and watching the flakes of snow. And then you know the strange silence that falls upon your heart – the same silence that comes just one minute before the curtain rises. I felt that and knew that I should write here. I wish that you would write a poem about that silence sometime, my bogey. It is so *peculiar* – even one's whole physical being seems arrested. It is a kind of dying before the new breath is blown into you. As I write I can almost see the poem you will make – I see the Lord alighting upon the breast of the man and He is very fierce. (Are you laughing at me?) So after this intense emotion I dashed out of the café bought some oranges and a packet of rusks and went back to the hotel. Me voici. The garcon has just polished the handles of the door. They are winking and smelling somethink horrible. The sky is still full of snow – but everything is clear to see – the trees against the tall houses – so rich and so fine and on the grey streets the shiny black hats of the cabmen are like blobs of Lawrence's paint. Its very quiet. A bird chirrups – a man in wooden shoes goes by. Now I shall start working. Goodbye, my dear one.

The same night. Very strange is my love for you tonight – don't have it psychoanalysed – I saw you suddenly lying in a hot bath, blinking up at me – your charming beautiful body half under the water. I sat on the edge of the bath in my vest waiting to come in. Everything in the room was wet with steam and it was night time and you were rather languid. "Tig chuck over that sponge." No, Ill *not* think of you like that – Ill shut my teeth and not listen to my heart. It begins to cry as if it were a child in an empty room & to beat on the door and say Jack – Jack – Jack and Tig – Ill be better when I've had a letter. Ah my God, how can I love him like this. Do I love you so much more than you love me or do you too – – feel like this?

Tig.

Saturday morning. Just off to see if there are any letters. I'm alright, dearest.

To a friend (1916)

For a period during the First World War, Mansfield and Middleton Murry lived near the writer D. H. Lawrence (1885–1930) and his wife, Frieda, the subjects of this letter.

Let me tell you what happened on Friday. I went across to them for tea. Frieda said Shelley's *Ode to a Skylark* was false. Lawrence said: "You are showing off; you don't know anything about it." Then she began. "*Now* I have had enough. Out of my house – you little God Almighty you. I've had enough of you. Are you going to keep your mouth shut or aren't you." Said Lawrence: "I'll give you a dab on the cheek to quiet you, you dirty hussy." Etc. Etc. So I left the house. At dinner time Frieda appeared. "I have finally done with him. It is all over for ever." She then went out of the kitchen & began to walk round and round the house in the dark. Suddenly Lawrence appeared and made a kind of horrible blind rush at her and they began to scream and scuffle. He beat her – he beat her to death – her head and face and breast and pulled out her hair. All the while she screamed for Murry to help her. Finally they dashed into the kitchen and round and round the table. I shall never forget how L. looked. He was so white – almost green and he just hit – thumped the big soft woman. Then he fell into one chair and she into another. No one said a word. A silence fell except for Frieda's sobs and sniffs. In a way I felt almost glad that the tension between them was over for ever – and that they had made an end of the "intimacy". L. sat staring at the floor, biting his nails. Frieda sobbed. Suddenly, after a long time – about quarter of an hour – L. looked up and asked Murry a question about French literature. Murry replied. Little by little, the three drew up to the table. Then F. poured herself out some coffee. Then she and L. glided into talk, began to discuss some "very rich but very good macaroni cheese." And next day, L. whipped himself, and far more thoroughly than he had ever beaten Frieda; he was running about taking her up her breakfast to her bed and trimming her a hat.

JACK LONDON

ORN IN SAN FRANCISCO, JOHN GRIFFITH LONDON (1876–1916) was successively a sailor, hobo, Klondyke gold-miner, before becoming a writer, most memorably of the children's classics, *Call of the Wild* (1903) and *White Fang* (1907).

To his daughter, Joan London (16 September 1915)

Dear Joan:

First of all, I had Aunt Eliza send you the check for $7.00 so that you might buy the two pairs of boots for yourself and Bess.

Second of all, I promised to reply to your letter.

Third of all, and very important, please remember that your Daddy is a very busy man. When you write to society people, or to young people, who have plenty of time, write on your fine stationery and write on both sides of the paper. But, please, when you write to Daddy, take any kind of paper, the cheapest paper for that matter, and write on one side only. This makes it ever so much easier for Daddy to read. A two-sheet letter, such as yours that I am now looking at, written on both sides, is like a Chinese puzzle to a busy man. I take more time trying to find my way from one of the four portions into which your two-sided sheet is divided than I do in reading the letter itself.

Some day I should like to see your French heeled slippers. Joan, you are on the right track. Never hesitate at making yourself a dainty, delightful girl and woman. There is a girl's pride and a woman's pride in this, and it is indeed a fine pride. On the one hand, of course, never over-dress. On the other hand, never be a frump. No matter how wonderful are the thoughts that burn in your brain, always, physically, and in dress, make yourself a delight to all eyes that behold you.

I have met a number of philosophers. They were real philosophers. Their minds were wonderful minds. But they did not take baths, and they did not change their socks and it almost turned one's stomach to sit at table with them.

Our bodies are as glorious as our minds, and, just as one cannot maintain a high mind in a filthy body, by the same token one cannot keep a high mind and high pride when said body is not dressed beautifully, delightfully, charmingly. Nothing would your Daddy ask better of you in this world than that you have a high mind, a high pride, a fine body, and, just as all the rest, a beautifully dressed body.

I do not think you will lose your head. I think, as I read this last letter of yours, that I understand that you have balance, and a woman's balance at that. Never forget the noble things of the spirit, on the other hand, never let your body be ignoble, never let the garmenture of your body be ignoble. As regards the garmenture of your body, learn to do much with little, never to over-do, and to keep such a balance between your garmenture and your mind that both garmenture and mind are beautiful.

I shall not say anything to you about your method of saving, about Bess's method of saving, but there is much I should like to say to you, and, in the meantime I think a lot about it. You are on the right track. Go ahead. Develop your mind to its leftmost beauty; and keep your body in pace with your mind.

Daddy

ROBERT GRAVES

R OBERT VON RANKE GRAVES (1895–1985), ENGLISH poet and novelist.

To Sir Edward Marsh (7 August 1916)
Graves served on the Western Front during the First World War; before

embarking for France his nose had been operated on as part of the development of a close-fitting gas mask.

My dear Eddie,

If I wasn't such a desperately honest chap I'd cover my wickedness by swearing that I'd written to you and that someone had forgotten to post the letter – but what really happened was I started writing then stopped because l was waiting to give you a bit of news which didn't arrive, then forgot and imagined I'd written. Such millions and billions and squadrillions of letters came condoling, inquiring, congratulating – I never knew I had so many friends. Mostly rather tedious. But three lovely ones today, the first from old Siegfried* (whom by the way I always call "Sassons" since Tommy was killed: he invented it) at Oxford and he's coming to see me in a week (Eddie, what is a spot on the lung? A wound, or tubercle or what?) and as I'm going to be able to travel in "a week or ten days" the medico says, I'm going to lug him up to Harlech (I hope you liked the Harlech part of the Caucasus letter: I wrote it within 50 yards of the dead Bosche in Mametz Wood!) and we'll have high old primitive times together.

By the way, Mark Gertler would paint the Bosche so well: do ask him sometime.

To resume, next was your letter which I'm endeavouring to answer in a manner that will show my appreciation. Next, a wonderful composition from dear old Ralph Rooper starting: "Oh my dear, dear Lazarus"; he has also been mourning me for a week. It's awfully jolly to have such friends: I'd go through it all again for those three letters I got today; straight I would.

I never knew S.S. was in England. I'm so relieved he's out of it.

I've had ridiculously little pain, the worst being when they tear the sticking plaster that holds my leg bandage in position... off the hairy part of my leg.

I had an immensely uncomfortable journey down to Rouen because they wouldn't risk tipping me off a stretcher onto a bed and

---

*Siegfried Sassoon, English poet and author.

a stretcher is agony after the first few minutes – no support for your back, if you can understand. Also, I sneezed by mistake this afternoon which was most painful. But I've not had a thousandth part of what I suffered when they cut my nose about at Millbank: that made this a beanfeast by contrast.

As a matter of fact, I did die on my way down to the Field Ambulance and found myself just crossing Lethe by ferry. I had only just time to put on my gas-helmet to keep off the fumes of forgetfulness but managed it and on arrival at the other side began to feel much better. To cut short a long story, old Rhadamanthus introduced himself as my judge but I refused to accept his jurisdiction. I wanted a court-martial of British officers: he was only a rotten old Greek. He shouted out: "Contempt of Court" but I chucked a Mills bomb at him which scattered the millions of the mouthless dead in about two seconds and wounded old R. in the leg and broke his sceptre. Then I strode away, held a revolver to Charon's head, climbed into the boat and so home. I gave him a Rouen note for 50 cm. which I didn't want particularly. Remained Cerberus whose three heads were, I noticed, mastiff, dalmatian and dachshund. He growled furiously and my revolver was empty, and I'd no ammunition. Happy thought: honeyed cakes and poppy seed. But none was handy; however, I had an excellent substitute – Army biscuit smeared with Tickler's "plum and apple" and my little morphia tablets carefully concealed in the appetizing conserve. He snapped, swallowed, slumbered. I tiptoed past him, a free man and found myself being lowered on the floor of the 99th Field Ambulance. The doctor was saying "hopeless case" (and this part of the tale is true, truer even than the rest) and I winked at him and said "dear old doctor" and went off again to sleep.

My sense of humour may have been enfeebled but I laughed till I was nearly ill yesterday over 100 copy lines which a Charterhouse master told my brother to write the other day, to the effect that he mustn't be a baby. I can't reproduce the original exactly, but the result was ludicrous and more so as it was written in the very choicest copper-plate handwriting. It went something like this for eight pages:

I must endeavour to emerge from my present phase of infantility.

The symptoms of babyhood must be eradicated from my composition.

It behoves me to comport myself in a manner less typical of extreme juvenility.

I am bound by a moral obligation to rid myself of the characteristics of a youthful and childish baby.

I must not be a baby. Oh God, save me from shrinking smaller and smaller, from boyhood to babydom and finally from vanishing completely away, etc., etc.

Don't you love the "youthful and childish baby"? It has a wonderful naiveté about it. Is the thing so funny because it was shown up to a master, or what?

I'm longing to see you on Saturday. Try to bring Ivor Novello with you. I'd love to meet him, if he wouldn't be bored and you, busy man, could kill two birds with one stone by coming up and back with him.

Peter has promised thro' my brother to act on my suggestion and write his folk a tragic letter of cold pathos and reproach about my death for my country and the way they've treated him and me. He'll do it well; he's an artist. Charterhouse is at Camp on the Plain now.

I'm afraid, great as is the love I bear you, Jane Austen is too hard a nut to attempt to bite at with these weak jaws. Thanks awfully tho'. I have my Sorley here: he's my chief standby.

I see in the *Mail* today that a damnably nasty German cousin of mine has been killed flying. I remember once my sister in her young enthusiasm told him: "Oh Wilhelm, what a lovely squirrel." Up went his rifle and the squirrel fell dead at her feet. He couldn't understand her tears of rage. She'd admired the squirrel: he'd got it for her and was prepared to skin it then and there for her.

The brute used to climb up the only greengage tree in the orchard (this was Bavaria) and throw us down the stones. How I hated him! I was too young to climb trees myself.

I hope to hear from Ruth Mallory soon about George: I wrote to her yesterday. I've not heard a word since he left Havre.

I'm looking forward to Arthur Parry's letter.

Now goodbye till Saturday. I must write to Ralph ere they dout my light.

Ever yours affectionately
Robert

Funny that in "The Queer Time" I should have talked about "clutching at my right breast": it's just what I did on the 20th July!

WILFRED OWEN

WILFRED OWEN (1893–1918), ENGLISH POET.

❧

To his mother, Susan Owen (4 January 1917)

The letter was sent from the Western Front; Owen had enlisted in the Army in 1915.

My own dear Mother,

I have joined the Regiment, who are just at the end of six weeks' rest.

I will not describe the awful vicissitudes of the journey here. I arrived at Folkestone, and put up at the best hotel. It was a place of luxury – inconceivable now – carpets as deep as the mud here – golden flunkeys; pages who must have been melted into their clothes and expanded since; even the porters had clean hands. Even the dogs that licked up the crumbs had clean teeth.

Since I set foot on Calais quays I have not had dry feet.

No one knew anything about us on this side, and we might have taken weeks to get here, and *must* have, but for fighting our way here.

I spent something like a pound in getting my baggage carried from trains to trains.

At the Base, as I said, it was not so bad. We were in the camp of Sir Percy Cunynghame, who had bagged for his Mess the Duke of Connaught's chef.

After those two days, we were let down, gently, into the real thing. Mud.

It has penetrated now into that Sanctuary my sleeping bag, and that holy of holies my pyjamas. For I sleep on a stone floor and the servant squashed mud on all my belongings; I suppose by way of baptism. We are 3 officers in this "Room"; the rest of the house is occupied by servants and the band; the roughest set of knaves I have ever been herded with. Even now their vile language is shaking the flimsy door between the rooms.

I chose a servant for myself yesterday, not for his profile, nor yet his clean hands, but for his excellence in bayonet work. For the servant always at the side of his officer in the charge and is therefore worth a dozen nurses. Alas, he of the Bayonet is in the Bombing Section, and is against Regulations to employ such as a servant. I makeshift with another.

Everything is makeshift. The English seem to have fallen into the French unhappy-go-lucky non-system. There are scarcely any houses here. The men lie in Barns.

Our Mess Room is also an Ante and Orderly Room. We eat & drink out of old tins, some of which show traces of ancient enamel. We are never dry, and never "off duty".

On all the officers' faces there is a harassed look that I have never seen before, and which in England, never will be seen – out of jails. The men are just as Bairnsfather* has them – expressionless lumps.

We feel the weight of them hanging on us. I have found not a few of the old Fleetwood Musketry party here. They seemed glad to see me as far as the set doggedness of their features would admit.

I censored hundreds of letters yesterday, and the hope of peace was in every one. *The Daily Mail* map which appeared about Jan 2 will be of extreme interest to you.

---

*Bruce Bairnsfather, artist.

We were stranded in a certain town one night and I saved the party of us by collaring an Orderly in the streets and making him take us to a Sergeants Mess. We were famishing, and a mug of beer did me more good than any meal I ever munched. The place was like a bit of Blighty, all hung with English Greetings and Mistletoe.

As I could I collected accoutrement, some here, some there, and almost complete: Steel Helmets, & Gas; improved Box Respirator, and etcetera.

The badge of the Regt. is some red tabs on the shoulder thus
I scarcely know any of the officers. The senior are old regulars. The younger are, several, Artists! In my room is an Artist of the same school as I passed. He is also a fine water-colour sketcher. I may have time to write again tomorrow. I *have* not of course had anything from you. I am perfectly well and strong, but unthinkably dirty and squalid. I scarcely dare to wash. Pass on as much of this happy news as may interest people. The favourite song of the men is

> "The Roses round the door
> Makes me love Mother more."

They sing this everlastingly.
I don't disagree.

Your very own *W.E.O.* x

To his mother (31 October 1918)

This is the last letter Wilfred Owen MC sent; he was killed in action on 4 November, a week before the signing of the Armistice.

Dearest Mother,

I will call the place from which I'm now writing "The Smoky Cellar of the Forester's House". I write on the first sheet of the writing pad which came in the parcel yesterday. Luckily the parcel was small, as it reached me just before we moved off to the line. Thus only the paraffin was unwelcome in my pack. My servant & I ate the chocolate in the cold middle of last night, crouched under a draughty Tamboo, roofed with planks. I husband the Malted Milk for tonight, & tomorrow-night. The handkerchief & socks are most opportune, as the ground is marshy, & I have a slight cold!

So thick is the smoke in this cellar that I can hardly see by a candle 12 ins. away, and so thick are the inmates that I can hardly write for pokes, nudges & jolts. On my left the Coy. Commander snores on a bench; other officers repose on wire beds behind me. At my right hand, Kellett, a delightful servant of A Coy. in *The Old Days* radiates joy & contentment from pink cheeks and baby eyes. He laughs with a signaller, to whose left ear is glued the Receiver; but whose eyes rolling with gaiety show that he is listening with his right ear to a merry corporal, who appears at this distance away (some three feet) nothing [but] a gleam of white teeth & a wheeze of jokes.

Splashing my hand, an old soldier with a walrus moustache peels & drops potatoes into the pot. By him, Keyes, my cook, chops wood; another feeds the smoke with the damp wood.

It is a great life. I am more oblivious than alas! yourself, dear Mother, of the ghastly glimmering of the guns outside, & the hollow crashing of the shells.

There is no danger down here, or if any, it will be well over before you read these lines.

I hope you are as warm as I am; as serene in your room as I am here and that you think of me never in bed as resignedly as I think of you always in bed. Of this I am certain you could not be visited by a band of friends half so fine as surround me here.

Ever *Wilfred* x

IVOR GURNEY

IVOR GURNEY (1890–1937), ENGLISH POET AND COM-poser. He suffered from depression and spent most of his later life in a London asylum; he died there of tuberculosis, exacerbated by a gassing received on the Western Front in 1917.

❧

To Marion Scott (11 April 1917), from the frontline, France

My Dear Friend

Tin whistles and mouth organs still going hard, and we waiting for dinner and moving afterwards, for a company of ours took two more villages last night, and we shift also of course.

We have been hard worked but still and all the same, this open country work is far preferable to trench life. This place is quite pretty, very pretty; and this morning I saw, at first dawn, one mystical star hanging over a line of black wood on the sky-line; surely one of the most beautiful things on earth.

I hope by the time this letter gets to you you will be trotting about in real Spring sunlight; it is cold here as yet, but no man may foretell of Aprils whims.

I told you of the death, a little time back of one of our most looked to corporals. Well, that was before the advance. About a fortnight after the movement started, we heard his grave had been discovered; and after tea one evening the whole company (that was fit) went down for a service there. Quite a fine little wooden cross had been erected there: the Germans had done well: it was better than we ourselves would have given him; and on the cross was

> "Hier ruht ein tapferer Engländer,
> Richard Rhodes", and the date.

Strange to find chivalry in sight of the destruction we had left behind us; but so it was. They must have loved his beauty, or he must have lived a little for such a tribute. But he was brave, and his air always gallant and gay for all his few inches. Always I admired him and his indestructibility of energy and wonderful eyes.

I am sorry to hear about the shortage of pianos, that may affect me and my tinklings.

/ April 4 or 5th.

I thought we were going over the top tonight, but it has been postponed – a state of things which will inevitably lead to soul-outpourings. My state of mind is – fed up to the eyes; fear of not living to write music for England; no fear at all of death. Yesterday we had a little affair with a German patrol, which made me interested for 5 minutes; after which I lapsed into the usual horrid state of boredom. O that the Nice Blighty may come soon! I do not bear pain and cold well, but do not grumble too much; so I reckon that cancels out. One cannot expect to have everything, or to make one's nature strong in a week. It snowed like anything yesterday, but today has been quite beautiful, and I have strolled about chatting of Maisemore Wood and such-like things of beauty. Your Kampote blocks came in very useful – what were left of them, and a warm drink now and then is salvation indeed; after the drink I settle down to think of the delightful cosy comfortable teas I will have one day, and of the music to follow; trying so to forget my feet. What an April! Well, we have had some bon fires not so many days back.

My dear friend, it has been very kind of you to write to my friends as you have, and I know they are grateful. It is something to know that my father realises his trouble and sacrifice have not been all wasted. He has been only too good always; especially considering the difference of our temperaments, and my long wasted time. Surely my life must lead to something. Surely the apprenticeship has almost passed?

I am afraid there are no poems again. The conditions are against it, but, thank Goodness rations are better now.

My friendships are mostly queer ones, and this is queer, but believe me, a very valued one. You have given me just what I needed, and what none other of my friends could supply to keep me in touch with things which are my life; and the actuality of which is almost altogether denied me. Well, perhaps it will not be long before I am back again, and having tremendous jaws about your book, and seeing you get stronger, and watching Audrey grow up, and seeing what her smile grows to be. Here we are called up.

Goodbye: Your sincere friend
Ivor Gurney

Next day

Our Q M S has told us that the 61st are mentioned in despatches. Is this true I wonder? We have risen a little in our own estimation if this is so; one does not wish to belong to a washout division. This morning was beautifully sunny, and daisies are poking their heads out here and there – without steel helmets! O the Spring, the Spring! Come late or early, you must give hope ever to the dwellers in the house of flesh. How does your frail tenement get on? I hope it is warmer and sunnier with you now, and you playing on your violin, revelling in sunlight of earth and music.

To Marion Scott (June/July 1917)

My Dear Friend,

Here am I, sheltered from the sun by the parados of a trench behind a blockhouse; reading *The Bible in Spain*. That's finished now, and *Robinson Crusoe* need not be begun for we are being relieved tonight, and O! the relief! 'Robinson' may follow; we shall have tomorrow off anyway. What a life! What a life! My memories of this week will be, – Blockhouse; an archway there through which a sniper used his skill on us as we emerged from the rooms at the side; cold; stuffy heat; Brent Young; Smashed or stuck Tanks; A gas and smoke barrage put up by us, a glorious but terrifying sight; Fritzes shells; One sunset; two sunrises; *The Bible in Spain*; The tale of the cutting up of the KRRs in 1914; of Colonel Elkington; of the first gas attacks also; of the Brigade Orderly; and of the man who walked in his sleep to Fritz, slept well, woke, realised, and bolted; Thirst; Gas; Shrapnel; *Very* H.E.; Our liquid fire; A first sight of an aeroplane map... Does it sound interesting? May God forgive me if I ever come to cheat myself into thinking that it was, and lie later to younger men of the Great Days. It was damnable; and what in relation to what might have happened? Nothing at all! We have been lucky, but it is not fit for men to be here – in this tormented dry-fevered marsh, where men die and are left to rot because of snipers and the callousness that War breeds. "It might be me tomorrow. Who cares? Yet still, hang on for a Blighty."

Why does this war of spirit take on such dread forms of ugliness and why should a high triumph be signified by a body shattered, black, stinking; avoided by day, stumbled over by night, an offence to the hardest? No doubt there is consolation in the fact that men contemplate such things, such possible endings; and are yet undismayed, yet persistent, do not lose laughter nor the common kindliness that makes life sweet – And yet seem such boys – Yet what consolation can be given me as I look upon and endure it? Any? Sufficient? The "End of War"? Who knows, for the thing for which so great a price is paid is yet doubtful and obscure; and our reward most sweet would seem to depend on what we make of ourselves and give ourselves; for clearer eyes and more contented minds; more contented because of comparisons ironically to be made... and yet

etc (Not quite correct)

Forgive all this; and accept it as a sincere reflection; a piece of technique; only one side of the picture; trench-weariness; thoughts of a not too courageous, not too well-balanced mind. Like Malvolio, I think nobly of man's soul, and am distressed. God should have done better for us than this; Could He not have found some better milder way of changing the Prussian (whom he made) than by the breaking of such beautiful souls? Now *that* is what one should write poetry upon. Someday I will say it in Music, after a while...

Now I must go into the Blockhouse, may get a Blighty doing so... and O if it were but a small hole in the leg! But I am lucky only in my friends, and existence has gone awry for me, not by any means wholly my fault. Maybe I am strong enough to prove the truth of "Character is Destiny" now. God, how I could work, how train myself in Blighty now, were it over! Dyspepsia or no dyspepsia, I'd "be a marvellous kid!" And yet (O the Shakespearian insight of me!) Had I used those earlier years, still I must have come out here for all my promise and accomplishments, and – there you are; here.

I have made a book about Beauty because I have paid the price which five years ago had not been paid. Someday perhaps the True, the real, the undeniable will be shown by me, and I forgive all this.

There is a great gap in my mind, very thirsty, which shall be filled with sunsets, trees, winds, stars, and children's faces; blossoming fairer after so long a drought my mind shall turn freely to that which once was effort to contemplate. I, even I, may experience Present Joy – but not yet. But were I home, with this new ability and Passion for my work, O then perhaps...

It is a hard thing to accustom oneself to the resigning of life at any moment, and to become aware and more aware of what that leaving means. Meanwhile, while I am thus thinking and writing, our guns pour almost incessantly a thin musical complaining watery trickle of shells; for what purpose one may rise up and see. "After all I might have gone to Liepsic, to Bonn, to Munich; and they might have been my friends and companions in Art." There goes a dud, and I am glad of it.

Who will dare talk of the glory of Waterloo or Trafalgar again?

There now, I have written myself out, and feel happier. (Theirs or ours? Theirs. Bash!)

I do not forget in my preoccupations to hope you are getting stronger, and that Mr Scott is now on holiday. Nor forget the funny side of things. A few yards away are three walking cases; perhaps "Blighty" men. To get to the Dressing Station is a slightly risky thing, but far less so than many ordinary things a soldier does. Will they risk it? In day light? Hardly! For they have that which is more precious than much fine gold.

Tea's up!

TEA!! O magic word.

Late reading with a pipe and a teapot. 5 oclock at Cranham. Willy Harvey and wonderful Mrs Harvey. Framilode. Twigworth.

O what not? All these memories have music in them. Bach and Schumann. Perhaps there are two men of that name over there:

Your sincere friend
Ivor Gurney

I wish I wasnt so lousy.

Dont trouble to sympathise. I take that for granted or would not have written comme ça.

ROSA LUXEMBURG

THE GERMAN SOCIALIST ROSA LUXEMBURG (1871–1919) was imprisoned for much of the First World War. On her release, she took part in the abortive Spartakist Uprising, and was murdered at its end in Berlin.

To Hans Diefenbach (29 June 1917), from Wronke jail

Good day, Hänschen!

...Every night while sitting at my barred window; where I can breathe in the fresh air and dream, with my legs stretched out on another chair, somewhere in the neighborhood the muffled sounds begin of someone diligently beating carpets, or something like that. I have no idea who is doing it or where. But I have already gained an intimate, though indeterminate, relation to whoever it is through the regular recurrence of those sounds. They awake in me some vague idea of competent housework, of a little place in which everything is sparkling clean. Perhaps it is one of our female officials, who finds time only late at night, after the daily work, to take care of her tiny household – a lonely old maid or widow, like the majority of prison officials, who uses the little leisure time she has to forever put her few rooms into meticulous order. Of course, no one ever enters these rooms, and she only rarely makes use of them herself. I just don't know; yet, every time, these rapping sounds bring me the feeling of ordered, circumscribed quiet and, at the same time, a slight feeling of being enclosed within the narrowness and hopelessness of a penurious existence – china cabinets, yellow photographs, artificial flowers, a hard sofa...

Do you also know this strange effect of sounds whose origin is unknown to us? I have experienced this in every prison. For example, in Zwickau, every night at exactly two o'clock, ducks who were living somewhere nearby in a pond, woke me with a loud "quack-quack-quack-quack!" The first of the four syllables was called in a high pitch with the strongest emphasis and conviction. From that point, it scaled down to a deep bass murmur. Awakened by the noise, for a few seconds I was always forced to reorient myself in the blackest darkness on a stone-hard mattress and remember where I was. That feeling of being in the jail cell, always somewhat oppressive, the special accentuation of the "quack-quack," the fact that I had no idea where the ducks were and that I only heard them at night, gave their call something mysterious and meaningful. It always sounded to me like some type of philosophical saying which, through its regular recurrence every night had something irrevocable about it, something that had been valid since the beginning of the world like some kind of coptic maxim.

> And on the nights of Indian air
> And in The deep of Egyptian graves
> Have I heard the sacred word...

That I could not decipher the meaning of this duck wisdom, that I only had a vague idea of it, called forth a strange disquiet in my heart every time, and I used to lie awake, anxious, for a long time.

It was completely different in Barnimstrasse. At 9 o'clock it was lights out, and I would always willy-nilly lie down in my bed though, naturally, I was unable to fall asleep. Shortly after 9, in the stillness of night, from some nearby tenement the crying of a two- or three-year-old boy would regularly begin. Then, after a few pauses, the little fellow would gradually sob his way into a true, plaintive crying which, however, had nothing vehement about it and which expressed no clear pain or desire. Instead, it only manifested a general discontent with existence, and an inability to come to terms with the difficulties of life and its problems, especially since Mommy was not by his side. The helpless crying lasted a good three-quarters of an hour. At exactly ten, however, I would hear the door opening firmly; light, quick steps resounded loudly in the little room, and a full-sounding young woman s voice, from which one could still sense the freshness of the street air, would say: "Why aren't you asleep? Why aren't you asleep?" At that point, three hearty smacks would follow from which one could clearly feel the appetizing roundness and bed warmth of that particular part of the little body. And – oh, wonder – the three smacks would suddenly solve all the difficulties and complex problems of life with ease. The whimpering would stop, the little boy would immediately fall asleep, and a quiet relief would rule again in the tenement.

This scene recurred so regularly every night that it became a part of my own existence. By 9 o'clock, I would be waiting with tensed nerves for the awakening and whimpering of my little unknown neighbour. I knew his whole vocal register in advance and could follow that crying, in which the feelings of helplessness in the face of life were fully communicated to me. Then I would wait for the young woman's return home, for the sonorous question, and especially for the liberating smacks. Believe me, Hänschen, that old-fashioned method of solving the problems of existence, by way of the little fellow's behind, also worked wonders in my own soul. My nerves would immediately relax with his and, every time, I would fall asleep at almost the same time as the little one. I never learned from which window decorated with geraniums, from which garret, those human threads stretched to me. In the harsh light of day, all the houses which I was able to see appeared equally grey, sober and sternly reserved. They all had the expression: "We know nothing." Only in the darkness of night, through the soft breath of the summer air, were spun the mysterious relations between people who neither knew nor saw one another.

Ah, what a beautiful memory I have of Alexanderplatz! Hänschen, do you know what Alexanderplatz is? That one-and-a-half-month stop-over there left me with grey hair and rents in my nerves which I shall never repair. And yet, I recall a small scene which breaks forth like a flower in my memory. The nights there began – it was late autumn, October, and there was no lighting at all in my cell – as early as 5 or 6 o'clock. There was nothing left for me to do in the 400-cubic-foot cell except stretch myself out on the cot, squeezed in between indescribable pieces of furniture. Into a hell's music of the incessantly thundering elevated trains, which shook the cell and struck red reflections of light on the rattling window panes, I would recite my Mörike under my breath. From 10 o'clock on, the diabolical concert of the trains would quiet down somewhat, and after, from the street, the following little episode could be heard. First a subdued masculine voice, which had something summoning and admonishing about it, and then, in response, the singing of an 8-year-old girl. Evidently she was singing a nursery song while skipping and jumping around; her silvery laughter resounded as pure as a bell. Probably the voice belonged to some tired and grouchy doorman calling his little daughter home to bed. The little rascal didn't want to obey. She played tag with her father, that bearded, gruff bass voice and fluttered around the street like a butterfly, teasing the feigned strictness with a lively nursery rhyme. You could practically see the short shirt flap up and down and the little legs fly into a dancing stance. In this jumping rhythm of the nursery song, in the bubbling laughter, there was so much carefree and victorious lust for life that the whole dark, mouldy building of the police presidium seemed enveloped in a coat of silvery mist; it was as if, all of a sudden, my malodorous cell smelled of falling dark-red roses. Thus, wherever we are we can gather up a little happiness from the street, and we are reminded again that life is beautiful and rich.

Hänschen, you have no idea how blue the sky was today! Or was it just as blue in Lissa? Usually, before the "lockup," I go out into the evening for a half-hour to water my little flower bed (self-planted pansies, forget-me-nots, and phlox!) with my own little can, and stroll around a bit in the garden. This hour before nightfall has its own peculiar magic. The sun was still hot, but one was happy to allow its slanted rays to burn one's neck and cheeks like a kiss. A low breath of air moved the bushes like a whispered promise that the coolness of evening would soon arrive and relieve the heat of the day. In the sky, which was a sparkling, glimmering blue, some dazzling-white cloud formations stood towering; a very pale half-moon swam between them like a phantom, like a dream. The swallows had already begun their nightly communal flight. Their sharp pointed wings cut the blue silk of space into pieces. They shot to and fro, somersaulting with shrill cries in the dizzying heights. I stood with my dripping water can in my hand. My head was held high, and I had an uncontrollable desire to plunge into the moist, shimmering blue above, to bathe in it, to splash in it, to give myself up to the foam and then disappear. Mörike came to mind – you know:

> Oh river, my river in morning light!
> Receive this once, receive
> This yearning body
> And kiss its breast and cheek!
> The sky, azure and or childlike purity,
> In which the waves are singing,

The sky is thy soul,
Oh let me permeate it!
With my mind and my senses I immerse myself
Into thy deepest azure
And cannot wing to its ends!...
Is anything as deep, as deep as this azure?
Only, only Love,
Love is never satiated, she never sates
With her ever changing light...

For God's sake, Hänschen, don't follow my bad example. Don't you also become so talkative. It won't happen again, I swear!!!

R.

E. M. FORSTER

EDWARD MORGAN FORSTER (1879–1970), AUTHOR OF *Howard's End* (1910) and *A Passage to India* (1924). During the First World War, Forster served with the Red Cross in Alexandria, where he began an affair with an Egyptian tram-conductor, Mohammed ed Adl ('A').

To Florence Barger (13 September 1917), from Alexandria, Egypt

Dearest Florence,

You enquire what A and I do. Talk mostly – you see our time together seldom averages over 2 hours a week. Occasionally chess but "I have learnt play but not learnt to think" he says – Ways and means are an increasing difficulty. His $1/2$ brother – "my brother and my enemy" – is still with him and squats blinking in the corner of the room that would otherwise be ours. While as for my room, my landlady has got the wind up: – I didn't – or hope I didn't – tell you this at the time, lest it worried you, and I tell you now because all is all right – she is calmed and has forgotten, being a simple soul. It didn't worry me the least, except as a practical problem: all my old awe of people's opinions has dried up, and A never had any. I told him why he couldn't come any more, and he nodded. Then we had 2 Sunday mornings together – one at Pompey's Pillar and the Catacombs, the other at Mouzha Gardens, and sometimes we meet of an evening in the Gardens in the middle of the town. We have laid down certain rules, and assume that so long as we keep them we are safe – that is the only sensible course, I think. We meet and part *at* the places – both in civilian costume – and never travel together on the trams. His other (third) suit – besides his uniform – is a long and rather unpleasing nightgown over which you button a sort of frock coat: bare feet in clogs. Thus attired he may walk with me in the neighbourhood of his room, but not elsewhere. He always wears a fez. He is unfortunately rather black – not as black as a child's face or ink, but blacker than Altounyan or Masood – so that our juxtaposition is noticeable. It was thoughtless of him to have been born that colour, and only the will of God Allah prevented his mother from tattooing little bluebirds at the corners of his eyes. Blobs on his wrist have sufficed her.

Last night – perhaps the happiest of my life – has left me very solemn at least though not outwardly. All is far greater than I have yet realised. I tell you one thing not as wanting to confide it even to you, but because I want it to be known if ever I should die. We had by good luck his room to ourselves, and he said suddenly "If we are to be friends for ever you must promise me something," I asked if he wanted wished to be friends for ever. He said "if you wish." I said "I do", and he went on – "You must promise me at once to tell me when if I wrong you, so that we may make the place clean. One two three four wrongs may not matter, but if more are left all turns we leave more all will turn evil." – That is all – . Then I told him about work and he went to the heart of *that* with "You stop the relations of those who are missing lost from having wrong ideas – thus you serve your King and Country better than by fighting, I think." Then he went to the heart of my possible return to England – he knew nothing of it before. "Give Mother money – not *enough* but *too* much – and do *not* go, for she will only be unhappy in case they make you a soldier."—And apart from the joy of all this I feel, more deeply, its solemnity, and think of what you once said that the possibilities of human intercourse are only beginning. I hate faith as a creed – but when something happens that gives you faith you're very near heaven. I was resting my head on him all the time I'd like you to know, too: and his hands were stroking it. Then he said "But I *must* be independent – if I do not want to meet you, I must say 'I do not', if I am not sure, I *must* be able to say 'perhaps', you must respect me as I respect you." – No more now, dearest Florence.

To Florence Barger (16 July 1918), from Alexandria

Dearest Florence

How I hope that this will reach you that you may share my happiness. I have just been to Mansurah for the week end, and it was even better than either of us hoped. Does one experience a *renewal* or a *deepening* of emotion each time? It feels so like the latter. Of course we have never before had perfect conditions – they have marked this meeting as one apart. I have told you of all his sorrow – death of father and, what is worse, death of brother by drowning. He has become – funny little fellow – a "householder": or rather the family own 3 houses. They are situate in a lane near the station: nearly nearly a slum – ducks & chicks paddle, and O my dear the sanitation! only means to of washing is to strip in the passage under the stairs and pour little tins of water over each other which slither away into a far yet not far enough latrine. "Perfect conditions!' – never before did I so bless my adaptability. Where would I be if I had gone in for "requiring" things like Plugs and Plates. I don't know that the room was very clean either, but I seldom touched bottom, as on entering you crawled straight on to a sofa, and big bed, table, and wardrobe paved the rest. The rest of the house was let. Food – delicious and very lavish. Once we had a tray of roast mutton potatoes, tomatoes and onions as big as the top of a drum, and amazing good tea in the morning. They were brought in by a semi-slave from outside, who squatted in the passage while we ate and gave vent to her views on the world.

We emerged fairly smart from our lair, and saw the sights of Mansurah – pleasantly situated on the Nile with an esplanade (not too formal) and cafés. We drove, went in a boat. I saw some of his friends – they looked good stamp: some of them spoke both French & English: uncle of one of them a doctor, had been at London University. None of them know what *he* did at Alexandria, he says. Curious state of affairs! Our main topic was the possibility of his marrying his brother's wife. I am rather in favour of it. He likes her and has often seen her, she likes him and approves the scheme – which originates with his sister. She requires no dowry, and – being a widow – there will be no expense over her wedding. She wants him to protect the child – aged 2 – of whom he is very fond. It wouldn't – as he agreed work in England, because he is not in love with her at all. But I see no disaster ahead in this country. They are so simple and the women simpler than the men. I wouldn't like him to miss a romantic marriage if it was possible, or if its romance was likely to outlast his curiosity. What do you feel for him about it?

He was awfully grave at first. The drowning was so inexplicable – cramp I think. He went to Tantah at once to see his sister in law and arrange business, but made no detailed enquiries about the death. "What is the use? I shall only increase my sorrow? – . If only it had been the rest of my family instead." The second day of my visit he cheered up – I felt so proud & happy. He started ragging me in bed just as H[arold] or E[vert] might – "Morgan I will hurt you – Edward I will kill you" and we went on fooling till we fell asleep. To put the lid on, I travelled 3rd. Quite comfortably. I theorised to him, by the way, rather deeply against R[espectability] – how afterwards I found its absence even more important than at the time. He said very gently "I quite understand" – so I have the happiness of knowing that things are sound even on an intellectual basis. He has given me for the time some nice gaiters and breeches, also consents to get measured for a suit a little too large for him which is to do for us both: advances towards communism we shouldn't have made a year ago. I don't see where things will end, so keep an open mind. Next month he should come to Alexandria to look for work. Reenlistment in the army he says is now *for duration*: this if true – and it's likely to be – renders it impossible. The net is falling on Egypt, though slowly. F[urness]'s failure to help me hurts very much. He has not mentioned the subject again. A. is so presentable and unscalliwagy – I'm more and more certain that something could have been done, but have no one else to turn to. One mistake, A. points out, we have made. He ought from the first to have given me Arabic lessons in my rooms.

On I go – I meant to insert a sheet on other subjects but it's time for my stupid work. It has grown so tedious, but it's the basis of my existence out here. Much love and thanks. My life would have split beyond mending if it wasn't for you.

Morgan.

T. E. LAWRENCE

THE BRITISH SOLDIER T. E. LAWRENCE (1888–1935) LED an Arab irregular force during the First World War, earning himself the soubriquet "Lawrence of Arabia"; his memoir of the time was later published as *Seven Pillars of Wisdom*. He turned his back on fame in 1922 and entered the RAF as an aircraftsman under the alias "John Hume Ross" but when newspapermen discovered his identity he joined the Tank Corps as "T. E. Shaw". In 1925 he transferred back to the RAF, serving in that force almost until his death in a motorcycle accident.

To George Bernard Shaw (17 August 1922)

George Bernard Shaw, Irish-born dramatist, critic and socialist.

Dear Mr Shaw

You will be puzzled at my writing to you: but Cockerell some months ago took me round to you and introduced me, and you did not talk too formidably.

I want to ask you two questions: the first one, "Do you still read books?", doesn't require an answer. If you still go on reading I'm going to put the second question: if you don't, then please skip the two inside pages of this note and carry over to my signature at the end, and burn it all without replying. I hate letter-writing as much as I can and so, probably, do you.

My real wish is to ask if you will read, or try to read, a book which I have written. It's about the war, which will put you off to start with and there are technical unpleasantnesses about it. For instance it is very long: about 300,000 words I suspect, though I have not counted them. I have very little money and do not wish to publish it: however it had to be printed, so I got it done on a lino. press in a newspaper office. That means it's beastly to look at, two columns on a quarto page, small newspaper type which hurts your eyes, and dozens of misprints, corrected roughly in ink: for only five copies exist, and I could not afford a proof. The punctuation is entirely the compositor's fancy; and he had an odd fancy, especially on Mondays.

That's the worst to be said on the material side. So far as concerns myself you must be told, before you commit yourself to saying "yes", that I'm not a writer, and successfully passed the age of 30 without having wanted to write anything. I was brought up as a professional historian, which means the worship of original documents. To my astonishment, after peace came I found I was myself the sole person who knew what had happened in Arabia during the war: and the only literate person in the Arab Army. So it became a professional duty to record what happened. I started out to do it plainly and simply, much as a baby thinks it's easy to talk: and then I found myself bogged in a confusion of ways of saying the easiest things, and unable to describe the plainest places: and then problems of conduct came along, and the people with me had to be characterised: – in fact I got fairly into it, and the job became too much for me. Your first book was not perfect, though it was a subject you had chosen for yourself, and you had an itch to write!

In my case, I have I believe, taken refuge in second-hand words: I mean, I think I've borrowed expressions and adjectives and ideas from everybody I have ever read, and cut them down to my own size, and stitched them together again. My tastes are daily mailish, so there's enough piffle and romance and wooliness to make a realist sick. There's a lot of half-baked thinking, some cheap disgust and complaint (the fighting fronts were mainly hysterical, you know, where they weren't professional, and I'm not the least a proper soldier): in fact all the sham stuff you have spent your life trying to prick. If you read my thing, it will show you that your prefaces have been written in vain, if I'm a fair sample of my generation. This might make you laugh, if the thing was amusingly written: but it's long-winded, and pretentious, and dull to the point where I can no longer bear to look at it myself. I chose that moment to have it printed!

You'll wonder, why if all this is true (and I think it is) I want any decent person still more a person like yourself* to read it. Well, it's because it is history, and I'm shamed for ever if I am the sole chronicler of an event, and fail to chronicle it: and yet unless what I've written can be made better I'll burn it. My own disgust with it is so great that I no longer believe it worth trying to improve (or possible to improve). If you read it or part of it and came to the same conclusion, you would give me courage to strike the match: whereas now I distrust my own judgement, and it seems cruel to destroy a thing on which I have worked my hardest for three years. While if you said that parts were rubbish, and other parts not so bad, and parts of it possible, (and distinguished those parts variously) then your standards might enable me to clear up mine, and give me energy enough to tackle the job again. (If you say it is all possible then I will reluctantly get rid of your own books from my shelves.)

All this is very unfair – or would be, if you knew me but deleting that twenty minutes with Cockerell we are utter strangers, and likely to remain so, and therefore there is no pressure on you to answer this letter at all. I won't be in the least astonished (indeed I'll write another of the same sort to a man called Orage whom I have never me, but whose criticism I enjoy): and my opinion of you will go up.

Yours with many apologies
T E Lawrence

Incidentally: I don't want people to know that the book exists. So whether you reply or not, I hope you will not talk of it.

*ambiguous: but I wanted to avoid expressing my liking for your work.

To Lionel Curtis (27 March 1923)

A letter written just after Lawrence's reluctant transfer to the Tank Corps from the RAF.

It seems to continue itself today, because I've been wondering about the other fellows in the hut. A main feeling they give me is of difference from the R.A.F. men. There we were excited about our coming service. We talked and wondered of the future, almost exclusively. There was a constant recourse to imagination, and a constant rewarding of ourselves therefore. The fellows were decent, but so wrought up by hope that they were carried out of themselves, and I could not see them mattly. There was a sparkle round the squad.

Here every man has joined because he was down and out: and no one talks of the Army or of promotion, or of trades and accomplishments. We are all here unavoidably, in a last resort, and we assume this world's failure in one-another, so that pretence would be not merely laughed at, but as near an impossibility as anything human. We are social bed-rock, those unfit for life-by-competition: and each of us values the rest as cheap as he knows himself to be.

I suspect that this low estimation is very much the truth. There cannot be classes in England much more raw, more free of all that the upbringing of a lifetime has plastered over you and me. Can there be profit, or truth, in all these modes and sciences and arts of ours? The leisured world for hundreds, or perhaps thousands of years has been jealously working and recording the advance of each generation for the starting-point of the next – and here these masses are as animal, as carnal as were their ancestors before Plato and Christ and Shelley and Dostoevsky taught and thought. In this crowd it's made startlingly clear how short is the range of knowledge, and what poor conductors of it ordinary humans are. You and I know: you have tried (Round Tabling and by mouth) to tell all whom you can reach: and the end is here, a cimmerian darkness with bog-lights flitting wrongly through its gas.

The pity of it is, that you've got to take this black core of things in camp, this animality, on trust. It's a feeling, a spirit which colours every word and action, and I believe every thought, passing in Hut 12. Your mind is like a many-storeyed building, and you, its sole tenant, flit from floor to floor, from room to room, at the whim of your spirit's moment. (Not that the spirit has moments, but let it pass for the metaphor's sake.) At will you can be gross, and enjoy coffee or a sardine, or rarefy yourself till the diaphancité [sic] of pure mathematics, or of a fluent design in line, is enough to feed you. Here –

I can't write it, because in literature such things haven't ever been, and can't be. To record the acts of Hut 12 would produce a moral-medical case-book, not a work of art but a document. It isn't the filth of it which hurts me, because you can't call filthy the pursuit of a bitch by a dog, or the mating of birds in springtime; and it's man's misfortune that he hasn't a mating season, but spreads his emotions and excitements through the year... but I lie in bed night after night with this cat-calling carnality seething up and down the hut, fed by streams of fresh matter from twenty lecherous mouths... and my mind aches with the rawness of it, knowing that it will cease only when the slow bugle calls for "lights out" an hour or so hence... and the waiting is so slow...

However the call comes always in the end, and suddenly at last, like God's providence, a dewfall of peace upon the camp... but surely the world would be more clean if we were dead or mindless? We are all guilty alike, you know. You wouldn't exist, I wouldn't exist, without this carnality. Everything with flesh in its mixture is the achievement of a moment when the lusty thought of Hut 12 has passed to action and conceived: and isn't it true that the fault of birth rests somewhat on the child? I believe it's we who led our parents on to bear us, and it's our unborn children who make our flesh itch.

A filthy business all of it, and yet Hut 12 shows me the truth behind Freud. Sex is an integer in all of us, and the nearer nature we are, the more constantly, the more completely a product of that integer. These fellows are the reality, and you and I, the selves who used to meet in London and talk of fleshless things, are only the outward wrappings of a core like these fellows. They let light and air play always upon their selves, and consequently have grown very lustily, but have at the same time achieved health and strength in their growing. Whereas our wrappings and bandages have stunted and deformed ourselves, and hardened them to an apparent insensitiveness... but it's a callousness, a crippling, only to be yea-said by aesthetes who prefer clothes to bodies, surfaces to intentions.

These fellows have roots, which in us are rudimentary, or long cut off. Before I came I never visualised England except as an organism, an entity... but these fellows are local, territorial. They all use dialects, and could be placed by their dialects, if necessary. However it isn't necessary, because each talks of his district, praises it, boasts of it, lives in the memory of it. We call each other "Brum" or "Coventry" or "Cambridge", and the man who hasn't a "place" is an outsider. They wrangle and fight over the virtues of their homes. Of solidarity, of a nation, of something ideal comprehending their familiar streets in itself – they haven't a notion.

Well, the conclusion of the first letter was that man, being a civil war, could not be harmonised or made logically whole... and the end of this is that man, or mankind, being organic, a natural growth, is unteachable: cannot depart from his first grain and colour nor exceed flesh, nor put forth anything not mortal and fleshly.

I fear not even my absence would reconcile Ph.K.* to this.

E. L.

---

*Philip Kerr, Marquess of Lothian, later Ambassador to the United States.

To Robert Guy (21 March 1923), from Bovington Camp

Guy was a young American in the RAF with whom Lawrence had developed a close, possibly homoerotic, friendship.

My rabbit

I do no good here. Out upon the army & all its clothes and food & words and works. You in the R.A.F. are as lucky as I thought myself in the old days, & as I used to tell you.

They give us great leisure. Five hours work a day on Monday and Thursday. Tuesday is an afternoon for sports. Wednesday is a half-day. On Friday our work is drawing pay, & wondering afterwards why they, out of all the possible payments in the world, should have given us just that little or that much. Saturday, needless to say is Saturday: and Sunday is Sunday.

I'm going to dazzle you, if ever I see you again, with the perfection of my salute: while at slow marching! I march slower and slower: the whole camp agrees that my slow marching is slow. Though some idiots this afternoon were arguing as to whether it was marching. God help them they are fools, & myself the solitary wise man in Dorset.

"Easter leave" did you say, in your exquisite letter? I get none. They dazzle us with the prospect of eight days' leave in August: – but to win that we must have done eighteen weeks upon the square, & must have reached, as a squad, the standard of finished squads. Horrors & horrors piled upon one another! Thanks be to God that I require no leave. Only, rabbit, I'm sorry, since that summer holiday in Oxford would have been perhaps a pleasure to you. There are no rabbits here (or at least no imitation ones) and it would give me contentment to see your queer but jolly face again. There are men from Brum but their accent isn't like yours (except when they miss an h) and their wishes are ordinary.

My attack upon you in the last letter was presumably a bad joke. I envy everyone who doesn't think continually.

Brough* is in London, & myself confined to camp.

R.

---

*His motorcycle.

Tell Jock that soldiers are men like Jimmy Carr, & that I can't do the weight. I might sham A.C.II-ship but this is too difficult.

I wasn't in Farnborough on Monday. Depot.

F. SCOTT FITZGERALD

FRANCIS SCOTT KEY FITZGERALD (1896–1940), AMERIcan author of the Jazz Age classic, *The Great Gatsby* (1925). He married Zelda Sayre in 1920, who subsequently became mentally unstable and was confined. Ridden by debt and alcoholism, Fitzgerald moved to Hollywood in 1937 to work as a screen writer.

❧

To Maxwell Perkins (c. 20 December 1924), from Rome, Italy

Perkins was Fitzgerald's editor at Scribner's publishing house.

Dear Max:

I'm a bit (not very – not dangerously) stewed tonight and I'll probably write you a long letter. We're living in a small, unfashionable but most comfortable hotel at $525.00 a month including tips, meals, etc. Rome does not particularly interest me but it's a big year here, and early in the spring we're going to Paris. There's no use telling you my plans because they're usually just about as unsuccessful as to work as religious prognosticators are as to the End of the World. I've got a new novel to write – title and all – that'll take about a year. Meanwhile, I don't want to start it until this is out and meanwhile I'll do short stories for money (I now get $2000 a story but I hate worse than hell to do them) and there's the never-dying lure of another play.

Now! Thanks enormously for making up the $5000. I know I don't technically deserve it, considering I've had $3000 or $4000 for as long as I can remember. But since you force it on me (inexecrable [or is it execrable] joke) I will accept it I hope to Christ you get 10 times it back on *Gatsby*– and I think perhaps you will.

For:

I can now make it perfect but the proof (I will soon get the immemorial letter with the statement "We now have the book in hand and will soon begin to send you proof." What is "in hand?" I have a vague picture of everyone in the office holding the book in the right hand and reading it.) will be one of the most expensive affairs since *Madame Bovary*. *Please* charge it to my account. If it's possible to send a second proof over here I'd love to have it. Count on 12 days each way– four days here on first proof and two days on the second. I hope there are other good books in the spring because I think now the public interest in *books* per se rises when there seems to be a group of them, as in 1920 (spring and fall), 1921 (fall), 1922 (spring). Ring's and Tom's (first) books,* Willa Cather's *Lost Lady*, and in an inferior, cheap way Edna Ferber's are the only American fiction in over two years that had a really excellent press (say, since *Babbitt*).

With the aid you've given me I can make *Gatsby* perfect. The Chapter 7 (the hotel scene) will never quite be up to mark– I've worried about it too long and I can't quite place Daisy's reaction. But I can improve it a lot. It isn't imaginative energy that's lacking– it's because I'm automatically prevented from thinking it out over again *because I must get all those characters to New York* in order to have the catastrophe on the road going back, and I must have it pretty much that way. So there's no chance of bringing the freshness to it that a new conception sometimes gives.

The rest is easy and I see my way so clear that I even see the mental quirks that queered it before. Strange to say, my notion of Gatsby's vagueness was O.K. What you and Louise and Mr Charles Scribner found wanting was that:

---

*Thomas Boyd, best known for his war novel *Through the Wheat*.

I myself didn't know what Gatsby looked like or was engaged in and you felt it. If I'd known and kept it from you you'd have been *too impressed with my knowledge to protest.* This is a complicated idea but I'm sure you'll understand. But I know now– and as a penalty for not having known first, in other words to make sure I'm going to tell more.

It seems of almost mystical significance to me that you thought he was older – the man I had in mind, half-unconsciously, was older (a specific individual) and evidently, without so much as a definite word, I conveyed the fact. Or rather I must qualify this Shaw Desmond trash by saying that I conveyed it without a word that I can at present or for the life of me trace. (I think Shaw Desmond was one of your bad bets– I was the other.)

Anyhow after careful searching of the files (of a man's mind here) for the Fuller Magee case and after having had Zelda draw pictures until her fingers ache I know Gatsby better than I know my own child. My first instinct after your letter was to let him go and have Tom Buchanan dominate the book (I suppose he's the best character I've ever done– I think he and the brother in *Salt* and Hurstwood in *Sister Carrie* are the three best characters in American fiction in the last twenty years, perhaps and perhaps not) but Gatsby sticks in my heart. I had him for awhile, then lost him, and now I know I have him again. I'm sorry Myrtle is better than Daisy. Jordan of course was a great idea (perhaps you know it's Edith Cummings) but she fades out. It's Chapter VII that's the trouble with Daisy and it may hurt the book's popularity that it's *a man's book*.

Anyhow I think (for the first time since *The Vegetable* failed) that I'm a wonderful writer and it's your always wonderful letters that help me to go on believing in myself.

Now some practical, very important questions. Please answer every one.

1. Montenegro has an order called the Order of Danilo. Is there any possible way you could find out for me there what it would look like – whether a courtesy decoration given to an American would bear an English inscription – or anything to give verisimilitude to the medal which sounds horribly amateurish?

2. Please have *no blurbs of any kind on the jacket*!!! No Mencken or Lewis or Sid Howard or anything. I don't believe in them *one* bit any more.
3. Don't forget to change name of book in list of works.
4. Please shift exclamation point from end of third line to end of fourth line in title page poem. *Please*! Important!
5. I thought that the whole episode (2 paragraphs) about their playing the "Jazz History of the World" at Gatsby's first party was rotten. Did you? Tell me your frank *reaction – personal*. Don't think! We can all think!

Got a sweet letter from Sid Howard – rather touching. I wrote him first I thought *Transatlantic* was great stuff – a really gorgeous surprise. Up to that I never believed in him specially and I was sorry because he did in me. Now I'm tickled silly to find he has power, and his own power. It seemed tragic too to see *Mrs Vietch* wasted in a novelette when, despite Anderson, the short story is at its lowest ebb as an art form. (Despite Ruth Suckow, Gertrude Stein, Ring, there is a horrible impermanence on it *because* the overwhelming number of short stories are impermanent.)

Poor Tom Boyd! His cycle sounded so sad to me – perhaps it'll be wonderful but it sounds to me like sloughing in a field whose first freshness has gone.

See that word?* The ambition of my life is to make that use of it correct. The temptation to use it as a neuter is one of the vile fevers in my still insecure prose.

Tell me about Ring! About Tom – is he poor? He seems to be counting on his short story book, frail cane! About Biggs – did he ever finish the novel? About Peggy Boyd – I think Louise might have sent us her book!

I thought *The White Monkey* was stinko. On second thoughts I didn't like Cowboys, West and South either. What about *Bal du Comte d'Orgel*? and Ring's set? and his new book? and Gertrude Stein? and Hemingway?

I still owe the store almost $700.00 on my encyclopedia, but I'll pay them on about January 10th – all in a lump as I expect my finances will

---

*Fitzgerald had circled "whose" in the preceding sentence.

then be on a firm footing. Will you ask them to send me Ernest Boyd's book? § Unless it has about my drinking in it that would reach my family. However, I guess it'd worry me more if I hadn't seen it than if I had. If my book is a big success or a great failure (financial – no other sort can be imagined I hope) I don't want to publish stories in the fall. If it goes between 25,000 and 50,000 I have an excellent collection for you. This is the longest letter I've written in three or four years. Please thank Mr Scribner for me for his exceeding kindness.

Always yours,
Scott Fitz—

~❧~

To his daughter, Frances Scott Fitzgerald (8 August 1933)

Dear Pie:

I feel very strongly about you doing [your] duty. Would you give me a little more documentation about your reading in French ? I am glad you are happy – but I never believe much in happiness. I never believe in misery either. Those are things you see on the stage or the screen or the printed page, they never really happen to you in life.

All I believe in in life is the rewards for virtue (according to your talents) and the *punishments* for not fulfilling your duties, which are doubly costly. If there is such a volume in the camp library, will you ask Mrs Tyson to let you look up a sonnet of Shakespeare's in which the line occurs *"Lilies that fester smell far worse than weeds."*

Have had no thoughts today, life seems composed of getting up a *Saturday Evening Post* story. I think of you, and always pleasantly; but if you call me "Pappy" again I am going to take the White Cat out and beat his bottom *hard, six times for every time you are impertinent.* Do you react to that?

I will arrange the camp bill.

Halfwit, I will conclude.

Things to worry about:
  Worry about courage

Worry about cleanliness
Worry about efficiency
Worry about horsemanship
Worry about...
Things not to worry about:
Don't worry about popular opinion
Don't worry about dolls
Don't worry about the past
Don't worry about the future
Don't worry about growing up
Don't worry about anybody getting ahead of you
Don't worry about triumph
Don't worry about failure unless it comes
  through your own fault
Don't worry about mosquitoes
Don't worry about flies
Don't worry about insects in general
Don't worry about parents
Don't worry about boys
Don't worry about disappointments
Don't worry about pleasures
Don't worry about satisfactions
Things to think about:
What am I really aiming at?
How good am I really in comparison to my contemporaries in regard to:
(a) Scholarship
(b) Do I really understand about people and am I able to get along with them?
(c) Am I trying to make my body a useful instrument or am I neglecting it?

With dearest love,
Daddy

P.S. My come-back to your calling me Pappy is christening you by the word Egg, which implies that you belong to a very rudimentary state of life and that I could break you up and crack you open at my will and I think it would be a word that would hang on if I ever told it to your contemporaries."Egg Fitzgerald." How would you like that to go through life with– "Eggie Fitzgerald" or "Bad Egg Fitzgerald" or any form that might occur to fertile minds? Try it once more and I swear to God I will hang it on you and it will be up to you to shake it off. Why borrow trouble?

Love anyhow.

ᴔᴁᴈ

To his wife and daughter, Zelda and Frances Scott (20 June 1940), from Hollywood, California

Dearest Zelda and Scottie:

I wish I were with you this afternoon. At the moment I am sitting rather dismally contemplating the loss of a three-year-old Ford and a thirty-three-year-old tooth, The Ford (heavily mortgaged) I shall probably get back according to the police because it is just a childish prank of the California boys to steal them and then abandon them. But the tooth I had grown to love.

In recompense I found in *Colliers* a story by myself. I started it just before I broke my shoulder in 1936 and wrote it in intervals over the next couple of years. It seemed terrible to me. That I will ever be able to recover the art of the popular short story is doubtful. At present I'm doing a masterpiece for *Esquire* and waiting to see if my producer can sell the "Babylon Revisited" screenplay to Shirley Temple. If this happens, everything will look very much brighter.

Scottie, I got the marks and was naturally pleased you were off probation at last. It brought back memories of phoning you from Los Angles to see if you were at the Harvard game, of the dean's gloomy picture a year ago last October, of years of distress about your work with threats and prayers and urgings and rewards and apologies and promises and then suddenly the first change about a year ago when you found that Vassar didn't care whether you studied or not – or whether you stayed in or not. It is a story of hair-breadth escapes, and extraordinary devices going back to the French schedule that we had at "La Paix." All sorts of people have been drawn into it. Hours, days and weeks have been consumed. Stories, scripts, trips have been put aside – all to achieve what might have been prevented if I had carried out my first plan– never to let you go near an American school, or else I should have let you become a doll. I couldn't leave you hanging –

The police have just called up telling me they've recovered my car. The thief ran out of gas and abandoned it in the middle of Hollywood Boulevard. The poor lad was evidently afraid to call anybody to help him push it to the curb. I hope next time he gets a nice, big, producer's car with plenty of gas in it and a loaded revolver in each side pocket and he can embark on a career of crime in earnest. I don't like to see any education left hanging in the air.

Enclosed find four checks, two of which (including one of yours, Scottie) should go to Mrs Savre for provisions, etc. By Monday I should be able to make some plans for you, Scottie. Meanwhile you will have written whether you would like to go to Harvard alone which I did not think should frighten you. You have those two Vassar credits to make up if you are going to get an A.B. degree and I presume this would do it.

From the larger attitude one doesn't know from day to day what the situation will be. We may be at war one week after the extinction of the British, an event which at present writing seems scarcely a fortnight away. It will probably mean our almost immediate embroilment both in Northern Canada and Brazil and at least a partial conscription. Scottie, you've been as lucky as anybody could be in your generation to have had a two months' look at Europe just before the end and to have gotten in two years of college in times of peace before such matters are drowned in the roar of the Stuka bombers. And you have seen the men's colleges as they may not be again in our time, with the games and proms. Maybe I'm speaking too quickly – if the British hold out two months until we can get aid to them – but it looks to me as if our task will be to survive.

Even so I would rather you didn't get tied up in any war work except of a temporary nature for the present. I want you to finish your education. If you have any plan for this summer that displaces summer school and is actually constructive please tell me immediately but I know you want to do something.

My thoughts are not so black as this letter sounds – for instance I'm now going to break off and hear the Louis and Godov fight which will prove Black Supremacy or Red Indian Supremacy or South American Inca Supremacy or something. I hope you are swimming a lot. I can't exercise even a little any more: I'm best off in my room. But I love to think of you two diving from great heights and being very trim and graceful in the water.

With dearest love to all,
{ Daddy
  Scott

ERNEST HEMINGWAY

Ernest Miller Hemingway (1899–1961), American short-story writer and novelist. During the 1920s he made several trips to Spain, the background for the novel *The Sun Also Rises* (1926).

To F. Scott Fitzgerald (1 July 1925)

Fitzgerald (see above), author of The Great Gatsby and a friend of Hemingway's from his Paris sojourn. Zelda was Fitzgerald's wife; Hadley, Hemingway's.

Dear Scott:

We are going in to Pamplona tomorrow. Been trout fishing here. How are you? And how is Zelda?

I am feeling better than I've ever felt – havent drunk anything but wine since I left Paris. God it has been wonderful country. But you hate country. All right omit description of country. I wonder what your idea of heaven would be – A beautiful vacuum filled with wealthy monogamists, all powerful and members of the best families all drinking themselves to death. And hell would probably [be] an ugly vacuum full of poor polygamists unable to obtain booze or with chronic stomach disorders that they called secret sorrows.

To me heaven would be a big bull ring with me holding two barrera seats and a trout stream outside that no one else was allowed to fish in and two lovely houses in the town; one where I would have my wife and children and be monogamous and love them truly and well and the other where I would have my nine beautiful mistresses on 9 different floors and one house would be fitted up with special copies of the Dial printed on soft tissue and kept in the toilets on every floor and in the other house we would use the American Mercury and the New Republic. Then there would be a fine church like in Pamplona where I could go and be confessed on the way from one house to the other and I would get on my horse and ride out with my son to my bull ranch named Hacienda Hadley and toss coins to all my illegitimate children that lived [along] the road. I would write out at the Hacienda and send my son in to lock the chastity belts onto my mistresses because someone had just galloped up with the news that a notorious monogamist named Fitzgerald had been seen riding toward the town at the head of a company of strolling drinkers.

Well anyway we're going into town tomorrow early in the morning. Write me at the Hotel Quintana

Pamplona

Spain

Or dont you like to write letters. I do because it's such a swell way to keep from working and yet feel you've done something.

So long and love to Zelda from us both,

Yours,
Ernest

To Paul Romaine (6 July 1932)

Dear Mr Romaine:

Thanks for the 15.00. I have not received the book [*Salmagundi*]. Are you sure you sent it to Scribners? They are usually very careful about forwarding – but I have been along the Cuban coast for 65 days and it might have been held up at Havana. When I came in to clear there was notification of a package at Post Office and I filled out a card to have it forwarded. Hope it will be your book and come through safely. Very sorry not to have answered your letters which I enjoyed reading. But I have quit writing letters myself.

As for your hoping the Leftward Swing etc has a very definite significance for me that is so much horseshit. I do not follow the fashions in politics, letters, religion etc. If the boys swing to the left in literature you may make a small bet the next swing will be to the right and some of the same yellow bastards will swing both ways. There is no left and right in writing. There is only good and bad writing.

Dreiser is different. He is an old man and old men all try to save their souls in one way or another.

Dos Passos doesn't swing. He's always been the same. To hell with all your swingers. E. Wilson is a serious and honest bird who discovered life late. Naturally he is shocked and would like to do something about it.

These little punks who have never seen men street fighting, let alone a revolution, writing and saying how can you be indifferent to great political etc. etc. I refer to an outfit in, I believe, Davenport, Iowa. Listen– they never even heard of the events that produced the heat of rage, hatred, indignation, and disillusion that formed or forged what they call indifference.

Now they want you to swallow communism as though it were an elder Boys Y.M.C.A. conference or as though we were all patriots together.

I'm no goddamned patriot nor will I swing to left or right.

Would as soon machine gun left, right, or center any political bastards who do not work for a living – anybody who makes a living by politics or not working.

And if we had a revolution ever and I hadn't been bumped [?] already and had a minute to spare would most certainly see that all limited edition publishers were shot and all their stinking little souls distributed to relieve sanitex shortage. Of all phony rackets that is certainly one of the phoniest. (I know you have to live and my metier is a good metier but when you are street sweeping you don't want to give advice to the horses.) And you wanted the Leftward swing to have a definite significance for me. Well well well.

Yours always,
Ernest Hemingway

VITA SACKVILLE-WEST

THE DAUGHTER OF THE 3RD BARON SACKVILLE, VITA Sackville-West (1892–1962) was the author of the long poem *The Land*, which won the 1927 Hawthornden Prize. She married the diplomat Harold Nicolson in 1913, and their marriage survived despite his homosexuality and her lesbian affairs with Violet Trefusis and the writer Virginia Woolf. Sackville-West is also remembered for the garden she designed at Sissinghurst, Kent.

To Virginia Woolf (21 January 1926), from Milan

I am reduced to a thing that wants Virginia. I composed a beautiful letter to you in the sleepless nightmare hours of the night, and it has all gone: I just miss you, in a quite simple desperate human way. You, with all your un-dumb letters, would never write so elementary a phrase as that; perhaps you wouldn't even feel it. And yet I believe you'll be sensible of a little gap. But you'd clothe it in so exquisite a phrase that it would lose a little of its reality. Whereas with me it is quite stark: I miss you even more than I could have believed; and I was prepared to miss you a good deal. So this letter is just really a squeal of pain. It is incredible how essential to me you have become. I suppose you are accustomed to people saying these things. Damn you, spoilt creature; I shan't make you love me any the more by giving myself away like this – But oh my dear, I can't be clever and stand-offish with you: I love you too much for that. Too truly. You have no idea how stand-offish I can be with people I don't love. I have brought it to a fine art. But you have broken down my defences. And I don't really resent it.

However I won't bore you with any more.

We have re-started, and the train is shaky again. I shall have to write at the stations – which are fortunately many across the Lombard plain.

Venice. The stations were many, but I didn't bargain for the Orient Express not stopping at them. And here we are at Venice for ten minutes only, – a wretched time in which to try and write. No time to buy an Italian stamp even, so this will have to go from Trieste.

The waterfalls in Switzerland were frozen into solid iridescent curtains of ice, hanging over the rock; so lovely. And Italy all blanketed in snow.

We're going to start again. I shall have to wait till Trieste tomorrow morning. Please forgive me for writing such a miserable letter.

V.

To Virginia Woolf (15 March 1926)

Sackville-West had accompanied her husband on his diplomatic posting to Teheran.

Today being the birthday of the Shah, (though common report has it that he knows neither his birthday nor his age, being of low extraction,) last night a dinner was given in his honour at the Foreign Office. So at 8.15, an immense yellow motor draws up at the door: Harold in uniform and gold lace, little sword getting between his legs; Vita derisive, but decked in emeralds; escort in scarlet and white, (the Minister is all for swank, – thinks it impresses the Persians;) the yellow motor proceeds down the street. Pulls up at the Foreign Office. Sentries present arms. The scarlet escort escorts. The sentries' boots are muddy; everything is very shoddy here. Seventy people to dinner; the china doesn't match, – not enough to go round, – the Persian ministers wear their robes of honour: grubby old cashmere dressing-gowns, with no collars to their evening shirts; dinner cold; I escape the awful fate of sitting between two Persians who talk nothing but their own language, and get Sir Percy, who is nice, and the Belgian minister, who tells me about the Emperor of Korea. (I never knew there was such a person; he sounds incredibly romantic; Hakluyt's voyages, and all that.) Suddenly, an awful pause, and we stand up to drink the health of the eleven states represented. But first their national anthems must be played; and, glass in hand, we endure God Save the King, the Brabançonne, (I feel the Belgian minister at my side stiffen to attention,) the International Soviet Hymn, the Marseillaise, the Wacht am Rhein, and six unidentifiable minor powers. An unfortunate incident ushers in the ceremony: all the dirty plates have been stacked under Sir Percy's chair, all the dirty knives and forks under mine, so as we rise to our feet shoving back our chairs there is a clatter… Having drunk to our respective sovereigns and presidents, we drink to the Shah. We adjourn. There are fireworks. Now the Persians are really good at fireworks. The garden, from the balconies, coruscates with wrestling babies of Herculean promise, I taxi-cabs with revolving wheels, aeroplanes with revolving propellers, catherine wheels, and VIVE SA MAJESTÉ IMPÉRIALE PAHLEVI in letters of gold reflecting in in the central tank– all very lovely, really, and fantastic, seen through clouds of smoke from above; while Tamur Tasch officially Minister of Works, but really the Power behind the Throne, enquires in my car as to the merits of Thos. Goode and Son, South Audley Street, and the Army & Navy Stores. This is diplomatic life.

This morning, the yellow motor again; and Sir Percy and Harold, both in uniform again, with fluttering plumes in their hats, (Sir Percy loving it, and Harold wretched,) going off to the Shah's reception, the scarlet-and-white servants and the Indian lancers trotting before and behind the car.

Do not imagine, however, that life is all like that. There are days of going into the mountains, and eating sandwiches beside a stream, and picking wild almonds, and of coming home by incredible sunsets across the plain. And every morning at seven we ride, and the freshness and beauty of the morning are inconceivable.

Then once a fortnight the muddy car comes in, and there are letters: the only rift opening on the outside world. Otherwise it is all very self-contained, – what with the old white horse who goes his rounds every morning, bringing two barrels of water to every house in the compound, and the Sanitary Cart, which drawn by a donkey performs a sordid emptying function henceforward unknown at Rodmell... There is a great deal of compound life. (The compound is really the Legation garden, surrounded by a mud wall; and, dumped down among the plane-trees, are the various houses: the Military Attaché's house, the Secretaries' house, the Counsellor's house, the Consul's house, and houses E.-and-F.-on the-office-plan, from which on Sunday mornings proceed the plaintive sounds of an harmonium.) Compound life means that at 8 a.m. the Consul's son aged ten starts an imitation of a motor horn; that at 9 a.m. somebody comes and says have I been letting all the water out of the tank; that at 10 a.m. the Military Attaché's wife strolls across and says how are your delphiniums doing; that at 11 a.m. Lady Loraine appears and says wasn't it monstrous the way the Russian Ambassador's wife cut the Polish Chargé d'Affaires' wife last night at the Palace; that at 12 noon a gun goes off and the muezzins of Tehran set up a wail for prayer; that at 1 p.m. it is time for luncheon, and Vita hasn't done any work.

Then in the evening the white stems of the plane-trees turn pink, and the stars come out, and the little owls begin to hoot, and Vita says to the servant in very careful Persian, thought-out in advance,

"If anybody calls say I'm not at home." And then gets our *Roget's Thesaurus* of the English language, a rhyming dictionary, and the proofs of her poem (alas alas alas that they don't bear the superscription of the Hogarth Press.)

This brings me to what I really wanted to say: that you upset me dreadfully about the central transparency. Because it is what I have always felt myself. Only how to do it? It only you had put down those unexpressed thoughts instead of letting them fall on the carpet! How invaluable they would have been.

You see from this that the muddy car has come in, and that I have had a letter from you (with a picture enclosed, which was an insult, – an insult to you, I mean.) You had fallen in love with being a stock-broker. Well... And I had galvanised you into asking Leonard to come to the South Seas; but, darling Virginia, that wasn't the point *at all*. The point was that you should come to Persia with *me*; that I should waft you to these brown plains; not that you should matrimonially disappear for a year out of my ken. Or were you teasing me? You see, it becomes clearer and more clear that I shall spend the next two years in tearing backwards and forwards across Europe and Asia, and it is my dream to take you with me. Leonard would like it too; he can fish and shoot here, if he likes that; and there are at least twelve horses to ride. Believe me, Burmah is not a patch on Persia; it has no classical traditions, and the architecture is abominable. As for the South Seas, I am sure they are over-rated; vulgar to a degree; and you wouldn't like hibiscus. Whereas this ancient country... This is the place for you. Indeed, if you won't come by kindness, I shall have to make you come by main force. But it would make me so happy, that I am sure no one as kind-hearted as you could refuse me that pleasure? We would come by the desert, and go back through Russia, which with your Soviet connections you would appreciate. Certainly it must be done.

25 March. Do you know what nice little job I have on hand now? Arranging the palace for the coronation. I go down there and put on an apron, and mix paint in pots in a vast hall, and wonder what the Persian is for "stipple". At one end of the hall is the Peacock Throne, and all round the walls are ranged glass cases containing every conceivable sort of object from Sèvres vases to the late Shah's toothbrush. This is known as the Museum. Lady Loraine is away, so I'm responsible. I've got to re-organise the Museum next week, and shall make Raymond help. He will trot about, under giant scaffolding, carrying alabaster bowls, while the paint drips on him from the brushes of the men skied up against the ceiling. I am sure the Shah will come to the coronation in tennis-shoes, with the twin-diamond of the Koh-i-Nur blazing in his hat. This is the principle upon which everything is conducted here.

Why do grammars only teach one such phrases as "Simply through the courage of the champion's sword" when what one wants to say is Bring another lamp?

Now this letter is long if apparently un-loving, but a lot of love gets spilt over them, like sand to dry the ink, of which no trace remains when the letter arrives, but which nevertheless was there, an important ingredient. And I send you a picture, much nicer than the one you sent me. I perceive there are a lot of questions I wanted to ask you, such as Who is Clive's new hand? (said by him to be more like the Knave than the queen of spades, – but girls will be boys,) also how is dear Grizzle? no longer like a rainbow trout, I trust; and why were you tired for two days? and is the Press overworking you? I suppose you will be motoring about France when this arrives; be careful, I pray; though I'm sure the dangers of motoring in France are nothing to the re-adjustment of standards which I have had to undergo here, with precipices and what-not. (I daren't however spin you too much of a traveller's tale, since Raymond is coming; he has squared my pitch badly.)

The little owls are hooting, and the bag leaves tomorrow on its long journey. You can write me only one more letter after you get this, for I shall be starting home. Or, if you are in France, address it to me here, and put it in a covering envelope addressed to Charles Hartopp Esq., The Residency, Cairo, and mark the inside envelope *By air-mail via Baghdad*. It will reach me quicker so. Your letters are always a shock to me, for you typewrite the envelope, and they look like a bill, and then I see your writing. A system I rather like, for the various stabs it affords me.

Now this letter is really getting disproportionately long, and you will be bored. It leaves such chasms of non-information, too; regular continents of unwrapped territory. I have added bits to my poem, but they are nothing without the context. As you may suppose, they are almost entirely Asiatic in character. I mind about that poem, never having minded about any other book. I hope you will think I have improved it. My interest in it is however almost completely cancelled by the fact that I couldn't give it to you. I do see that it would have been impossible, but nevertheless am full of resentment.

What fun it will be to sit on your floor again and stick on stamps. And to carry you off in the little blue motor. If you knew what you meant to me, you might be pleased.

Your
V.

❧

To Virginia Woolf (15 January 1927), from Knole, Kent

You've no idea of the intrigues that have been going on here to ensure your getting the room I wanted you to have, – how I have lied shamelessly, tucked Olive away in a room she never has, bundled her clothes out, bribed the housekeeper, suborned the housemaids. You have a curious effect of making me quite unscrupulous, of turning me into a sort of Juggernaut riding over obstacles. Now all is well, – do I expect you by the 5.18? or when? Telephone Sevenoaks 146 to say. But as early as possible, please. I look on it as a swansong. (Not a permanent swansong; only a temporary one.)

My mother was an angel; I adore her.

I send you lots and lots of money.

Eddy told me he had seen you last night, little pig. He returned, looking rather dissipated and rather charming – I'm going to the film society with him tomorrow – Wish I could come to see you, but you will be otherwise engaged.

I've got a lovely full moon (or nearly) for you – I've just been out looking at the court; it's now midnight; I like the battlements in the moonlight and the frost. You *will* stay over Tuesday night, won't you? and I'll motor you up to London on Wednesday morning. Do remember what a dreadfully long time it will be before I see you again.

I don't know, by the way, why I assume that you won't come till the evening; come any time you can.

I suppose I can manage to exist till Monday but I'm not sure.

Your
V.

Eddie Marsh says I'm the best living poet under 80 – so there.

⊷✤⊶

To Harold Nicolson (25 June 1929), from Long Barn, Kent

What is so torturing when I leave you at these London stations and drive off, is the knowledge that you are *still there* – that, for half an hour or three-quarters of an hour, I could still return and find you; come up behind you, take you by the elbow, and say "Hadji".

I came straight home, feeling horribly desolate and sad, driving down that familiar and dreary road. I remembered Rasht and our parting there; our parting at Victoria when you left for Persia; till our life seemed made up of partings, and I wondered how long it would continue.

Then I came round the corner on to the view – our view – and I thought how you loved it, and how simple you were, really, apart from your activity; and how I loved you for being both simple and active in one and the same person.

Then I came home, and it was no consolation at all. You see, when I am unhappy for other reasons, the cottage is a real solace to me; but when it is on account of you that I am unhappy (because you have gone away), it is an additional pang – it is the same place, but a sort of mockery and emptiness hangs about it – I almost wish that just *once* you could lose me and then come straight back to the cottage and find it still full of me but empty of me, then you would know what I go through after you have gone away.

Anyhow, you will say, it is worse for you who go back to a horrible and alien city, whereas I stay in the place we both love so much; but really, Hadji, it is no consolation to come back to a place full of coffee-cups – there was a cardboard-box lid, full of your rose-petals, still on the terrace.

You are dearer to me that anybody ever has been or ever could be. If you died suddenly, I should kill myself as soon as I had made provision for the boys. I really mean this. I could not live if I lost you. I do not think one could conceive of a love more exclusive, more tender, or more pure than I have for you. I think it is immortal. a thing which happens seldom.

Darling, there are not many people who would write such a letter after sixteen years of marriage, yet who would be saying therein only one-fiftieth of what they were feeling as they wrote it. I sometimes try to tell you the truth, and then I find that I have no words at my command which could possibly convey it to you.

JOHN STEINBECK

JOHN STEINBECK (1902–68) WAS THE AUTHOR OF *THE Grapes of Wrath*, which won him the 1940 Pulitzer Prize.

To Carl Wilhelmson (late 1930)

Dear Carl:

It is a gloomy day; low gray fog and a wet wind contribute to my own gloominess. Whether the fog has escaped from my soul like ectoplasm to envelope the peninsula, or whether it has seeped in through my nose and eyes to create the gloom, I don't know. Last night I read over the first forty pages of my new novel and destroyed them – the most unrelieved rot imaginable. It is very sad.

We went to a party at John Calvin's in Carmel last week. These writers of juveniles are the Jews of literature. They seem to wring the English language, to squeeze pennies out of it. They don't even pretend that there is any dignity in craftsmanship. A conversation with them sounds like an afternoon spent with a pawnbroker. Says John Calvin, "I long ago ceased to take anything I write seriously." I retorted, "I take *everything* I write seriously; unless one does take his work seriously there is very little chance of its ever being good work." And the whole company was a little ashamed of me as though I had three legs or was an albino.

I am very anxious to see a copy of Midsummer Night. When I can afford to, I will buy it. It was different with my own first novel. I outgrew that before I finished writing it. I very definitely didn't want you to have it just as I didn't want to have it myself. I shall be glad to arrive at an age where I don't outgrow a piece of work as children outgrow shoes.

This letter would seem to indicate that I am unhappy. Such is not the case. As long as I can work I shall be happy (except during moments of reflection) regardless of the quality of the work. That is a curious thing but true.

There was a great fire last night. The Del Monte bath house burned to the ground. We got up and went to it and stood in the light and heat and gloried in the destruction. When Cato was shouting in the Roman Senate "Carthago delenda est," I wondered whether in his mind there was not a vision of the glorious fire it would make. Precious things make beautiful flames. The pyre that Savonarola made of all lovely and profound, wise and beautiful things of northern Italy must have been the finest fire the world has seen. I believe there is an account which says that when Caesar burned the great library at Alexandria, the populace laughed and groaned in exquisite despair.

You say you are striving for tenseness in your ms. I feel increasingly that you and I are the only ones of our entire acquaintance who have retained any literary responsibility and integrity. That is worth while regardless of the badness of my work.

Modern sanity and religion are a curious delusion. Yesterday I went out in a fishing boat – but in the ocean. By looking over the side into the blue water, I could quite easily see the shell of the turtle who supports the world. I am getting more prone to madness. What a ridiculous letter this is; full of vaguenesses and unrealities. I for one and you to some extent have a great many of the basic impulses of an African witch doctor.

You know the big pine tree beside this house? I planted it when it and I were very little; I've watched it grow. It has always been known as "John's tree." Years ago, in mental playfulness I used to think of it as my brother and then later, still playfully, I thought of it as something rather closer, a kind of repository of my destiny. This was all an amusing fancy, mind you. Now the lower limbs should be cut off because they endanger the house. I must cut them soon, and I have a very powerful reluctance to do it, such a reluctance as I would have toward cutting live flesh. Furthermore if the tree should die, I am pretty sure I should be ill. This feeling I have planted in myself and quite deliberately I guess, but it is none the less strong for all that.

I shall stop before you consider me quite mad.

Sincerely,
John

To Elaine Scott (6 June 1949)

Steinbeck had met Elaine Scott, the then wife of actor Zachary Scott, in Hollywood. A week later he wrote this letter; Steinbeck's interest was reciprocated and they later married.

Dear Miss West Forty-seventh Street
between Eighth and Ninth:

Am a widower with 10,000 acres in Arizona and seven cows so if you can milk I will be glad to have you give up that tinsel life of debauchery and sin and come out to God's country where we got purple sage. P. S. Can you bring a little sin and debauchery along? You can get too much purple sage but you can only get just enough sin.

I am really glad that you got some rest and that you feel somewhat restored. I guess it is that purple sage. I think I will try to bottle it.

Annie Rooney [Ann Sothern] called to say that the skirts had arrived [Chinese men's ceremonial skirts he had sent them as presents]. I would like one too but I ain't pretty enough. This has been my tragedy – with the soul to wear a scarlet-lined opera cape and small sword I have the physical misfortune always to be handed a hod. I have never quite got over this sadness. Let me know whether you want me to get another. I have been tempted to buy the whole stock because there will never be any more. The new regime is not going to approve of them I guess and they are unique as far as I know.

I was sad when you two bugs went away. Now I haven't even a half-assed reason for not working.

I am told that darling Louella tagged Annie and me last night. This will henceforth be known as The Seven Days That Shook the Pine Inn. Running naked through the woods with flowers in your hair is against the law and I told you both but you wouldn't listen.

Sometime during the summer I will drift down your way.

[Next day]

Neale is flying a twin engine Cessna to New York on the 15th. He'll have a little vacation and bring back my kids on the 1st.

Love to you and Annie.

J.

⚜

To Joseph Bryan III (17 December 1957)

YES, JOE, THERE IS A SANTA CLAUS IF YOU BUT LOOK ABOUT. HE IS:
  In the wistful eyes of a general writing Santa for one more star;
  In the homeward tread of a call girl whose date wanted to dance;
  In gay, song-driven garbage men;

In the earnest loft burglar with twelve fur coats for his mother;
In the selflessness of Richard Nixon and of his wife Pat and of his
children whose names I do not know.

SANTA IS ALWAYS THERE IF YOU HAVE EYES TO SEE. YOU WILL FIND HIM:
When you hit your funny bone on the bathroom door, Kris Kringle
is nigh;
He dwelleth on the top floor of the FBI Building at 69th and Third
Avenue;
You will glimpse him in the subway at 5:15;
His cheery hand reaches for the cab door you thought you had;
When your show closes out of town – look for reindeer droppings;
Santa speaks in the kindly voice of the income tax collector;
He lurketh under the broken filling – peereth from behind the
ulcer and caroleth in the happy halls of Mattewan.

Yes, Joe, there is a Santa Claus if we but seek him – BEFORE HE SEEKS
US.

MERRY CHRISTMAS TO ALL

AND

GOODNIGHT

When you slip in the bath tub and land on your ear
hallelulia in excelcis
Kris Kringle is near
(Sorry, Virginia)

J. and E.

JAWAHARLAL NEHRU

EDUCATED IN BRITAIN, NEHRU (1889–1964) JOINED THE
Indian Congress Committee on his return to India in
1918. He was first arrested for civil disobedience against

British rule in 1921 and spent eighteen of the next twenty-five years in prison. In 1947 he became India's first prime minister.

~❦~

To the Superintendent, District Jail, Dehra Dun (11 July 1932)

Dear Sir,

You were good enough to show me today the reply of the Officiating Inspector General of Prisons to my letter dated the 22nd June. I am informed therein that, in the course of an interview with Mr R.S. Pandit in the Allahabad District Jail on May 27th, my wife handed a letter to Mr Pandit, and the Jailer not allowing this, my mother "used insulting language to the Jailer and was impertinent."

As this account of what occurred is untruthful and is a perversion of the facts, and further, as the action taken by Government raises wider issues, I am writing to you again on the subject and shall be obliged if you will forward this letter to the Government.

During the interview with Mr Pandit on May 27th, information was given to him about his three little daughters, aged three, five and eight, who are at a school in Poona. This information was contained in a letter or report from the School. My daughter, who attends the same school and who was spending her holidays in Allahabad, had this report or letter, and she read it out to Mr Pandit, and later gave it to him to see for himself. The Jailer took objection to this and was generally offensive and particularly to Mr Pandit. Apart from the insult to Mr Pandit, the Jailer's behaviour was an affront to my mother and wife. My mother hardly spoke to him.

Three days later, on May 30th, I had my usual fortnightly interview with my mother, wife and daughter in the Bareilly District Jail. I was then informed of what had happened. I was surprised to learn that anyone should have behaved so discourteously to my mother and I expected some expression of regret from the Jail officials for what had occurred. Instead of that, I now find that the Government have chosen to punish my mother and wife. I presume this has been done on some statement made to them by the Jailer. No reference was made, so far as I am aware, to my mother or my wife to find out what had happened. Without any further enquiry or effort to find out the truth, the Government have not hesitated to insult my mother and wife, and have done so in such a way as to cause the maximum inconvenience to all parties concerned.

It may be that it is an offence under the jail regulations to show a school report about one's children. If Government wish to treat even this as worthy of punishment, I have no grievance. Nor shall I object if my interviews are stopped for a month or a year. I have not come to prison for the sake of my health or for pleasure.

But there are certain matters which I cannot pass in silence. I cannot tolerate even the suspicion of an affront or insult to my mother. I have noticed with deep regret that Government have not shown my mother the courtesy which I would have expected from them under any circumstances. For the Inspector-General to say that my mother "used insulting language to the Jailer and was impertinent" shows that he is strangely lacking in a sense of proportion and knows little of Indian society.

The action that Government have taken, and the manner of taking it, makes it clear that those who seek to interview me in jail are always liable to be insulted by Government officials or by Government itself. On no account am I prepared to take the slightest risk of further insult to my mother and wife. Under the circumstances, the only course open to me is not to have any interviews, so long as I do not feel that such interviews can be had with dignity and with no fear of discourtesy to those who come to see me. I am therefore informing my people not to take the trouble to come for interviews with me in future, even after the month of punishment is over.

I shall be glad if the Offg. Inspector-General will take the trouble to spell my name correctly in future.

Yours faithfully,
Jawaharlal Nehru

DYLAN THOMAS

DYLAN THOMAS (1914–53), WELSH POET AND DRAMA-tist. After an unrequited love affair with Pamela Hansford Johnson he married Caitlin Macnamara in 1936. For nearly ten years he worked intermittently on a radio play about a Welsh seaside village, which was first broadcast as *Quite Early One Morning*, but became famous as *Under Milk Wood*, published in 1954, a year after Thomas' death from alcohol abuse.

❧

To Pamela Hansford Johnson (27 May 1934)

Pamela Hansford Johnson (1912–81), the author of The Unspeakable Skipton. *She later married the novelist C. P. Snow.*

Question	One.	I can't come up
	Two.	I'm sleeping no better
Question	Three.	"No" I've done everything that's wrong
	Four.	I daren't see the doctor
Question	5.	Yes I love you

I'm in a dreadful mess now. I can hardly hold the pencil or see the paper. This has been coming for weeks. And the last four days have completed it. I'm absolutely at the point of breaking now. You remember how I was when I said goodbye to you for the first time. In the Kardomah [café] when I loved you so much and was too shy to tell you. Well imagine me one hundred times worse than that with my nerves oh darling absolutely at the point of breaking in little bits. I can't think and I don't know what I'm doing When I speak I don't know if I'm shouting or whispering and that's a terrible sign. It's *all* nerves & no more But I've never imagined anything as bad.

And it's all my own fault too. As well as I can I'll tell you the honest truth. I never want to lie to you. You'll be terribly angry with me I know and you'll never write to me again perhaps   But darling you want me to tell you the truth don't you.

I left Laugharne on Wednesday morning and went down to a bungalow in Gower. I drank a lot in Laugharne & was feeling a bit funny even then. I stayed in Gower with Cliff, who was a friend of mine in the waster days of the reporter's office. On Wednesday evening [...] his fiancée came down. She was tall & thin and dark with a loose red mouth & a harsh sort of laugh. Later we all went out & got drunk. She tried to make love to me all the way home. I told her to shut up because she was drunk   When we got back she still tried to make love to me wildly like an idiot in front of Cliff. She went to bed and Cliff and I drank some more and then very modernly he decided to go & sleep with her. But as soon as he got in bed with her she screamed & ran into mine.

I slept with her that night & for the next three nights   We were terribly drunk day & night   Now I can see all sorts of things, I think I've got them.

Oh darling, it hurts me to tell you this but I've got to tell you because I always want to tell you the truth about me. And I never want to share It's you & me & nobody. But I've been a bloody fool & I'm going to bed for a week I'm just on the borders of DTs darling, and I've wasted some of my tremendous love for you on a lank redmouthed girl with a reputation like a hell. I don't love her a bit I love you Pamela always & always But she's a pain on the nerves. For Christ knows why she loves me Yesterday morning she gave her ring back to Cliff.

I've got to put a 100 miles between her & me

I must leave Wales forever & never see her

I sees bits of you in her all the time & tack on to those bits   I've got to be drunk to tack on to them

I love you Pamela & *must have you* As soon as all this is over I'm coming straight up. If you'll let me. No, but better or worse I'll come up next week if you'll have me. Don't be too cross or too angry What the hell am I to do? And what the hell are you going to say to me? Darling I love you & think of you all the time. Write by return And don't break my heart by telling me I mustn't come up to London to you becos I'm such a bloody fool.

XXXX Darling. Oh Darling.

To his wife, Caitlin Thomas (n.d. probably 1952)

Caitlin,

Please read this.

That letter you saw was horrible, it was dirty and cadging and lying. You know it was horrible, dirty, and cadging and lying. There was no truth in it. There was no truth meant to be in it. It was vile, a conscientious piece of contrived bamboozling dirt, which *nobody* was supposed to see – not you, or that Marged gin woman. I wrote it as I will tell you. The fact that you read it has made me so full of loathing & hatred for myself, and despair, that I haven't been able to speak to you. I haven't been able to speak to you about it. There was nothing I could say except, It isn't true, it's foul, sponging lies. And how could I say that when you'd seen it? How could I tell you it was all lies, that it was all made up for nothing, when you'd seen the dirty words? You'd say, If you didn't mean the dirty words, why did you write them? And all I could answer would be, Because I wanted to see what foul dripping stuff I could hurt myself to write in order to fawn for money. I'd as soon post that muck as I'd swim, I was going to tear it up in a million bloody bits. Marged told me, when she was drunk with that [...], to write to her about what I owed the Insurance things & others, or that's what I gathered – as much as anyone could gather. Or perhaps that's what I wanted to gather. Anyway, I put the Insurance thing summons in an envelope & explained, in a note, that I'd spent the other half of the money she'd given us for that, & that there were other real debts too. Then I went on writing something else – those endless rotten verses of mine, which I almost agree with you about – and then, when I came to a dead bit, to a real awful jam in the words, I saw – on the other broken table – when I'd written to Marged & started writing a proper sycophantic arselicking hell letter, putting in pretentious bits, introducing heart-throb lies, making, or trying to make, a foul beggar's lie-book of it. I only just avoided tuberculosis & orphans. There's no excuse for my writing this. I'd no idea it would go further than the floor of this shed. I was all wrong to drivel out this laboured chicanery. So wrong, & ashamed, I haven't been able to say a word to you about it. The misery I'm in can't make up for, or explain the misery I've made for you by my callous attempt at a mock-literature of the slimiest kind.

I love you.
Dylan

~⚜~

To Caitlin Thomas (20 April 1953)

In April 1953 Thomas took his third trip to the USA. He died there in the course of a lecture tour.

Oh Caitlin Cat my love my love, I love you for ever & ever, I LOVE YOU CAT, if only I could jump over this rocking ship-side into the awful sea and swim to you now, I want to be with you all the time, there isn't one moment of the endless day or night on this hell-ship when I'm not thinking about you, feeling through the dark and the rolling and the wind for you and talking to you. Don't be lost to me, darling; forgive me for all my nastiness, mad-dog tempers, of the last days & weeks: they were because I didn't want to go, I didn't want to leave you in old dull Laugharne with children and loneliness, I didn't want, I promise you before God, to move at all, except with you. I longed to be with you, terribly close as we very often are, as we nearly always are, sitting in the shed and writing, being with you, & in your arms at night. And here I am, on this huge hot gadget-mad hotel, being tossed and battered; the sea's been brutal all the time; I can hardly write this at all, in the tasteful, oven-ish, no-smoking library-room, for the rattle & lurch; everybody's been sick every day; for one whole day, full of dramamine, I groaned in a fever in the cabin which I do not share, alone in my horrible rocking hothouse where there's no time, no night or day; occasionally now I manage to rock, like a drunk, to the bar where a few pale racked men are trying the same experiment as me, and then, after an ice-cold couple, stagger back to my room, to pray that I was with you, as I always wish to be, and not on this eternal cocktail-shaker of a ship – or if I *have* to be on it, which God knows I don't have to be, then oh Cat oh my sweetheart, then why why aren't you with me too. I've spoken hardly a word to anyone but one stout barman; the people who share my table – when any of us is well enough to appear – are a thousand times worse than those dumpling (Dolly's kind of dumpling) Dutchmen: there's a middle-aged brother & sister, and a little sophisticated German woman; the little German woman's beastly, and told me, when the brother & sister weren't there, that she'd thought of asking the purser to move her to another table: "I don't like," she said, "having my meals in the company of a woman who reminds me of my cook" – which seems one of the oddest things I ever heard said. There is also a German count, or mock-count, with whom I have exchanged half a dozen words: he looks, speaks, & acts like Charles Fisher. Otherwise, not a word to anyone. Every one is very clean & well-dressed and moneyed; the only one possible thing I have in common with them is that we all feel ill. It is nine o'clock in the morning; tomorrow we dock at New York; breakfast has been & gone. I love you, Caitlin, oh my darling I love you. To think that *I* was angry because *you* did not want me to go away. I was angry, really, only with myself, because I did not want to go away and yet was going. But I shall bring money back & we will go [to] the sun very soon: that is sure. I'll write properly when I'm on land: this rocking is getting unsteadily worse. And I'll send some money in the letter, just as soon as I get any. Higham's number is TEMPLE BAR 8631 in case you feel like ringing him about the letter I wrote to him on the morning of my going away: I told him then to send any money coming to me *direct* to you. I love you. Please, my darling, try to love me, and wait for me. Wait for me, dear, I'll hurry like hell through this sad month-and-a-bit. I can see you now. You're more beautiful than ever, my own true love. Kiss the children and beat them to death. I hope the sun is out, and that you can buy the canoe. Be good to me: you are everything,. Why did I snarl when you only wanted me to stay? I love you.

Now I am going to the bar for a cold beer, then back to the bloody cabin to lie on the unmade bed & to fall into a timeless dream of you and of all I love – which is only you – and of the sea rocking & the engines screaming and the wind howling and the despair that is in everything except in our love.

Oh, Cat,
I love you
Dylan

JAMES AGEE

J AMES AGEE (1909–55), AMERICAN CRITIC and writer. The publication of *Let Us Now Praise Famous Men* (1941) made him a literary celebrity, and he was persuaded to go to Hollywood, where he wrote the scripts for *The African Queen* and *Night of the Hunter*, among other films.

❧

To Father Flye (30 October 1934)

Father Flye, an Episcopalian priest, was Agee's oldest friend.

Dear Father Flye:

In two or three days, when I can get hold of another copy, I want to send you a copy of my book of poems [*Permit Me Voyage*], not out of any pleasure in them myself but because I expect you would like to see and have them: if a dying man passed out his hair and his toenails to friends he would not be thought vain of hair, toenails, or his friendship. Not a dying man, and you are more than a friend, but the reason for all this elaborateness of diffidence is more genuine than it looks: I am in most possible kinds of pain, mental and spiritual that is. In this pain the book and its contents are a relatively small item, only noticeable in the general unpleasantness because they are tangible. The rest of the trouble is even more inexpressible, and a lot more harm, but revolves chiefly around the simple-sounding problem of how to become what I wish I could when I can't. That, however, is fierce and complicated enough to keep me balancing over suicide as you might lean out over the edge of a high building, as far as you could and keep from falling but with no special or constant desire not to fall. It works many ways: one is apathy, or a sort of leady, heavy silt that, always by nature a part of my blood, becomes thicker and thicker, and I, less pleasant and less bearable to live with, or to live within. Another is that without guidance, balance, coordination, my ideas and impressions and desires which are much larger than I can begin to get to paper, are loose in my brains like wild beasts of assorted sizes and ferocities, not devouring each other but in the process tearing the zoo to parts. Or more accurately like the feeling they are loose wires highly charged which cross and short-circuit and send burning spasms all through me, with nothing connecting long enough to hold, and give power or light. The wise answer of course would be that there is only one coordinator and guide, and that he is come at through self-negation. But: that can mean nothing to me until or unless I learn it for myself. Without scrupulousness I am damned forever, and my base, if I ever find it, must be of my own finding and understanding or it is no sort of base at all. Well, it cannot be solved. Not at any rate in process of this rotten letter. I can I think quite surely promise you that I shall not suicide. Also be sure I am sorry and ashamed for this letter, in every way but one, that being that between friends even the lowest cowardliness is not to be shut away and grinned about, if worse comes to worst. Aside from all these things, there is much to enjoy and more to be glad for than I deserve, and I know it. but they are mostly, by my own difficulty, out of my reach.

Much love to you and to Mrs Flye.

LION FEUCHTWANGER

FEUCHTWANGER WAS THE AUTHOR OF *JUD SUSS* AND *Erfolg*, a satire on Hitler's abortive 1923 Munich putsch. In March 1933, when the Nazis eventually assumed state power in Germany, Feuchtwanger was visiting the USA and his house was confiscated and given to a prominent member of the National Socialist Party.

To Mr X, the Nazi occupant of Feuchtwanger's confiscated house (1935)

Dear Sir

I do not know your name or how you came into possession of my house. I only know that two years ago the police of the Third Reich seized all my property, personal and real, and handed it over to the stock company formed by the Reich for the confiscation of the properties of political adversaries (chairman of the board: Minister Goering). I learned this through a letter from the mortgagees. They explained to me that under the laws of the Third Reich confiscations of property belonging to political opponents concern themselves only with credit balances. Although my house and my bank deposits, which had also been confiscated, greatly exceeded in value the amount of the mortgage, I would be obliged to continue the payment of interest on the mortgage, as well as my German taxes, from whatever money I might earn abroad. Be that as it may, one thing is certain – you, Herr X, are occupying my house and I, in the opinion of German judges, must pay the costs.

How do you like my house, Herr X? Do you find it pleasant to live in? Did the silver-grey carpets in the upper rooms come to grief while the S.A. men were looting? My houseman sought safety in these upper rooms, as, I being in America at the time, the gentlemen seemed to determine to take it out on him. Those carpets are very delicate, and red is a strong colour, hard to eradicate. The rubber tiling in the hallways was also not primarily designed with the boots of the S.A. men in mind.

Have you any notion why I had the semi-enclosed terrace built on the roof? Frau Feuchtwanger and I used it for our morning setting-up exercises. Would you mind seeing to it that the pipes of the shower don't freeze?...

I wonder to what use you have put the two rooms which formerly contained my library? I have been told, Herr X, that books are not very popular in the Reich in which you live, and whoever shows interest in them is likely to get into difficulties. I, for instance, read your Führer's book and guilelessly remarked that his 140,000 words were 140,000 offences against the spirit of the German language. The result of this remark is that you are now living in my house. Sometimes I wonder to what uses bookcases can be put in the Third Reich. In case you should decide to have them ripped out, be careful not to damage the walls...

By the way, is our street still called Mahlerstrasse? Have the masters of your Reich overlooked that the composer, Gustav Mahler, for whom the street is named, was a Jew, or had Richard Strauss brought this fact to their attention?

And what have you done with my terrarium which stood at one of the windows of my study? Did you actually kill my turtles and my lizards because their owner was an "alien"? And were the flower beds and the rock garden much damaged when the S.A. men, shooting as they ran, pursued my sorely beaten servant across the garden into the woods beyond?

Doesn't it sometimes seem odd to you that you should be living in my house? Your Führer is not generally considered a friend of Jewish literature. Isn't it, therefore, astounding that he should have such a strong predeliction for the Old Testament. I myself have heard him quote with much fervour, "An eye for an eye, a tooth for a tooth" (by which he may have meant, "A confiscation of property for literary criticism"). And now, through you, he has fulfilled a prophecy of the Old Testament – the saying, "Thou shalt dwell in houses thou hast not builded."

With many good wishes for our house,

Lion Feuchtwanger

P. S. On the other hand, perhaps you think my statement that your "Führer" writes bad German is justified by the fact that you are now living in my house?

JAMES THURBER

JAMES GROVER THURBER (1894–1961), AMERICAN cartoonist and humorist, the author of *The Secret Life of Walter Mitty* (1946).

❧

To Herman and Dorothy Miller (August 1935)

The Millers were friends of Thurber from his home town, Columbus, Ohio.

Dear Herman and Dorothy,

… Helen and I have just returned from dinner at the Elm Tree Inn in Farmington, some twenty miles from our little cot. It was such a trip as few have survived. I lost eight pounds... I can't see at night and this upset all the motorists in the state tonight, for I am blinded by headlights in addition to not being able to see, anyway. It took us two hours to come back, weaving and stumbling, stopping now and then, stopping always for every car that approached, stopping other times just to rest and bow my head on my arms and ask God to witness that this should not be.

Farmington's Inn was built in 1638 and is reputed to be the oldest inn in these United States. I tonight am the oldest man... A peril of the night road is that flecks of dust and streaks of bug blood on the windshield look to me often like old admirals in uniform, or crippled apple women, or the front end of barges, and I whirl out of their way, thus going into ditches and fields and up on front lawns, endangering the life of authentic admirals and apple women who may be out on the roads for a breath of air before retiring...

Five or six years ago, when I was visiting my former wife at Silvermine, she had left the car for me at South Norwalk and I was to drive to her house in it, some five miles away. Dinner was to be ready for me twenty minutes after I got into the car, but night fell swiftly and there I was again. Although I had been driven over that road 75 or 100 times, I had not driven it myself, and I got off onto a long steep narrow road which seemed to be paved with old typewriters. After a half hour of climbing, during which I passed only two farm boys with lanterns, the road petered out in a high woods. From far away came the mournful woof of a farm hound. That was all. There I was, surrounded by soughing trees, where no car had ever been before. I don't know how I got out. I backed up for miles, jerking on the hand brake every time we seemed to be falling. I was two hours late for dinner.

In every other way I am fine. I am very happy, when not driving at night. And my wife is very happy too, when not being driven by me at night. We are an ideal couple and have not had a harsh word in the seven weeks of our married life. Even when I grope along, honking and weaving and stopping and being honked at by long lines of cars behind me, she is patient and gentle and kind. Of course, she knows that in the daytime, I am a fearless and skilled driver, who can hold his own with anyone. It is only after nightfall that this change comes upon me. I have a curious desire to cry while driving at night, but so far have conquered that, save for a slight consistent whimpering that I keep up – a sound which, I am sure, is not calculated to put Helen at her ease.

Looking back on my hazardous adventures of this evening I can see that whereas I was anguished and sick at heart, Helen must have felt even worse, for there were moments when, with several cars coming toward me, and two or three honking behind me, and a curved road ahead, I would take my foot off of everything and wail, 'Where the hell am I?' That, I suppose, would strike a fear to a woman's heart equaled by almost nothing else. We have decided that I will not drive any more at night. Helen can drive but she has been out of practice for some years. However, she is going to get back into it again. She can see. She doesn't care to read, in the *Winsted Evening Citizen*, some such story as this:

Police are striving to unravel the tangle of seven cars and a truck which suddenly took place last night at 9 o'clock where Route 44 is crossed by Harmer's Lane and a wood road leading to the old Beckert estate. Although nobody seems to know exactly what happened, the automobile that the accident seemed to center about was a 1932 Ford V-8 operated by one James Thurberg. Thurberg, who was coming into Winsted at 8 miles an hour, mistook the lights of Harry Freeman's hot-dog stand, at the corner of Harmer's Lane and Route 44, for the headlight of a train. As he told the story later: he swerved out to avoid the oncoming hot-dog stand only to see an aged admiral in full dress uniform riding toward him, out of the old wood road, on a tricycle, which had no head-lights. In trying to go in between the hot-dog stand and the tricycle, Thurberg somehow or other managed to get his car crosswise of all three roads, resulting in the cracking up of six other cars and the truck. Police have so far found no trace of the aged admiral and his tricycle. The hot-dog stand came to a stop fifteen feet from Thurberg's car.

We got the Ford on Martha's Vineyard, where we spent July. Now we are at Colebrook, Conn., or rather three miles out of it at the summer cottage of Helen's parents. It is a delightful place and why don't you motor here and visit us for a while?... You'll like my wife and she already knows she will like you. She is as calm as ice when I am driving at night, or as cold anyway.

Love,
Jim

To Ada Laura Fonda Snell (8 July 1949)

Miss Ada Laura Fonda Snell
Mount Holyoke College
South Hadley, Massachusetts

Dear Miss Snell:
...Fifteen years ago and more, I sometimes talked briefly at English classes at Ohio State, on which frightening occasions my nervousness made the class nervous, setting up a nervous cycle. We were both glad when it was over. Since 1940, when I lost the ability to read and to get around by myself, I have had to abandon what one friend called my public apparitions...

I was pleased and honored, so was Helen, to receive your invitation, and I am distressed that I have to decline, since I love Mount Holyoke. The idea of addressing the flower of American womanhood would terrify me even if I could see. I am like the tough American soldier, loose in no-man's-land during the First War, who had invaded a dozen enemy trenches with a lone companion, capturing a hundred Germans, and who suddenly came upon a dark, mysterious, and deep hole in the ground. He peered into it cautiously. "You goin' down there, Mac?" asked his friend. Mac looked at the hole again. "I wouldn't go down there," he said, "if they was Fig Newtons down there."

Your name is like a waving flag and should never be furled in abbreviation. Helen joins me in thanking you for your invitation, and we send you our joint regrets. I hope that I will have the pleasure someday of meeting you.

Cordially yours
James Thurber

To Robert Leifert (4 January 1958)

Dear Robert

Since a hundred schoolchildren a year write me letters like yours – some writers get a thousand – the problem of what to do about such classroom "projects" has become a serious one for all of us. If a writer answered all of you he would get nothing else done. When I was a baby goat I had to do my own research on projects, and I enjoyed doing it. I never wrote an author for his autograph or photograph in my life. Photographs are for movie actors to send to girls. Tell your teacher I said so, and please send me her name...

One of the things that discourage us writers is the fact that 90 percent of you children write wholly, or partly, illiterate letters, carelessly typed. You yourself write "clarr" for "class" and that's a honey, Robert, since *s* is next to *a*, and *r* is on the line above. Most schoolchildren in America would do a dedication like the following (please find the mistakes in it and write me about them):

> To Miss Effa C. Burns
> Without who's help
> this book could never
> of been finished it,
> is dedicated with

gartitude by it's
arthur.

Show that to your teacher and tell her to show it to her principal, and see if they can find the mistakes...

Just yesterday a letter came in from a girl your age in South Carolina asking for biographical material and photograph. That is not the kind of education they have in Russia, we are told, because it's too much like a hobby or waste of time. What do you and your classmates want to be when you grow up – collectors? Then who is going to help keep the United States ahead of Russia in science, engineering, and the arts?

Please answer this letter. If you don't I'll write to another pupil.

Sincerely yours,
James Thurber

ALBERT EINSTEIN

ALBERT EINSTEIN (1879–1955), SCIENTIST. THIS LETTER to the then President of the United States, Franklin Delano Roosevelt, led to the construction of the atomic bomb.

~❧~

To F. D. Roosevelt, President of the United States (2 August 1939)

Sir:

Some recent work by E. Fermi and L. Szilard, which has been communicated to me in manuscript, leads me to expect that the element uranium may be turned into a new and important source of energy in the immediate future. Certain aspects of the situation seem to call for watchfulness and, if necessary, quick action on the part of the administration. I believe, therefore, that it is my duty to bring to your attention the following facts and recommendations.

In the course of the last four months it has been made probable – through the work of Joliot in France as well as Fermi and Szilard in America – that it may become possible to set up nuclear chain reactions in a large mass of uranium, by which vast amounts of power and large quantities of new radium-like elements would be generated. Now it appears almost certain that this could be achieved in the immediate future.

This new phenomenon would also lead to the construction of bombs, and it is conceivable – though much less certain – that extremely powerful bombs of a new type may thus be constructed. A single bomb of this type, carried by boat or exploded in a port. might very well destroy the whole port together with some of the surrounding territory. However, such bombs might very well prove to be too heavy for transportation by air.

The United States has only very poor ores of uranium in moderate quantities. There is some good ore in Canada and the former Czechoslovakia, while the most important source of uranium is the Belgian Congo.

In view of this situation you may think it desirable to have some permanent contact between the administration and the group of physicists working on chain reaction in America. One possible way of achieving this might be for you to entrust with this task a person who has your confidence and who could perhaps serve in an unoffical capacity. His task might comprise the following:

(a) To approach government departments, keep them informed of further developments, and put forward recommendations for government action, giving particular attention to the problem of securing a supply of uranium ore for the United States.

(b) To speed up the experimental work which is at present being carried on within the limits of the budgets of the university laboratories, by providing funds, if such funds be required, through his contacts with private persons who are willing to make contributions for this cause, and perhaps also by obtaining the cooperation of industrial laboratories which have the necessary equipment.

I understand that Germany has actually stopped the sale of uranium from the Czechoslovakian mines which she has taken over. That she should have taken such early action might perhaps be understood on the ground that the son of the German Undersecretary of State, von Weizacker, is attched to the Kaiser Wilhelm Institute of Berlin, where some of the American work on uranium is now being repeated.

Yours very truly
A. *Einstein*

SIR JOCK DELVES BROUGHTON

SIR JOCK DELVES BROUGHTON (1888–1942), ENGLISH aristocrat. A principal member of the expatriate community based in Happy Valley, Kenya, Broughton was charged in 1941 with the murder of the Earl of Erroll, one of his second wife's lovers, but acquitted. The following letter, written to his second wife, caused him to be questioned in Britain but he committed suicide before any action could be brought.

To Diana Delves Broughton (n.d.)

Diana,

I am determined to punish you for ruining my life in the way you have done. Up to the time we left England, universally popular, respected, millions of friends, and welcome everywhere. I worshipped the ground you stood on, and got divorced in order to marry you. On board the boat you became a stranger to me and a completely different human being. You started a fuck with Tony Mordant under my eyes and I discovered the copy of the letter you wrote to your Italian; the most violent love letter written when living with me on Doddington writing paper. This was the first time I knew you had double crossed me. On the boat you were regretting the whole time that you had not stayed in England and married Rory Moore O'Farrel.

We got to South Africa where at Cape Town you were bloody to me most of the time. When being thoroughly fed up I said I should like to return to England in front of the Bailes family you said "I shall stay in South Africa, why don't you return to England?" Charming for me. You made such a farce of our marriage that the Registrar almost refused to marry you. If I had not adored you I should not have been fool enough to marry you, but I worshipped you. We came up to Kenya where, for about six weeks, I was happy. You then started double crossing me with Erroll. Do you think any woman has ever treated any man as badly as you did me? Letting him be divorced from a wife he has lived with not unhappily for 25 years, and then telling him she was leaving him two months after she had married him because she herseif had fallen in love. Millions of people fall in love, but they have feelings of decency and do not behave like you did. If you had returned to England you would have of course got over it. Erroll was murdered. You say yourself it never even occurred to you to connect me with it till the Police put it into your head. You then in your evidence did all in your power to get me hung. Later you say yourself you were convinced that I had nothing to do with it. After the verdict you were charming to me and were perfectly happy in Ceylon and India. We came back and were quite happy till we went on safari with Gilbert Colville. Since that moment everything has gone wrong. You knew he was the richest settler in Kenya, could be useful to you, was easy money and laid yourself out to ensnare him, quite regardless of how you knew how unhappy and miserable it made me.

Like a fool I bought Oserian [Lord Erroll's farm] because you said you were unhappy at Karen. We have never been anything else but unhappy since we went there on March 1st. I never objected to you having people to stay, but when we had rows you always dinned into me how you were still in love with Erroll. This, your very fervent friendship with Colville and your obvious dislike of being ever alone with me made me depressed, unhappy and hating the place, people, country – everything connected with it. In addition, I was ill with malaria for four months.

I thought things were going better when you had Hugh Strickland to stay, liked him and enjoyed having him, and you were apparently quite happy. Like the poor fool I was I had no idea of what was happening or why you put him in a room with no lock on the door opening straight out into your rooms till Chappy Bailes told me that he was seen kissing you in your bedroom at the Stanley by a highly amused crowd from Torr's Hotel. Even then, thinking that you had always told me the truth about your "cold temperament" I didn't suspect what was going on till you were so very anxious to get me off to bed one night with a sleeping draught. I watched through the window of your bathroom, and saw you actually go and fetch him and return to your bedroom with him, and then listened to him fucking you through the gauze in your bedroom window not more than three yards away. By the way the whole bed rocked you evidently enjoyed it, like you used to with me. I waited and watched the next two nights, but you both had chills and I saw nothing. The next night I asked for a sleeping draught and went to bed early, and watched, and saw him walk into your bedroom and get into bed, and you followed and got into bed with him. I then took action. After this you had the cheek to suggest that he stayed another four days till you could take him to Nairobi. Like the fool I was, still loving you, I forgave it, but since that moment, you have been more vile to me than anyone would think possible ...

I have always been suspicious as to what you had inside the deed box you gave me to give George Green to keep for you.* I have cabled him to take it to my solicitors; I have given my agents here a sealed letter with instructions inside it to cable my solicitors at home to open the box, and if my suspicions are correct, to send the

---

*The deed box contained a string of pearls belonging to Diana that she had declared lost and fraudulently claimed £12,000 insurance on.

contents to the place where they were purchased for verification, and if so verified to send the box and contents to Scotland Yard, on my instructions, and to ask them to await an air mail letter I am sending in duplicate. You will then be sent home for trial. If you were only an accessory it would be exactly the same thing and make no difference. The penalty for this "offence" is 14 years hard labour. You are now nearly 29 and by the time you were taken home for trial and tried and sentenced it might take nine months and this would keep you from double crossing me and popping into bed with any strange man until you are 44, and prison is very ageing, and I don't think you would find men so easy then. I could, moreover, divorce you for having committed a criminal offence. Moreover any accomplices you may have had would be equally involved (if my suspicions are verified). Do not think this is an empty threat because nothing in this world will stop me doing it. I want you to be punished for ruining my life by ruining yours and punished you shall be, regardless of what happens to me. I should change my name after the trial and go and live where no one knows me. I have no doubt that I can get someone I am fond of to live with me. You have changed me into a fiend thirsting for vengeance. I think of nothing else day and night. I never sleep for thinking of it.

As I said hate and love are very akin, and I still love you. I hate you sometimes like you do me, but I miss you every hour of the day and night, and want you back, and am determined that swine Gilbert Colville, who is the cause of all this shall not have you. When you told me that he and you were going to share Oserian, which of course means that he would have to keep you, and thought how I could punish you both and this is how I am going to do it.

I will give you one last chance and one only. If within ten days of receiving this letter you have packed up all your belongings, and put them on the train for Mombasa and have gone down there yourself to catch the first boat to England, and come back and live with me wherever I elect to live, I will do nothing. You say that you and Colville have fixed up Oserian so that you have the house and he the land. Right, leave it at that. The place will be yours, or I will get Spring Valley to advance the money for taking over the house if he lends the money on mortgage and takes it over, I will settle it on you in strict settlement, but will take no more chances of being a cipher in *your* house to be treated like dirt and turned out when you wish.

EVELYN WAUGH

WAUGH (1903–66) WAS THE AUTHOR OF SCOOP and *Brideshead Revisited*. During the Second World War he served as junior officer with the British Commandos.

❧

To Laura Waugh (25 February 1940)

Laura Waugh (née Herbert), Evelyn Waugh's second wife.

Darling Laura

…My stock is high. I gave a twenty-minute lecture on reconnaissance patrols which was greeted with universal acclaim. On the other hand I was overheard by Major Cornwall speaking with contempt of the head of the Hythe School of Small Arms and was rebuked, so that may have put me down a bit.

Yesterday was an alarming day. The Brigadier suddenly accosted Messer-Bennetts & me & said, "I hear you are staying in camp for the week-end. You will spend the day with me." So at 12.30 he picked us up in his motor-car and drove all over the road to his house which was the lowest type of stockbroker's Tudor and I said in a jaggering way "Did you build this house, sir?" and he said "Build it! It's 400 years old!" The Brigadier's madam is kept very much in her place and ordered about with great shouts "Woman, go up to my cabin and get my boots". More peculiar, she is subject to booby-traps. He told us with great relish how the night before she had had to get up several times in the night to look after a daughter who was ill and how each time she returned, he had fixed up some new horror to injure her – a string across the door, a jug of water on top of it etc. However she seemed to thrive on this treatment & was very healthy & bright with countless children.

So after luncheon we were taken for a walk with the Brigadier who kept saying "Don't call me 'sir'." He told us how when he had a disciplinary case he always said, "Will you be court martialled or take it from me". The men said, "Take it from you, sir," so "I bend 'em over and give 'em ten of the best with a cane."

When we came back from our walk he showed me a most embarrassing book of rhymes & drawings composed by himself and his madam in imitation of *Just So Stories*, for one of his daughters. I had to read them all with him breathing stertorously down my neck. Then we did the cross-word puzzle until a daughter arrived from London where she is secretary to a dentist. She told me she had been a lift girl at The Times Book Club and had lost her job because at Christmas time, she hung mistletoe in the lift. The Brigadier thought this a most unsuitable story to tell me. When he is in a rage he turns slate grey instead of red. He was in an almost continuous rage with his daughter who is by a previous, dead madam. After that she & I talked about low night clubs until I thought the Brigadiers colour so unhealthy that I ought to stop. Most of the madam's reminiscences dealt with appalling injuries to one or other member of the family through their holiday exercises. The Brigadier says that the only fault he has to find with the war is that he misses his hockey. A very complex character. A lot of majors & their madams came to dinner; oddly enough all foreign – a Russian, a German and a Swede – a fact on which the Brigadier never ceased to comment adding "I suppose I can't really tell 'em what I think of their benighted countries." Then he asked very loudly whether it was true that he ought not to smoke his pipe with vintage port and if so why, so I told him and he got a bit grey again.

He said, "There's only one man in Egypt you can trust. Hassanin Bey. Luckily he's chief adviser to the King. He is a white man. I'll tell you something that'll show you the kind of chap he is. He and I were alone in a carriage going from Luxor to Suez – narrow gauge, single track line, desert on both sides, blazing heat. Ten hours with nothing to do. I thought I should go mad. Luckily I had a golf ball with me. So I made Hassanin stand one end of the corridor and we threw that ball backwards & forwards as hard as we could the whole day – threw it so that it really hurt. Not many Gyppies would stand up to that. Ever since then I've known there was at least one Gyppy we could trust."

Your friend Bailey came very near being expelled from the Brigade owing [to] the worst possible reports from all his instructors but has been given a second chance. The Brigadier said, "I hope I'm not giving away his identity when I tell you I meant to turn one of you out. Then he said he'd been a reporter on the *Star* in civil life and I thought that a good enough excuse". I said, "You have given away his identity but I can assure you he is all right." "Yes, he spoke up for himself very well". I did not like to ask whether he had caned him.

Capt. Macdonell has just been in here with his madam. He says he thinks that it will be o.k. for us to live out in a week or two. Yesterday he told me the Colonel had said no one was to live out. That shows how things change from day to day.

He also said, "I hope you aren't taking a lot of notes about us all to make fun of us in a book. There was a nasty bloke called Graves wrote a book called *Goodbye To All That*. Made fun of his brigadier. Bad show!" I thought it lucky he did not know what was in this letter.

All love
Evelyn

❧

To Nancy Mitford (5 January 1946)

Nancy Mitford (1904–73), English writer and the originator of the "U" (i.e. Upper Class) and "Non-U" classification of behaviour.

Darling Nancy

Death is not certain; blindness & baldness are. Still it will save you from seeing Picasso & wigs are easier on girls than chaps.

Please, before your sight fails, order Mrs F Greene to send you *The Tablet* and read my opening chapter of the life of the Empress Helena. I want your opinion on it.

This Prod-worship* is not healthy. Clever perhaps – good no. You must get a nun to nurse you through your fever. She will explain what goodness is.

I am very jealous of R. Mortimer. and Debo.† It was unfeeling of you to tell her he was like a wild beast. She was clearly very much over excited before his visit. I hope it was a bitter disappointment.

Picasso is the head of the counter-hons. I went to his disgusting exhibition to make sure. Klee rather old-maidish & sweet in a finicky way. It is a pity you do not read *The Times* Newspaper it has been full of tremendous art balls lately. I have had a great fan mail about Picasso – all from Surrey.

Miss Hunter Dunn is a real person. Her sister is engaged to be married to a Major this morning.

With your resistance weakened by so many dinners at the Dorchester the fever may prove fatal.

My two eldest children are here and a great bore. The older alternates between strict theology & utter silences; the boy lives for pleasure and is thought a great wit by his contemporaries. I have tried him drunk & I have tried him sober...

How nice to be able to read Proust in his own lingo. I tried in Scottish and couldn't get on at all. *Take Henrietta Temple* (Disraeli) to the lazar house.

I have just got to work again on Helena – now the Cinema company from whom I have been happily drawing money all these years suddenly demand my services. It is a great nuisance.

Yesterday I went to an excruciating Pantomime at Bristol. I asked Maria Teresa how she had enjoyed it. "All except the jokes, papa."

In a moment of Christmas sentiment I wrote to the nuns who had this house during the war to say I would let them off paying the damages & losses (assessed at £214 by the agents). The Mother Superior wrote to say that she was "glad our little difficulty was forgotten".

---

*"Prod" was the nickname of Mitford's husband, Peter Rodd.
†Deborah Mitford, Nancy's sister

Our nursery maid at Pixton has fallen ill so Laura goes off there next week leaving me alone here.

A chap I know was lately possessed by the devil and has written a very interesting account of the experience.

I saw Bowra drunk in White's with Smarty. Smarty never comes in now except on Saturdays when one is allowed a guest to luncheon.

The first thing Maria Teresa asked for on her arrival from her middle class convent was a "serviette-ring".

Counter Hon Quennell behaved well about *Love* in his *Daily Mail*, I was glad to see, I look for other reviews but don't see them. Your cousin Ed thought the communist part particularly good.

Try not to die. It is the strong ones who go under easiest.

Love
Evelyn

⊷⊰⊱⊶

To A. D. Peters (12 June 1947)

Peters was Waugh's agent.

Dear Pete

No, not for 12 guineas.

Price for television £50 in a false beard. With the naked face £250.

Yours
Evelyn

MARTIN BORMANN

MARTIN BORMANN (1900–?45), REICHSMINISTER OF the German Nazi Party. Effectively Hitler's deputy during the last years of the Second World War, he remained with the Fuehrer until the last. His fate is uncertain, but in all probability he was killed during the battle of Berlin in May 1945.

❧

To his wife, Gerda Bormann (21 January 1944)

"M" was an actress, who became Bormann's mistress.

My dear Mummy-Girl,

…During the next few weeks I intend to have nothing but apple juice and a teaspoon-full of magnesia for breakfast. At Obersalzberg I noticed that I was ten pounds over weight.

You said that M. must be an incredible girl because she managed to persuade me of the virtues of magnesia. But, my sweet, it is not she who is an incredible girl – I am an incredible fellow! You know that before there was nothing at all between M. and me, I just found her attractive because she was such a thoroughly good sort. When I met her again last October after all those years, I was simply overjoyed, beyond all measure. You can't imagine how overjoyed I was. She attracted me immensely. And in spite of her resistance I kissed her without further ado and quite scorched her with my burning joy. I fell madly in love with her. I arranged it so that I met her again many times, and then I took her in spite of all her refusals. You know the strength of my will, against which M. was of course unable to hold out for long. Now she is mine, and now – lucky fellow! – now I am, or rather, I feel doubly and unbelievably happily married.

M., good girl that she is, suffers the most violent pangs of conscience: she used to have quite a different view of women who "carry on with a married man". And, above all, M. has a bad conscience towards you. Though this is sheer nonsense – it was I who conquered her by force of my will!

What do you think, beloved, of your crazy fellow? I don't need your reply, for I know you. You can't imagine how I rave about you to M. All the same she still believes that you couldn't help feeling angry with her and would never like her again!

What will come of it? Well, obviously we aren't proclaiming our union to the four winds!

M.'s father, the high civil servant and jurisconsult, hasn't the faintest inkling. M. poured out her heart to her mother, who is a very nice woman, and the mother shed a few tears and – worries only about you! M. insists that she would never be able to match your largemindedness. This has its advantages. I must never make her jealous, or she would run away from me.

Oh, my sweet, you can't imagine how happy I am with the two of you! Really, Heaven has been kind to me. All the happiness you have given me through your self and all the children, and now I have M. in addition! I shall have to be doubly and trebly careful now, and see that I keep well and fit.

Fond love,
Your M.B.

❧

Gerda Bormann to Martin Bormann (21 January 1944)

My dearest, best Daddy,

Thank you very, very much for your dear long letter. I had sensed for some time that there was something between you and M., and when you were here last I felt sure of it. I am so fond of M. myself that I simply cannot be angry with you, and the children too love her very much, all of them. In any case she is far more practical and housewifely than I am [NOW COME COME].* When she stayed in

---

*When too busy to pen a full reply, Borman annotated his wife's letters with comments and answers, and returned them to her. These marginalia are shown here in upper case and enclosed in [ ].

Pullach, she and I did the packing of our whole white china set, that is, she did the packing and I made the list, and only one plate was broken on the long transport. Altogether, in the last few years there has been nobody, except Ilse R., with whom I got on so well as with M. Funny that both girls are from D. and have both lost their fiancés in the war. M.'s fiancé was killed some time ago in Spain, that is why she has had time to get over it, while Ilse R.'s was killed as recently as at Stalingrad and she still feels it very deeply – to get over it, she is burying herself in work as she does. It is a thousand pities that fine girls like these two should be denied children. In the case of M. you will be able to alter this, but then you will have to see to it that one year M. has a child, and the next year I, so that you always have a wife who is mobile. [WHAT A WILD IDEA!] Then we'll put all the children together in the house on the lake, and live together, and the wife who is not having a child will always be able to come and stay with you in Obersalzberg or Berlin. [THAT WOULD NEVER DO! EVEN IF THE TWO WOMEN WERE THE MOST INTIMATE FRIENDS. EACH STAYS BEST BY HERSELF. VISITS, ALL RIGHT, BUT EVEN THAT WITHOUT EXAGGERATION.] There is only one thing I don't quite like: that you went together to Alt-Rehse [WHAT'S THAT?], because I don't care a hoot about Helmut Vehrs, but I hope Frau Vehrs didn't smell a rat, she is so narrow-minded and might comment on it, as Frau Deuschel did that time with the little Swedish girl who died afterwards. You'd better take M. here with you, then nobody can say a thing. Once she has a child she can't go on as an actress anyway, so she will be much better off here. That she shouldn't have a child is something which seems to me out of the question, you being you. [YOU'RE STUPENDOUS!] Only, I must first get rid of Aunt Hilde who is difficult anyhow. As soon as the holiday evacuee children go home, she can go too. With our own children she has no contact at all, none of them can stand her. We all like M., we like her much better even than Aunt Anni. In her hands, I wouldn't mind leaving the children at any time, without worrying. She would bring them up with the same tenderness and in the same spirit as I do. Only in one thing, dearest, you will have to be careful with her and educate her very gently. She isn't a churchwoman, but at the same time she is not yet quite free of the Christian faith. If you attack Christianity you will only make her stubborn, [TRUE] not because she is a Christian by conviction, but purely out of a spirit of contrariness. [TRUE, THAT SPIRIT IS VERY STRONGLY DEVELOPED IN HER!] Give her enlightening books, but do it discreetly, and then she is sure to come to the right conclusion in due course. Well, now I've said everything I wanted to say. You see, I love you so much, all I wish for is that you should always be happy and that all our children should be all right.

Good-night, my Sweetheart, don't diet too much for your slimming, or you will only get bad nerves, and that is something I can't bear because it always affects me and, through me, the children. We want a daddy who is healthy and cheerful.

I love you more than I can say [AND VICE VERSA].

Your Mummy.

Martin Bormann to his wife (7 October 1944)

My beloved girl,

You cannot imagine how much I am looking forward to life after I'm pensioned off. I fail to understand those old men who, in times of peace, get indignant when they have to make room for youth. Obviously they are simply too old to assess their own senile decay. My own attitude is quite different. As soon as our Fuehrer no longer needs me, or as soon as there is a new Fuehrer, I shall retire to private life and live – at last – a few years in peace according to my inclinations.

Then I am going to devote myself to:

1. My family.
2. The garden or manor (this depends on what we are going to be allotted).
3. The library.

Even from the Reichstag I shall resign at once.

I shall no longer read any letters of political content, such as still might be sent to me by acquaintances or strangers. We shall leave it to a secretary to return the letters, with a printed slip, to the respective departments or senders.

I have seen it too often that retired officers turn into perpetual grousers and bitter critics. This danger, which besets all "have-beens", all those "on the retired list", is something I mean to evade by a complete separation from my present work and surroundings.

I shall not go to any Party Conference, and as a rule never even listen to political broadcasts. Otherwise it would be only too easy to slip into the totally mistaken attitude – very frequent in old people towards the young – that "before" this or that had been better, so much better, that one would have acted differently oneself, and so on and so forth.

All these are rocks which anyone runs up against, willy-nilly, and on which many people founder intellectually and morally; I intend wisely to avoid them from the outset. My contentment will be the greater, the more I concentrate it deliberately, with commonsense and prudence, on cabbage and cabbage-butterflies, on all the tomes I have been buying without having had a chance to know what is in them, on wind and weather, on house and farm.

Oh, Mumsy dear, it will be a beautiful life, if I live to see it. And I have great hopes that I shall.

You know, I've come to know in excess all ugliness, distortion, slander, nauseating and false flattery, toadying, ineptitude, folly, idiocy, ambition, vanity, greed for money, etc., etc., in short, all unpleasant aspects of human nature. Already when I was in charge of the Assistance Fund, I found to my astonishment – candid fool that I was – that good Nazis, who had courageously given battle to Communists and had been hurt in the fight, suddenly stayed on the sick-list as long as possible to go on drawing assistance from the Fund.

Therefore, when I am pensioned off at the end of the war, I can say with a sigh of relief: "I've had enough!"

No – only as long as the Fuehrer Adolf Hitler needs me – and then I disappear from the political scene! An irrevocable decision! And you know my irrevocable decisions, after all. I stick to them, my girl: we'll continue our honeymoon journey, which was interrupted in 1929, and no one is going to call us back from it this time. We'll stay, quietly and unknown, in lonely inns. We'll go again to the Bergle and climb the rocks in the Scheiding, as we did once. I'm eagerly looking forward to it already now.

Oh, my girl, even now I'm looking forward to it! But until then I will have to work very hard really to deserve peace and rest afterwards.

I am all your
M.

EDITH SITWELL

DAME EDITH SITWELL (1887–1964), ENGLISH POET. She was the sister of the equally eccentric Osbert and Sacheverell Sitwell.

❧

To John Lehmann (29 August 1945)

John Lehmann (1907–87), poet and publisher.

My dear John,

Thank you a thousand times for your most kind, most understanding and sympathetic letter. It did me a great deal of good. You always understand everything, with such intuition and heart.

I am delighted with the beautiful poem, which is deeply moving. The fourth section is particularly lovely. And I find the idea of the reaper very moving and lovely: but there are, in this section (2) fair lines which I feel are not *quite* the equal of the rest of the poem; I am doubtful about these:

And strained to watch them, while his lips repeat
"Brave lads – the best of all…"

It is especially the second half line that I am doubtful about. Also,

> Poor blinking heroes, like those towns below,
> Their souls be roasting – though their lives were cheap.

I may be wrong. *Will you I think it over?*

Dear me, how well you manage the A-B-A-B 10-syllable line. That scheme, like the open-shut open-shut scheme or its reverse, are extraordinarily difficult to handle. You do it with such ease that it is like a swan floating. You gain *great* effects of beauty from this complete ease, for the A-B-A-B 10-syllable line quatrain is very lovely when properly handled, and quite awful when badly done. When Emily Dickinson uses the same rhyme scheme in an 8-syllable line, she wobbles like a jelly. You always float, or fly.

Apropos of my beloved father's goings-on. Now, Osbert realises he (my father) actually got through at least £200,000 of the family money, above and beyond his annual income. It isn't bad, is it? And all spent on his own whims. Sachie is badly hit by all this. The old man played ducks and drakes with Sachie's money (*without* telling him, and he had no right to touch it) – he then, out of vanity, made up Sachie's income out of his own (my father's money) and now of course Sachie finds a large part of his income gone.

Osbert will not get the £1,200 a year he should have had. He will have nothing to leave, and the old man seized and squandered everything that was not entailed. Osbert with great nobility is giving up the £20,000 to Sachie.

I have my small family allowance. Owing to having had to leave home owing to my mother's conduct and habits, I had great charges of honour and gratitude, and so have had, in the past, and still have, to pay out a part of my income. But I have the house in Bath (a present) and I have an allowance, and I can earn money. And I never, never mention the charges I have spoken of, because it is so terribly painful to the helpless, generous and noble-minded person concerned – and was to the one who is now dead. I should have been lost if it had not been for them.

When I am told by the left-wing boys that I can't write poetry because I have not proletarian experiences, I often wonder how many of them, at the age of 17, have been sent to pawn false teeth – parental false teeth!!!!! You get 10/5 on them. And whisky was then 12/6d. My handwriting at that point became wonky from an attack of fou rire. Mind you, I couldn't sympathise more with the owner of the teeth, as regards that. The life would have driven anyone to it. But I did not lead exactly a "sheltered life" as a child and young girl!

When do you get to Paris? I don't want to bother you about poor Evelyn Wiel, and if you have not the time to see her, I shall more than understand. If you *do* go, No. 129 Rue Saint Dominique is between the Avenue Bosquet and the Avenue de la Bourdonnais. The house is exactly above the Fountain (a landmark.) The flat is the top floor right-hand one. Evelyn Wiel is one of the most wonderful women I know. (I lived in the flat before the war, and she looked after me like a mother. She is the sister of my dear Helen Rootham, who brought me up, and who is now dead.) E.W. may startle you by her *maquillage* effects. These are worn to prove to herself that *nothing* can conquer her, neither having starved in the past (she used to live on *25 shillings a week*) – *nor* having had frightful operations (not cancer, but terrible anyhow) – *nor* being in constant pain – *nor* being old (she is nearly seventy, if not quite) – *nor* having been beaten and then deserted by her Norwegian husband, who was at the Legation in Paris – deserted with no money.

She is terrifically brave, and is covered with decorations for bravery as a nurse in the last war. The Germans bombed a hospital full of liquid-fire cases. All the nurses and doctors ran for their lives, excepting Evelyn and two doctors, who remained with the delirious patients.

She has no brain in particular, but a heart of gold, and one of the most lovely natures I have ever known…

To Minnie Astor and James Fosburgh (26 December 1953), from Hollywood

Dearest Minnie and Jim,

I am so ashamed that this letter is so late, but it is so for two reasons, into which I will go later. [...]

I do hope you had a wonderful Christmas – but I know you did, for I have never seen two people so happy, with a heavenly happiness spread to everyone round you. [...]

The reasons for my being so late in writing: A. I had, like a fool, come away without your address, and had to wait till Osbert and David arrived to get it, as I was not sure where Betsey was, so could not send it to be forwarded. B. I have had to work *all* day (copying in the morning, being roared at by Walter in the afternoon) including Christmas Eve and Christmas Day. C. I have had a very bad shock – (coming straight on top of Dylan Thomas's death: it was I who found him, so to speak, and it was I who made his very great fame).

The other day, at the St Regis, as we were leaving the restaurant and Natasha was coming in, she introduced a playwright called Peter Ustinov (Osbert knew him already). I *thought* his manner was most odd: he behaved exactly like a blackbeetle that thinks it is going to be killed – tried to crawl into the wall. (Excepting that he was like a fat white slug.) Well, a few days after I arrived here, I found out *why*. On the 2nd of December, or 3rd, he produced a play of his at the Savoy in London, *written for the purpose of grossly insulting Osbert and me*. There can be no question it was meant for us. We are given the name of *D'Urt*!!!

Miss D'Urt is a famous "poetess in a turban" (I used to wear these many years ago). Sir Mohammed D'Urt is a famous writer who is a baronet, and they have an eccentric old father. Both of us, apparently, are sex maniacs of an advanced kind. The baronet was described by one paper as "a lecherous pontiff" and I hunt unwilling gentlemen in and out of bedrooms. *The Daily Express* has said, in *so many words*, that it is meant for us. Can you imagine anything *so foul* as to do this to a poor man who is known, by the whole of London, to have a most terrible disease that is made *infinitely* worse by any kind of shock or worry?

However – the play was booed off. On the first night, every entrance of the actors and actresses was booed and yelled at by the gallery. One line of Miss D'Urt's ran, "We forgive everything" to which a voice replied, "We don't. We'll never forgive this." The brave Mr Ustinov who has insulted a helpless cripple had to hide in his box. The play was withdrawn after nine days...

George said I was to give you his love when I write. He hadn't got your address, which I shall now give him.

It is heavenly weather here, but I have been too busy to go out more than three times – I having dined with George, who is working fearfully hard all day. I have given a strong impression, in George's household, that I am, to say the least of it, not quite in my right mind. (I *am*, of course, rather dotty, but there is nothing *actually* wrong with the grey matter.)

Immediately on my arrival, I received a telegram from the *Sunday Times* asking me to fly straight back to London at their expense in order to be third mourner (after his wife and mother) at Dylan Thomas's Memorial Service arranged by them. It was in that paper that I made his fame originally.

I told you I would keep a kind of diary for you, Mrs Whitney and Natasha. So far, there has only been one *really* terrible scene. That was at dinner with George, two nights after I arrived. The enormous black poodle! – the size of a large carthorse (I adore him) – was chasing one of the dachshunds across the sofa, over my lap (trampling on my appendix) backwards and forwards. George mentioned Miss Jean Simmons, whereupon Walter, who hates her, began to shriek imprecations in a really piercing manner. I have never heard such yells. George said, "Damp down, Walter, damp down." After about five minutes of this, the dachshund suddenly turned, just as it was being chased over my lap, and put its head into the poodle's mouth, where it became fixed – I thought irrevocably. The poodle's eyes were distended with fear and suffocation. Walter stopped yelling and pulled, violently, at the dachshund's back legs. The dachshund, thinking Walter was trying to tear it in two, as its head was held as in a vice, shrieked down the poodle's throat – making the poodle's fear and suffocation far worse. George tried to prise open the poodle's mouth. Myrtle, George's housekeeper, who worships the poodle (as do I) was standing outside the door with her hands clasped in an agony of apprehension. For some minutes the commotion was indescribable. I *still* cannot think how the dachshund was dislodged, but it was, at last. George said, rather huffily, when I expressed wonderment and condolence, that it is always happening.

I am sending you Dylan Thomas's great and wonderful poems, from the Gotham Book Mart.

Best love to both and all, *all* best wishes for the happiest New Year you have ever known. A million thanks for my lovely present.

Edith

MALCOLM LOWRY

MALCOLM LOWRY (1909–57), NOVELIST. BORN IN England, Lowry spent much of his life in a self-built shack in Vancouver, where he wrote his masterpiece, *Under the Volcano* (1945). He was married to the writer Margerie (Margie) Bonner.

To Conrad Aiken (Autumn 1945)

Conrad Aiken (1889–1973), American poet and novelist.

Dear old Conrad:

Thanks for yours and have been meaning to write a really fat informative and diverting letter – in fact made all the notes for same, but I want to get this letter off now so it will be in time to wish you bon voyage, therefore I must make a sacrifice of the other for the time being. Yes, the phoenix clapped its wings all right all right, in fact gave such a bloody great resounding clap that the poor bird nearly broke its neck and had to be immolated all over again. As you know we went east after the fire. The grave preceded us however. The interminable golden bittersweet awful beautiful Eastern Autumn (which I'd never before experienced) restored Margie, whose childhood was in Michigan, to *some* extent, but me it almost slew. It had a worse effect upon me in fact than on Henry Adams, though the Noxons' Niagara-on-the-Lake is something to see: really beautiful. I was in shocking bad form and worse company so all in all, though I was very disappointed not to see you – albeit I *heard* you – it was perhaps just as well that I didn't. How the Noxons bore with me – if they really did – I don't know. Actually the business of the fire seemed to drive us both slightly cuckoo. Its traumatic effect alone was shattering. We had to live through the bloody fire all over again every night. I would wake to find Margie screaming or she would wake to find me yelling and gnashing my teeth. Apart from these diversions (fortunately the Noxons were sound sleepers but when we moved to a house of our own it grew much worse), fire itself seemed to follow us around in a fashion nothing short of diabolical. Betty had painted a picture of a neighbor's house in Oakville that Margie and I had thought of renting for the winter because it vaguely resembled our old home, and one day when everyone was out I sat in the attic studying this picture which I liked very much. My concentration on the picture was somewhat marred by the fact that in my imagination the house kept bursting into flames and sure enough, about a week later, that's precisely what the house did, they couldn't get the fire engines through the woods, nothing of the kind had happened for fifty years in that rural route, and there was a terrific to-do, through all of which Margie and I, for once, calmly slept. Then when we went down to Niagara-on-the-Lake the house next door to ours, one night while we were over at the Noxons, went up in a blaze. We heard the shouts and bells and saw the awful sun (I don't know why so much Emily Dickinson today) and of course thought it was *our* house and ran over in a panic, so much so that Margie was not even convinced it was *not* our house, by the time we had got there, and took all our manuscripts out into the street. And to cap everything when we returned here, it turned out that the house where someone had been good enough to let us store our bedding and some few things we had left after *our* fire, had in our absence itself burned down, totally demolished, and our bedding and stuff with it, the house mysteriously bursting into flame for no reason at all apparently one calm mild evening when the owners weren't even there. Margie and I had invented a horror story, a murderer, a black magician, one of whose specialities was the starting of fires by means of incomprehensible talismans. This fictitious gent's name was Pell and the MSS concerning him I had happened to rescue from our fire. S'welp me bob if the owners of this house don't turn out to be Pell too, though there had been no connection at all originally. And so forth; altogether about fifty other odd senseless sad terrifying and curiously related things that make me sometimes think (taking it all in all) that maybe I am the chap chosen of God or the devil to elucidate the Law of Series. Unfortunately it would seem to involve one in such rotten bad art: or need it not? At all events, I have been reading Kant's *Critique of Pure Reason* to see if that would help.

When we arrived back here too it was to find that someone, strangers and vultures, had disregarded our burned stakes and notices and built smack on half our old site, blocking our southerly view, a great tall ugly creation to be full in the summer of rackety rickety children and hysterical fat women who meantime had pulled down the flags we left – perhaps too dramatically – flying on our poor old ruin, thrown dead mice down our well, and shat – even on the wall – all over our toilet. This of course is a crime, according to the local folkways, the mores, or whatever, though we had no legal toehold in the matter, pioneer's and squatter's rights having been abolished: our few fishermen friends – with ourselves the only permanent inhabitants – arrived back too late from Alaska to prevent it, and our local Manx boat-builder only got insulted and nearly beaten up when he tried to put a stop to it. They had no excuse; knew we were coming back. We could have knocked their house down ourselves and had the support of even most of the summer community, but like a fool or not I decided to be Christlike about it with the result that we had them in our hair all summer while we were building on what space was left for us, our new neighbours even calling us greedy because we made the most of that, until one day the owner came over and asked why we wouldn't speak to them more often and accused me of putting a curse on them and on their house, that they couldn't be happy there, that the youngest child had almost drowned the day before, and so on, and that they'd had one misfortune after another, ever since they'd built there, to which I replied that while we forgave them, all right, they had never had the charity to perceive that there was anything to forgive, moreover if you built on top of a guy's soul, you couldn't be sure what would happen, and if something you didn't like did happen, it was no use coming round complaining to us and looking as if they'd swallowed Paddy Murphy's goat and the horns were sticking out of their arse. All round, quite an ethical problem.

To be frank, it is ourselves who have had most of a share in this misfortune. Margie ran a nail through her foot the first day we got the lumber in – cellulitis set in, then blood poisoning, shortage of doctors, and finally hospital, and probings, and a horrible awful anxious time that was. Meanwhile she received the first part of her proof for her novel but we are still waiting for the promised proofreader's copy of the second part, Scribners having held her first novel now for over four years (it is getting into the fifth year) without publishing it, and although they signed a contract for a second novel with a time limit set for publication date at this fall, it is already this fall and still Margie hasn't had so much as a smell of the proofs of this second novel, which was supposed to be at the printers last Christmas, so it looks as though a breach of contract looms, with what small comfort that is for the poor author. I then proceeded to cut off the end of my thumb while doing some ripsawing with an ordinary saw, which set us back with the building and for the last two months I have been in bed practically unable to move with a toxaemia caused by an osteomyelitis due to a tooth that became abscessed and had to be removed. There is a shortage of dentists – they will not take new patients, even if you are hopping with agony as I was, and on V.J. Day too, with the drugstores all shut.

But on the other hand there is apparently also a surplus of dentists: they are threatening to open offices on the street because of the housing shortage. But I myself have not been able to find a trace of these dentists. Meantime there has been an average of two murders a week here, most of them by or of children: a pet slayer likewise is at large who has disembowelled thirteen goats, several sailors' monkeys, twelve pet rabbits, and is doubtless also somewise responsible for the apparition of half a cocker spaniel in a lane near West Vancouver. Just the same we have built our house and paradise has been regained. I forgot to say that no sooner had paradise been regained than we received the notice that a new law had gone through and that all our lovely forest was to be torn down and ourselves with it within a year and turned into "autocamps of the better class." This placed our new house – which by the way has the distinction of being the last example of such pioneer activity on the Vancouver waterfront property – under a sentence of death that was finally too much for our sense of humours and my temperature went up within a quarter of an hour to 103. A sad story, you say, almost as poignant as the "Triumph of the Egg." Not a bit of it. Reprieve has come. There will be no autocamps of the better class, and no neighbours either, of the worse class. We may live here for three years at least, as we are doing, without molestation or paying any rent at all and then buy the land too, that is the part we want and we are being given first choice – for a reasonable price. Thus does your old Malc, if still a conservative Christian Anarchist at heart, at last join the ranks of the petty bourgeoisie. I feel somewhat like a Prometheus who became interested in real estate and decided to buy up his Caucasian ravine.

At the moment we are living in the house without inside walls, it's pouring with rain, and it doesn't leak. What triumph. Herewith our handiwork – also the pier we built ourselves, all that was left of our old house – it used to come out of our front door: the vultures wedged themselves in just- beyond, hoping to use our pier too, not to say our well.

My novel – [Under the] Volcano – seems to have gone smack into the void, no intelligent comments so far or encouragement. I think it is really good, though *The Lost Weekend* may have deprived it of some of its impact – alack, prosaic justice? – if not confused with *The Last Week End* by John Sommerfield, in which it actually is old Malc who goes all too recognizably down the drain, and pretty feebly too. I was planning to send you the *Volcano* in some trepidation but with some pride too, but I don't like to saddle you with the only copy in my possession and I don't at present see how I can get back the only available other one before you sail. So please take the will for the deed for the time being. I'll learn 'em eventually, as Mr. Wolfe once said, I feel.

The only difference in my present status since I wrote the above is that while we are still living in the house without inside walls the roof is leaking in six different places. But now your letter about the *Collected Poems* has arrived and I hasten to make some reply in time, though please forgive me if what I say seems hastily digested. In brief, these are the ideas which immediately occur to me and I hope they are not merely confusing. I think the idea of reversing the chronological order is very good, in fact as good as can be – though I think perhaps "The Soldier" might profit by being dislocated out of the new order and being placed, if not actually among the symphonies, somewhere near them in the second volume. What I mean is if the poem does not belong to the symphonies, "The Soldier" does to the notion of the Divine Pilgrim. Houston Peterson or somebody once put the possibly erroneous idea in my head that you had once thought of including "Tetélestai" also under the Divine Pilgrim heading, and even if this is erroneous and "Tetélestai" not a symphony this is worth thinking of if you haven't already rejected it. As for the early poems I would certainly put in everything that can possibly be of use to the fellow-poet and student of your work – "Discordants with Youth that's now so bravely spending" and as many of the actual "Cats and Rats" turns and movies as you have space for. They latterly certainly stay with me as unique and powerful work, whatever you may think of them. I would also take the opportunity of exhuming from undeserved limbo such pieces as "Red petals in the dust under a tree," "Asphalt," "Tossing our tortured hands to no Escape" (though not very early, 1925 model? but very fine) and even the "Succubus you kissed" lampoon you wrote agin the Imagists which has a historical interest, and giving the dates of all these.

I don't know about a selection from "Earth Triumphant," but I would be inclined to make a short one – possibly you are right to disown it, but I myself cannot forget the "unaccustomed wetness in my trousers" with which I read it at your Uncle Potter's. The only other departure that comes to me would be to start the whole collected poems with "The Morning Song of Senlin" and end them with "The Coming Forth by Day of Osiris Jones." I must say I like this notion per se exceedingly, if it would not play too much hob with your reversed chronology. Whatever you do, I am very glad a *Collected Poems* is coming out and very best luck with them.

If, by the way, you have any old *Harper's Bazaars*, *Vice Versas*, *Southern Reviews* or what not you are thinking of throwing away – no old *Dials*, alack – we would be immensely beholden if you would wrap a paper around them and shoot them in this direction C.O.D. or something, for we are absolutely stuck here for such reading matter, all intelligent American magazines having been unprocurable for donkey's years: on the other hand it occurs to me it is probably a poor time to ask, what with you packing and all: so if it's too much trouble, just forget it.

Well, bon voyage, old fellow and our very best love to you both and best wishes for Mary's success and our very best again to her and you and also to Jeakes.

Malc

To David Markson (10 May 1954)

Dear old Dave:

I should have written you weeks ago – and indeed I did write, and more than once – but owing to certain auxiliary circumstances... Yeah. Well, the first auxiliary circumstance was that a pigeon nesting in the airvent head on the apartment roof fell down the said airvent shaft and got trapped in the wall behind our bed, which bed came out of the wall like a drawer. I was going to make the rescue of said bird coincident with the second circumstance, though in fact the latter preceded it; a cut forehead, no more than a scratch it seemed, while messing about with these city chores more unfamiliar than trapped pigeons: but suddenly the scratch had turned into Grand Guignol – I'd severed a bloody artery. Worse to follow: Margerie, on going to the rescue, got trapped in the elevator. I mean that the elevator chose that very moment to stop between floors when her benighted husband was bleeding to death in the bathroom. Pandemonium: save from me, who having let out the third bathful of Lowry gore felt at the top of his form, and even less disposed to holler for help myself than I was to put a tourniquet round the wound in question: I have not, I said to myself, got an artery in my head, so how can I put a tourniquet on it? Perhaps what I meant was any brains but at all events there was a happy ending and we were saved in the nick, on the stroke of midnight, in St Paul's Hospital, having been conveyed thence at 117 miles an hour by an air force officer who up to then had been slightly drunk in the corridor below when he'd been having an affair with his half-sister. "And did you do this yourself?" asked the midnight interne grimly, to which I replied, "Christ no, it was that bloody pigeon." All went well for a week or so, when someone supplicated our own aid in a manner almost as urgent as we had – or Margie had – the air force officer, though the urgency in this case was more psychological or interfamilial, and implied a journey, through the wet and wilderness – long live the wet and the wilderness yet! – of some seventy miles to a remote island – the very island upon which lives a friend of yours by the way, should you ever need him, and whom I once mentioned to you – and with a couple of cracked ribs, I mean mine, also perhaps suffered as in combat with the holy bird, and growing increasingly more painful, the more so since to reach our friend's house, one has to descend a precipice some six hundred feet in depth and at a gradient – where steps go down – of about 1 in 2.

Back in the apartment of the holy bird (the janitor suggested that despite the rules we might feed the poor thing on the window-sill after its exertions that night) it was to discover that the cracked ribs had succeeded in apparently paralyzing my innards: in endeavouring to remedy this in the approved Gandhi-esque manner – my enema the Douche, as Haile Selassie put it – there was, after many fruitless attempts, suddenly a sound of breaking and crepitous (though alas, not crapitus, had it been crapitus might have been better) enough to awaken the dead, the dead being me, to a sense, again, of the illogical or brute fact: ribs (and I have broken them all before) seemed to me malleable creatures, designed for give and take – and sway and scend and every kind of pressure from the outside: but apparently not from the inside – horrendous thought (one redthroated loon, one foolish seagull trying to steal a fish off one beautiful merganser, burning oil waste in the refinery, the first star – is the scenery outside from the room you know) like those dams in Holland during the floods of yesteryear, the ribcage was giving under the water-pressure, and it wasn't any use sticking one's finger in the dam. Or up one's arse for that matter. This time Margie got her instructions by telephone, nobly – and embarrassing though it must have been (our doctor lives in North Vancouver) – bind sheet tightly around patient to give support; more enema the douche: cascara: 2 tablespoonsful of epsom salts: an infusion of rosemarine: and caper several times boldly about the room, taking deep breaths of smog. And brandy, said I, should be given to the dying. It was, but by Monday night – that had been Sunday – it still hadn't done any good. "If nothing happens by 8, get to the hospital." Our last call was cut off by the cry Emergency from somebody else: so I made my own emergency this time under my own steam – I mean I walked – nach dem Krankenhaus. St Paul's again: (the first and last scenes of the whole Volcano – The Voyage That Never Ends – are supposed to be there too, but this was nightmarish a little: I ought to have been writing this, not living it or dying it, mutters Malc to himself, chuckling thoughtlessly – you oughtn't to chuckle thoughtlessly, old man, with broken ribs under such circumstances, and I warn you not to try it should you ever be unfortunate enough to be in the same position. So our North Vancouver doctor sent an emergency doctor after me, x-rays were taken, drugs given, and suffice it – with a temperature that was now rising much as it does when you go down into the engine-room of a bauxite freighter—

Several mescals later...

FASTING

behind the bed.

And at the foot a picture of the infant Jesus, apparently being instructed, with a view to the corollary of constructing a cross (since there was one above) while he looked rather like Dylan, when absolutely blind tight, being instructed, as I say, by his father Joseph, in the art of what can be done with a hammer and a nail – a truce to this. (unposted)

Our very dear old Dave:

I am terribly sorry not to have (unwritten)

Very dear old Dave:

Extremely sorry not to have written for so long, or rather not have posted any letters to you, especially when you were so sporting to write us para-psychologically suspecting some Lowry misery-grisery, and at that so entertainingly, brilliantly and sympathetically, so often at that point – (unposted)

– to cut a long story short (and incidentally I wrote you another long unposted letter, which didn't mention our troubles, but concentrated on what we thought might be your own, not posted, because of the supernatural idea that perhaps the troubles didn't really exist but stating them might somehow and obscurely beget some of them for you, god damn it, all this when I know very well that all you might have wanted was for a fellow to say oh or shit or something (as you see I couldn't say shit very well, as the poet said when he shouted Fire, having fallen down the sewer) – to cut that long story short anyhow, we are thinking of coming east this summer, in fact with the object of seeing you before we depart for Tel Aviv up the S.S. ΟΙΔΙΙΙΟΥΣ ΤΥΡΑΝΝΟΣ. though actually we are bound for Sicily, or at least the kingdom of the 2 Sicilies – if not under dat ole King Bomba (who made a law that stopped the trains every night at 6 P.M. making it obligatory that they hold a religious service on board) – there to live, if not in turn like that old Typhoeus, beneath Mount Etna. Previous to this, Prospero-wise, we aim to return to

Milan, in which city the Volcano of your own better (or bitter) discovery is shortly to erupt: or fizzle out. We wondered if you could put us up in New York for a few days previous to this, under a bed or wherever, while we were on our way: said request not being made for financial reasons, but rather from Love, whatever that entity is. If you want, you can have our house when we're gone if you want to go west though don't swear we won't haunt it and sing hot teleported tunes at you: but more likely you won't want and more likely still you'll be crossing the seas like us or whatever. Actually we don't know exactly what ship we'll be going on from New York: whether a Greek, Egyptian, Israeli, or Italian freighter. Or the exact date. But the Italian Consul is letting us know. As the said Consul remarked to Margie the other day: "This ship for lady-nice – has a friend who know the Commandante: the captain: but I must see friend. But maybe wait 5 or 6 day New York. But is friend I will try... No, it is my privilege for lady-nice and friend-boy, or is he your housebound?"

At all events, you won't be too far away even if you are; but let us know, as we shall: and meantime HOLD THAT NOTE, ROLAND! BLOW THAT HORN! Hold that note! God bless from us both, Margie and me, and from the shack and many mergansers and other wild and profound sea-foul (not written).

Malcolm

HUMPHREY BOGART

H UMPHREY DE FOREST BOGART (1899–1957), AMERI-can movie actor.

To Time Magazine *(1948)*

It has come to my attention that in your Current & Choice section, Lauren Bacall has consistently been left out of the cast of *Key Largo*.

Inasmuch as there are those of us in Hollywood, Miss Bacall among them, who would rather make Current & Choice than win an Academy Award or make Men of Distinction, won't you please include her in the cast of *Key Largo* in Current & Choice just once, as she is my wife and I have to live with her. Miss Bacall is extremely tired of being labeled *et al*.

Humphrey Bogart
Beverly Hills

GROUCHO MARX

GROUCHO MARX (1895–1977) WAS THE LEADER OF the Marx Brothers comedy team.

To Warner Bros (1948)

Warners, the studio which had made Casablanca, *was seeking to prevent the Marx Brothers calling their new film* A Night in Casablanca.

Dear Warner Brothers,

Apparently there is more than one way of conquering a city and holding it as your own. For example, up to the time that we contemplated making this picture, I had no idea that the city of Casablanca belonged exclusively to Warner Brothers. However, it was only a few days after our announcement appeared that we received your long, ominous legal document warning us not to use the name Casablanca.

It seems that in 1471, Ferdinand Balboa Warner, your great-great-grandfather, while looking for a shortcut to the city of Burbank, had stumbled on the shores of Africa and, raising his alpenstock (which he later turned in for a hundred shares of the common), named it Casablanca.

✓ I just don't understand your attitude. Even if you plan on re-releasing your picture, I am sure that the average movie fan could learn in time to distinguish between Ingrid Bergman and Harpo. I don't know whether I could, but I certainly would like to try.

You claim you own Casablanca and that no one else can use that name without your permission. What about "Warner Brothers"? Do you own that, too? You probably have the right to use the name Warner, but what about Brothers? Professionally, we were brothers long before you were. We were touring the sticks as The Marx Brothers when Vitaphone was still a gleam in the inventor's eye, and even before us there had been other brothers – the Smith Brothers; the Brothers Karamazov; Dan Brothers, an outfielder with Detroit; and "Brother, Can You Spare a Dime?" (This was originally "Brothers, Can You Spare a Dime?" but this was spreading a dime pretty thin, so they threw out one brother gave all the money to the other one and whittled it down to, "Brother, Can You Spare a Dime?")

Now Jack, how about you? Do you maintain that yours is an original name? Well, it's not. It was used long before you were born. Offhand, I can think of two Jacks – there was Jack of "Jack and the Beanstalk," and Jack the Ripper, who cut quite a figure in his day.

As for you, Harry, you probably sign your checks, sure in the belief that you are the first Harry of all time and that all other Harrys are imposters. I can think of two Harrys that preceded you. There was Lighthouse Harry of Revolutionary fame and a Harry Appelbaum who lived on the corner of 93rd Street and Lexington Avenue. Unfortunately, Appelbaum wasn't too well known. The last I heard of him, he was selling neckties at Weber and Heilbroner.

Now about the Burbank studio. I believe this is what you brothers call your place. Old man Burbank is gone. Perhaps you remember him. He was a great man in a garden. His wife often said Luther had ten green thumbs. What a witty woman she must have been! Burbank was the wizard who crossed all those fruits and vegetables until he had the poor plants in such a confused and jittery condition that they could never decide whether to enter the dining room on the meat platter or the dessert dish.

This is pure conjecture, of course, but who knows – perhaps

Burbank's survivors aren't too happy with the fact that a plant that grinds out pictures on a quota settled in their town, appropriated Burbank's name and uses it as a front for their films. It is even possible that the Burbank family is prouder of the potato produced by the old man than they are of the fact that from your studio emerged *Casablanca* or even *Gold Diggers of 1931*.

This all seems to add up to a pretty bitter tirade, but I assure you it's not meant to. I love Warners. Some of my best friends are Warner Brothers. It is even possible that I am doing you an injustice and that you, yourselves, know nothing at all about this dog-in-the-Wanger attitude. It wouldn't surprise me at all to discover that the heads of your legal department are unaware of this absurd dispute, for I am acquainted with many of them and they are fine fellows with curly black hair, double-breasted suits and a love of their fellow man that out-Saroyans Saroyan.

I have a hunch that this attempt to prevent us from using the title is the brainchild of some ferret-faced shyster, serving a brief apprenticeship in your legal department. I know the type well – hot out of law school, hungry for success and too ambitious to follow the natural laws of promotion. This bar sinister probably needled your attorneys, most of whom are fine fellows with curly black hair, double-breasted suits, etc., into attempting to enjoin us. Well, he won't get away with it! We'll fight him to the highest court! No pasty-faced legal adventurer is going to cause bad blood between the Warners and the Marxes. We are all brothers under the skin and we'll remain friends till the last reel of *A Night in Casablanca* goes tumbling over the spool.

Sincerely,
Groucho Marx

To the President of the Franklin Corporation (1961)

Dear Mr Goodman:

I received the first annual report of the Franklin Corporation and though I am not an expert at reading balance sheets my financial adviser (who, I assure you, knows nothing) nodded his head in satisfaction.

You wrote that you hope I am not one of those borscht circuit stockholders who get a few points' profit and hastily scram for the hills. For your information, I bought Alleghany Preferred eleven years ago and am just now disposing of it.

As a brand new member of your family, strategically you made a ghastly mistake in sending me individual pictures of the Board of Directors. Mr Roth, Chairman of the Board, merely looks sinister. You, the President, look like a hard worker with not too much on the ball. No one named Prosswimmer can possibly be a success. As for Samuel A. Goldblith, PhD., head of Food Technology at MIT, he looks as though he had eaten too much of the wrong kind of fodder.

At this point I would like to stop and ask you a question about Marion Harper, Jr. To begin with, I immediately distrust any man who has the same name as his mother. But the thing that most disturbs me about Junior is that I don't know what the hell he's laughing at. Is it because he sucked me into this Corporation? This is not the kind of a face that inspires confidence in a nervous and jittery stockholder.

George S. Sperti, I dismiss instantly. Any man who is the President of an outfit called Institutum Divi Thomae will certainly bear watching...James J. Sullivan, I am convinced, is Paul E. Prosswimmer photographed from a different angle.

Offhand, I would say that I have summed up your group fairly accurately. I hope, for my sake, that I am mistaken.

In closing, I warn you, go easy with my money. I am in an extremely precarious profession whose livelihood depends upon a fickle public.

Sincerely yours
Groucho Marx
(temporarily at liberty)

HARRY S. TRUMAN

HARRY S. TRUMAN (1884–1972) WAS THE 33RD PRESIdent of the USA. His daughter Margaret harboured singing ambitions

❧

To Paul Hume (6 December 1950), from the White House, Washington)

Paul Hume the music critic of the Washington Post. *He had reviewed a concert performance by Margaret Truman, concluding "Miss Truman cannot sing very well".*

Mr Hume:

I've just read your lousy review of Margaret's concert. I've come to the conclusion that you are an "eight ulcer man on four ulcer pay."

It seems to me that you are a frustrated old man who wishes he could have been successful. When you write such poppy-cock as was in the back section of the paper you work for it shows conclusively that you're off the beam and at least four of your ulcers are at work.

Some day I hope to meet you. When that happens you'll need a new nose, a lot of beefsteak for black eyes, and perhaps a supporter below!

Pegler, a gutter snipe, is a gentleman alongside you. I hope you accept that statement as a worse insult than a reflection on your ancestry.

H. S. T.

E. B. WHITE

E LWYN BROOKS WHITE (1899–1985), AMERICAN
novelist and parodist.

❧

To the American Society for the Prevention of Cruelty to Animals (12 April 1951)

Dear Sirs:

I have your letter, undated, saying that I am harboring an unlicensed dog in violation of the law. If by "harboring" you mean getting up two or three times every night to pull Minnie's blanket up over her, I am harboring a dog all right. The blanket keeps slipping off. I suppose you are wondering by now why I don't get her a sweater instead. That's a joke on you. She has a knitted sweater, but she doesn't like to wear it for sleeping; her legs are so short they work out of a sweater and her toenails get caught in the mesh, and this disturbs her rest. If Minnie doesn't get her rest, she feels it right away. I do myself, and of course with this night duty of mine, the way the blanket slips and all, I haven't had any real rest in years. Minnie is twelve.

In spite of what your inspector reported, she has a license. She is licensed in the state of Maine as an unspayed bitch, or what is more commonly called an "unspaded" bitch. She wears her metal license tag but I must say I don't particularly care for it, as it is in the shape of a hydrant, which seems to me a feeble gag, besides being pointless in the case of a female. It is hard to believe that any state in the Union would circulate a gag like that and make people pay money for it, but Maine is always thinking of something. Maine puts up roadside crosses along the highways to mark the spots where people have lost their lives in motor accidents, so the highways are beginning to take on the appearance of a cemetery, and motoring in Maine has become a solemn experience, when one thinks mostly about death. I was driving along a road near Kittery the other day thinking about death and all of a sudden

I heard the spring peepers. That changed me right away and I suddenly thought about life. It was the nicest feeling.

You asked about Minnie's name, sex, breed, and phone number. She doesn't answer the phone. She is a dachshund and can't reach it, but she wouldn't answer it even if she could, as she has no interest in outside calls. I did have a dachshund once, a male, who was interested in the telephone, and who got a great many calls, but Fred was an exceptional dog (his name was Fred) and I can't think of anything offhand that he wasn't interested in. The telephone was only one of a thousand things. He loved life – that is, he loved life if by "life" you mean "trouble," and of course the phone is almost synonymous with trouble. Minnie loves life, too, but her idea of life is a warm bed, preferably with an electric pad, and a friend in bed with her, and plenty of shut-eye, night and days. She's almost twelve. I guess I've already mentioned that. I got her from Dr. Clarence Little in 1939. He was using dachshunds in his cancer-research experiments (that was before Winchell was running the thing) and he had a couple of extra puppies, so I wheedled Minnie out of him. She later had puppies by her own father, at Dr. Little's request. What do you think about that for a scandal? I know what Fred thought about it. He was some put out.

Sincerely yours,
E. B. *White*

MALCOLM X

MALCOLM X (1925–65), BLACK NATIONALIST LEADER, born Malcolm Little. The son of a Baptist preacher, he joined Elijah Muhammad's Nation of Islam (on which he assumed the name Malcolm X), but following a visit to Mecca he rejected the organization's separatist views in favour of a philosophy which combined Islam with socialism and racial solidarity. A power struggle within the Nation of Islam ensued and Malcolm X was assassinated by opponents as he spoke at a rally in Harlem.

୶ଋୡ

To his followers (1965)

Never have I witnessed such sincere hospitality and the overwhelming spirit of true brotherhood as is practiced by people of all colors and races here in this Ancient Holy Land, the home of Abraham, Muhammad, and all the other prophets of the Holy Scriptures. For the past week, I have been utterly spellbound by the graciousness I see displayed all around me by people of all colors.

I have been blessed to visit the Holy City of Mecca. I have made my seven circuits around the Ka'ba, led by a young *Mutawaf* named Muhammad. I drank water from the well of Zem Zem. I ran seven times back and forth between the hills of Mt Al-Safa and Al-Marwah. I have prayed in the ancient city of Mina, and I have prayed on Mt Arafat.

There were tens of thousands of pilgrims, from all over the world. They were of all colors, from blue-eyed blonds to black-skinned Africans. But we are all participating in the same ritual, displaying a spirit of unity and brotherhood that my experiences in America had led me to believe never could exist between the white and the non-white.

America needs to understand Islam, because this is the one religion that erases from its society the race problem. Throughout my travels in the Muslim world, I have met, talked to, and even eaten with people who in America would have been considered "white" – but the "white" attitude was removed from their minds by the religion of Islam. I have never before seen *sincere* and *true* brotherhood practiced by all colors together, irrespective of their color.

You may be shocked by these words coming from me. But on this pilgrimage, what I have seen and experienced has forced me to *re-arrange* much of my thought-patterns previously held and to *toss aside* some of my previous conclusions. This was not too difficult for me. Despite my firm convictions. I have been always a man who tries to face facts, and to accept the reality of life as new experience and new knowledge unfolds it. I have always kept an open mind, with every form of intelligent search for truth.

During the past eleven days here in the Muslim world, I have eaten from the same plate, drunk from the same glass, and slept in the same bed (or on the same rug) – while praying to the *same* God – with fellow Muslims, whose eyes were the bluest of blue, whose hair was the blondest of blond, and whose skin was the whitest of white. And in the *words* and in the *actions* and in the *deeds* of the "white" Muslims, I felt the same sincerity that I felt among the black African Muslims of Nigeria, Sudan, and Ghana.

We were *truly* all the same (brothers) – because their belief in one God had removed the "white" from their *minds*, the "white" from their *behavior* and the "white" from their *attitude*.

I could see from this, that perhaps if white Americans could accept the Oneness of God, then perhaps, too, they could accept in *reality* the Oneness of Man – and cease to measure, and hinder, and harm others in terms of their "differences" in color.

With racism plaguing America like an incurable cancer, the so-called "Christian" white American should be more receptive to a proven solution to such a destructive problem. Perhaps it could be in time to save America from imminent disaster – the same destruction brought upon Germany by racism that eventually destroyed the Germans themselves.

Each hour here in the Holy Land enables me to have greater Spiritual insights into what is happening in America between black and white. The American Negro never can be blamed for his racial animosities – he is only reacting to four hundred years of conscious racism of the American whites. But as racism leads America up the suicide path, I do believe, from the experiences I have had with them. that the whites of the younger generation, the colleges and universities, will see the handwriting on the wall and many of them will turn to the *spiritual* path of *truth* – the *only* way left to America to ward off the disaster that racism inevitably must lead to.

Never have I been so highly honored. Never have I been made to feel more humble and unworthy. Who would believe the blessings that have been heaped upon an *American Negro*? A few nights ago, a man who would be called in America a "white" man; a United Nations diplomat, ambassador, a companion of kings, gave me *his* hotel suite, *his* bed. By this man, His Excellency Prince Faisal. who rules this Holy Land, was made aware of my presence here in Jedda. The very next morning, Prince Faisal's son, in person, informed me that by the will and decree of his esteemed father, I was to be a State Guest.

The Deputy Chief of Protocol himself took me before the Hajj Court. His Holiness Sheikh Muhammad Harkon himself okayed my visit to Mecca. His Holiness gave me two books on Islam. with his personal seal and autograph, and he told me that he prayed that I would be a successful preacher of Islam in America. A car, a driver, and a guide, have been placed at my disposal, making it possible for me to travel about this Holy Land almost at will. The government provides air-conditioned quarters and servants in each city that I visit. Never would I have even thought of dreaming that I would ever be a recipient of such honors – honors that in America would be bestowed upon a King – not a Negro.

All praise is due to Allah, the Lord of all the Worlds.

Sincerely,
El-Hajj Malik El-Shabazz
(Malcolm X)

ELVIS PRESLEY

IN 1970 ELVIS PRESLEY (1935–77) IMPROBABLY ENOUGH, applied to President Nixon to become a "Federal Agent at Large" in the war against drugs in USA.

To President Richard M. Nixon (December 1970)

Dear Mr President,

First, I would like to introduce myself. I am Elvis Presley and admire you and have Great Respect for your office. I talked to Vice President Agnew in Palm Springs three weeks ago and expressed my concern for our country. The drug culture, the hippie elements, the SDS, Black Panthers, etc. do *not* consider me as their enemy or as they call it, The Establishment. I call it America and I love it. Sir, I can and will be of any service that I can to help The Country out. I have no concerns or Motives other than helping the country out. So I wish not to be given a title or an appointed position. I can and will do more good if I were made a Federal Agent at Large and will help out by doing it my way through my communications with people of all ages. First and foremost, I am an entertainer, but all I need is the Federal credentials. I am on this plane with Senator George Murphy and we have been discussing the problems that our country is faced with.

Sir, I am staying at the Washington Hotel, Room 505–506–507. I have two men who work with me by the name of Jerry Schilling and Sonny West. I am registered under the name of Jon Burrows. I will be here for as long as it takes to get the credentials of a Federal Agent. I have done an in-depth study of drug abuse and Communist brain-washing techniques and I am right in the middle of the whole thing where I can and will do the most good.

I am Glad to help just so long as it is kept very Private. You can have your staff or whomever call me anytime today, tonight, or tomorrow. I was nominated this coming year one of America's Ten Most Outstanding Young Men. That will be in January 18 in my home town of Memphis, Tennessee. I am sending you the short autobiography about myself so you can better understand this approach. I would love to meet you just to say hello if you're not too busy.

Respectfully,
Elvis Presley.

P. S. I believe that you, Sir, were one of the Top Ten Outstanding Men of America also.

I have a personal gift for you which I would like to present to you and you can accept it or I will keep it for you until you can take it.

MONICA LEWINSKY

L EWINSKY (1969–) WAS A WHITE HOUSE INTERN WITH whom US President Bill Clinton had an "inappropriate" relationship. The affair became public when Linda Tripp, a friend in whom Lewinsky had confided, sold the story to the media. As a consequence of "Monica-gate", impeachment proceedings were begun against President Clinton but failed to secure a majority vote in the Senate.

❧

To Linda Tripp (4 February 1997 2:15PM (e-mail))

Thank God for you! Oh Linda, I don't know what I am going to do. I just don't know what went wrong, what happened? How could he do this to me? Why did he keep up contact with me for so long and now nothing, now when we could be together? Maybe it was the intrigue of wanting something he couldn't have (easily) with all that was going on then? Maybe he wanted to insure he could have variety and phone sex when he was on the road for those months? AAAAH!!!!! I am going to lose it! And where is Betty's phone call? What's up with all this shit? oh, well, bye.

❧

To Bill Clinton, President of the USA (29 June 1997)

Dear Handsome

I really need to discuss my situation with you. We have not had any contact for over five weeks. You leave on Sat. and I leave for Madrid w/the SecDet on Monday returning the 14th of July. I am then heading out to Los Angeles for a few days. If I do not speak to you before you leave, when I return from LA it will have been two

months since we last spoke. *Please do not do this to me*. I feel
disposable, used and insignificant. I understand your hands are tied,
but I just want to talk to you and look at some options. I am begging
you from the bottom of my heart one last time to please let me come
see you visit Tuesday evening. I will call Betty Tues. afternoon to see
if it is o.k.

M

SOURCES

Peter Abelard, *The Love Letters of Abelard and Heloïse*, ed. H. Morten, J. M. Dent 1901

James Agee, *Letters of James Agee to Father Flye*, George Brazillier Inc. 1962

Louisa May Alcott, *Louisa May Alcott: Her Life, Letters and Journals*, ed. E. D. Cheney 1889

Mark Antony, *Life of Augustus* by Suetonius, trans. J. C. Rolfe, Loeb Classical Library 1952

Jane Austen, *Jane Austen's Letters to her Sister Cassandra*, ed. R. W. Chapman, OUP 1952

Elizabeth Barrett, *The Letters of Robert and Elizabeth Barrett Browning*, Smith Elder & Co 1899

Alban Berg, *Alban Berg's Letters to His Wife*, ed. Bernard Grun, Faber & Faber 1971

William Blake, *The Letters of William Blake*, ed. Geoffrey Keynes, Rupert Hart-Davis 1956

Humphrey Bogart, *Time* magazine 1948

Anne Boleyn, *The Life and Death of Anne Bullen, Queen Consort of England*, G. Smeeton 1820

Napoleon Bonaparte, *Letters of Napoleon*, J. M. Thompson, Basil Blackwell 1934

James Boswell, *Letters of James Boswell*, ed. C. B. Tinker 1924

Charlotte Brontë, *The Brontës*, Clement Shorter, Hodder & Stoughton 1908

Robert Browning, *The Letters of Robert and Elizabeth Barrett Browning*, Smith Elder & Co 1899

Rupert Brooke, *The Letters of Rupert Brooke*, ed. Geoffrey Keynes, Faber & Faber 1968

The Duke of Buckingham, *Facsimiles of Autographs in the British Museum*, ed. George F. Warner 1899

Fanny Burney, *Selected Letters and Journals*, ed. Joyce Hemlow, Oxford, Clarendon Press 1986

Lord Byron, *Byron's Letters and Journals*, ed. L. A. Marchand, John Murray 1973

Jane Welsh Carlyle, *Jane Welsh Carlyle: A New Selection of Her Letters*, ed. Trudy Bliss, Victor Gollancz 1950

Thomas Carlyle, *The Correspondence of Emerson and Carlyle*, ed. Joseph Slater, Columbia University Press 1964

Thomas Carlyle, *The Collected Letters of Thomas and Jane Welsh Carlyle*, ed. Charles Richard Sanders *et al*, Duke University Press 1970

Lewis Carroll, *The Selected Letters of Lewis Carroll*, ed. Morton N. Cohen, Pantheon Books 1982

Sir Robert Cecil, *Facsimiles of Autographs in the British Museum*, ed. George F. Warner, British Museum 1899

Lord Chesterfield, *Chesterfield's Letters to His Son*, 1813

Winston Churchill, *Winston S. Churchill*, by Randolph Churchill, Heinemann 1966

Marcus Cicero, *Letters to Atticus*, trans. G. E. Jeans, reprinted in *Voices from the Past*, by James and Janet Maclean Todd, Readers Union 1956

John Clare, *The Letters of John Clare*, ed. Mark Storey, Oxford, Clarendon Press 1985

William Cobbett, *The Emigrant's Guide in Ten Letters*, Mills Jowett & Mills 1829

Samuel Taylor Coleridge, *Letters*, ed. E.L. Griggs, Clarendon Press 1959

Joseph Conrad, *The Collected Letters of Joseph Conrad*, ed. Frederick R. Karl & Laurence Davies, Cambridge University Press 1983

Oliver Cromwell, *Oliver Cromwell Letters and Speeches with elucidations by Thomas Carlyle*, Bernhard Tauchnitz 1861

Charles Dickens, *Charles Dickens: Selected Letters*, D. Parossier, Macmillan 1985

John Donne, *John Donne: Complete Poetry and Selected Prose*, ed. John Hayward, Nonesuch Press 1929

Frederick Douglass, *North Star*, 8 September 1848

Fyodor Dostoyevsky, *Dostoyevsky: His Life and Letters*, Chatto & Windus 1923

Albrecht Dürer, *The Voice of the Middle Ages*, by Catherine Moriarty, Lennard 1989

John Dryden, *The Letters of John Dryden*, ed. Charles E. Ward, Duke University Press 1942

Albert Einstein, *Einstein. The Life and Times*, World Publishing 1971

Elizabeth I, *Original Letters Illustrative of English History*, ed. H. Ellis, Harding, Triphook & Lepard 1824

Elizabeth I (letter to King Erik of Sweden), *The Word of a Prince: A Life of Elizabeth*, Maria Perry, Boydell & Brewer 1990

Lion Feuchtwanger, *Treasury of the World's Greatest Letters*, ed. M. Lincoln Schuster, Simon & Schuster 1948

F Scott Fitzgerald, *The Letters of Scott Fitzgerald*, ed. Andrew Turnbull, The Bodley Head 1964

Gustave Flaubert, *Selected Letters*, trans. Geoffrey Wall, Penguin 1997

E.M. Forster, *Selected Letters of E.M. Forster*, ed. Mary Lago & P.N. Furbank, William Collins 1983

Benjamin Franklin, *Mr Franklin, a Selection from his Personal Letters*, ed. Leonard W. Labaree and Whitfield J. Bell, Yale University Press 1956

André Gide, *The Correspondence between André Gide and Paul Claudel 1889–1926*, ed. J.Russell, Martin Secker & Warburg 1972

Vincent Van Gogh, *The Complete Letters of Vincent Van Gogh*, ed. J. van Gogh-Bongerand and C. de Dood, Thames & Hudson 1958

General Gordon, *Gordon: Martyr and Misfit* by Anthony Nutting, Constable 1966

Joey Grimaldi, *The Faber Book of Letters*, ed. Felix Pryor, Faber & Faber 1988

Ivor Gurney, *Ivor Gurney: War Letters*, ed. R. K. R. Thornton, Mid Northumberland Arts Group 1983

Nell Gwyn, *The Camden Miscellany, Volume the Fifth*, Camden Society 1864

William Hazlitt, *The Letters of William Hazlitt*, ed. Herschel Sikes, W.H. Bonner & Gerald Lahey, Macmillan 1979

Ernest Hemingway, *Selected Letters: 1917–1961*, ed. Carlos Baker, Charles Scribner's Sons 1981

Anthony Henley, *Christmas Cracker*, ed. John Julius Norwich, Penguin Books 1982

Henry VIII, VAT 3731–A letter 15, Biblioteca Apostolica Vaticana Henry VIII, *Intimate Letters of England's Kings*, British Museum 1959

Gerard Manley Hopkins, *The Letters of Gerard Manley Hopkins to Robert Bridges*, ed. Claude Colleer Abbot, Oxford University Press 1935

James Howell, *Epistolae Ho-Elianae, 1645–55*

David Hume, *The Letters of David Hume*, ed. J. Y. T. Grieg, Oxford University Press 1932

James I, *Intimate Letters of England's Kings*, British Museum 1959

Saint Jerome (letter to Asella), *Roman Letters*, Finley Hooper & Matthew Schwartz, Wayne State University Press 1991

Samuel Johnson, *The Letters of Samuel Johnson*, ed. R. W. Chapman, Oxford, Clarendon Press 1952

John Keats, *The Letters of John Keats*, ed. Robert Gittings, Oxford University Press 1970

Charles Lamb, *The Letters of Charles Lamb*, Everyman's Library, J. M. Dent & Sons 1909

D. H. Lawrence, *The Letters of D.H. Lawrence*, ed. J. T. Boulton, Cambridge University Press 1979–93

T. E. Lawrence, *The Letters of T. E. Lawrence*, ed. Malcolm Brown, J. M. Dent 1988

Monica Lewinsky (letter to President Bill Clinton), quoted in *The Guardian*, 22 September 1998

Monica Lewinsky, e-mail to Linda Tripp, quoted in *The Times*, 23 September 1998

Abraham Lincoln, *Abraham Lincoln: Speeches and Letters*, ed. Peter J. Parish, J. M. Dent 1993

The Lisle Family, *The Lisle Letters, an abridgement*, ed. Muriel St Clare Byrne, Martin Secker & Warburg 1983

Malcolm Lowry, *Selected Letters of Malcolm Lowry*, ed. Harvey Breit & Margerie Bonner Lowry, Jonathan Cape 1967

Rosa Luxemburg, *The Letters of Rosa Luxemburg*, ed. Stephen Eric Bronnen, Westview Press 1978

Katherine Mansfield, *The Collected Letters of Katherine Mansfield*, ed. Vincent O'Sullivan & Margaret Scott, Clarendon, Oxford 1984

Cotton Mather, *Selected Letters of Cotton Mather*, ed. Liz Smith, Louisiana State University Press 1971

Groucho Marx, *The Groucho Letters*, Simon & Schuster 1967

Karl Marx, *The Marx–Engels Correspondence*, ed. Fritz J. Raddatz, trans. C. Ewald Osers, Lawrence & Wishart 1981

Lady Mary Wortley Montagu, *Letters*, Everyman's Library, J. M. Dent & Sons 1906

Wolfgang Mozart, *The Letters of Mozart and His Family*, ed Emily Anderson, Macmillan & Co 1938

Jawaharlal Nehru, *A Bunch of Old Letters*, Oxford University Press 1960

Lord Horatio Nelson, *Nelson's Letters*, ed. Geoffrey Rawson, J. M. Dent & Sons 1960

Cardinal Newman, *The Letters and Writings of Cardinal Newman*, ed. Charles Stephen Dessain and Edward E. Kelly, Nelson 1971

Lord Nelson, *Nelson's Letters*, ed. Geoffrey Rawson, J. M. Dentt 1960

Wilfred Owen, *Wilfred Owen: Selected Letters*, ed. John Bell, Oxford University Press 1985

Petrarch, *The Voice of the Middle Ages*, ed. Catherine Moriarty, Lennard Books 1989

Pope Pius II, *Treasury of the World's Greatest Letters*, ed. M. Lincoln Schuster, Simon & Schuster 1948

The Younger Pliny, *The Letters of the Younger Pliny*, trans. Betty Radice, Penguin 1963

Elvis Presley, *Letters of a Nation*, ed. Andrew Carroll, Kodansha 1997

The Duke of Queensberry, *Catalogue of Collection of Autograph Letters and Historical Documents formed by Alfred Morrison*, 1891

Sir Walter Raleigh, *The Life of Sir Walter Ralegh . . . Together with his Letters*, Edward Edwards, Macmillan & Co. 1868

Vita Sackville-West, *The Letters of Vita Sackville-West to Virginia Woolf*, ed. Louise DeSalvo and Mitchell A. Leaska, Hutchinson & Co 1984

Vita Sackville-West, *Harold Nicolson. Diaries and Letters*, vol. 1, 1930–39, ed. Nigel Nicolson, Wm. Collins & Sons 1967

George Sand, *The Letters of George Sand*, ed. Veronica Lucas, George Routledge & Sons 1974

Erik Satie, *The Literary Clef*, ed. Edward Lockspeiser, John Calder 1955

Captain R. F. Scott, *Scott's Last Expedition* ed. Leonard Huxley, John Murray 1913

Madame de Sévigné, *Madame de Sévigné: Selected Letters*, Penguin 1982

George Bernard Shaw, *Bernard Shaw: Collected Letters*, ed. Dan H. Laurence, Max Reinhardt 1965–8

Mary Shelley, *Treasury of the World's Greatest Letters*, ed. M. Lincoln Schuster, Simon & Schuster 1948

Sir Philip Sidney, *The Prose Works of Sir Philip Sidney*, ed. Albert Feuillerant, Cambridge University Press 1912–26

Edith Sitwell, *Selected Letters of Edith Sitwell*, ed. Richard Greene, Virago Press 1997

Sydney Smith, *The Letters of Sydney Smith*, ed. Nowell C. Smith 1953

John Steinbeck, *Steinbeck. A Life in Letters*, ed. Elaine A. Steinbeck, Penguin 1975

Harriet Beecher Stowe, *Collected Letters*, Bowling Green 1982

Jonathan Swift, *The Correspondence of Jonathan Swift*, ed. Harold Williams, Oxford, Clarendon Press 1963

Dylan Thomas, *Collected Letters of Dylan*, ed. Paul Ferris, J. M. Dent 1985

Henry David Thoreau, *The Correspondence of Henry David Thoreau*, ed. Walter Harding & Carl Bode, New York University Press 1984

James Thurber, *Selected Letters of James Thurber*, ed. Helen Thurber

& Edward Weeks, Little Brown & Co. 1981

Mark Twain, *The Selected Letters of Mark Twain*, ed. Charles Neider, Harper & Row 1982

Esther Vanhomrigh, *Vanessa and Her Correspondence with Swift*, Selwyn & Blount 1921

Leonardo da Vinci, *Treasury of the World's Greatest Letters*, ed. M. Lincoln Schuster, Simon & Schuster 1948

Horace Walpole, *Horace Walpole's Correspondence with Thomas Gray, Richard West, and Thomas Ashton*, ed. W. E. Lewis, George L. Lam, Charles H. Bennett, Yale University Press

Horace Walpole, *The Yale Edition of Horace Walpole's Correspondence*, ed. W. S. Lewis, Oxford University Press 1941

George Washington, *Writings of Washington*, George Washington Bicentennial Commission 1931

Evelyn Waugh, *The Letters of Evelyn Waugh*, ed. Mark Amory, Weidenfeld & Nicolson 1980

Edith Wharton, *The Letters of Edith Wharton*, ed. R. W. B. Lewis & Nancy Lewis, Scribner 1988

Oscar Wilde, *The Letters of Oscar Wilde*, ed. Rupert Hart-Davis, OUP 1979

Mary Wollstonecraft, *The Collected Letters of Mary Wollstonecraft*, ed. R. M. Wardle 1974

Virginia Woolf, *The Monks House Papers*, University of Sussex Library

Virginia Woolf, *The Letters of Virginia Woolf*, ed. Nigel Nicolson, Hogarth Press 1975–1980

William Wordsworth, *Letters of William Wordsworth: A New Selection*, ed. Alan G. Hill, Oxford University Press 1984

Malcolm X, *The Autobiography of Malcolm X*, by Malcolm X and Alex Haley, Random House 1964

Emile Zola, *Treasury of the World's Greatest Letters*, ed. M. Lincoln Schuster, Simon & Schuster 1948

ACKNOWLEDGMENTS

The editor has made every effort to locate all persons having any rights in the letters appearing in this anthology and to secure permission from the holders of such rights. Any queries regarding use of material should be addressed to The Editor, c/o Robinson Publishing, England. For permission to reprint the letters in this volume the editor gratefully acknowledges the following:

Curtis Brown on behalf of the Estate of Sir Winston Churchill for *Winston S. Churchill* by Randolph S. Churchill, Heinemann 1996; Duke University Press for the *Letters of John Dryden*, ed. Charles Ward; Faber & Faber Ltd for *The Letters of Rupert Brooke*, ed. Geoffrey Keynes, and *Alban Berg's Letters to His Wife*, trans. copyright © Bernard Grun 1971; HarperCollins for *Harold Nicolson Diaries and Letters*, volume 1, ed. Nigel Nicolson, copyright © 1967 Nigel Nicolson and *Selected Letters of E.M. Forster volume 1*, ed. Mary Lago & P.N. Furbank, © Provost and Scholars of King's College, Cambridge 1983: The Hebrew University of Jerusalem, Israel, for *Einstein: Life and Times* by Ronald W. Clark; David Higham Associates for *The Collected Letters of Dylan Thomas*, ed. Paul Ferris, copyright © 1957, 1966 and 1982 The Trustees for the Copyright of Dylan Thomas, and *Selected Letters of Edith Sitwell*, ed. Richard Greene, Virago; Hogarth Press for *The Letters of Virginia Woolf*, ed. Nigel Nicolson, copyright © 1977 Quentin Bell and Angelica Garnett; Hutchinson for *The Letters of Vita Sackville-West to Virginia Woolf*, ed. Louise DeSalvo & Mitchell A. Laska, Virago, copyright © Nigel Nicolson 1985; Little Brown & Company for *The Selected Letters of James Thurber*, ed. Helen Thurber & Edward Weeks, copyright Helen Thurber © 1981; Louisiana State University, for *Selected Letters of Cotton Mather* compiled by Kenneth Silverman, copyright © 1971 Louisiana State University; John Murray and Harvard University Press for *Byron's Letters and Journals*, ed. Leslie A. Marchand; New York University Press for *The Correspondence of Henry David Thoreau*, ed. William Harding & Carl Bode; Oxford University Press for *Jane Austen's Letters*, ed. Alan G. Hill, *The Letters of John Keats*, ed. Robert Gittings, *William Wordsworth Letters*, ed.

Alan G. Hill, *Wilfred Owen: Collected Letters*, ed. Harold Owen & John Bell: Oxford Clarendon Press for *The Collected Letters of Samuel Taylor Coleridge*, ed. Earl Leslie Griggs, *The Letters of John Clare*, ed. Mark Storey, *The Letters of Sydney Smith*, ed. Nowell C. Smith; Penguin Books Ltd for *Gustave Flaubert: Selected Letters*, trans. Geoffrey Wall, copyright © Geoffrey Wall 1997, *The Letters of The Younger Pliny*, trans. copyrigh © Betty Radice and *Madame de Sevigné: Selected Letters*; Laurence Pollinger Ltd and the estate of Frieda Lawrence Ravagli for *The Letters of D.H. Lawrence*, ed. James T. Boulton; Random House for an extract from *Dostoevsky's Letters to Family and Friends*, trans. copyright © Ethel Coburn Mayne, *The Autobiography of Malcolm X*, copyright © 1964 Alex Haley and Betty Shabazz, *Selected Letters of Malcolm Lowry* © 1965 Margerie Bonner Lowry; Scribner, a division of Simon and Schuster, for © *The Letters of F. Scott Fitzgerald*, ed. Andrew Turnbull, copyright © 1963 Frances Scott Fitzgerald Lanahan, *Ernest Hemingway: Selected Letters 1917 to 1961*, ed. Carlos Baker copyright © 1981 Carlos Baker and The Ernest Hemingway Foundation, and *The Letters of Edith Wharton*, ed. R.W.B. Lewis and Nancy Lewis, copyright © R. W. B. Lewis, Nancy Lewis and William Tyler, reprinted by permission of William Royall Tyler, proprietor of the Edith Wharton Agency and The Watkins Loomis Agency; Simon & Schuster for *The Letters of Groucho Marx*, copyright © Groucho Marx 1967; The Society of Authors on behalf of the Bernard Shaw estate for *Bernard Shaw: Collected Letters*, Dan. T. Laurence; Trustees of the Seven Pillars of Wisdom Trust for *The Letters of T.E. Lawrence*; *Time* Magazine for the letter of Humphrey Bogart, copyright © 1983 Time Inc; Virago Press for *Selected Letters of Edith Sitwell*, ed. Richard Greene copyright © 1997, F.T.S. Sitwell, and Richard Greene; A.P. Watt Ltd on behalf of the estate of David Garnett for *Carrington: Letters and Extracts from her Diaries*, ed. David Garnett; Viking Penguin and Methuen, London, for *Steinbeck: A Life in Letters*, ed. Elaine A. Steinbeck and Robert Walsten, copyright © 1952 by John Steinbeck, copyright © 1969 by the Estate of John Steinbeck, copyright © 1975 Elaine A. Steinbeck and Robert Wallsten; Weidenfeld & Nicolson Ltd for *The Letters of Evelyn Waugh*, ed. Mark Amory; Yale University Press for *Horace Walpole's Correspondence with Thomas Gray, Richard West and Thomas Ashton*, ed. W.E. Lewis, George G. Lam, Charles H. Bennett.

And special thanks to Sharron O'Gorman and Golden Valley Finance for photocopying above and beyond the call of duty.

Other titles available from Robinson Publishing

The Führer Konrad Heiden £9.99 [   ]
'Incomparably the most brilliant and comprehensive treatise yet written about the master of the third Reich.' *New York Times*

Son of Oscar Wilde Vyvyan Holland £7.99 [   ]
The classic biography by his son, newly revised with an introduction by Merlin Holland, 'A biographical tour de force.' *Observer*

**The Mammoth Book of
War Diaries & Letters** Ed. Jon E. Lewis £7.99 [   ]
A unique collection of letters and diaries from the battlefields of the last two centuries – moving and compelling.

The Mammoth Book of Cats Ed. Mark Bryant £6.99 [   ]
Anthology of the best writing about cats from over 2,000 years of literature.

Robinson books are available from all good bookshops or direct from the publishers. Just tick the titles you want and fill in the form below.

TBS Direct
Colchester Road, Frating Green, Colchester, Essex CO7 7DW
Tel: +44 (0) 1206 255777
Fax: +44 (0) 1206 255914
Email: sales@tbs-ltd.co.uk

UK/BFPO customers please allow £1.00 for p&p for the first book, plus 50p for the second, plus 50p for each aditional book.

Please send me the titles ticked.

NAME (Block letters)..

ADDRESS...

....

POSTCODE..

I enclose a cheque/PO (payable to TBS Direct) for...

I wish to pay by Switch/Credit card

Number...

Card Expiry Date...

Switch Issue Number...